BLACK BROTHERS, INC.

The Violent Rise and Fall of Philadelphia's Black Mafia

BLACK BROTHERS, INC.

The Violent Rise and Fall of Philadelphia's Black Mafia

Sean Patrick Griffin

Milo Books Ltd

Sean Patrick Griffin
Black Brothers Inc: The Violent Rise and Fall of Philadelphia's Black Mafia

Includes bibliographical references and index.

ISBN 1 903854 36 9
ISBN-13 978 1 903854 36 5

First published in 2005 by Milo Books Ltd
Revised and updated editon published in 2007.

Typeset by e-type

Printed in the United States of America

MILO BOOKS LTD
www.milobooks.com

CONTENTS

PROLOGUE

T HOUGH SEVERELY TRAUMATIZED, he survived the diabolical ordeal, as did his mother and brother. His sister was not as fortunate, succumbing to the bullet wounds in her head. Some thirty-three years passed before the phone call came. A television producer introduced himself, and announced his intentions. "I'm doing a show on Philadelphia's Black Mafia, and would like to speak to you about what happened to your family," the producer opened. Without hesitation, the victim of one of the Philadelphia area's most infamous crimes interrupted, "If you're a gentleman, you'll hang up. If not, I'll be forced to hang up on you." As the producer started his next sentence attempting to allay the victim's concerns, whatever they were, he heard the click of the phone going down. Returning to that horrific event, to those trying times – for even a moment – was too much.

Such was the recurring theme in 2007 for Henry Schipper as he tracked down dozens of victims of, and witnesses to, Black Mafia mayhem. Schipper is the executive producer of the episode on Philadelphia's Black Mafia for Black Entertainment Television's popular *American Gangster* program. Many victims and witnesses essentially told him, "What benefit would there be to do the show? It is depressing to relive this." According to Schipper, the common theme of people not wanting to be interviewed, much less on screen, was that the Black Mafia history was "painful and frightening."

After many months spent immersing himself in the story, Schipper said, "The main thing I couldn't get over was the level of fear. I have never experienced that before." Most incredibly, a former assistant district attorney who prosecuted one of the most notorious Black Mafia cases, said he would agree to be interviewed, but not on camera. Asked why he was hesitant to go on camera, there was a long pause before the retired prosecutor said one word, "Safety." In fact, Schipper noted, "Some people even told me that *I* should be concerned about *my* safety for doing the show on Philly's Black Mafia."

*

Black Brothers Inc. was first published in July 2005, resulting in a rash of media inquiries relating to historical and, more commonly, contemporary matters discussed in the book. Because part of the story told in "*BBI*" was still unfolding as the book went to press in December 2004, there have been many events that necessitated an updated edition. Readers will find these, predictably, in the back of the book, along with a commentary on my experience researching Philadelphia's Black Mafia.

I can't imagine another project will ever be as fascinating and gratifying as the research and writing was for *Black Brothers Inc.* Academicians spend most of our time presenting our work to each other, and the routine offers little excitement and only slightly more reward. The "*BBI* experience", as I have come to call it, has consumed me for more than four years, dating to the original research and writing. Throughout the process, in particular since the book's first publication, I have very much enjoyed the give-and-take (a lot of take, incidentally) with readers who have their own experiences, comments, and criticisms to relate. These exchanges have also produced a surprising number of people expressing gratitude for documenting the Black Mafia story. To me, this was a curious reaction to a true crime book. However, after speaking with so many observers, it is clear to me these are precisely those who, unlike me, had lost so much as the syndicate's numerous affiliates terrorized, polluted, and looted their neighborhoods. It never made sense to them that the Black Mafia was still treated as a legend on the street, rather than a significant, disturbing part of the city's history. In their view, with which I agree, they have been victimized still further by the media and academia, who have all but refused to investigate and narrate this history.

Working with people like the production team for the BET program, and the staff working on a National Geographic show on Philadelphia's underworld, has been a treat. It is also important, in my view, that the topic is reaching a vast and diverse audience, far beyond the historians and criminologists who would normally see such work if written in the expected academic prose. The book has been optioned to be made into at least one major motion picture, and if the film project pans out, it will be the next step forward for those who have yearned for the story to be told on a grand stage.

Before being asked to produce the one-hour show on the Black Mafia, Henry Schipper had never heard of the syndicate. Reflecting on his experience producing the show, Schipper recently said, "The fact the Black Mafia story is little known is important. It should be well known." I, along with many faceless others, couldn't agree more.

Sean Patrick Griffin
July 2007

INTRODUCTION ★
THE BUG

AT 7:15 A.M. on 7 October 2003, Philadelphia police officers conducting a supposedly routine sweep for electronic devices in the Mayor's Office at Room 215, City Hall, found a sophisticated listening apparatus hidden in the ceiling. The "bug" in Mayor John F. Street's office was a battery-powered device with various microphones that transmitted to a nearby, undisclosed location. Officers alerted Police Commissioner Sylvester Johnson, who immediately contacted the local office of the Federal Bureau of Investigation to report the discovery. FBI agents responded to the call and retrieved the device – knowing all the while that it was their own.

By 9 A.M., word of the discovery had made its way to news organizations, and the story was about to explode. The City of Philadelphia was less than four weeks away from a tight mayoral election pitting Democrat incumbent Street, an African-American, against white Republican Sam Katz. By late in the afternoon, Democratic operatives were telling reporters the apparent investigation was a Republican smear. One prominent Street supporter, labor leader John Dougherty, said, "You have an African-American Democratic mayor who's starting to pull ahead in the polls ... and suddenly there are ewly-placed listening devices in the mayor's office?" *Draw your own conclusions*, was his implication.

An FBI spokeswoman wound up stoking the fires in Mayor Street's camp when she said that, while she could not comment on the specifics of the investigation, she could state that it was not "election-related." Thus the public was left with the unmistakable inference that something criminal was being investigated involving the mayor. By the following day, when FBI agents raided the home and office of a prominent African-American Muslim cleric and Street supporter, Shamsud-din Ali, the story was national news.

Mayor Street's press secretary, Frank Keel, sensing events were getting out of hand and could irreparably damage the re-election campaign, went on the offensive. "I let it rip," he later said. "I was giving voice to what a lot of people were feeling in Philadelphia, that this thing just smelled bad and that it was entirely within the realm of the Republican Party, in an effort to wrest control of the city of Philadelphia from the Democratic machine to set up a win in Pennsylvania for [President George W.] Bush."

The Democrat plan was to suggest it was part of a smear campaign. They declared that the timing of the bug's discovery was suspicious, and that Attorney General John Ashcroft's Department of Justice should not be intervening in a competitive mayoral race with national election implications. Numerous local, state and national political operatives adopted this line in the ensuing weeks. On October 9, however, news agencies reported that investigators were looking into corruption in the city's no-bid contracts – those awarded without open competition and therefore susceptible to cronyism – especially those involving Philadelphia International Airport. A few days later, it was learned the FBI was looking into contracts dealing with the city's Minority Business Enterprise Council (MBEC), responsible for certifying firms for set-aside programs, which stipulate a certain percentage of business must be given to firms owned or predominantly staffed by minorities or women. On October 16, the media frenzy flared up again when the FBI raided three city agencies and the law office of Ronald A. White, another influential, black Street supporter and fundraiser who was also a major player in the city's government bond business, in which people can purchase shares in a municipal bond to finance substantial public works. White was asked why he was being investigated in conjunction with the corruption probe. "Because I am a black man in America doing what I think needs to be done, and people resent that," he replied. "They resent that black men in America are supposed to be bowing down all the time and not doing nothing but having babies and not taking care of them."

The key subjects of the probe appeared to be the powerful triumvirate of Mayor Street, Ron White and Shamsud-din Ali, and the city agencies involved included the finance department, the treasurer's office, MBEC, the board of pensions, and the Philadelphia Housing Authority. As events played out in the weeks between the bug's discovery and the November 4 election, conspiracy theories took hold among various segments of the electorate, particularly in the city's black neighborhoods. "There are some people, particularly in the African-American community, that believe this is too much of a coincidence to be a coincidence," said Street, stirring the pot. The three men publicly supported each other throughout the campaign and routinely questioned the motivation behind of the investigation.

A race that was tight before the bug discovery ended in a landslide re-election for John Street. "The bug, playing on skepticism of the federal government and the GOP, was the defining moment of the campaign," said one election analyst. "It moved undecided voters into the Street camp and firmed up supporters who were lukewarm toward the Mayor, making them more determined to get out and vote." Others agreed that the probe "energized Street's base of black supporters skeptical of the federal government's intentions." As the dust settled, the citizens of Philadelphia continued to grapple with the apparent size and scope of the investigation. By this point, federal authorities had seized boxes of documents and countless computer files from a variety of individuals, municipal offices, and companies. Though specifics were still lacking, this much was clear: the FBI, the IRS and perhaps other agencies were investigating allegations of extortion, mail and wire fraud, bank fraud and racketeering, and links to campaign donations. In essence, the feds were looking into the city's "pay-to-play" system, which awarded contracts only to those who "donated" to the ruling political machine.

Though the election had passed, cries of racism persisted, and now the media, too, became a target. A. Bruce Crawley, head of Philadelphia's African-American Chamber of Commerce and a friend of Street's, held a press conference and said the city's two main newspapers were engaging in "racial profiling" by covering the probe. Crawley, who was joined at the conference by Shamsud-din Ali, demanded that the newspapers put an end to their "mean-spirited focus on black businesses and exclusive focus on contributions made to the city's black mayor." He continued admonishing the media, and asked reporters, "If you think it's a story, are you guided only by what the FBI had done?" He also said FBI inquiries were "suspect ... especially when you know the FBI has been politically inspired against the African-American community ... The FBI has a history that causes African-Americans to be suspicious of its intentions."

As 2003 came to an end, it was widely rumored that the corruption probe actually originated with an unrelated investigation into narcotics trafficking. More specifically, it was said that the Ali, the Muslim cleric, had been picked up talking on an FBI drug wiretap. Furthermore, some news reports mentioned that Ali was once a kingpin in Philadelphia's "Black Mafia." For his part, Ali smiled, declared, "There's no African-American mobsters ... it is unbelievable what they can do to an African-American," and added that he was under attack for being a Muslim.

So in addition to questions about the city administration, supposed corruption, and allegations of racism and religious persecution on the part of the government, observers were now asking more fundamental questions. Who was Shamsud-din Ali? What was the Black Mafia? And what connections, if any, were there between Ali, the Black Mafia and the extraordinary corruption probe? Answers to these questions trace back decades, through some of Philadelphia's most fascinating, controversial and complex history. They have their origins in the development of a crime syndicate whose members were as feared as any in recent times, who were among the most ruthless, malevolent killers ever spawned in the U.S., and who became untouchable because no one dared testify against them. Yet the biggest mystery of all was why this ferocious group of racketeers has remained virtually unknown outside the city limits for several decades.

The answer would seem to be a failure – by law enforcement, the media and academics – to acknowledge the specific phenomenon of African-American organized crime. Books on the Italian Mafia proliferate, and are increasingly squeezed on the shelves by tomes about Irish, Jewish, Russian, and Asian mobsters. Organized or semi-organized black criminals, however, have received attention almost exclusively at the level of street gangs. Any notion of black crime syndicates on a par with the other ethnic mobs mentioned is all but absent. The study of organized crime has generally been a sociological pursuit, and the response of academics has typically been to say either that African-Americans do not organize crime, or that even to research the topic is evidence of racial bias and should be discouraged.

The story of the Black Mafia belies that view, which is itself a form of prejudice. Its members were not just street thugs. They manipulated political ties, expropriated government funds, extorted countless businesses, taxed drug dealers, held regular board meetings, appointed titular heads, assassinated rivals, planned and executed hundreds of crimes, and had an umbilical link with the most militant black religious movement of the times. Indeed the questions raised by the sensational 2003 probe also have answers in the history of the Black Muslims, the Nation of Islam. Specifically, they go back to the mid-1960s, to a time when Philadelphia's Black Muslims were led by Shamsud-din Ali's mentor, Minister Jeremiah X. Shabazz, and the city was in racial turmoil.

CHAPTER 1 ★
THE KENNEDY PLAN

A MASSIVE MIGRATION of African-Americans from the southern states of the U.S. to the urban centers of the North began in earnest in the 1940s. Twenty years later it was still going strong, despite the decline in demand for unskilled labor that initially drove it. "During the 1940s and 1950s blacks in effect were piped aboard a sinking ship, welcomed into the urban industrial age just as that age was dying, with industrial cities losing population and jobs," summed up the historian Roger Lane. Predictably, black unemployment rocketed, and the related problems of crime and family instability began to climb too. Northern cities in particular saw a big increase in ghetto poverty. The likes of New York, Chicago, Detroit and Philadelphia were losing scores of jobs in manufacturing, wholesale, and retail enterprises just as their populations were becoming "minority dominant." Joblessness, crime and social disorganization were aggravated by the "white flight" to the suburbs, which eroded substantial tax bases from several cities and further isolated minority communities.

The dire circumstances of America's cities, and their black populations, accounted at least partly for a movement away from the peaceful political protests of the early 1960s to a more militant push as the decade hit its midpoint. Activity grew in Black Nationalist movements in the North, some of which sought to penetrate urban decision-making systems. At the same time, President Lyndon Johnson was rolling out his government's so-called Great Society program in an attempt to repair the rifts in American life. The model for Johnson's "War on Poverty" – community-coordinated attacks on social injustice, stimulated but not controlled by federal monies – grew out of the Committee on Juvenile Delinquency and Youth Crime. Established in 1961 by President John F. Kennedy and lasting through 1964, the committee was led by Attorney General Robert Kennedy and included the Secretaries of Labor and Health, Education, and Welfare. Its signature initiative was the creation of community action agencies, grassroots organizations aimed at ferreting out "real" solutions to urban ills that distant bureaucrats could not identify, much less understand or solve. These agencies required "maximum feasible participation" by ghetto residents, who were to engage in making and implementing policies on community development, job training and health care. Local neighborhood councils would coordinate the distribution of funds. Some of these grant projects were doled out in fear of racial demagogues' vitriol and of threatened civil unrest by black militants. Importantly, because these initiatives targeted a criminogenic environment, career criminals were frequently the recipients of the funds.

It eventually became clear the Kennedy-inspired juvenile delinquency policies were not having the intended effect. The broader anti-delinquency campaign was publicly branded a "dismal failure" by one of its chief congressional sponsors, and one former Kennedy staffer concluded that "it caused political and civil rights controversies in nearly every city it entered ... and can nowhere be shown to have actually reduced juvenile delinquency." One of Robert Kennedy's advisers dismissed the community action agencies as "bitching societies," while some of the measures served actually to embolden black militants and to intimidate the general population. In Chicago, an exasperated Mayor Daley asked the Johnson Administration, "What the hell are you people doing? Does the President know he's putting M-O-N-E-Y in the hands of subversives?" Yet when pressed on why he was courting known criminals, Robert Kennedy replied, "These are the people we have to reach. Some people may not like it, but they are in the street and that is where the ball game is being played."

Even as the Johnson Administration implemented and promoted its War on Poverty, fires burned across the country. In the summer of 1964, race riots in Harlem and in Rochester, N.Y., left several dead and hundreds injured. Then, over the course of three days in late August 1964, riots erupted along North Philadelphia's Columbia Avenue in a downtrodden area cynically referred to as "The Jungle." Two people died, more than 300 were injured, dozens of white-owned shops were wrecked by fire, and property worth an estimated $3 million was destroyed. The following summer, the world watched part of Los Angeles go up in flames. Watts, a part of the L.A. ghetto, saw rioting that put the previous year's disturbances into the shade. Thirty-five people, most of them African-Americans, were killed and hundreds more were injured. For two days after the National Guard arrived, Watts took on the aspect of a theater of war. More than 4,000 people were arrested and property damage was estimated at over $35 million.

The riots of 1964 and 1965 only served to reinforce Robert Kennedy's views on the problems of America's inner cities. He renewed the earlier call by the Committee on Juvenile Delinquency to put more ghetto dwellers to work through community action programs. When more than twenty cities suffered disturbances in 1966, the federal government responded by providing still more money for job-training and recreation – diversionary field trips, playgrounds and sports leagues. Not surprisingly, a 1966 national survey indicated the most important domestic problem was race relations, with the related issue of crime ranking second. The summer of 1967 saw the last serious rioting, but four years of bitter racial discord had exacted a toll on many cities and citizens. Approximately 130 civilians, mainly blacks, and twelve civil personnel, mainly whites, were killed. Around 4,700 people were injured and over 20,000 people were arrested during the unrest, while property damage ran into the hundreds of millions of dollars. Many neighborhoods resembled warzones.

FBI Director J. Edgar Hoover's response was to create a massive and ultimately infamous intelligence database; a far-reaching, controversial counterintelligence program called COINTELPRO-Black Nationalist Hate Groups. Its officially stated purpose was "to expose, disrupt, misdirect, discredit, or otherwise neutralize the activities of black nationalist, hate-type organizations and groupings, their leadership, spokesmen, membership and supporters, and to counter their propensity for violence and civil disorder."

Crime, which had grown worse throughout the riotous years, so dominated the public consciousness that the Omnibus Crime Control and Safe Streets Act was enacted in 1968. This sweeping legislation provided law enforcement with more funding and a variety of legal tools and resources, including some specifically targeting organized crime. It also focused on the problem of inner-city gang warfare by providing funds for the community action initiatives. These came with very little in the way of checks and balances, because it was felt the federal bureaucracy was part of the problem in the first place. As history was about to demonstrate, there were all too many individuals and groups – in Philadelphia and elsewhere – willing to exploit the lack of oversight.

*

Philadelphia's overall population was declining at the same time as its black population was substantially increasing. In 1940, African-Americans accounted for thirteen per cent of the city's residents; by 1960, they were more than twenty-six per cent of a total population of just over two million, and a decade later they made up a third of the total. By 1980, when L.A. supplanted Philly as the nation's third-largest city, blacks made up thirty-eight percent of a total population that had fallen to 1.68 million.

Historically, Philadelphians lived in ethnically-homogenous neighborhoods, and this continued as whites fled the city. The social isolation of black Philadelphia was only part of a complex race problem. The black unemployment rate, for instance, was roughly twice the rate of whites dating back to 1950. This worsened as the number of jobs, in general, declined in the city, and several major firms moved their headquarters to the suburbs. Like other cities in similarly dire straits, Philadelphia turned to the federal government for assistance.

The city administration paralleled the federal government's progressive bent, and was led by Mayor James Tate. A Democrat, Tate was elected, along with a handful of Democratic, reformer councilmen, in 1962. As a result, African-Americans ascended to numerous high city posts, including deputy mayor, and headed the city's anti-poverty and urban improvement programs. Nearly one-third of Philadelphia's budget came from President Johnson's Great Society programs, which some saw as "a pipeline to the federal government." There were in fact any number of public, private and public-private programs targeting poverty and community development in Philadelphia from 1965, and all were greatly influenced by the War on Poverty's mandate to give power to the people.

While the city tried innovative measures to deal with the broader socio-economic problems, its Police Department relied upon more traditional methods. Police-minority relations were strained for a host of reasons, and this was exacerbated in 1964 with the creation of the department's Civil Defense (CD) Squad in response to the street disturbances. The CD Squad was designed to "muzzle a growing number of public demonstrations without confrontation" but quickly expanded its mission. It gained a reputation for developing informants, whose mandate was primarily to infiltrate so-called radical groups. CD officers, and at times their wives, were also to mingle with the radicals to develop intelligence. Undercover CD officers primarily targeted groups thought to be espousing Communist ideals, but they also infiltrated their share of Black Nationalist groups, including the burgeoning Nation of Islam. The Squad also enjoyed the cooperation of the FBI, which often shared intelligence and provided informants.

Another source of animosity in the black community was the Department's "history of excessive use of arrests and failure to provide adequate protection for minorities," and some strongly argue that its dubious history was further sullied by the tenure of Police Commissioner Frank Rizzo. Rizzo was appointed to the post in 1967 by Mayor Tate and served until 1972, when he was himself elected Mayor. He became one of the best known and most controversial police commissioners in modern urban history, partly because of the extent to which allegations of police brutality and racism increased during his tenure. Before leaving the post, Rizzo engendered great acrimony among segments of the black community.

A contributing factor to the problems of black Philadelphia was the lack of a primary group, let alone a single galvanizing personality, heading a progressive movement. Two of the more prominent African-American leaders, Robert Nelson Cornelius Nix, Sr., and Cecil B. Moore, also happened to be close with the Nation of Islam (NOI), and its leader in Philadelphia, Minister Jeremiah Shabazz. These high-profile figures became intertwined with what would soon become the social system of the "Black Mafia."

Robert Nix, Sr. began his law career in 1925 and gained a reputation as an excellent criminal attorney. He became active in Democratic politics and was elected to represent Philadelphia's 4th Congressional District (then North Philadelphia) in May 1958, becoming Pennsylvania's first black congressman. At the time, only three other African-Americans sat in Congress, and of them, a quote-making machine called Adam Clayton Powell Jr., of New York, was undoubtedly the star, or at least commanded the most attention. Powell proudly claimed he was the "first bad nigger in Congress." In 1962, Powell and Nix helped to thwart a congressional probe into the controversial Nation of Islam. Among other actions, Nix wrote a letter stating that NOI leader Elijah Muhammad's teachings on liberty and freedom were "consistent with statements by Thomas Jefferson, Benjamin Franklin, John Adams, and other founders of this republic."

Nix allied with Cecil B. Moore, a fellow lawyer, community leader, NOI supporter, and one of Philadelphia's most controversial personalities. Like Nix, Moore was close with Adam Clayton Powell, and was considered by some to be one of the most significant leaders of Philadelphia in the Twentieth Century. Elected president of the Philadelphia Chapter of the National Association for the Advancement of Colored People (NAACP) in 1962, he built the local branch into the country's largest. That success did not last long. Membership in 1963 was estimated at over 20,000 but by October 1965 was down to 3,855, and some blamed Moore for the branch's disunity and poor organization. One indisputable Moore achievement, however, was the integration of Philadelphia's Girard College. He led thousands of followers in protesting its policy of racial segregation and, following two years of protests and court proceedings, the college admitted its first black students in 1968.

Moore was at various times described as loud, effective, outspoken, vigorous, flamboyant, profane, fanatical, caustic, fiery and militant. "Confrontational and in-your-face, he angered and alienated not only those in the white power structure but also many in the black power structure as well," judged one columnist. In 1966, during a period of extreme civil conflagration, he told the press, "What we need is a few more riots. I'm in full accord with Black Power. You name me a Negro who isn't anti-white." His stridency disturbed many blacks as well as whites, and he was criticized by some NAACP colleagues for his close relationship with the Black Muslims. In 1967, in an effort to lessen his influence, the NAACP divided the Philly branch into five chapters, and Moore resigned soon afterward.

In addition to being a civil rights leader, a community activist and a politician, Moore found time to party with some of the era's most fascinating people. His favorite stomping ground was West Philadelphia's 52nd Street Strip, a reinvigorated area of bars and nightclubs where black entrepreneurs began buying drinking establishments formerly owned by whites. The area was embodied by a popular joint called Mr. Silk's Third Base, known to one and all as Silky's and owned by Moore's friend Gus Lacy, a former postal worker who got his nickname from selling lingerie on the side out of his car trunk; the car had "Stockings to Step-Ins from Mr. Silk" stenciled on it. Like many black entrepreneurs of that era, Lacy had borrowed the money to start his business in the 1950s from a neighborhood numbers banker, numbers being the illegal street lottery played by many in poorer areas. According to Lacy, black gamblers often invested in legitimate businesses to help their neighborhoods: "A lot of these numbers bankers, man, supported small businesses in the community. If you came to them for a loan, there was no twenty-five cents on the dollar. Then they kept the money in the community, kept money generating ... if you wanted $2,500, they would lend it to you."

Silky's played a key role in Philadelphia's nightlife throughout the 1960s and '70s. Popular with blacks and whites, its patrons included Muhammad Ali, Billy Eckstine, Joe Frazier, Teddy Pendergrass and Stevie Wonder, as well as many members of the Philadelphia Eagles and Phillies teams. "Late model Cadillacs and Rolls-Royces dominated the street's parking area," according to one reporter. It was, said another commentator, "the place where straight-lifers in conservative clothes mixed easily with pimps and hustlers in diamond rings and wide-brimmed hats." Lacy's motto for the club was, "You have to touch Third Base before you go home."

Lacy was also involved with several civil rights causes, and formed motorcades for Cecil Moore during the struggle to integrate Girard College. His closest friend, Stanley Branche, was also tight with Moore. The relationships between Jeremiah Shabazz, Nix, Moore, Branche and Lacy would become more extensive, formal and significant over time.

★

Concern in Philadelphia about the bleak outlook for the African-American community and the related crime epidemic was so great that a novel organization called the Black Coalition was founded in the spring of 1968. The group's origin was outlined in one of its reports:

> The Black Coalition, Inc., is a neighborhood organization made up of a cross section of the Black community, ranging from Black

judges to the grass-root and militant gang member. For quite some time before the riots of 1964 and since then, certain responsible members of the Philadelphia business community, realized that many of the efforts currently underway in many cities across the nation to establish a fruitful and meaningful dialogue between Blacks and Whites were failing. This group of civic minded Philadelphians believed that this failure was because no overt attempt had been made to communicate with the so-called grass-root element of the city. Convinced of the necessity for bold and innovative thinking, a meeting was planned for Good Friday 1968. To this meeting was invited a broad cross section of the Black and White community, including a number of Black Gang members. As a result of this meeting, the Black Coalition was formed.

The Coalition's by-laws listed its two main purposes: to "advance and promote the socio-economic conditions primarily of Black citizens and those of Negro ancestry and other citizens disadvantaged in the Philadelphia metropolitan area" and to "develop, carry out and promote such cultural, educational and economic programs to accomplish these purposes."

Soon the Coalition, hailed as "the black man's own community project," announced it had obtained pledges of more than $1 million in seed money from banks and businesses to "attack the full spectrum of ghetto ills." With summer – and its usual threat of riots and increased gang conflict – fast approaching, some speculated that the new body was merely a temporary measure to diffuse seasonal tensions, but the Coalition strongly denied this.

Its executive director was Stanley Branche, another fiery, outspoken civil rights activist who had headed an NAACP branch before being forced out for allegedly mishandling funds. He served on President Kennedy's Task Force on Poverty and continued working with President Johnson's anti-poverty team. It was said that in the early 1960s, Branche turned to headline-grabbing politician Adam Clayton Powell for help so often that Powell once sarcastically said, "Niggah, I'm not your congressman. Get out of here." Described by one observer as "a sepia-toned Jack Armstrong, the black all-American boy grown to shrewd manhood," Branche was no stranger to Philly politics, and worked with fellow firebrand Cecil B. Moore on several endeavors, most notably the effort to desegregate Girard College. A 1968 *Philadelphia Magazine* profile said Branche "wears two costumes, a guerrilla outfit when he is communing with the guerrillas and conventional expensive duds when he is dealing with the straight world." Those in the underworld and in the nightlife scene knew the Branche who wore stylish clothes and who drove in comfortable rides. This Branche declared that "in the ghetto, to survive, we all have to be damn good hustlers," and was a very close friend of a flamboyant con artist called Major Coxson, a leading figure in underworld circles.

Branche enlisted the media to get the word on the street that the Black Coalition was in business. He also dismissed worries that he was selling out by now working from the smart Black Coalition office. "Some people are saying we used to be militants, but now we've turned into moderates," he said. "Don't you believe it, baby. We don't intend to be subservient to anybody, and we don't intend to lessen our protest against the white bigots who consider all black people nothing more than niggers. We're responsible to the black community and nobody else." The Coalition had an impressive and eclectic sixteen-member board of directors that included a few personalities who, along with Branche, would factor into the Black Mafia history: Judge Robert N.C. Nix, Jr., Jeremiah Shabazz, and Gus Lacy. Though the official records suggest otherwise, con artist and drug financier Major Coxson told anyone who would listen that he was also one of the founders of the Black Coalition, and at least one media account reported that Coxson helped found the Coalition "and then was ostracized from it by the power grabbers."

Regardless of whether Coxson was formally part of the endeavor, the nature of the players involved meant that Philadelphia's CD Squad and the FBI kept a close watch on Black Coalition activities.

★

The FBI's Philadelphia Office was also attempting to fuel discord between the Nation of Islam and the militant Black Panther Party. To this end, the Feds interviewed Nation minister Jeremiah Shabazz in his home, using as their pretext a supposedly imminent clash between the NOI and the Panthers. Shabazz clearly sensed what the agents were trying to do, and said there was nothing to the rumors. At the conclusion of the interview, agents asked Shabazz to keep them informed if he received information "which might indicate a riot situation threatening life and property was imminent in Philadelphia." According to an FBI memo, "[Shabazz] said he would consider the information before furnishing it as he did not intend to place himself in the position of informer."

As the City of Philadelphia searched for answers to its social problems, Shabazz's Temple 12 was thriving. Throughout the tumultuous times, Shabazz traveled extensively in recruiting and enlightenment drives, often in the company of boxer and Black Muslim convert Muhammad Ali. In October 1966, Shabazz spoke at an NAACP rally led by Cecil B. Moore and supported the group's demonstrations at Girard College. A few months later, Muhammad Ali headlined a special meeting of Temple 12 at Philadelphia's famed Blue Horizon Auditorium.

Some of Shabazz's converts were also flourishing in the Philadelphia underworld as small bands of criminals who were slowly making connections that would assist each others' conspiracies. One of his followers was a bull of a man with a formidable past and even more frightening future. His name was Sam Christian.

CHAPTER 2 ★
SUPERFLY

S AM CHRISTIAN FIRST encountered the justice system in 1953, at the age of fourteen. He was arrested and convicted for armed robbery with three other teens, and his criminal course was set. He later took a handful of pinches for "gambling on the highway" – likely shooting craps on street corners, which was popular in the late 1950s. As the decade ended and Christian came to adulthood, his street reputation was about to soar.

Powerfully built at five feet ten and 215 pounds, he was once succinctly described as a "thick-necked bully." In fact, he was the bully of all bullies. Christian began organizing stick-ups of crap games, and from October 1959 he amassed multiple arrests for serious offenses such as robbery, aggravated assault, carrying a concealed deadly weapon and violating the Uniform Firearms Act. In October 1964, he was arrested for robbing a card game and shooting one of the players when the man reached to protect the game's pot. Christian and his two fellow robbers wore stocking masks to conceal their identities, a tactic Christian would often employ, especially when the targets were people he or his crew knew personally. In this case, Christian's mask slipped off during the robbery, allowing three of the card players to identify him. Yet almost all cases against Christian would be dropped because people so feared testifying against him.

Fear was his greatest weapon, and would become the bedrock upon which the Black Mafia built its empire during the next two decades. Christian and the cohort of the ferocious, the psychotic and the downright evil he gathered around him, could terrify by their mere presence. Their aura became such that overt threats were rarely necessary; their street rep alone was enough.

In the mid-1960s, Christian became a Black Muslim, joining Temple 12 of the Nation of Islam. The sincerity of his religious conviction is unknown, but the Muslims were recruiting heavily among disenchanted black youths in the poorer districts of America's northern cities, and many hoodlums and gang members joined up. His membership became public knowledge in dramatic fashion when, in September 1967, Christian caused mayhem at a voter registration drive in North Philadelphia. Forty people were waiting in line at a mobile registration unit at 18th Street and Columbia Avenue when Christian got into a fight with a bunch of men. Outnumbered, he fled, vowing to return with a gun. Apparently a man of his word, at least in this case, Christian came back and fired four .38 caliber shots into the crowd. Dozens of prospective voters ducked behind and under cars, in doorways and in nearby homes, while Christian stood defiantly, waving the gun over his head. One man was wounded in the hip. When arrested, Christian told police he was now a Black Muslim with a new name, Sulieman Bey, or Beyah.

A few months later, in April 1968, Christian was arrested with Walter Hudgins and Roosevelt "Spooks" Fitzgerald for assaulting police officers during a narcotics inquiry by the Philadelphia Police Department's Special Investigations Squad. Like Christian, Fitzgerald was a Black Muslim convert and also went by a Muslim name, Roosevelt Bey. Within months, this trio would serve as the foundation for a newly formed African-American syndicate calling itself the Black Mafia, with Christian as its leader.

There is debate about precisely when the syndicate formed, some suggesting it was as early as 1965, and there is also some doubt about the identity of all the founders. Nevertheless, according to law enforcement, by 1968 the Black Mafia leadership, in order of importance, consisted of:

Samuel "Sam" Christian, 29 years old
Eugene "Bo" Baynes, 30
Ronald Harvey, 28
Robert "Nudie" Mims, 28
Grady Dyches, 29
Roosevelt "Spooks" Fitzgerald, 39
Donald "Donnie" Day, 28
Robert "Bop Daddy" Fairbanks, 33
Clyde "Apples" Ross, 30
Richard "Pork Chops" James, 34
Jerome Barnes, 23
Charles "Black Charles" Toney, 31
Walter Hudgins, 33
Nathaniel Williams, 23.

All of the founders already had extensive arrest records, mostly involving violence. Much less is known about their private lives; nearly all were married, but many also had several girlfriends. Most of the charter members had spent the previous few years holding up crap games and extorting drug dealers, numbers men and other illegitimate businessmen. Such targets made great victims because they were accessible, plentiful, and they typically dealt in cash. A supervisor in the Philadelphia Police Department's Intelligence Unit added the last part of their strategic targeting of victims: "They would intimidate persons who would not report them to police."

However, while Christian and friends were successful criminals, and each was developing his own reputation, they lacked the necessary notoriety to engage in large-scale extortion. That changed in September of 1968, when they adopted the name "Black Mafia." It was a term deliberately evocative of the Italian Mob, designed to suggest organization, ruthlessness and violence, and most importantly, to evoke fear, the commodity that remained Sam Christian's greatest weapon.

One founding member who flew solo before 1968 was Nudie Mims. Mims was first arrested back in 1954, when he was a mere ten years old. At the age of fourteen, he was one of four suspects arrested in the fatal beating of a half-blind eighty-seven-year-old man. The murder charge against him was dropped, but he was sentenced to reformatory school for assault. In 1961, Mims caused a riot in the juvenile detention room in the basement of Philadelphia's Municipal Court Building. He had just been sentenced – for assaulting two pedestrians with milk bottles and for molesting a woman – when he gave an order to about thirty juveniles, resulting in a melee. The event foreshadowed Mims's ability to organize and motivate groups of people.

Some of the syndicate's founding members knew each other from years of hustling together, often in pairs or groups. Walter Hudgins, for instance, was arrested in November 1966 with "Bop Daddy" Fairbanks and Alfred "Sonny" Viner for stealing $50,000 worth of fur coats, stoles and jackets from Gittleman's Sons' fur shop on Chestnut Street in Center City. They broke into the store during the night by knocking down a basement firewall that separated it from an adjacent building.

At this early stage, the Black Mafia engaged almost exclusively in robbery and extortion, and their activities were confined to the city's predominantly African-American neighborhoods in North, West, South and Southwest Philadelphia. For the most part, Black Mafia members did not deal narcotics themselves, but rather taxed drug dealers in the group's territories. Things began to change in the summer of 1970, when they started trafficking in narcotics.

Heroin was the drug of choice in Philadelphia, especially in black neighborhoods that found cocaine too pricey. The heroin market in the U.S. at that time was dominated by a black distributor named Frank Matthews, who operated out of New York. A pivotal figure in the history of the U.S. drug trade when barely out of his teens, Matthews was one of the nation's largest narcotics dealers in the 1960s and early 1970s, and commonly handled multi-million-dollar shipments. He became a major dealer in twenty-one states, with quality overseas contacts for both heroin and cocaine. The DEA stated that Matthews imported heroin from Turkey by way of processing plants in Marseilles, France, and cocaine from Latin America. He had contacts with Cuban wholesalers who controlled vast portions of the South American coke trade to the United States. Locally, he eliminated middlemen by handling the narcotics all the way to the street sales. In other cities, he sold to distributors who handled the street sales themselves.

The Matthews operation was so large that in one notorious raid on a Brooklyn house where drugs were cut, federal narcotics agents found 2.5 million glassine bags and two thirty-two-gallon plastic garbage cans used for mixing. One informant told authorities that when he visited Matthews to make a payment, he was told to put the money in a closet. He opened the double doors to find money piled from the floor to eye-level. Frank Matthews lived the life of a millionaire, renting several lavish apartments and owning a fleet of luxury cars and a $200,000 mansion he had custom-built in Staten Island's exclusive Todt Hill. He did not lack for confidence. In one oft-cited act of hubris, Matthews warned an Italian-American mobster, "Touch one of my men and we'll drive down to Mulberry Street … and shoot every wop we see."

Matthews's key Philadelphia contacts were all Black Mafia operators. They included John "Pop" Darby, Thomas "Cadillac Tommy" Farrington, Tyrone "Fat Ty" Palmer, and, most importantly, Major Coxson. All were drug dealers, but Coxson alone also orchestrated financial scams and forged great contacts within the Italian-American underworlds in Philadelphia and New York. One of his associates was Angelo Bruno, the head of Philadelphia's Cosa Nostra family.

The Black Mafia adopted a formal structure, holding regular meetings at several locations in its early years and making distinctions between general meetings and those convened exclusively for its hierarchy. General meetings were held at various spots along the 52nd Street strip and the Storybook Inn in South Philadelphia. Executive meetings were held at the Johnson Homes public housing project in North Philadelphia. Minutes taken at several of the general meetings indicate that the average number of attendees ranged from forty to sixty. General meetings were governed by several written procedures, all of which were included in the group's explicit overall rules. One rule that applied specifically to security read: "Each member must be searched upon entering the designated meeting place by the authorized and only those designated by the executive shall bear any offensive weapons. Members are cautioned to exercise extreme caution when attending."

Some Black Mafia members were blindfolded when they were transported to executive meetings in order to keep locations secret. When sensitive topics were raised, they were ordered out of the room. Secrecy was also addressed in the group's oath, taken by selected members:

I, in the presence of the brethren of the honorable assembly and council, do hereby promise and swear by all that I consider to be good, decent, respectable, pure, and/or sacred, yea, even by the blood that sustains my children, that I will never divulge any pertinent information, or secrets that pertain to the family, and I shall ever be on guard against those who would and report any such violations to members of higher authority to see that the violations are properly acted upon. I swear by my own life that I will not communicate any information to any law-enforcement official or anyone else in any way, that which could endanger the safety or freedom of another member.

There are few similar examples of any organized crime syndicates convening formal, business-like meetings, complete with attendance rosters and minutes. The Black Mafia's predilection for bureaucracy was therefore novel – and perilous, because the underworld requires a delicate balance between organization, to increase the probability of illicit ventures, and *dis*organization, to avoid becoming too predictable and thus an easier target for competitors and law enforcement.

Though no one could predict what was in store for the new syndicate, two things were not in question: this was an impressive collection of violent cons, and two of them stood out – Sam Christian and Ron Harvey. This utterly ruthless duo probably instilled more terror than any pair in Philadelphia's history. They were often suspected of committing crimes in concert, and were once arrested together for assaulting a police officer. Christian had already earned his place among the criminal elite, and was known to be a hired gun. "Sam was the kind of guy, if you were a financier and you hadn't been paid, you reached out for, for a price, and he would make everything right," said one street source. Harvey was also more than a just founding member of the Black Mafia; reporters and officials who investigated the syndicate speak in awe of his street status. A flamboyant, big spender who had a voracious appetite for women, often enjoying several simultaneously, Harvey was known for one thing over all others: violence. Even among fearsome colleagues, he was feared. According to his attorney, the five foot eleven, 200lb Harvey "looked athletic; he was built as strongly as anyone I've ever known." The attorney also said Harvey was a "religious fanatic in that he followed the word of Islam to its fullest degree."

Legend has it that Christian and Harvey once walked into a speakeasy to get in on a major craps game that was run and patronized by some of the most dangerous street hoods of the time. When the pair entered the joint, the game's participants fell over themselves to offer up the pot: "Take it! Just take it!" The crowd was comforted when one of the two Black Mafia chieftains said they were simply there to hang out and shoot craps, not steal the pot. Christian and Harvey were *superfly* personified. In short, they owned the streets of Black Philadelphia, and their reputations served as a great recruiting tool for their syndicate. Indeed, their predilection for fine women, group sex, stylish clothes and late model Cadillacs would be emulated by many of their Black Mafia brethren, though none ever evoked the same fear and paranoia.

The early Black Mafia years brought plenty of new members, associates, and arrests. Importantly, though, law enforcement officials, who at that time were unaware of the group as an organized entity, had difficulties prosecuting Black Mafia members because witnesses would rarely cooperate, fearing retaliation, and cases were usually dropped. This not only permitted the gangsters to continue their criminal activities, but also allowed their reputation for "untouchability" to flourish, enhancing their influence on the street. Many syndicate crimes went unreported, and the term "Black Mafia" would not itself become public currency for several years.

★

It was Saturday night, and Nathaniel "Rock and Roll" Williams, one of the Black Mafia's youngest founding members, was decked out in a green knit shirt, green pants, green loafers, a brown leather jacket and a "jeff" cap. Williams had quite a reputation for the fast – and dangerous – life, as evidenced by his lengthy criminal record. His rap sheet listed seventeen arrests for crimes ranging from gambling, theft and robbery to weapons violations and aggravated assaults. He also had a rep for reckless bravado. "The old people around the way had a saying that Nate was 'Death Struck,'" said one source. "I mean that he was not afraid of anything. I once saw him walk up to a guy who had a loaded shotgun pointed at him, punch the guy in the face and [take] the shotgun."

On 19 April 1969, Williams, as was his custom, orchestrated a craps game, this time over Junior's Barber Shop on South Street. Perhaps not satisfied with the modest proceeds from running the game, Williams dreamed up a plot to rob his own game. He recruited Ernest West and Edward Simpkins and another person known only as Upchurch, all said to be members of the Clymer Street Gang. West and Simpkins traveled together to the barbershop, where Upchurch had already settled in with the crowd. After hanging out at the craps game for a while, West gave the signal and, with guns drawn, they took the pot and ran to a waiting car a block away. Williams let all three men into the car and drove to 13th and Kater to split up the take.

Williams was ecstatic. The heist had gone off without incident and the take was enough for a decent share each. He had made one major miscalculation, however. He had organized the craps game with a partner, the formidable Robert "Bop Daddy" Fairbanks, and Fairbanks was at the game with other Black Mafia leaders when it was robbed. It wasn't lost on them that the youthful Williams was absent from his own game. The search for him and his confederates began immediately.

Fairbanks and Walter Hudgins got word that one of the robbers was at the Postal Card Bar, an elaborately decorated and well-stocked bar/restaurant located at 1504 South Street. They visited the bar, where they quickly found Edward Simpkins. Fairbanks told Simpkins, who had already heard they were looking for him, to step outside, and he readily complied. As the door closed behind them, Bop Daddy stepped away from Simpkins, looked up and down the street, and pulled a gun from his coat pocket. In front of a crowd of thirty people that had gathered around, Bop Daddy shot Simpkins in the chest, then kept the gun pointed at him as he grilled him on the whereabouts of his co-conspirators. Someone in the crowd pleaded for Fairbanks to let Simpkins get to a hospital, as the wounded man insisted he had no idea where the other stickup men had gone. Frustrated, Fairbanks and Hudgins considered taking Simpkins in their car to search the area for the others, but decided to leave without him. "Sissy motherfucker," snarled Fairbanks as he departed.

Bop Daddy and Hudgins returned around ten o'clock, this time with one Jerome Barnes, and parked Hudgins's car in front of the Postal Card. All three Black Mafia enforcers entered the bar, along with their top man, syndicate founder Sam Christian. They were now searching specifically for their own Rock and Roll Williams, ringleader of the holdup.

Williams was in the bar standing next to another legend in this crowd, James "P.I." Smith, when the quartet of embittered gangsters entered. Jerome Barnes took up a post at the door, with Christian at a nearby phone booth, leaving Hudgins and Fairbanks to find their target. Openly brandishing guns as they searched, they found Williams midway through the bar, sipping a drink. They pointed their guns at his head in front of the large crowd, and promptly ordered him outside. Christian walked out with the group and left. His three henchmen put Williams in Hudgins's steel gray Cadillac, distinguished by its black vinyl top, and sped off with Barnes at the wheel.

They drove Rock and Roll to a dark and desolate area on 26th Street, just south of Penrose Avenue, and stopped. Whatever pleas he may have made were to no avail. Hudgins and Fairbanks took him from the car, shot him four times in the back and dumped him on the highway. An employee of the nearby U.S. Naval Base found his body just after midnight. Williams lay face up, with his jacket thrown open and his shirt pulled up to his chest, exposing his bloodied stomach. Some of his personal items littered the pavement beside him.

Police properly termed it a "Black Mafia execution." Fairbanks and Hudgins were each arrested in their homes in the early hours of June 30. When police searched Hudgins's residence, they found a loaded .32

revolver, 186 bags of heroin, hypodermic needles and a syringe. Hudgins had a remarkably lengthy arrest record dating back to 1951; some of his twenty-three collars were for burglary, aggravated assault, weapons violations, rape, and robbery. Fairbanks and Barnes had been arrested eighteen and ten times respectively. Barnes was not apprehended for the slaying until August 12, when he was pulled over by police for driving through a stop sign. As the officer started asking routine questions, Barnes grabbed the officer's gun and wrestled it away, then fled into a nearby home as scores of police responded to the scene. He was found hiding under a bed, with the gun placed in a clothes hamper.

Police never found the murder weapon, and the case relied on the testimony of eyewitnesses to the craps game stickup and the ushering out of Williams from the Postal Card Bar. One witness, Yvonne "Bonnie" Bell, claimed Barnes had discussed the incident with her in detail, implicating himself, Hudgins and Fairbanks and corroborating much of what police had learned from other witnesses. But after the prime witness refused to appear in court, fearing for his safety, little evidence remained against Hudgins and Fitzgerald, and charges against the two were dropped. The charges against Barnes stood, however, and he went to trial in October. One of the key remaining prosecution witnesses recanted his earlier statements to police, while Yvonne Bell's otherwise compelling testimony was clouded by the fact that she was in custody at Philadelphia's House of Correction, serving time for "operating a motor vehicle without a serial number." The arrest was just one of fifteen that Bell, *aka* Cookie Rump, had amassed in a criminal career that consisted largely of thefts of one kind or another. The Barnes jury returned a not-guilty verdict, prompting the presiding judge to tell them, "This man is guilty, but the Commonwealth was hindered by a witness who had a bad past."

Of particular importance to the history of the Black Mafia, the investigation into Williams's murder was the first to turn up substantive intelligence about the group. Very few in law enforcement had even heard of the Black Mafia in 1969, and fewer still had any idea of the group's members or activities. Homicide detectives were taken aback by references to a Black Mafia given by witnesses to the murder. Asked about the organization, one witness said, "All I know is that it exists and it is true. They are a group of black men who are monopolizing the illegal things down South Philadelphia and everything is run by them."

Another source visited the Police Administration Building, PPD headquarters, on May 12 to provide information concerning the Black Mafia, particularly as it related to the murder of Rock and Roll Williams. He confirmed the motive behind the slaying, and also said that the group was responsible for a recent murder inside a record store at 52nd and Spruce Sts. This source provided law enforcement with the first known list of Black Mafia members, naming Richard James, Sam Christian, Donald Day,

Robert Fairbanks, Jerome Barnes, Charlie Block and Leonard Chaplin as some of the members. All but Block and Chaplin would go on to make names for themselves in the underworld as progenitors of the Black Mafia. None of this information, however, was disseminated to the department's Organized Crime Unit (OCU).

Federal authorities were also, independently, developing their first intelligence on the Black Mafia as a syndicate. The Bureau of Narcotics and Dangerous Drugs (BNDD) noted, "An organization known as the Black Mafia is active in the Philadelphia area and is composed of several Negro criminals who have set up a racket of selling protection to Negro narcotics violators in South Philadelphia, Pennsylvania." Another sign of a more formal criminal alliance was documented in a federal intelligence report that stated, "There appears to be a loosely formed Black crime syndicate in Philadelphia made up primarily of narcotics traffickers who are defended by the same defense attorneys ... operating for the benefit of the syndicate and not their individual clients."

None of this information was forwarded to the Philadelphia Police Department's OCU either, and the Black Mafia would not face a concerted effort by law enforcement for more than three years. Ironically, intelligence records have a few scattered references to a group of African-American men meeting at various locations along the 52nd Street strip in West Philadelphia starting in 1969. It was not until several years later, however, that officials realized what they had unwittingly observed were the meetings of the newly-created Black Mafia.

*

While law enforcement authorities were finding hints of a Black Mafia in April 1969, the controversial Black Coalition was facing its downfall less than one year after its incorporation. During its brief existence, the Black Coalition faced its share of ups and downs. Soon after formation, the Coalition tried to host an exhibition boxing match featuring Jeremiah Shabazz's friend and most famous convert, Muhammad Ali. The Coalition wanted to host a fight and/or an Ali training camp in Philadelphia to raise funds. Ali was at the time without a boxing license because of his refusal to enlist in the armed forces, and Shabazz was lining him up for a variety of speaking engagements and other events. Shabazz vowed that Pennsylvania would be "overrun with black militants" if the state rejected their efforts to get the exhibition sanctioned. Nonetheless, Pennsylvania Governor Raymond P. Shafer refused to permit the bout, prompting Stanley Branche to complain, "This is just another injustice directed at the black man by a governor who has never demonstrated any concern for black people." He added, "The Governor has revealed himself as a racist bigot – as much a bigot as any Southerner in the country."

In September 1968, the Coalition held a fundraising drive, ostensibly for youth education, and staged a motorcade fronted by the hustler Major Coxson (Major was his given first name) that started at his West Philadelphia home, traveled through the city, and ended at Gus Lacy's hot spot, Silky's. The event turned heads because each of the Cadillacs and Lincoln Continentals in the motorcade carried an attractive young woman, and because Muhammad Ali joined his new friend, Coxson, in the procession. "As a member of the Muslims," Ali said, "we are taught we must do something for our people. I am not here to lecture or to preach, but to help in this effort to raise money to educate black youth." As a sign of the complex times, Coxson went out of his way to thank Police Commissioner Frank Rizzo for assisting in the motorcade.

Muhammad Ali's presence in Philadelphia was significant because it lent credibility to the Black Muslims and, by extension, the Black Mafia, as the two were becoming increasingly interlinked. His alliance with persons embedded in the Black Mafia social system also created public relations difficulties for the authorities, and fed the concern of victims and witnesses that law enforcement would not take their complaints seriously.

On a couple of occasions, the militant factions within the broader Black Coalition effort engaged in internal power struggles, resulting in assaults, injuries, and bad publicity. In January 1969, Stanley Branche announced his intention to step down as executive director, stating that the organization needed a leader with a college education, "someone who knows administration and program designing." He added, "I was a fighter, but the days of the street demonstration are over." Weeks later, U.S. District Court Judge A. Leon Higginbotham, Jr., resigned from the Coalition board, citing poor book-keeping among the reasons. "I feel very strongly that we have not considered the $1 million commitment by the business community a trust rather than an outright gift," he added.

Soon after, the Coalition officially disbanded after infighting over use of funds and other matters. In April, it issued a statement that noted "businessmen were unable to deliver on a commitment for jobs for blacks at the rate promised, several gang-oriented programs failed and procedures and relationships between the Black Coalition and the [board of ten white businessmen supporting the initiative] proved cumbersome." In approximately ten months, the Black Coalition had spent $825,273 of the funds pledged on various projects and overhead. The pittance that remained was turned over to Philadelphia's Urban Coalition, another non-profit civic group with a similar set of mandates. Never one to turn up a self-promotion opportunity, Major Coxson seized on the demise of the Black Coalition, maintaining that he was forced out of the group's leadership. "I would have made something of the Black Coalition," he boasted.

While the Black Coalition experiment had broadly illustrated the problems facing Philadelphia and the commensurate difficulties in addressing them, it also had ramifications for the burgeoning Black Mafia crime syndicate. Beyond the public face of the Black Coalition and its efforts, a subtle message was being conveyed on the streets. In African-American neighborhoods, many took notice of the Black Coalition players who had "made it." Stanley Branche, Gus Lacy and Jeremiah Shabazz were now on the fringe – if not part – of the establishment, and other significant ties were growing. Branche and Lacy had both developed relationships with Police Commissioner Frank Rizzo. Branche's older brother Gilbert had worked his way up the ranks in the Philadelphia Police Department under Rizzo before leaving and becoming chief of county detectives within Arlen Specter's District Attorney's Office. In 1972, Commissioner Rizzo left the department after being elected Mayor. For the rest of his political career, he often popped into Lacy's Third Base, and the 52nd Street Strip was his locus of power in the black community, with Branche and Lacy leading the way.

Among other mutual endeavors, Branche and Lacy started the Advance Security Agency, Inc. in 1972. Advance Security garnered no-bid contracts from Philadelphia's Redevelopment Authority in 1974 because it was supposedly the only security agency available to provide the required services. This was immediately disputed by competitors who claimed they were shut out of the process because of Rizzo's close relationship with Branche and Lacy.

There was yet another connection between the Black Coalition crowd and the so-called establishment. Jeremiah Shabazz married Elizabeth Lee in 1954. Elizabeth's brother was Edward S. Lee, a former boxer who served as a task force coordinator in the Urban Coalition, the *de facto* successor to the ill-fated Black Coalition. People took note of Eddie Lee's relationship to Shabazz when Lee was elected Philadelphia Clerk of Courts in 1972 on the Democratic ticket under Frank Rizzo, who personally campaigned with Lee, an African-American, to garner white votes for him. Lee's term as Clerk of Courts was marked by several scandals, and his ties to the Black Mafia came under scrutiny by law enforcement when informants described meetings between him and high-ranking crime syndicate leaders. One informant said the Black Muslims had "plans for Eddie" and that he fit "into their master plan." This mix of inter-relationships would continue for the next two decades, providing the alliances of convenience commonly found in the social system of organized crime. Such networks confused and intimidated the Black Mafia's victims because they suggested the group was piped into the establishment through connections with power brokers like Shabazz, Branche and Lacy.

As one community-based initiative with ties to the Black Mafia went down in flames in April 1969, another was about to begin. Gang warfare had become a major problem in Philadelphia by 1968. Though tracking gang crimes is an imperfect science, the District Attorney's office estimated the numbers of gang-related deaths rocketed from one in 1962 to thirty in

1968. D.A. Arlen Specter concluded that innovative efforts were needed, and garnered funding from a private foundation to hire juvenile gang leaders to work in his office in the summer of 1968. Assistant D.A. Paul A. Dandridge, chief of the office's Community Rights Division, selected the gang members, who were paid $50 per week to perform messenger chores and to watch how the court system operated. The aim was to give gang members something constructive to do, to compensate them, to build respect for law enforcement, and to encourage them to disseminate what they learned to their peers. Though one of the participating gang members was arrested soon after the experiment, the D.A.'s Office was encouraged by the experience. As gang violence increased throughout 1968-69, Municipal Judge Dandridge (the former assistant D.A. was sworn in in January 1969), D.A.'s Detective Heywood Matthews, and Bill Wilcox, the executive director of another non-profit called the Greater Philadelphia Movement, accompanied several juvenile gang members on a rural retreat for "group therapy" in the spring of 1969.

Around this time, Specter used his connections to obtain money from the Department of Justice for a nonprofit corporation called Safe Streets, Inc., first envisioned by Bill Wilcox. The plan was to open and manage youth centers in ghetto areas that would serve as safe harbors and mentoring facilities. Specter said Safe Streets would "provide an alternative to the corner culture of the gangs, supplement or provide educational experience, stimulate family cohesiveness by involving other family members." The program was to "provide attitude training through retreats with group therapy experience, coordinate with the police to effect peace treaties among rival gangs to prevent or reduce violence, coordinate services with such groups as settlement houses, supplement existing recreational programs." Judge Paul Dandridge was picked to head the Safe Streets board, which included Specter, Wilcox, Matthews, A.D.A. Walter W. Cohen, James T. Giles, an attorney, and D.A.'s Detective Gilbert Branche, brother of fireball activist and entrepreneur Stanley Branche. According to Giles, the key premise of the program was to "go into the streets". He added that the Safe Streets concept was "purely one of interceding at places and at times where gangs had conflict before a firefight". Safe Streets, Inc. was awarded $80,267 from the federal government, and the Greater Philadelphia Movement added $25,000. Specifically, the federal funds came from the Law Enforcement Assistance Administration (LEAA), an outgrowth of the 1968 Omnibus Crime Control and Safe Streets Act.

Predictably, some in the D.A.'s office debated whether this was an appropriate approach to street crime, and if resources could have been better utilized. Police Commissioner Rizzo, despite his friendship with Branche, joined the critics by deriding the Safe Streets program as "soft" on crime. Nevertheless, Safe Streets, Inc. had opened two centers by August 1969 in West and North Philadelphia. Each center was run by a unit director, who was responsible for planning and supervising activities; an assistant director, who worked directly with the gangs on the street; a coterie of youth workers that consisted mostly of former gang members, who were responsible for working with gang members in the centers; teachers; and community organizers. Each center also had recreational activities, such as ping-pong and pool, card games and checkers.

Nineteen sixty-nine saw forty-three gang-related deaths, and it seemed the Safe Streets centers could not have opened soon enough. The unit director of the North Philadelphia center was Clarence Fowler, a thirty-one year-old Black Muslim and former gang member. Interviewed soon after his center opened, Fowler said times had changed for the worse on the street. "I was a gang member and we had some fights," he admitted, "but it was nothing like these boys do today. When they go for each other they arm themselves for total war. We want the boys to look beyond their present situation. We want them to see that there is no future in being a gang member." In time, many would question the oversight of Safe Streets, Inc. – and whether Clarence Fowler could heed his own words.

CHAPTER 3 ★
THE MERGER

AT SOME POINT in 1969, criminals within Philadelphia's Black Muslim community began competing with the Black Mafia for lucrative narcotics and extortion networks. They brought with them levels of discipline, hierarchy and image-awareness previously unknown among the anarchic, competing groups of the black underworld. Law enforcement intelligence files contain numerous informant references to the "Men in the Dark Suits," the criminal element within Philadelphia's Nation of Islam Temple 12, headed by Minister Jeremiah Shabazz.

Shabazz was born Jeremiah Pugh in Philadelphia on 27 November 1927 and grew up in the area of 25th and Master Streets. His parents had settled in North Philly from South Carolina. According to Jeremiah, he was raised a Christian – indeed his father's forenames were Martin Luther – but at age fourteen he was introduced to the teachings of Islam by a barber who'd been imprisoned with some Muslims down in Virginia. "I'd never heard of Islam before," he recalled. "I'd heard about Muhammadanism before, but the way this brother was talking, even though it was strange to me, it definitely had the ring of truth." By "Muhammadanism," he specifically meant the Black Muslim movement emanating from Detroit and Chicago. Within two years he was following the teachings of a man named Elijah Muhammad, and the course of his life was set.

The Black Muslim movement was born in the summer of 1930, when a traveling salesman named Wallace D. Fard began teaching African-Americans in Detroit about their "true religion – not Christianity, but the religion of the Black men of Asia and Africa." One of Fard's earliest understudies was Elijah Poole, who later adopted an Arabic surname, Muhammad. Under Fard, each proselyte was required to discard his "slave" name for his "original" Islamic name. Over time, changing names became a proud ritual for Fard's followers. There was a grace period for one to be awarded a Muslim name, and in the interim Black Muslims adopted the practice of replacing their slave surname with an X. A Nation of Islam official named Abass Rassoull, formerly Clarence Byrd, explained, "The names that the black man in America has are names that were given to their foreparents by former slave masters, and consequently are not a true indication of their origin, the continent of Africa, from which the black slave was brought here ... For example, if my grandfather or great grandfather worked on a plantation owned by a man by the name of Green, when they were freed they adopted the name Green ... Consequently, for the black man here in America, those names are not the names of their true foreparents. The teachings of the Honorable Elijah Muhammad were that by utilizing the X it nullified the slave master's name, it freed the man from the hold of the slave master because he taught us that if you go in the name of a man you belong to him, he has claim to you. The X nullified that. James X Smith, for example, nullified the name Smith."

Elijah Muhammad proclaimed that Fard was the earthly incarnation of Allah, and preached his idiosyncratic theories that Islam was the original faith of blacks prior to slavery and that whites were a race of devils created, according to some accounts of Fard's teaching, by an evil scientist. He offered blacks a credo of moral and cultural superiority to their white "oppressors," and the NOI's goals included establishing a separate nation state in the United States, within the framework of the law. After Fard's mysterious disappearance in 1934, Elijah Muhammad took on his work. He became "The Messenger" and eventually oversaw dozens of mosques nationwide, each numbered by city. He wanted to demonstrate that African-Americans would thrive under self-rule. The Black Muslims so focused on separatist rhetoric – it was a standard practice to refer to whites as "devils" – that observers often questioned the merits of this new "religion." One prominent scholar at the time wrote that the Black Muslims were an African-American "protest group," one which "like the NAACP, (is) frequently before the courts – but only on behalf of their own membership ... They want justice and fair play, but unlike the NAACP, they do not really expect the courts to give it to them through the normal processes of American jurisprudence, because they assume that whites are by nature incapable of justice towards Blacks. By nature they are devils." The public face of the Black Muslims was often the bluesuited, stone-faced members of the Fruit of Islam (FOI), an elite paramilitary guard responsible for investigating prospective members and protecting officials and property.

Jeremiah Pugh graduated from Philadelphia's Benjamin Franklin High School in January 1945 and enlisted in the regular Army in April 1946. He was honorably discharged as a "Technician – 5th Grade" at Camp Stoneman, California in October 1947, when he declared his intention not to re-enlist. Pugh had served one year and nineteen days in foreign service in the Pacific Theater, and was awarded the World War II Victory Medal and the Army Occupational Medal, Japan. His military records show that his character and efficiency ratings ranged from unknown to excellent. He returned to Philadelphia, got fired from a job with the U.S. Postal Service because of his unsatisfactory work ethic and absenteeism, and joined the Army Signal Corps Supply Depot as a mail and file clerk.

His life changed in 1954. First, he married Elizabeth Shirley Lee; secondly, Malcolm X came to Philadelphia to open the Temple of Islam Number 12. Malcolm X was by now the flamboyant, headline-making spokesman of the NOI movement, and at times overshadowed The Messenger himself. Formerly Malcolm Little, his life was representative of many NOI followers, and included poverty and prison. After stints as a bootlegger, a numbers runner, and a drug dealer, he converted to the Nation in 1948 while in prison, and began his rise within the NOI when he gained back his freedom in 1952. Malcolm X personified the civil rights movement's tilt toward militancy, and he spoke derisively of the peaceful sit-ins led by people like Reverend Martin Luther King. "Anybody can sit," he said. "An old woman can sit. A coward can sit ... It takes a man to stand." He pointedly admonished whites, "You might see these Negroes who believe in nonviolence and mistake us for one of them and put your hands on us thinking we're going to turn the other cheek – and we'll put you to death just like that."

Malcolm X found a loyal follower and a quick study in Jeremiah Pugh, and Brother Jeremiah soon rose to the rank of captain in Temple 12's Fruit of Islam guard. Jeremiah and Malcolm became virtually inseparable, and roomed together at 2516 W. Nicholas Street in North Philadelphia until Malcolm moved to New York. "Malcolm lived in a room with another brother and me for a year. So I got to know him well," recalled Pugh. "I woke up next to him every day, and went to bed next to him every night."

Though it was Malcolm who commanded the television cameras and the print media, upstart Pugh was doing his share to spread Elijah Muhammad's message throughout the country, building a significant following in Philadelphia and all the while honing his sales pitch. His oratorical skills were mesmerizing, and his stylish appearance – topped off by his large-framed eyeglasses – added to his mystique. He was a captivating speaker with a clear, direct message. "What we taught was different from what Martin Luther King was teaching," he later explained. "We dealt with the reality of the situation, not the way everybody wanted it to be. We taught first that God is a black man. Everybody else has a God like them. The Chinese have a Buddha who looks Chinese. Africans have a God on a stick that looks like them. The Europeans have a Jesus. And as far as white people were concerned, we taught that the white man was the devil. There's no devil in the ground ... To us, God is real, the devil is real, heaven is a place here on earth. When you die, you're finished. You go in the ground but there's no hell in the ground ... Hell is here on earth."

As Pugh quickly rose in stature within the Nation of Islam, the federal government became increasingly interested in his activities. The FBI started investigating him as early as September 1954. At the time, the Bureau was still compiling a list of the most significant communists and "racial agita-tors" called the Security Index, which listed these persons according to their estimated "degree of dangerousness." The Index, also called the Emergency Detention Program, dated back to 1939 and was "intended to facilitate mass arrests in the event of a national emergency." The authorities deter-mined that Pugh's former position in the Army, combined with his rank in the NOI – then referred to by the Bureau as the Muslim Cult of Islam – amounted to a potential national security threat. Within a few months, the FBI contacted his supervisors to advise them of his role in the movement and his status on the Security Index. As a result, he was suspended from his position in June 1955 and afforded a hearing to fend off dismissal.

On August 3, Pugh was charged with being an "active member of the Muslim Cult of Islam in Philadelphia which disavows allegiance to the United States, teaches and advocates civil disobedience, and teaches military drill, tactics and discipline in preparation for the destruction of the Government of the United States by force of arms and violence." It was claimed he was an officer within the Fruit of Islam, the "military branch" of the Cult designed to engage in force against "constituted authority." Because all federal employees signed an agreement upon appointment stating they vowed to "support and defend the Constitution of the United States ... SO HELP ME GOD," the panel asserted that Pugh's membership in the Muslim Cult of Islam was a violation of his employment agreement. To the consternation of the hearing's panel, Pugh repeatedly denied being a part of the so-called Muslim Cult and artfully dodged any questions of substance. Nevertheless, he resigned his position the following day, and went to work as a door-to-door salesman hawking massage equipment and Avon products while spending more and more time spreading the word of The Messenger.

Though obviously now aware of at least some of the law enforcement interest in him, Pugh and his NOI peers persevered and, indeed, prospered. Embodying the black militant ethos that would characterize the mid-to-late-1960s, the NOI grew exponentially, with Pugh as one of its main players. His passion for the movement can be sensed from "The Message" he preached:

> When somebody does to a people what whites have done to us for no reason whatsoever other than that our skin is black, then they must be evil for the sake of evil. And that makes them the devil. Their hatred of us has no grounds. There's no reason for it. We didn't do anything to them. It'd be different if there had been a war between Europe and Africa and Europeans had to wage war and take prisoners and then make slaves to save lives. But what hap-pened to us had no reason for it except greed, where they brought us over here to use our labor. And after using it, then they turned

on us and killed us and treated us worse than animals. They used us up until we couldn't serve them no more, and then they killed us ... Black people made America what it is today. The country became great because it had hundreds of years of cheap labor and black slaves ... Why are we so hated and despised when we've done nothing but work and slave for the white man all of our days? Today it's sophisticated slavery, but we're still slaves and the white man still hates us ... And I still don't know why ... All black people are doing is going to church singing songs, and praising the God white people taught us about, and they're still beating us and killing us and burning our homes."

Still ranked as a captain in the FOI, Jeremiah Pugh was effectively in charge of Temple 12. Malcolm X was the formal overseer of the Temple, but remained in New York and on the road, leaving the reins to his friend. Having established himself with the leadership, Pugh was put on salary in February 1956. He was promoted to Minister of Temple 15 in Atlanta in January 1958, and became the Nation's Minister over the Deep South. Of the experience, he later said, "Whenever we talked to black people, they had misgivings about what we were saying because black people generally feared whites, particularly in the South. That's what I saw at my post when I first went to Georgia. The biggest thing I saw down there was fear. And my leader, the Messenger, had told me to teach those people to overcome that fear because every black person knew one thing about the white man – if you said something he didn't like, he was going to get you, and fear of the white man's retribution was greater than any fear of God."

In Atlanta, Pugh went by the names Jeremiah X and Jeremiah Shabazz, and recruited and lectured throughout the South. Responsible for all mosques in Alabama, Georgia and Florida, he became enmeshed in a much-debated sequence of historical events regarding the NOI's relationship with the Ku Klux Klan. According to the FBI and others, Shabazz hosted a December 1960 meeting in his Atlanta home that included Malcolm X and the head of the Klan. The purpose was to broker a deal whereby the Black Muslims could create The Messenger's envisioned separate nation state within the U.S. The NOI was considering buying a large, county-sized tract of land in Georgia or South Carolina, and had been told the Klan, with its own ethos of racial separation, was supportive of such a proposal. The FBI concluded that Elijah Muhammad wanted to "induce Negroes to migrate and make it appear that his program of a segregated state or separate state was feasible." When the FBI interviewed Shabazz five years later, he denied involvement. Importantly, however, he disclosed two other occasions where he did meet Klan leaders. According to Shabazz, an attorney and KKK member named James Venable, who had been retained by the NOI on a prior occasion, brokered a 1963 meeting in Atlanta between Shabazz, Malcolm X and a Klan official. Shabazz, however, refused to say what was discussed at the meeting. He also admitted attending a public Klan meeting in March 1964, as a correspondent for *Muhammad Speaks*, the NOI's newspaper, and that he had no knowledge of discussions between the Nation and the Klan regarding a land purchase agreement. Regardless of which version of events is true, nothing ever came of the supposed NOI efforts to procure land for a state of their own.

One of Shabazz's most heralded achievements while in the South was the 1961 courting of a young fighter named Cassius Clay to the Nation of Islam. The NOI minister in Miami, Ishmael Sabakhan, introduced Clay, who had been brought up a Christian, to the teachings of Elijah Muhammad, and Shabazz was brought down to meet him. "He told me that he liked what he'd heard; he'd never heard anything like it before," said Shabazz. "It was new, it was strange, but it was also the truth, and he said he'd seriously consider becoming a Muslim. So we continued to talk with him, encouraging him to come to our meetings, which he did."

What Shabazz said to Clay during his recruitment is illustrative of the oratorical skills he employed during his rise in the Nation of Islam. He gave him his "no devil in the ground" speech about how the white man hated blacks and later insisted Clay was happy with the idea. "Cassius didn't have problems with our claim that the white man was evil," he said later. "Sometimes he'd ask questions like, 'Wait a minute, what about a baby? A baby is born white, how is it the devil?' And I'd explain, if a lion gives birth, it can't give birth to anything except a lion … This was in 1961, and there was a lot of outright injustice going on … You could pick up the newspaper every day, and see white police cracking black skulls and [setting] dogs on us. And the thing that really got Cassius was when we began to explain that, for someone to do this to other human beings, they can't be what he thought they were. They can't be God's people and mistreat other people the way white folks were doing. He was a young man, but a wise young man, so he was able to see that what we were teaching had truth.

"The more Cassius saw, the more he questioned; and the more he questioned, the more he convinced himself that what we were telling him was right. He'd seen the white man mistreating black people, saw his father and mother being disrespected and mistreated. So the real problem we had with him was not convincing him we were right. It was fear.

"He wanted to know how we could believe these things and say these things and keep walking around without the white man retaliating, because white people were killing black people every day. Cassius wasn't fearful of being shot or hung, but he had this great respect for the white man's power. From the President on down, the white man was it, and Cassius was asking, 'How are you going to overcome it? Even if what you're saying is right, how are you gonna beat the white man?' We had to convince him that the

God we served was greater and more powerful than the white man; that Allah had power over all things."

The two men would become great friends, and remained so for the rest of Shabazz's life. The boxer, however, initially kept his conversion quiet because, he said, "I was afraid if [the public] knew, I wouldn't be allowed to fight for the title." As Pulitzer Prize-winning author David Remnick wrote: "Ali knew that the few white people who did know something about the Nation of Islam saw it is as a frightening sect, radical Muslims with a separatist agenda and a criminal membership."

Reports of Clay attending NOI events, and of him spending time with Malcolm X, filtered into news reports and became common gossip. He finally disclosed what was obvious to any casual observer on 26 February 1964, the day after his momentous title victory over Sonny Liston in Miami. Elijah Muhammad took advantage of the great opportunity for exposure, proclaiming that Cassius Clay had won thanks to Allah and his Messenger, and soon announced in a radio address that he had given Clay his Muslim name, Muhammad Ali.

Years later, boxing aficionado and Ali confidant Ferdie Pacheco summed up Ali's rationale for joining the Nation. "Ali understood strength," he said. "Just like Sonny Liston understood the Mafia, Ali understood that you did not fuck with the Muslims. He liked their strength. He turned his head away from the fact that, especially in the early days, the Nation was filled with a lot of ex-cons, violent people who would go after you if you crossed them." Pacheco also believed Ali was paid top dollar for his fights partly because high-profile promoters feared someone like Jeremiah Shabazz might be behind Ali's business manager, ready to act as an enforcer if the promoters attempted to put one over on Ali.

After spending just over five years successfully establishing the NOI in the Southeastern United States, Shabazz was transferred back to Philadelphia in April 1964. Now one of Elijah Muhammad's closest advisers, he returned to his hometown as a minister with national influence and connections. As head of Temple 12, he was responsible for Southeast Pennsylvania, Southern New Jersey, and Delaware, and played upon the poor conditions of the city's African-Americans to recruit, exploiting the resurgence in black pride. He also took advantage of the acrimonious relationship between the black community and the police department. Shabazz was not back in Philadelphia more than four months when he witnessed the three days of Columbia Avenue race riots. He appears to have been no more than a spectator; when the FBI investigated any role he might have played in the riots, it concluded he'd had nothing to do with them and had instructed his followers to stay away from such incidents.

Meanwhile, the NOI's most famous figure was about to make a fateful decision. Malcolm X took the traditional pilgrimage to Mecca in 1964, and returned a changed man. Greatly influenced by the sight of, and from bonding with, Muslims from different backgrounds, Malcolm X turned increasingly toward Orthodox Islam, rejecting racial separatism. He also began arguing publicly with Elijah Muhammad and other NOI leaders, sparking rumors about what the consequences for such impropriety would be. In November 1964, an FBI informant inside Washington's Temple 4 told the Bureau that an announcement had gone out to the Fruit of Islam: Malcolm should be attacked on sight. On December 4, Louis Farrakhan (then known as Louis X) wrote in *Muhammad Speaks*, "If any Muslim backs a fool like Malcolm ... he would be a fool himself ... Only those who wish to be led to hell, or to their doom, will follow Malcolm. The die is set, and Malcolm shall not escape ... Such a man is worthy of death." A cartoon of a cemetery accompanied the article; on the tombstones were the names of infamous traitors such as Judas, Brutus, and Benedict Arnold, and the cartoon depicted Malcolm's decapitated head bouncing into a bed of bones with a tombstone marked with his name.

When Malcolm and his bodyguards arrived at a Philadelphia radio station for an interview on December 29, a crew from Temple 12 met them, and fought with Malcolm's guards in their effort to get at him. A police detective happened to be in the area, and managed to break up the fistfight. The crew sent to attack Malcolm was led by Sterling X. Hobbs, a gangster who was usually called upon when the need for physical force was expected. Hobbs would make headlines a decade later, but for now his importance was tied to Jeremiah Shabazz. He was close to Shabazz and thus the attack on Malcolm suggested that Shabazz had allied with Elijah Muhammad against his former friend and roommate.

Another article in *Muhammad Speaks* predicted that 1965 would be "a year in which the most outspoken opponents of the Honorable Elijah Muhammad will slink into ignoble silence." Malcolm X took the threats seriously, and told anyone who knew him that his life was in danger. His concerns were validated on February 14 when his house was firebombed. Malcolm survived and continued to speak out against Elijah Muhammad. On February 21, he was on the stage again, about to speak, when he was shot dead. Elijah Muhammad expressed no sympathy for Malcolm's death, stating instead that "Malcolm died according to his preachings. He preached violence and violence has taken him away."

The public assassination of Malcolm X served notice that virtually no one was untouchable or out of the NOI's lengthening reach. Federal authorities, of course, watched with a keen interest. J. Edgar Hoover's Security Index was increasingly listing Black Militants rather than Communists. That did not satisfy Hoover, however, and he instituted a refined listing called the Rabble Rouser Index for "individuals who have demonstrated a potential for fomenting racial discord." It included Jeremiah X. Shabazz, and listed several of his aliases: Jeremiah Pugh, Jerry Gerado, Geronimo, Jermal Shabazz, and Jamal Shabazz.

★

As the 1960s came to an end, Philadelphia's Black Muslim membership was roughly 10,000. The number of criminals within the Mosque was never estimated. Nevertheless, there is no doubt the criminal subgroup within the NOI far outnumbered the nascent Black Mafia in numbers of affiliates and weapons as early as 1969. It was inevitable that the two groups would come into contact, and given the uncompromising nature of both, a violent clash seemed likely. Yet any notions Sam Christian and his men may have had that they could simply take over Black Muslim territories they way they had with many neighborhood gangs were dispelled by several high-profile Black Muslim shootings. Faced with a turf war that they would undoubt-edly lose, the Black Mafia opted to become, in essence, the extortion arm of Temple 12. Christian and other Black Mafia members were already Muslims and knew many members of the mosque. It was the formality of the relationship, and the conversion of many underlings, that made the deal significant.

Depending on a Black Mafia affiliate's standing in the "Muslim faith," ability to generate money, and prior history of violence, he could be incor-porated into the intimidating Fruit of Islam. Sam Christian was immediately made a captain in the FOI. He would be responsible for sanc-tioning murders and other criminal acts, and reported directly to Jeremiah Shabazz. Roosevelt "Spooks" Fitzgerald became Brother Investigator to Shabazz, and reviewed prospective members, complaints on active members, and possible security leaks. The informal absorption of the Black Mafia into the Mosque was never complete, however. Many Black Mafia affiliates chose to forsake becoming Muslims, and were therefore excluded from positions of power. These affiliates continued to operate, however, with the permission of the Black Mafia leadership, although they now paid a higher percentage of their profits in tribute to their bosses.

The new structure provided several benefits. For both the criminal element in the Black Muslims in Philadelphia and Chicago, and the Black Mafia, the take would be greater, since there would be a virtual monopoly on the narcotics trade in several significant sections of the city and the trade would have the backing of some of the city's most notorious criminals. The newly-formed group's presence on the street also had an intimidating effect on witnesses to their activities. Victims and witnesses generally would not testify against either group prior to the merger; now, the prospect of facing in court one of a 200-strong criminal supergroup of "hardened street soldiers" was even more frightening. The Black Mafia now felt comfortable expanding their extortion to include many legitimate businesses. They and the Black Muslims had avoided a fight in the streets that would have been costly both in manpower and in business, as any such battle would have drawn heat from the cops. The Muslims had much to gain, as they would now receive portions of the Black Mafia's narcotics and extortion rackets, while maintaining the profits from their own illicit activities. Perhaps the biggest beneficiaries, however, were low and mid-level Black Mafia affiliates who opted not to enter the Mosque. Though they kept a smaller percentage of their profits – because both the Black Mafia and the Black Muslim commands were now getting a cut – all of these affiliates now had more recognition, backing, and power on the street. They faced less competition, their territories expanded and they had more business and job security than before the merger. The Black Mafia's highest command seemingly had less to gain, since they would now be sharing some of their profits with the Mosque. Law enforcement sources placed the group's contribution to the Black Muslims as high as $4,000 per month. For them, however, security was worth the tribute they now paid.

The merger afforded the Black Mafia the opportunity to create a more powerful political problem for authorities, for it was no longer simply race but religion too that could be exploited as needed. In addition to the public relations challenges the alliance presented to authorities, the syndicate now routinely attempted to exploit the legal system. Two defendants in one high-profile case appealed their convictions on the grounds of "racial and religious prejudice." In another noteworthy case, Black Mafia attorneys criticized the *voir dire* process with particular respect to the purported anti-social propensities of the Black Muslims. Specifically, defense counsel "urged that the court ask six specific questions of the individual jurors designed to elicit the jurors' attitudes to the Black Muslims. The court refused, and instead directed general questions to the panel at large with respect to prejudice on the basis of race, religion, or membership in the Black Muslims." In this atmosphere, otherwise nondescript robbery and extortion trials assumed serious racial and religious undertones. One high-profile case involved a prospective juror admitting she "might be confusing the so-called 'Black Mafia' with the Black Muslims." On appeal, defense counsel argued that the court "failed to fully explore the prejudices of potential jurors against members of the Black Muslim faith."

Another benefit of the merger, which would be essential to several of the Black Mafia's elite, was the ability of the Muslims to hide wanted criminals throughout their national chain of mosques. Philadelphia alone had at least five mosques. For authorities, it was inherently more difficult to obtain search warrants for the mosques because they were, at some level, places of worship. The mosques also employed Black Mafia fugitives as needed, and some mosques doubled as warehouses for the group's arsenal of weapons. Police received detailed information regarding the existence of stored weapons in the two largest Philadelphia mosques, along with the protocol for how they were to be maintained and accessed. Intelligence sources also described a mosque in Pittsburgh with a firing range in its basement.

The Black Mafia gained further stability, continuity and recruits from the Black Muslim prison networks. At some point in the 1960s, many prisons, particularly in the Northeastern United States, became the province of the Black Muslims. Intelligence came through that the Muslims were "in control of the major prisons" and were considered by inmates to be the best form of protection. Young prisoners with lesser sentences would join the Muslims for the purposes of protection, and were then schooled in criminal ways. Generally speaking, Black Muslim prison leaders were lifers and had nothing to lose by committing acts of violence and insubordination. If a top Black Muslim was transferred to another institution, his rank and position was retained, and the recruitment continued. Their protection was to be paid back through various means once the convict returned to the outside. Often this meant simply that financial deals were brokered, while on other occasions it involved providing various resources for family members and girlfriends. For the highest level of Black Muslims, beneficiaries of their protection who got out of prison were to retain drug territories once held by the hierarchy and remit a percentage of the proceeds.

In Philadelphia's Holmesburg Prison and Pennsylvania's Graterford Prison, forty-five minutes northwest of the city, *Muhammad Speaks* was a popular read. The Black Muslim populations there were significant enough that it was not uncommon for Jeremiah Shabazz to be called upon to help settle disputes. Indeed, NOI activities were so pervasive in Philadelphia prisons that several employees voiced concerns for their safety. "I used to love my job," said one Holmesburg guard. "Now I mark the calendar each day and say, well, that's another day toward retirement. The Muslims have close-order drill and practice karate. All I and the other guards can do is see that they go in and come out of their cells at the right time. They are calling the shots in there." Another Holmesburg worker said part of the reason he quit his job was the growth of the Black Muslim movement.

The Black Mafia also exploited some of the several Black Muslim businesses in the city. For instance, there were two Shabazz Bakeries, one located at Broad Street and Susquehanna Avenue and one on South 60th Street. The Shabazz Steak Shop was located at 6406 Stenton Avenue, and Spooks Fitzgerald operated the Shabazz Steak and Take on South 24th Street. Each of these locations came under extensive surveillance because law enforcement believed they were fronts for illicit Black Mafia activities. The vast majority of Black Mafia affiliates arrested listed one of these locations as their place of employment, while others listed themselves as employees of *Muhammad Speaks*.

One aspect of the loosely-knit Black Mafia-Temple 12 fabric was clear: a percentage of all money from Black Mafia activities was to be remitted in some fashion to the Philadelphia Mosque, headed by Jeremiah Shabazz. Each mosque, while under his ultimate control, was run by a lieutenant who was responsible for picking up protection money and the proceeds from other illegal operations in his designated territory each week.

According to a police informant, Shabazz was "confident and not at all worried about law enforcement agencies probing the Black Mafia, since he had kept himself far removed from actual involvement." His right-hand man was identified only as Lieutenant Gerald X, and was described by street sources as a ruthless murderer. Gerald would travel throughout the city's black neighborhoods with a select few Black Mafia members to commandeer lucrative drug corners. Law enforcement authorities and numerous street sources firmly believe that, after Shabazz took his percentage of the proceeds, his Philadelphia Mosque then sent a portion back to Elijah Muhammad in Chicago.

This confusing merger caused outsiders grief when trying to understand the groups involved. It is also why references since have intermittently referred to Philadelphia's Muslim Mob or Muslim Mafia. In fact, what those who use these terms are referencing was the newly syndicated Black Mafia criminal subgroup of Temple 12.

By the time Sam Christian and the rest of the Black Mafia were more formally incorporated into the Mosque, the foundation for underworld success was laid. Temple 12 was thriving under Jeremiah Shabazz and exploiting the militant strand of the black pride movement that rationalized many dubious acts under the ends-justifies-the-means philosophy, or as Malcolm X once famously put it, "By any means necessary." Shabazz's local Black Coalition and national NOI connections would also come in handy for his pursuits and for the syndicate.

One of Shabazz's Philadelphia converts, who would also make a name for himself in the Black Mafia, was overwhelmed by his introduction to the NOI. John Griffin (*aka* Omar Jamal) went to Temple 12 and saw a stage with a blackboard, just beside the podium, with a compelling message. "On one side was a drawing of the American flag, a cross, and a black man hanging from a tree," said Griffin. "The words on that side said, 'Slavery, Suffering and Death equals Christianity.' On the other side, it read, 'Freedom, Justice, and Equality equals Islam.' And, right in the middle of the board, were the words, 'Which one will survive Armageddon?'" Griffin was impressed with other things he saw that day, but came away most influenced by the talk given by Jeremiah Shabazz. "I was amazed, never had I heard such things. Never had I even thought of us in comparison with others in God's creation. Nor had I ever been in the midst of so many single-minded black people thinking about and being concerned with their own." Around the time the Black Mafia was being more fully absorbed into the Mosque, Griffin was arrested with Spooks Fitzgerald and Edward Sistrunk for possessing loaded firearms, one of which was stolen, following a car stop. After their arrest, a robbery victim identified Sistrunk and Fitzgerald as two of the three men who had broken into his home the week before, tied up his wife and daughter, and hit him on the head with a gun before taking $500.

By then, the impressive, intimidating presence of Temple 12 members on the streets of black Philadelphia was palpable. It was said that someone could park a car in a rough neighborhood with the windows down and the keys in the ignition and only needed to place a copy of *Muhammad Speaks* on the dashboard to ensure no one would touch it. Yet Jeremiah Shabazz was taken off the FBI's Agitator Index after the Bureau concluded, "He is interested in furthering the cause of the NOI, but is not interested in joining other groups that were involved in racial disturbances. During past racial disturbances Shabazz has instructed his members not to take part. It is not felt he would engage in treason, rebellion, insurrection or other such acts which would result in interference with, or a threat to, the survival and effective operation of national, state or local government."

The merger had taken place, the criminal powerbase within the Mosque was greater than ever, yet to the FBI, Minister Shabazz was the acceptable face of the area's Black Muslim movement.

CHAPTER 4 ★
THE ENFORCERS

T HE RAP sheet of Richard "Pork Chops" James included, among many entries, an arrest for "assault and battery with a sledge-hammer." His brutish nature made him a valued member of the Black Mafia's muscle platoon. Little more than a month after the murder of Rock and Roll Williams, James was handpicked to deal with an official called David Trulli, who headed the enforcement division for Pennsylvania's Insurance Department in the state capital, Harrisburg. On 29 May 1969, Trulli received a call at his home in South Philadelphia from someone identifying himself as "Frank," who told him, "We have some documents that you might be interested in." Trulli was preparing to take the witness stand in a major fraud trial the following week, and he assumed the proposal was related to the case. He was directed by the caller to Ellsworth Street and Cobbs Creek Parkway in West Philadelphia, and promptly drove alone to the location.

When he arrived, at approximately 11 P.M., he was met by a man who asked him to identify himself. Trulli did and was told that Frank was around the corner and would be back in a few minutes. A second man soon joined them and asked Trulli if he was from the Insurance Department. They then suggested the three of them walk to Frank's location. Now suspicious, Trulli refused, but they jumped him. One held him down while the other beat him on the head with a lead pipe. Before he collapsed, bleeding and on the verge of unconsciousness, he screamed for help, and someone from the neighborhood came to his aid as the assailants fled. Trulli lost three teeth, and required twenty-six stitches to close his wounds.

Authorities believed this was a cut-and-dried case of intimidating a witness to prevent him from testifying. "There is no question that there was a contract in this case," said Assistant D.A. Richard Phillips. "This is definitely the work of the Mafia." Phillips was half right – it was the work of the *Black* Mafia, now officially in the business of contracting violence.

Six months later, James was arrested in New York City for murdering a woman and child during a botched "hit" in which he only wounded the intended target. On 21 February 1971, before he could be brought back from jail for questioning about the Trulli attack, he was found dead from a heroin overdose. James had a history of thirty-two arrests, including the sledgehammer assault, and Camden Police Department intelligence files state that he was sent to New York on the orders of Bo Baynes to fulfil a contract of murder. They further state that his subsequent overdose in jail was, in fact, a "hot shot" given to him by members of the Black Mafia, arranged to ensure his silence in a Black Mafia-related assault case.

★

When the Omnibus Crime Control and Safe Streets Act of 1968 was passed, and identified street gang warfare as one of its main targets, Philadelphia was one of the cities at the forefront of the concerns. It had more than 100 street gangs. Among the most infamous was the 20th and Carpenter Streets gang in South Philly, and when the city attempted to broker peace agreements between warring factions to reduce the rising number of gang-related deaths, the 20th and Carpenter crew was one of the keys to success. Two of the gang's more influential members by 1967 were Charles Robinson, aged twenty-two, and James Fox, eighteen. They too were troubled by the fighting and drug dealing in their community, and decided enough was enough. With the aid of community leader Jimmie Lester, their gang became the first to lay down its weapons. Robinson and Fox also opened a youth center, the Council for Youth and Community Development (CYCD), in March 1970, at 20th and Pemberton Streets. A court stenographer was one of its incorporators and served as an adviser, and its supporters included Judge Paul Dandridge and City Councilman Thomas Foglietta. The stated purpose of the non-profit center was identified in its incorporation documents as, "charitable, scientific and educational."

Robinson was in the process of becoming an influential, positive force in the community while Fox was being groomed by civic leaders such as Jimmie Lester to run for political office. Despite Fox's criminal background (he had been arrested four times – twice for assault with intent to kill, once for robbery, and once for assaulting a police officer), councilman Foglietta once called him "the next Martin Luther King, Jr." He came from a crime-ridden environment, and many of his family had criminal histories, but, unlike many others in similar predicaments, he graduated from Edward Bok Vocational High School in 1966. He was employed by a men's clothing store as a presser until he left for the CYCD. Fox was a tough, stocky, imposing figure but also a polished, well-dressed young man, known for his deft social skills.

The CYCD center, a former police facility, was designed to provide a place for gang members to hang out, away from the violence of the streets. The city rented it to the CYCD for $1 a year. It had a pool table and other recreational amenities, and was said to support causes like the Police Athletic League. In addition to Robinson and Fox, its six incorporators included Robinson's brother William and one Russell Barnes. William Robinson was also a former 20th and Carpenter gang member, while Barnes was a Purple Heart Vietnam veteran who would soon make a name for himself in the Philadelphia underworld. At the time he had only one arrest on his record, for operating an automobile without the consent of the owner.

At some point in 1971, CYCD went the way of Temple 12. Founder Charles Robinson was on the way out, while two of his co-incorporators, James Fox and Russell Barnes, manipulated the center as part of the extortion enterprise operating out of the mosque. People close to Fox noticed striking changes in his appearance and attitude. The once subdued All-American boy began wearing flashy suits and slouch hats, and drove in expensive Cadillacs and Lincoln Town cars. He became a frequent spectator at boxing matches, often in the company of several women.

★

Black Mafia founding member Walter Hudgins and his wife, Josephine, hosted an after-hours party at their Federal Street apartment in the early morning of 5 April 1970. The crowd of twenty or so included co-founder Bop Daddy Fairbanks and a man with ties to the Black Mafia, Nate Swint. Swint had been convicted of second degree murder just three weeks earlier, and was out on bail. At some point during the party, he made a comment to Fairbanks about holding someone up, resulting in a heated argument between the two. Swint left, only to return a short time later in the company of his brother, Robert, and ring the apartment's doorbell. Walter Hudgins answered the door and, with the Swint brothers and Hudgins in the vestibule, Fairbanks opened fire, wounding Nate and killing Robert. Hudgins was also hit and wounded.

Fairbanks was convicted of second-degree murder, but the conviction was later overturned because of prosecutorial error, namely comments made by the prosecutor during the proceedings regarding Fairbanks's position in the Black Mafia. The prejudicial comments were several, including, "The reason [Fairbanks] was there ... is that he is an enforcer for a group that's loosely called the term or termed the Black Mafia." Furthermore, the prosecutor argued that Nate Swint was ambushed upon entering the apartment, and, "all of a sudden he sees his brother fall, no more than eight feet away he sees Mr. Fairbanks. Bop Daddy, the enforcer, the executioner, standing behind the kitchen wall firing a .38 caliber at his brother and then firing at him. They walked right into a death trap ... "

Though it was thought the dispute between Fairbanks and Swint concerned a disputed $700 Hudgins owed Swint for cocaine, outsiders have never fully understood what happened that night. Importantly, though,

Swint was soon a Black Mafia member and went on to establish himself as a player in the Philadelphia underworld.

The slaying of Rock and Roll Williams, the assaults on David Trulli and the Swint brothers, and other Black Mafia activities up until the spring of 1970, were creeping into the consciousness of the Philly underworld. A reporter who interviewed a prisoner about drug use was told of a group calling itself the "Black Mafia" that was approximately five years old. The prisoner, visibly nervous about spilling information on these men, explained that the rising syndicate was led by seven to ten main members who orchestrated its activities, including the control of much of the drug trade within the black community. The first hints of witness intimidation were already evident, he said, and there was a lot of fear in the community because this group had a reputation for carrying out contract killings. He added that their main drug operations were in North Philadelphia along Columbia Avenue between Broad and 19th Streets, and along the 52nd Street Strip in West Philly "because that's where Major is." The source was referring to the legendary Major Coxson, by then a main distributor for New York heroin kingpin Frank Matthews. One former junkie who bought heroin from Black Mafia-controlled dealers said that any dealers who came up short on payments usually got a second chance to make good on their debts. Often, the Black Mafia gave the dealer more stuff to sell. "If he fucked up again, it's his ass," he said.

Both law enforcement officers and reporters were also starting to catch wind of some of the group's activities, though no one grasped the totality of what was happening. One of the first Philadelphia detectives to develop serious intelligence on the Black Mafia came across them in early 1970 while investigating a series of drug-related shootings. Street sources mentioned someone named "Leon the Enforcer" as one of the toughs with this emerging group. "Leon would be called in if a pusher took a consignment of narcotics and went south with either the money or narcotics," said the officer. A prosecutor on one case said there was a group trying to cash in on the fear of the Mafia by letting itself be called the "Black Mafia." The tag also caused problems for the police who, when referring to the syndicate, ran the risk of being accused of racism at a time when race was at the top of the agenda in Philly.

In a May 1970 speech at a West Philadelphia church, a former police officer and Korean War veteran spoke about the political problems inherent in attacking the Black Mafia. The Reverend Melvin Floyd, who had just founded a grassroots group called Neighborhood Crusades, Inc., said authorities "would be faced with the possibility of offending the black community, and police can't really make a target out of the Black Mafia or make them a priority unless the politicians send down the word." In a sign of things to come, the Black Mafia marched on, untouched and unaffected.

★

Clarence Fowler was born in Oakfield, Georgia, where his family grew cotton and corn on a farm. In time, they moved to Philadelphia, and lived in a home on Randolph Street in South Philly. Fowler joined the Nation of Islam in 1965, just after Jeremiah Shabazz had returned to Temple 12 from his stint as regional head in the South. In fact, it was a sermon by Shabazz that moved Fowler to switch from Christianity. By 1970, Fowler was a captain in the NOI's paramilitary faction, the Fruit of Islam. He was also a unit director in D.A. Arlen Specter's Safe Streets, Inc. anti-gang initiative, having been picked to head the North Philadelphia office in August 1969. Unlike many of his FOI peers, Fowler didn't have a police record, but that was about to change.

Reverend Dr. Clarence M. Smith had been a minister at the Wayland Baptist Church at 25th Street and Columbia Avenue in North Philadelphia from 1937. The popular cleric had briefly been a member of the Pennsylvania House of Representatives, was active in numerous civic organizations, and in 1964 was honored with the "Above and Beyond the Call of Duty" award by the local chapter of the NAACP. He lived several blocks north of his church, took great care in his gardens, and neighbors gave him the credit for their block standing out as an oasis of freshness in the bleak North Philly ghetto. One remarked, "You look up and down this street, and go around to look at the backyards, the grass, the flowers, the neatness, and you'll see what Dr. Smith has worked for and influenced." He provided beat cops with iced tea on hot summer days. Everybody liked him, it seemed.

In 1970, Dr. Smith was sixty-seven years old and lived with his sixty-four-year-old wife, Lena, who had developed a heart condition. On May 18, their daughter, Beulah Hopewell, came over to check on her mother, and settled in at the breakfast room table. As she read the newspaper over a cup of coffee in the early afternoon, the doorbell rang. Her father answered it, and then she heard the voices of at least two men in the living room. She sensed someone was in the breakfast room, and turned to find a man standing in the doorway. "Don't look at me," he commanded. "Cover your eyes." Beulah's initial thought was that they were boys from the church joking or playing some sort of game. "Okay," she said, and turned back around, covering her eyes. The man quickly changed his mind, and ordered her to get up and come into the other room, where her father and the other man were. As she did, he again said, "Don't look at me," and put his hand in her face. Beulah noticed a gun in his free hand and hurriedly closed her eyes, realizing this was no prank.

Another man was standing in the living room with his back to her and handed a white envelope to her father. Upon opening it, he found a note with neat typewriting that read, "This is a stick up. Be cool. Do not move."

Beulah was made to lie face down on the dining room floor, and from her position she heard her father say, "You must be kidding. I have a sick wife upstairs." Smith also insisted he did not have a large stash of money in the home. Beulah's harasser was apparently frustrated with the scene, and admonished his partner, "Don't argue with the man. Just shoot the bastard." Reverend Clarence Smith was summarily shot twice in the chest at point-blank range in his living room, with his daughter powerless on the floor mere feet away, and his wife unaware upstairs. As he collapsed to the floor, he feebly called to his wife, "Sugar, I've been shot." He died within minutes, the would-be thieves leaving empty-handed.

As police scoured the scene for clues, Beulah Hopewell gave a description of the two men who entered the home. Both were black and wore dark suits, white shirts, ties and straw hats. The taller of the two wore gold-rimmed glasses, carried a long-barreled revolver, and was the man who handled her throughout the ordeal. That evening, Clarence Fowler was picked up by police, questioned for several hours, and consented to having his photo and fingerprints taken before being released the same night.

Speculation centered on the possibility the robbers thought Rev. Smith had the collection proceeds from Sunday's services, but one grieving colleague said, "They could not have known who he was to do this kind of thing. He was truly a great man and few other men commanded the respect from clergy, businessmen, workers – all classes – that he did. He has instituted youth programs, helped black businessmen, worked in his community, promoted civic pride – there's no end to the things that this man did. His death like this makes no sense at all, absolutely no sense at all."

The investigation lasted several months, before Beulah Hopewell picked out Fowler as the taller man who assaulted her, and he was ultimately arrested in August 1970. The intruder who handed Dr. Smith the note was never identified. Three days after the arrest, NOI Minister Jeremiah Shabazz called a press conference to announce that Temple 12 would defend Fowler. He also charged that the "vicious police" arrested Fowler solely because he was a Black Muslim, and decried police harassment of his followers after the murder. Fowler was convicted on November 9, 1972 of murder in the first degree, conspiracy, aggravated robbery, and burglary, and sentenced to life in prison. His conviction was controversial, and would later factor into the larger Black Mafia history. Meanwhile, Fowler would serve time in the Philadelphia-area prison system, where his leadership and power-broking skills would be honed and make him a legend in certain circles.

Three years after the event, investigators would question if robbery was, in fact, the motive for the Smith murder. The assailants did not take anything from the home, nor the wristwatch and $162 in cash Smith had on him. It would be a couple of years before law enforcement agencies discovered an extensive extortion racket run by the Black Mafia targeting churches. By then, it was essentially too late to return to cases such as the Smith murder, never mind the challenge of getting witnesses to testify against certain members of Temple 12.

★

Many crooks who had their own rackets up and running long before the Black Mafia existed were finding themselves in competition with the syndicate or being targeted for extortion. One was Eugene "Foo-Foo" Ragan, who split his time between running Foo-Foo's Steak House at 52nd and Locust Streets and managing a significant numbers business. By August 1970, Ragan had an impressive history of fifty-four arrests, mostly for numbers writing. On forty-two occasions, the cases were discharged, though he had been given three-to-five years in Georgia in 1955 for murder, and in 1962 he was sentenced to a brief term inside for corrupt solicitation and illegal lottery. His notoriety in the black community grew when he was shot twice in a gun battle in front of his steak shop. Ragan, who survived, believed someone named Dennis Swift was one of his assailants. One week later, Swift was shot twice, but he too survived. A few days later, Ragan was a passenger in a car which was pulled over by police. When the officer spotted three revolvers in the car, Foo-Foo offered him cash to ignore the discovery and was promptly arrested. It was soon established that one of the guns had been used in the Swift shooting.

Notwithstanding Ragan's criminal history, he soon found himself as an extension of the Black Mafia's racket. "The older heads like [Gus] Lacy and Ragan were given a choice: come in out of the rain or stay out there in the cold," said one informer. "They hadn't salted any money away and they were too old to take on the opposition, so they fell into line. The old saying used to be, 'You can't fight City Hall.' Now the saying is, 'You can't buck the system, and this is the system.'"

Though a numbers man at heart, Foo-Foo became a drug dealer of some renown as a middleman for a wealthy California businessman who supplied heroin to the Philadelphia area for the Black Mafia. Ironically, he was such a well-known numbers writer that his attorney, Robert Simone, used this fact as an unsuccessful defense against drug trafficking charges: "Foo-Foo Ragan is a numbers man, not a dope man," he announced to the court.

Ragan's decision to work with, or under, the Black Mafia was no doubt influenced by the syndicate's growing reputation. Shortly after the Ragan/Swift shootings, a Black Mafia crew of Ron Harvey, Donnie Day and Grady Dyches walked into the Lambert Bar on W. Susquehanna Ave., shot the bartender, and robbed him of $250. Predictably, the charges were *nolle prossed* when witnesses would not cooperate. Word on the street was spreading.

★

Harry G. Dubrow owned and operated Dubrow's Furniture Store on South Street. As 1971 began, his store had not been robbed in fifty-four years, a remarkable feat for an establishment in that bustling, crime prone South Philly area. Even pay phones were not immune – a diner across the street from Dubrow's had one removed because it was broken into so many times. Dubrow's luck was about to be tested, however; the Black Mafia was making extortion pushes throughout the South Street corridor, and the furniture store sat in the heart of their targeted area.

January 4, 1971, was going just as the Dubrow's employees expected for the first Monday following the New Year. As a rule, Mondays were slow, and the recent holiday only served to reduce the number of customers. Louis Gruby was the greeter for the store, responsible for meeting people as they entered and directing them to one of the two floors. In the early afternoon there was not a single customer, until Gruby's spell of boredom was broken when two men entered Dubrow's at 2 P.M. One of the them had noticeably protruding ears and was big, standing at least six feet four and *solid*. Gruby didn't the big man's identity or his background, but it was Black Mafia heavy Robert "Nudie" Mims. He asked Gruby if a salesman named Mort Grossman was around. Gruby said he was out on lunch break, and the two "customers" said they would wait for his return.

Two more men entered the store and asked Gruby where to find rugs, and he directed them accordingly. Several minutes later, another two men approached Gruby, asking to see some furniture. Soon, a seventh man came in, asking to see shag lamps, and yet another followed him. The men strategically placed themselves throughout the store, awaiting a signal from their leader. As the eighth Black Mafia affiliate entered, Gruby sensed something was wrong, but before he could take any action, Nudie Mims put a gun to his head.

"Do as I tell you or I'll blow your brains out," he said.

Several of the Black Mafia men in various parts of the store announced a hold-up and drew guns. One employee was on the phone when a gun was put in his face and he was told, "Don't say anything. I'll take the phone." Another was in her office when she heard, "Get on the floor or we'll kill you." She later said her assailant was "so cool and calm you would have thought he was asking you to dance." All of the employees were next herded together into the rear of the store, where they were told, "Be calm and you won't get hurt … If you move, we'll blow your brains out." Gruby and the twenty-three other employees were forced to lie face down on the floor, and the Black Mafia employed their trademark by binding each of them hand and foot, this time with tape and electrical cord.

Two handymen, Alton G. Barker and Daudis Burney, were about to exit a freight elevator just as the terror was unfolding, and tried to flee. "Hold it, hold it!" yelled a gangster, before shooting Barker just under his heart at point-blank range, dropping him near the elevator. Barker was then shot twice more in the back, one bullet fired with the gun pressed against him. Burney was struck in the right arm and left hand. Barker's hands were bound behind him using his belt, and he was dropped into the elevator, where a couple of Black Mafia members joined the injured Burney. On the way down to the first floor, one of the intruders asked Burney for the key to the store's rear door. He had it in his back pocket, and the robbers used it to gain entrance to the back alley, where a five-gallon can of gasoline had been placed before the assault.

Morton Grossman returned from lunch and, failing to grasp the situation, approached one of the Black Mafia members to see if he could be of assistance. The salesman was hit in the head, tied up and placed in the back room with his co-workers. Grossman next had his wallet, $400 cash, a wristwatch and a ring taken from him. His assailant tried to get a second ring from him, but couldn't get it off of his finger. Enraged, the robber struck Grossman in the head again, then shot him in the arm and back. While he was being worked over, the rest of the employees were also robbed, beaten and pistol-whipped, and another worker was shot.

William Dubrow, one of the owners, returned to the store and quickly became part of the hostage pool. The robbers took $315 from him, along with his watch and ring, before tying him up and dumping him on top of two other hostages in the rear room. Dubrow pleaded for mercy, explaining that he was having trouble breathing because of a heart condition, to which one of the marauders retorted, "If you don't shut up you won't breathe at all." The crew next ransacked the offices on both floors of the store, flipping over file cabinets and rummaging through them, apparently looking for cash and any worthwhile documents. In fact, there was little money in the store, beyond a trivial amount of petty cash found in a safety box.

The robbers began spreading gasoline over rugs, in offices and on paper strewn on the floors throughout the store. The terrified employees, who were still tied up in the rear of the store, watched in disbelief as *they* were doused with gasoline. One female employee had papers and coats piled on top of her, apparently to fuel the impending fire. As the gang prepared to leave, they set five fires throughout the store on both floors. Dubrow's employee Robert Porreca was hit on the head with a pistol and told to lie on the floor, after which gasoline was poured on his legs. One of the assailants flicked a match and dropped it on Porreca, setting him on fire.

The smoke from the multiple fires activated the fire alarm, forcing the eight intruders to hastily escape. They left Alton Barker dead, two employees shot, another in flames, and the rest tied up, beaten, terrorized, and all expecting to die in the spreading blaze. Adding insult to injury, as the Black Mafia henchmen left, they purposely stepped on the back of Mort Grossman, who was laying face down on a hallway floor, wounded from the shooting. They took $1,803 in cash, some jewelry and credit cards. Fortunately a few of the employees were able to untie themselves, and escorted the others out safely before the building could become consumed in fire. A combination of factors prevented a grand-scale inferno, primarily a lack of oxygen because the store was well-sealed and prompt reactions from some employees before the arrival of fire officials. "If a window or a door had been open, the place probably would have gone up in a matter of seconds," said a fire department spokesman.

"I have seen many crimes in my long police career," said Police Commissioner Frank Rizzo, "but this is the most vicious one I have ever come across." He went on to say that if the defendants faced the death penalty, "given the chance, I'd pull the switch myself." One Dubrow's employee said, "It was like a Western movie," while another said, "It was chaos. It was like being in a war. There were shots, men were being whipped, they were moaning and crying. And there were shouts, 'Shut up or we'll kill you.'" Store owner Harry Dubrow was confused. "I don't understand it," he said. "Who would rob a store on a Monday afternoon, and the Monday after New Year's at that?"

The motivation may have been robbery alone – the Black Mafia had quite a track record there – but police also received information that the store management had refused to pay protection money, and so may have been targeted for their non-compliance. This explanation made more sense to police, who pointed out the anomalies in the "robbery" – the intruders shot victims who offered no resistance, and the timing was curious, as there would have been little loot to steal.

Two days after the assault, Louis Gruby and another employee were shown more than 100 photographs of possible suspects. They both picked Nudie Mims as the man who first entered the store and who engineered the crimes. Intriguingly, police officers who arrived at the Dubrow's store observed Sam Christian standing across the street, but apparently no witnesses identified him during the investigation. Police immediately set up surveillance at Mims's home, his place of employment, his hangouts and, of course, at Temple 12. Authorities didn't get a whiff of Mims, however, and for good reason; he was already in Chicago being protected by the NOI. In Chicago, Mims served as bodyguard to Elijah Muhammad, spiritual leader of the Lost Society of Islam. He used various aliases, first among them being Robert 59X and Robert Green. When federal authorities finally tracked him down in September 1974, his wallet contained eighteen different identification cards in the name of Robert L. Green.

While awaiting trial and out on bail, Mims – Robert 28X in Philadelphia – listed his employment as circulation manager of Temple 12, the Black Mafia's primary headquarters. He went to trial in April 1975 and denied the charges, claiming he had moved to Chicago the day before the Dubrow's robbery and producing several witnesses from the Philadelphia and Chicago temples who corroborated his story. His main witness in this regard was Abass Rassoull, who identified himself as the National Secretary for the Nation of Islam. A jury rejected his alibi, and Mims was convicted of murder in the first degree, arson, two counts of aggravated robbery, three counts of aggravated assault and battery, and conspiracy.

The trial included a colorful exchange between Mims and prosecutor Frank DeSimone, when the Black Mafia founder said, "After I beat this rap, I want you to come up and have dinner on me at my restaurant," which was in the city's Ogontz section. DeSimone politely declined, and later joked, "In our Mafia, they kiss them on both cheeks before they take them out to dinner and lower the boom." Mims was sentenced to life imprisonment for the murder, with a concurrent five-to-ten year sentence for arson.

Police could only develop cases against three of the eight intruders: Mims (also known as Abdul Ameen Jabbar), Edward Sistrunk (Omar Askia Ali) and Ronald X. Boelter (Ahmad Abdus-Sabur). At the time of the robbery, the threesome had impressive rap sheets. Mims was first arrested in 1959, and amassed eight more arrests through 1969. His sheet was almost exclusively filled with crimes of violence, including aggravated assaults, robberies, weapons violations, and assaults on police. Sistrunk had been arrested ten times, beginning in 1959, and his record included several crimes of violence. Boelter had been picked up and charged by police three times before 1969, and was out on $4,000 bail for two violations of the Uniform Firearms Act. Like Mims, Sistrunk and Boelter were ultimately convicted of the Dubrow's attack.

The *Philadelphia Daily News* called the Dubrow's event "one of the most bizarre holdups in the annals of Philadelphia crime." A columnist for the *Philadelphia Inquirer* said, "It was one of the most coldblooded and inhuman acts in the long criminal history of this town," and a "showcase of savagery". Another said it "was an outburst of incomprehensible cruelty by a band of criminals whose motivation can't be explained by the lure of a day's receipts." The crime's notoriety inspired W.E.B. Griffin to write a novel, *The Witness*, based on it.

*

The Dubrow carnage bore similarities to other Black Mafia robberies, most of which involved at least one member of the Sam Christian-Ronald Harvey-Russell Meade triumvirate. On February 5, 1971, a month after Dubrow's, Harvey and Meade robbed the Uptown Dock Company in Philly's East Oak Lane section. They ordered all employees to strip at gunpoint, beat them, and took $5,000. On February 23, John W. Clark led Darrell Anthony Jackson and at least four others to the Southeastern National Bank in Exton, Pennsylvania. Two initially remained outside to guard the doors while the others entered the bank. Two of the four who entered were dressed in business attire, one was dressed as a priest, and John Clark wore a police uniform. Immediately, they pulled their guns and threatened to kill anyone who didn't cooperate, then herded employees and customers into the vault. The two lookouts joined their compatriots inside when another customer visited the bank. Their total take was $7,448.61, but they had made a significant mistake. Unlike the mom-and-pop shops they robbed with abandon, the bank had a surveillance system, which was activated just as the robbery began. The group's success at victim and witness intimidation became irrelevant at trial when they faced literally hundreds of quality photos taken throughout the robbery.

Robbery was second only to extortion as a Black Mafia moneymaker in the early years of the group, and though the robberies drew attention from authorities, they also increased the group's legend on the streets of black Philadelphia. Such notoriety is a fundamental component to the success of predatory networks, particularly extortion syndicates. Throughout 1971, the Black Mafia held up legitimate establishments while also extorting and robbing numerous individuals, particularly numbers writers and drug dealers. According to a June 1971 police intelligence report, for instance, African-American heroin dealers Eligah Jackson and Vernon Gregg "were robbed on several occasions by members of the Black Mafia and ... both fled the Philadelphia (PA) area when they feared a 'Black Mafia Contract' had been placed on them."

Around this time, the FBI was receiving information on Black Mafia activities in the drug trade. Specifically, the "Pennsylvania State Police (PSP) advised [the FBI] that a syndicate of blacks controls heroin traffic in Philadelphia." The document identified the leader as Major Coxson, and named other top Black Mafia figures including John Darby, James "P.I. Smith", Tyrone Palmer, George Glover and Eugene Baynes. Several of the listed individuals lived or conducted business in Camden, New Jersey. Thus, it was not surprising when Camden Police received information that Coxson had joined the party in the West Village Apartments on West Conshohocken Ave. Federal agencies considered the apartment complex a "beehive of narcotics activity." Several significant drug dealers – each of whom were Coxson associates – rented apartments there, and used them as safe houses and distribution centers.

Coxson's racket developed a bit earlier than the Black Mafia infrastructure. He had engaged in financial scams, car theft rings and drug networks from the late 1940s. He also had developed strong ties to quasi-legitimate businessmen along West Philadelphia's 52nd Street Strip. The 52nd Street crowd wasn't necessarily part of Black Mafia activities, but rather was alternately exploited and extorted. The relationship between independent drug dealers, financiers and grifters on the strip and the Black Mafia was complex, and consisted of numerous conspiracies, dual roles and inter-relationships. Three roughly autonomous social systems had been developing since 1965: Coxson and his multifarious crew, including actors from the 52nd Street Strip; cliques of African-American gangsters, mostly from South Philadelphia, who were slowly developing into a formalized group led by Sam Christian; and the more general criminal element of Philadelphia that would gain from membership in a criminal fraternity. It was not the manipulative opportunist Coxson who was the main link between all three worlds, though; it was Sam Christian.

★

In the early morning hours of 20 June 1971, police officers inside the city's 17th District in South Philadelphia were milling around the operations room when they were interrupted by a man who hurried into the building yelling, "There's four guys around my house with guns!" Two officers went with the man, Obie Scott, to his home on Titan Street to investigate. As their car turned onto Titan Street, Scott pointed to two black males on his doorstep and said, "That's them." The cops approached but the men ran down the steps and one threw a gun under a parked car. The other man briefly tripped and his gun discharged when he hit the ground, but he held on to it. The officers chased the suspects on foot, during which the man with the gun fired five shots at the officers but missed. The offenders escaped but Scott was able to identify all four: Sam Christian, Eugene Baynes, Ron Harvey and Ronald Woodruff. Police speculated that Scott was a numbers writer being extorted by the Black Mafia.

The following week, investigators were notified of a robbery of a numbers kingpin in Sharon Hill, Delaware County. Men burst into the target's home, only to find his wife home alone. They opted to bind and gag her, placed a bag over her head and waited for the numbers man to return. When he arrived, he was robbed of more than $10,000, but the crew let the couple live. Others would not fare so well.

Late in the evening of July 15, Dorothy Smythe was alone at her friend Harry Petros's Ardmore Court apartment in the suburb of Lansdowne, less than three miles from the 52nd Street strip, when two men knocked on the door, announcing themselves as Havertown Township police officers. Smythe let the pair in, and was held hostage for the next three-and-a-half hours as they awaited Harry Petros's arrival. The two intruders frequently phoned a third man who was stationed outside at a phone booth keeping watch. When Petros finally arrived, he was robbed of $2,000, and the crew left him and Smythe handcuffed and gagged. Somehow, Smythe got a phone off its hook and explained her ordeal to a phone operator.

As the late night turned to early morning, terror was now on its way to residents of a rural community in Delaware County, ten miles west of Ardmore Court. Gerald and Ruth Shoemaker lived in the quiet Middletown Township. Just before one o'clock in the morning, three men flashing silver badges and claiming to be FBI agents greeted Gerald when he answered a knock on his door. The bogus agents suddenly rushed into the house, placed Gerald in handcuffs and asked him if his name was "Marra." When told the "agents" were looking for black market cigarettes, Gerald pleaded ignorance, and the Shoemakers argued with the assailants in their living room for fifteen minutes. It was clear something was amiss, as the group tried to sort things out for almost thirty minutes, conferring with each other and making a phone call to confirm some information. The Black Mafia crew soon realized they were at the wrong house. Before splitting, the crew robbed the couple of several hundred dollars, and then handcuffed and suspended them upside down from the pipes and rafters in the cellar. Roughed up, robbed and traumatized, the Shoemakers would fare better than their neighbor, the intended target, who was also about to get unwelcome visitors.

James Mollo was a successful cigarette smuggler from South Philadelphia who had used the proceeds from his trade to move to the sticks west of the city. Every Wednesday and Friday, a truck made the trip from North Carolina to Delaware County with his illicit haul. Mollo lived next door to the Shoemakers with his wife, Philomena, and their three children. The family was home when the trio with bad intentions arrived, stepping onto the porch and knocking on the door. Mollo was in the basement tending to approximately 5,000 cartons of untaxed cigarettes, and didn't hear the knock. Philomena turned on the porch light and could see the visitors through a window.

"FBI!" one shouted. "Contraband cigarettes! Open up!"

Frightened, Philomena refused to open the door and rushed to get her husband, who came up the stairs, stopping just behind the cellar door in the kitchen. He also refused to open the door. One of the "agents" broke a glass window next to the front door and fired a shot at the cellar door that hit Mollo and sent him tumbling into the basement. Two men then burst in and Philomena rushed through the house to the back door in an attempt to flee. She was met by a voice yelling, "Get back inside. The place is surrounded."

As her husband lay dying from his wounds, Philomena was held in the kitchen and grilled by one of the gunmen, who produced a badge and continued the FBI charade. He wanted to know about the proceeds from the cigarette traffic, and where they could be found. The Mollo's daughter was now by her mother's side, and trembled as the gun was held beside her. Philomena unsuccessfully pleaded with the man to put the gun away and the group moved upstairs. They went into her son's bedroom and one of the attackers advised her of her rights, police-style, and asked her more questions. Unhappy with her responses, they put her in handcuffs and rummaged for her husband's neckties. Five children were in the home, including two guests, and each was bound with neckties while Philomena was paraded into the basement. When she saw James alive but in dire shape on the floor, she begged for someone to call an ambulance, to no avail. She divulged where the men could find $12,000 in the home, and they took the money and fled, sparing her life and the lives of the children. James Mollo, however, was out of luck and died soon after the men left. "There are more angles to this investigation than you could imagine," said one investigator on the case. "Organized crime, interstate thefts and murder are just hitting the surface in this puzzle." A police informer noted the Black Mafia had intelligence files that included "names, license numbers, car descriptions, associates, and the known haunts of all of us."

Not surprisingly, police have always thought the back-to-back events were related. The prime suspect in the Petros robbery was Russell Meade, the handcuffs used in the Shoemaker robbery were traced back to Sam Christian via a pawn shop in South Philadelphia, and the man later convicted of shooting and killing David Mollo was a member of Temple 12, Ronald J. Connolly. Interestingly, considering his crowd's relationship with the hustlers along the 52nd Street Strip, Connolly claimed to have been in a taproom at 52nd and Spruce at the time of the murder, some twenty minutes away from the crime scene.

Another Christian partner in crime was Harold Leon Baker, *aka* Leon the Enforcer, one of the cadre of toughs the Black Mafia employed on the street. In one span during this period of 1971, three separate shooting incidents were said to involve Leon firing one round into the left legs of the victims. On September 7, Labor Day, seven heavily-armed Black Mafia members entered the dimly-lit, smoke-filled Adelphia Bar in a decaying area of the fading resort town of Atlantic City, New Jersey. Led by Sam Christian, Russell Meade and Roosevelt Fitzgerald, they approached a barmaid and asked her for the combination to the bar's safe. When she told them she did not know it, the gangsters bound twenty-five patrons with rope and tape and awaited the return of the manager. Customers were herded into a back room where they waited for several hours until the manager arrived. He also denied knowledge of the combination and was instantly pistol-whipped. The mobsters took the till as well as cash and jewels from the crowd, worth a total of approximately $14,360. As they fled, they fired several shots into the bar's sign and sped off in two cars.

Two of the bandits were in a blue Buick and soon outdistanced the police on the Atlantic City Expressway and escaped. The remaining five were in a Buick Electra when they were spotted by police, resulting in a wild, 125mph chase on the Atlantic City Expressway. The robbers' car crashed, overturning after passing the Egg Harbor toll plaza. Roosevelt Fitzgerald and Russell Meade were arrested but the three other occupants fled on foot. When police searched the wreckage, they found Black Muslim literature and papers belonging to Samuel Bey, an alias of Sam Christian.

The following month, a sweeping grand jury investigation into narcotics trafficking in Philadelphia tripped up two Black Mafia members,

James Enoch and Leroy "Chinaman" Griffin. They were arrested along with several others for possession and conspiracy to distribute. Despite this minor hiccup, the law was way behind the curve when it came to the Black Mafia, and Sam Christian and Russell Meade were at it again with the help of another gangster, Lester Pointer. The trio, helped by three women and another man, stormed into the Charles and Charles Record Store in Harlem and robbed one of the owners at gunpoint. When he refused to hand over the store's cash, three of the gang went outside and kidnapped a passerby. They brought him in front of the owner and threatened to kill him if the owner didn't cooperate. The owner handed over $5,000 from the store's safe.

Another passerby saw what was happening and notified police, who arrived while the crime was in progress. As police entered the store, Lester Pointer tried to hold the owner and the hostage at gunpoint, and one of the officers shot him dead. At least one of the gunmen then fled into a loft with the other officer in pursuit. As the cop clambered up he was shot in the right arm by Sam Christian's .357 Magnum. A gunfight erupted, and as reinforcements arrived at the store, Christian was shot in the collarbone. It was an extraordinarily claustrophobic event, with most of the bullets fired at the police officers from a distance of no more than six feet. A total of twenty-three shots were exchanged before, somehow, four members of the crew – one man and the three women – got away. Christian and Meade were arrested for robbery and attempted murder. Christian used the alias "Richard Carter," of Brooklyn, New York, and eventually jumped bail.

Inevitably, dribs and drabs of these shocking episodes made their way into bars, speakeasies, pool halls, and seeped into conversations on the front steps of row houses throughout black Philadelphia. The legend of Sam Christian and his crew was growing rapidly.

CHAPTER 5 ★

MR. MILLIONAIRE AND THE CLUB HARLEM

A CROWD OF regulars gathered inside the Reynolds Wrap Lounge on October 27 to celebrate the birthday of the owner, Ed Reynolds. The bar sat on the southeast corner of 18th and South Street, below two floors of apartments. Like many taprooms in the city at intersections within residential neighborhoods, the Reynolds Wrap's main entrance opened to the street corner and a second entrance was located along one of the bar's sides. The joint was a mere sixteen feet wide and fifty-eight feet deep, and patrons who entered through the front door had to squeeze through the bar, with wooden stools on the left and the jukebox and a bowling/shuffle board game on the right. A checkerboard ceiling of black and white tiles topped the mahogany-paneled walls, while the floor was pedestrian vinyl. Multi-colored party balloons hung throughout the bar and a poster above the bowling machine announced a forthcoming concert by an up-and-coming singer called Billy Paul.

Velma Green, a twenty-three-year-old housewife, arrived with two girl-friends. She knew a number of the crowd inside, including her brother Wardell. A year younger than his sister, Wardell's smallish stature belied a rough reputation and he had prior arrests for assault and battery, robbery, and even murder. Just a few days earlier, however, he had stepped out of his league. Wardell and a friend had made the mistake of exchanging words with two relatives of Council for Youth and Community Development incorporator Russell Barnes. To Green, this was probably a garden-variety clash of machismo between two sets of men – until his friend was shot two days later. Given his own background, he had to suspect that he would be getting a visit, too. It was simply a matter of when.

Velma and her girlfriends decided to head out for a quick bite before the festivities at the Reynolds Wrap began in earnest, and went two doors down to the Chicken Shack, returning to the bar just before nine o'clock. Music was playing when they got back and people were dancing in the tight quarters. Soon after, Timmy Barnes showed up, parking himself next to the bowling machine, and was quickly joined by his nephew, Russell. The sight of Russell sparked Velma and her friend, the wife of Wardell's pal who had been shot, to huddle around Wardell and warn him.

Velma had no sooner finished speaking than Timmy asked Wardell to play the bowling game. Once they were next to the machine, Russell engaged Wardell. "I hear that you had a little trouble down here over the weekend," he said, referring to the previous Saturday's altercation. "Yeah, we did," responded Green, to which Barnes said, "Well, it don't make no sense." Green nervously replied, "No man, it don't."

Russell told Wardell to put a quarter in the machine and Green complied. Russell then went outside and sat in his new Cadillac, parked in front of the bar, while Timmy and Wardell played the game for a short time. Timmy next excused himself outside, joining his nephew in the car, and Wardell, probably relieved at their departure, walked to the rear of the bar and into the restroom.

When Wardell walked back out of the bathroom, he was confronted by an armed Russell Barnes blocking the side door. Timmy Barnes was back, too, standing near the front door. There was nowhere for Green to run, but he tried in vain to duck for cover as Russell opened fire.

Wardell Green was shot three times from behind. One bullet lodged in his left hip and others ripped into his back, piercing his black leather jacket, one shot tearing straight through his body and out of his stomach. People inside the bar initially thought balloons were popping but then saw Green crash to the floor. Russell pushed his way through the packed bar, following Timmy, who had a head start. Timmy hopped into the waiting car with a getaway driver at the wheel, but sped away before Russell could get in, leaving the gunman to flee on foot. Police were later tipped off that the over-keen wheelman was Russell's best friend, CYCD founder and Black Mafia up-and-comer James Fox. Meanwhile, Green was rushed to Graduate Hospital, but his injuries were fatal.

Russell Barnes had been busy marketing his skills as a contract killer and acting as the muscle for many of the Black Mafia's street hustles. In this case, it isn't entirely clear if he was genuinely upset about the slight to his family, if he was making a calculated business decision to demonstrate his flair for the dramatic kill, or both. Certainly, Barnes could have chosen any number of scenarios to kill Wardell Green that would have been less conspicuous and not invited dozens of witnesses. The question of motivation would actually never be answered, but word of incidents such as this was spreading throughout Philadelphia and the Black Mafia was happy to capitalize on its growing reputation.

Prominent defense attorney A. Benjamin Johnson surrendered Barnes to police on November 3. He was charged with murder and held without bail pending a trial, so it was an understandable shock to Wardell Green's mother when she ran into Barnes on her street in May 1973, while she was still waiting for the case to come to trial. Unbeknown to the Green family,

Barnes's attorney had successfully applied for bail and he was released on a $5,000 bond in June 1972. The case was eventually scheduled for September 1973; in the meantime, Barnes was out and about.

The case against him relied upon the testimony of Green's sister, Velma, the primary remaining witness. The many others who saw the killing in the Reynolds Wrap Lounge no doubt feared for their safety, considering the Black Mafia's penchant for killing witnesses. Velma was in her home on Rodman Street on 18 September 1973, pondering the fact that in a week she would have to relive the awful experience of watching her brother die, when she went to answer a knock at her door. As soon as she appeared in view and before she had even reached the door, Russell Barnes fired a high-powered pistol through it, killing her instantly.

Barnes's trial for the Wardell Green killing commenced as scheduled under heavy security. Velma's preliminary hearing testimony was read into the record as part of the three-week trial, but on October 12 Barnes was acquitted. Assistant District Attorney Michael Stiles said Velma's absence was the turning point in the case. Barnes had successfully wiped out the main threat to his freedom, and one more witness had paid the price for daring to testify against the Black Mafia.

They didn't always get off. Founding member Walter Hudgins was convicted in 1972 of involvement in two armed bank robberies, sentenced to concurrent fifteen-year prison sentences, and sent to the Lewisburg Penitentiary. As of February 1972, however, the Philadelphia Police Department had still to formally address the Black Mafia as a syndicate. Whatever efforts the department had employed simply targeted individual offenders for specific offenses. There was no intelligence gathering beyond a select few officers and detectives who were collating their own notes and drafting their own flow charts. Yet, with each successive robbery and act of extortion, the Black Mafia's street reputation grew, and with it, their power. Fewer victims and witnesses were willing to come forward as word in the African-American community – especially in the black underworld – spread about this growing and seemingly untouchable menace.

In March, the group struck again, and this time the target was essentially one of their own. Earl Walden, the thirty-four-year-old owner of a variety store, claimed to have real estate dealings, but was suspected of being a big-time drug dealer who was being extorted by the Black Mafia. He, an employee of his and a neighbor were unloading merchandise into his West Philly home one afternoon when a man walked into his garage with a gun in his hand, presented a badge and said, "Earl, if you move, I'll kill you. I'm from the Philadelphia Police Department." The Black Mafia script continued as the gun was pressed against his head and two other intruders appeared. Walden recognized one, prompting another to openly chastise his fellow robber. "I told you not to let Earl see us," he said. Walden, his employee, his neighbor and the neighbor's two-year-old daughter were taken at gunpoint upstairs to the kitchen as the robbery crew searched for cash and other valuables. A safe was found in the kitchen and Walden was asked to provide the combination. At first he gave a bogus set of numbers but the prompt of a click from the hammer of the gun as it was cocked behind his head persuaded him to reveal the genuine information. The take from the safe was $4,000, much less than the crew had expected to find.

Walden's twelve-year-old daughter walked into this scene as she returned home from school and was immediately taken hostage. The three men and two children were placed in the basement game room and bound hand and foot with clothesline and electrical cord. Walden and his daughter were grilled by their captors for the location of the sought-after money. Apparently, they were telling the truth, $4,000 cash was all there was, and the Black Mafia crew took off, leaving the neighbor bloodied from a pistol-whipping for not leaving his daughter's side. The haul netted a total of $37,000, including the cash, $30,000 in jewelry, mink coats, a television, a shotgun, and a revolver. When police pressed Walden for a description of the intruders, in particular the man he recognized, he claimed he could not recall. He undoubtedly knew the consequences and probably only reported the incident for insurance purposes.

*

As the Black Mafia grew in size and stature, and as killers like Russell Barnes bolstered its ruthless reputation, it was also commandeering vast segments of the city's lucrative drug trade. The sale of heroin and cocaine in black Philadelphia was controlled by a handful of large, independent distributors, led by Tyrone "Fat Ty" Palmer, known on the street as Mr. Millionaire because, at the age of just twenty-four, he was exactly that. He was the key Philadelphia-area contact for New York City's Frank Matthews and poised to rise to the top of the underworld.

Palmer was born in South Carolina but grew up in Philadelphia, graduating from Simon Gratz High School after using his squat, 273-pound frame as a lineman on the football team. Fat Ty began dealing drugs in 1966 at the age of eighteen, and was arrested twice the following year, receiving probation terms of one and two years, respectively, for the offenses. A quick learner, he soon devised a plan whereby he would buy pre-packaged heroin, rather than purchasing it in kilo form and cutting it himself. He had calculated that the risks inherent in cutting heroin were too substantial – the process lasted eight hours, was susceptible to police interference, and required employing cutters and testers who might steal from him.

In no time, Palmer's connections, influence and wealth grew, resulting in the material niceties many street criminals treasured. His conspicuous consumption included a harem of attractive girlfriends, a partying lifestyle in which he was the star, a late-model Cadillac, and a fortress-like home, complete with bars on the windows, on N. Wanamaker Street. The authorities knew Mr. Millionaire had no means of financial support, and put him under surveillance. He was arrested a third time for his narcotics business and on this occasion more than a dozen witnesses were paraded into court, each describing Palmer's vast network. On 7 July 1971, he was sentenced to prison for two to seven years, but released pending appeal. Though Tyrone Palmer dealt extensively with the Black Mafia, and was close with several of its leaders, he had not joined the group more formally. Independence had its benefits, though Fat Ty would soon learn its rather weighty costs.

In October 1971, Palmer flew – first class, of course – to Atlanta for an important, indeed extraordinary, conference arranged by Frank Matthews. Matthews had called a mass meeting of black and Hispanic dealers and financiers to find ways to streamline the importation of heroin and cocaine, and to address related issues concerning the predominant Italian-American crime families in the Northeast. More than forty representatives arrived from locations such as New York, Chester (PA), Rhode Island, Baltimore, Chicago and Baton Rouge (LA). Entrepreneurs Tyrone Palmer, James "P.I." Smith, Major Coxson, and some Black Mafia affiliates represented the Philadelphia area at the meeting. P.I. Smith was considered to be a lieutenant of Palmer's, and Coxson was a hustler *par excellence* who doubled as a moneyman between various drug factions, including Philadelphia's Black Mafia and some of New York City's Italian-American gangsters.

Networks, conspiracies, and relationships in the underworld are inordinately complex and fleeting, rife with mixed motives and an overflow of machismo. Trying to split hairs between who among the black Philadelphia gangsters was more independent or more aligned with the Black Mafia than with Frank Matthews and his crowd, and so on, is next to impossible. For the moment, there was consensus among the parties at the conference, and several deals were made between the participants. Philadelphia and Atlanta police each received tips about the meeting, and law enforcement was waiting for Palmer at Philadelphia International Airport when he returned to the city. Fat Ty had no drugs on him, and he was not subject to arrest for any other matters. Police let him go, disappointed, though they realized that at least some of their information was accurate.

Apparently unfazed by the fact police knew of the Atlanta meeting, within weeks Palmer drove back to Atlanta in the company of James "P.I." Smith and a few others, and returned to Philly with a large shipment of cocaine. As is often the case with illicit transactions, the wheels came off when the cocaine was split up for distribution. P.I. Smith took $240,000 worth of blow on consignment and things got interesting. P.I. was supposed to distribute Palmer's cocaine to the dealers in his smallish South Philadelphia market, and repay Palmer as the proceeds came in. One of

P.I.'s dealers, Richard "Red Paul" Harris, apparently stiffed him, and P.I. was not able to cover the loss to Palmer.

Gunmen soon found Harris – he was shot dead in February 1972 as he drank in a North Philadelphia bar at 17th and Dauphin Sts. Police received information the shooters did the job on behalf of P.I. Smith. Rumors soon spread that Fat Ty Palmer, who was still out the $240,000-worth of cocaine, placed a $15,000 contract on P.I.'s life for the loss. On March 2, police found P.I. Smith with two bullet holes in the back of his head in a parking lot on Brown Street. Palmer had gotten payback and could finally put the frustratingly muddled deal to rest – or so he thought. He took a trip to Bermuda, and returned in time for Easter Sunday – exactly one month after the slaying of P.I. Smith – and decided to treat himself to the "Easter Panorama" show that evening at Atlantic City's popular Club Harlem.

The Club Harlem sat a block away from the city's famed boardwalk on Kentucky Avenue, Atlantic City's main street for entertainment at the time. Club Harlem was the crown jewel of the Avenue. Opened in 1934, it had its own orchestra – fronted by a legend in the area, drummer Crazy Chris Colombo – and hosted some of the greatest blues and rhythm and blues acts in the country. The list included Cab Calloway, Al Green, Count Basie, Lena Horne, Duke Ellington, B.B. King, Billy Daniels, Pearl Bailey, Sarah Vaughan, and Sammy Davis, Jr. Longtime Philadelphia-area rock and roll DJ Jerry Blavat, also known as "The Geator with the Heator", looked back fondly on that scene: "There used to be the breakfast show at 6 A.M. ... and everyone who was in town – Sinatra, Dean Martin, whoever – would come." The club was also once described as a "brassy nightspot in a dismal, two-story brick building" where "the black elite of Philadelphia and South Jersey" gathered. Club Harlem was such a local institution that when it was demolished in 1992, its red front doors were taken to the Kentucky Avenue Museum for display. For all its glitz, the club also had a rougher side, namely the hustlers and cons who blended in among the crowd of societal elites and other "movers and shakers". It was certainly a vibrant, eclectic place, with a buzz of allure and excitement.

Billy Paul headlined the Easter Panorama bill, and a crowd of 600-800 people filled the dimly lit club. Ty Palmer, with a gathering of twenty-something females surrounding him, had a table right next to the stage. His stable of bodyguards topped off the group, and the entourage admired the scene of Paul taking the stage with lights reflecting off the mirrored walls. Across the room, a table of five determined men watched Palmer's actions intently as it turned 2 A.M. As Billy Paul ended his opening number, "Magic Carpet," the ominous quintet, led by a big, bull-necked man in a dark suit, walked across the crowded dance floor and surrounded Palmer's table. Sam Christian asked to speak with Fat Ty, while his lieutenant Larry Starks began to argue – perhaps by design as a diversion – with Palmer's twenty-five year-old bodyguard, Gilbert "Malik" Satterwhite. Palmer was barely out of his seat when, following a very brief exchange of words, Christian shot him in the face. As he fell, Christian reached over the table and shot him twice more. When Satterwhite reached for his gun, he was shot twice in the back of the head and fell into his girlfriend's lap. His gun never left its holster.

The other bodyguards drew their guns and as many as six people wound up exchanging fire as Billy Paul and his band scattered off the nearby stage. Screaming patrons ducked for cover under tables and in restrooms, and rushed for the exits as some of the twenty shots fired inevitably missed their marks. Glass shards covered the club floor from the bottles and glasses broken when tables were overturned and also from the wall's shattered mirrors. Atlantic City Police Commissioner Mario Florani said that following the shots, "bedlam broke loose – tables were flying, chairs were flying, bottles were flying – it was a shambles." The Black Mafia hit squad fought with the crowd to make their exit, and once outside they were spotted by a responding police officer. The gunmen waved their pistols in the air as they fled the scene, and fired at least one shot at the officer.

Larry Starks remained behind because of his injuries; he had been shot, presumably by Palmer's bodyguards, five times in the back and thigh. Christian went into another bar across the street from the Harlem, while James Enoch, Eugene Hearn and Richard Smith sped away. The police set up roadblocks on major highways around Atlantic City, and a high-speed chase ensued. It ended an hour after the shooting, on the Walt Whitman Bridge joining Philadelphia to New Jersey. The three men were brought back to Atlantic City and held as material witnesses until the following day.

The assault had left five dead: Tyrone Palmer, Gilbert Satterwhite and three women in their company. More than twenty people were wounded – eleven from bullets and fragmented glass, the rest from the mayhem that ensued. As Larry Starks recovered from his wounds in Atlantic City Hospital, he was served with an arrest warrant for murdering Satterwhite. A thirteen-state teletype alarm, serving as an arrest warrant for other departments, went out for a "former Black Panther, Black Muslim and now reputed member of the Black Mafia" named Samuel Christian, who was wanted for the slaying of Mr. Millionaire, Fat Ty Palmer. Satterwhite's death piqued the curiosity of law enforcement because he doubled as a bodyguard and investigator for prominent civil rights activist and attorney Cecil B. Moore. Police informants later disavowed any nefarious connections between the legendary attorney and the event. In addition to the $900 police found on Palmer's body, they later discovered $30,000 back in the safe of his hotel room.

There are three main theories regarding the Tyrone Palmer execution, and each has its merits. The most obvious is that the Black Mafia was exacting revenge for the murder of P.I. Smith. Smith was very close with the Black Mafia elite, and had even given his car to Walt Hudgins when he bought a new Cadillac for himself. Smith was also believed to be the brother of the Black Mafia's Richard Smith.

Others hypothesize that the Black Mafia helped finance Palmer's large cocaine purchase in Atlanta, and were therefore stiffed by Palmer just as Palmer had been stiffed by P.I. Smith, who himself had been stiffed by Richard "Red Paul" Harris. This line of reasoning gained some credence when, in the days following the Palmer killing, informants claimed that "Tyrone's killing was a mistake." It may well have been the Black Mafia didn't know Palmer was shorted by his own people. Of course, even if one was to accept either of these two explanations, there is still the matter of why the killing would be executed so publicly.

The Black Mafia had more than its share of experience with crimes of violence and could surely have picked a better venue as far as witnesses and notoriety were concerned. Then again, if they were confident that witnesses wouldn't dare testify against them and/or if they *wanted* as many witnesses and as much exposure as possible, the plot made sense. Organized crime groups, particularly those that are predatory (involved in robberies, shakedowns, contract killings and so on) *require* a certain amount of public displays of violence to lend credibility to their threats and to ward off competitors, and to deter victims and witnesses from testifying. In fact, Frank Matthews was convinced they were sending him a message for not kicking back enough of the drug proceeds he generated on their turf to them. Perhaps thinking too highly of himself, Matthews felt the Black Mafia killed Smith for similar reasons. As one of Matthews's chief lieutenants, Charles W. "Swayzie" Cameron, said, the Black Mafia felt they were "invincible ... they killed and killed and killed until people paid off. They kept killing and scared the other people ... After a while, 'Hey, let's pay off. Give them ten per cent'." The Black Mafia eventually murdered three of Matthews's Philadelphia intermediaries as it asserted itself in the lucrative heroin and cocaine trades. As Cameron noted, at that time in the early to mid-1970s the Black Mafia "controlled all the drug traffic in Philadelphia. Got their percentage. Anybody big was paying."

The Black Mafia's motivations for the Palmer killing have never been sufficiently explained. As far as the homicide investigations were concerned, they ended up as many Black Mafia cases did back in the day – charges were dropped when victims and witnesses refused to come forward and testify. Multiple messages were sent that Easter Sunday – the Black Mafia could murder influential criminals, in public *sans* disguises, and law enforcement was impotent without the help of victims and witnesses – and none were hopeful for the vast segments of Philadelphia who would face this growing, virulent parasite in the coming years.

Sam Christian fled to Chicago and Detroit, all the while being hidden in various Nation of Islam mosques. Detroit was considered the "strongest [Black] Muslim town in the country" by law enforcement at the time.

Intelligence sources had Christian starting another African-American crime group called the "Sons of Africa", with major heroin traffickers Edgar Thomas and Anthony Williams, in Detroit while avoiding the homicide charge in New Jersey.

★

The killing of Fat Ty was momentous for another reason: it was the incident that caused the Philadelphia Police Department to begin its investigation into the Black Mafia. A PPD OCU memo, "INFORMATION RE: BLACK MAFIA", dated 7 November 1973, summarized the circumstances as follows:

> On April 2, 1972, in Atlantic City, New Jersey, Tyrone PALMER was shot and killed by Sam CHRISTIAN and others inside CLUB HARLEM.
>
> The Atlantic County Prosecutor's Office requested assistance from the Organized Crime Unit. Assistance was provided to them, and, from the information gathered, it appeared to be a group of persons involved who called themselves the BLACK MAFIA.
>
> Due to extreme difficulties encountered in obtaining complainants concerning this group, it was thought, in the best interest of law enforcement, to notify and request assistance from the below listed agencies:
>
> Federal Bureau of Investigation
> Internal Revenue Service
> New Jersey State Police, Intelligence Division
> Bureau of Alcohol, Tobacco & Firearms

Early in the investigation into the Black Mafia, the Philadelphia Police Department Intelligence Unit developed information that, "in September of 1968 a group of hoods, all well known to one another, got together for the purpose of holding up craps games, poker games and extortion. There didn't seem to be any particular ringleader at that particular time, they just acted as a group. No one man issued orders in the group."

The group's members were thought to be mostly from South Philadelphia, and their activity seemed to concentrate in West Philly. Unbeknownst to the police department, the District Attorney's Office also had a very small file on this cast of characters. Their sources detailed numerous meetings at several sites along the 52nd Street Strip. Informants said Bo Baynes ran most of the meetings along the Strip and that he wouldn't usually start the meetings until Sam Christian gave the okay (assuming he was present). One informer claimed that at one of these routine meetings, James Enoch, Sam Christian and Leroy "Chinaman" Griffin "took the floor and said they would take care of Tyrone Palmer." A list of suspected meeting attendees included many now-familiar names: Alfred "Sonny" Viner, Eugene "Foo-Foo" Ragan, Dave Anderson, Jerome Barnes, Ron Harvey, Earl Walden, Jeremiah X. [Shabazz], and Carl Banks. The D.A.'s Office file, which was essentially nothing more than a folder, was labeled "BCL" for "Black Coalition League". Though they had also heard the term "Black Mafia" used with the group, the office also received information that others were using the BCL label. Of course, this made perfect sense when considering the links to the ill-fated Black Coalition: Major Coxson, Gus Lacy, Stanley Branche, and, most importantly, Jeremiah Shabazz. Minutes confiscated from a Black Mafia meeting on May 30, 1972, listed their organization as follows: Co-Chairmen, Samuel Christian, Ronald Harvey; Co-Treasurers, Robert Smith, Eddie Brinson; Secretaries, Roosevelt "Spooks" Fitzgerald, Larry "Large" Starks; Sergeants-at-Arms, Eugene Hearn, Richard "P.I." Smith.

Following Ty Palmer's death, Frank Matthews had to re-organize his Philadelphia operation. Aware of the danger, he brought one of his major distributors, Pop Darby, to New York City. Darby's wife, Thelma "Flossie" Darby, remained in Philly to keep a general eye on things. Except for a brief stint in prison on a gun charge in September 1972, Pop Darby continued his Philadelphia operations from a distance.

Matthews' remaining chief connection with the Black Mafia in Philadelphia was, like Palmer, an independent entrepreneur with business interests throughout Philly and South Jersey. The death of Ty Palmer opened up opportunities for Major Benjamin Coxson.

CHAPTER 6 ★
THE MAJE

I T WAS A bout none of the fight crowd wanted to miss. Muhammad Ali, banned from the ring for three-and-a-half years and stripped of his title, had returned to the ring only to lose to incumbent champion Joe Frazier. Now he was on the comeback trail, and the self-styled "Greatest" was still boxing's biggest name. He wanted his heavyweight title back, and his return match with tough "white hope" Jerry Quarry, whom he had already beaten unsatisfactorily on his return from suspension, was one more step on the ladder. At least one experienced judge thought Quarry, a rugged, plodding fighter with a great left hook in an era of quality heavyweight competition, was the "best fighter in the world who never became a champion." It was guaranteed to be one of the sports events of the year.

The weigh-in took place on the morning of 27 June 1972, at the Las Vegas Convention Center, the site of that evening's fight. The thirty-year-old Ali checked in at six foot three and 216½ lbs, while his twenty-seven-year-old opponent stood just over six feet and weighed 198. Their bout headlined a double bill, with light-heavyweight champion Bob Foster defending his crown against Quarry's younger brother Mike, the first time in history that a world title fight received second billing to a non-title match. Such an anomaly could only have happened with Ali on the marquee, who in the lead-up to the event dubbed it "The Soul Brothers versus the Quarry Brothers."

Muhammad Ali had been sanctioned back in 1967 for draft evasion, and had been out of boxing until October of 1970, when he beat Jerry Quarry in Atlanta. That had been more of a happening than a sports event; it was written the city of Atlanta "had never seen such a conglomeration of the glamorous and the curious, the grifters and the slicks, the limo class and glittering dressers, from Diana Ross to Bill Cosby to Budd Schulberg." Mixed in among the celebrities was a handful of leading African-American gangsters from New York, including Jack Brown and Frank Moten, career criminals who had risen to become major narcotics figures along the eastern seaboard. Their strongest connections were in Atlanta, Washington, D.C., and Philadelphia, while their main partner in New York was the infamous

Benny Intersimone. But the fight itself was a dud, with Quarry losing in the third round when a cut above his left eyebrow was so deep the ring doctor said you could look down and see his eyeball.

By the time of their rematch, Quarry was the number two contender, but the result was again not expected to be in question, with the resurgent Ali a 5-1 favorite. The undercard was even more lopsided, with Foster an 8-1 pick over his challenger, and the most interesting betting line regarded whether *either* Quarry would last the distance. None of this affected the draw or the television audience, as a crowd of 6,549 set a Nevada record for a boxing gate and the broadcast was contracted to more than 150 closed circuit TV locations in the U.S. and Canada and forty-two other countries around the world. In all, more than thirty-nine million viewers would see Ali-Quarry II, grossing more than $2 million.

As the crowd gathered in the Convention Center around eight o'clock, a lot was going on behind the scenes. For any high-profile match, there are spectators of ill-repute, hustlers of one kind or another, if not outright violent cons, blending in among the connected set of celebrities, politicians, businessmen and other legitimate members of society at ringside. Though the celebrity quotient didn't quite match Ali-Quarry I in Atlanta, the mob presence in Vegas – white and black – certainly did.

Frank Matthews, by then one of the world's most important players in the heroin and cocaine trades, decided to host another meeting of his most important distributors. Ali-Quarry II in Vegas was perfect for a conference of black gangsters, since the massive convergence of people with varied backgrounds would be difficult to track. Matthews revered Ali. He traveled to Vegas with Pop Darby and others close to him, and once there entertained his guests at the Sands Hotel. His conference included some of the most influential people in organized crime along the East Coast, from drug dealers to money launderers and credit scammers.

As luck would have it, FBI agents sent to investigate other hoodlum connections to the night's program found themselves seated among the Matthews crowd at ringside. The U.S. Attorney's Strike Force Against Organized Crime in California was investigating mob links to the fight promoters. Specifically, the FBI was concerned that California gangster Nick Licata and New Orleans mob boss Carlos Marcello were involved in raising money for the fight. An FBI airtel of May 1972 stated, "Informants of the Los Angeles Office have furnished information regarding the involvement of several hoodlum and con-men type individuals being involved in the promotional aspect of a proposed boxing match between Mohamed Ali and Jerry Quarry on 6/26/72, in Las Vegas, Nevada." The FBI conducted surveillance at the Convention Center and throughout the Sands Hotel, and were also looking into dummy corporations and money transfers between banks in California, Nevada and the Bahamas. Suffice it to say, Ali-Quarry II in Vegas was quite a scene – above board and below.

The fight itself saw Ali showboating in between dominating the exchanges. At the end of the sixth round, he pleaded with the referee to stop the fight for Quarry's sake, and the ref concurred, pleasing the sizable Matthews entourage and most of the crowd. As the fighters' cornermen spilled into the ring, along with the usual mix of promoters, security guards and others close to the scene, the broadcast crew approached Ali for the staple post-fight interview. Ali was aware of the sizable television audience, and wanted to take advantage of the opportunity to help a close friend who was running for political office. Before entertaining a single question about the fight, he looked into the camera and said that he was dedicating the victory to the "next Mayor of Camden, New Jersey, Major Coxson."

★

Mention of the name Major Coxson is greeted with a laugh and a shake of the head from most who knew him. A Philly-South Jersey legend, he was variously described as a political candidate, flamboyant entrepreneur, media darling, civil rights activist, inner-city power broker, fraudster, drug financier, and intermediary between Italian mob families in New York and Philadelphia and the Black Mafia. He was also friendly with his fair share of African-American and white politicians and community leaders. King of the area's old-school hustlers, Coxson also did "edgework," orchestrating scams and drug deals with otherwise violent crime organizations. In sum, Major Coxson was a one-man poster boy for what academics call the *social system of organized crime*, illustrating the interrelated worlds of crime, politics, labor leadership, politically-related business, sports and night life – communities whose value systems idolize dealmakers.

Major Benjamin Coxson was born on 29 June 1928, and raised in Western Pennsylvania. He later said his family moved from Uniontown to North Philadelphia in 1942 so that he and his brothers could avoid following their father into the coal mines. As a teenager, he parked cars, ran shoeshine stands and car washes, and pursued any number of small-scale schemes. He also attended, however infrequently, Benjamin Franklin High School, and ran for president of his senior class. As he proudly liked to recall, he won with 2,700 votes, which was curious because there were only 2,200 students in the school.

After graduation, one of his jobs was parking cars at the Gimbels concession parking lot in Center City. Coxson proposed a car washing service on site to the owner, so that patrons could have their cars washed while they shopped. Yet another Coxson enterprise was created, and before long he owned eight carwash joints and employed more than 100 people. Next was detailing for car dealers, whereby dealers would send cars to Coxson to prep them for display on their lots. "People credit me with being a good supersalesman," boasted Coxson. "They say I have the ability to sell ice to an Eskimo, fire to the devil, sand to an Arab." He soon invested his various profits into used car lots, a new car agency, and a car leasing business, among other endeavors. "The Maje," salesman, businessman, investor, entrepreneur and hustler extraordinaire, was born.

A consummate "people person", Major Coxson was known as much for his mannerisms as for his shady deals. His hearty laugh – like he was dying from laughing – was as much a trademark as his wide-brimmed Stetson hats. "His nose crinkles up," wrote one journalist, "and his bony black face lights up with the widest, biggest, toothiest grin in the world, then he grabs his stomach, like he's laughing so hard it's hurting him, his knees bend and come together and his chin almost touches the floor as he doubles over in breathtaking guffaws."

Coxson also amassed an extensive arrest record from at least 1949, when he was first pinched in Philadelphia for fraud, and he served minor stints in local and federal correctional facilities, including a twenty-two-month stay in a Lewisburg federal prison on a fraud conviction. When he came out in 1962, the *Philadelphia Tribune*, the city's acclaimed African-American newspaper, hailed the return of "the local 'playboy-sports-man-auto-king.'" Coxson paid $15 to get the story planted. Through 1970, he had been arrested seventeen times in Philadelphia for a variety of theft- and fraud-related offenses, including check scams and car theft rings. One of his swindles made headlines in three states, and left a co-conspirator dead – the Consolidated Automobile scam in the Bronx, New York.

Coxson, Harold Gelvan, Richard Berman and Alzie "Count" Kelly orchestrated a scheme in 1967 whereby Gelvan and Berman sold non-existent cars in the Bronx, and the checks involved in the sales were transported to Philadelphia and cashed by Coxson and Kelly. Berman was formerly a West Philadelphia used car salesman, and Kelly – who had a violent criminal background – was a good friend and business associate of Coxson. Kelly portrayed a tough image, wearing black suits and black snap-brim hats, with an ever-present toothpick in the corner of his mouth. Police agencies developed intelligence identifying a Renwick Mitchell of Philadelphia as the runner between the city and New York. This particular scheme was relatively minor, netting only $23,751, but was part of a much larger operation run by Gelvan and Berman that operated in the U.S., Puerto Rico, the Dominican Republic and the Canal Zone.

Consolidated Automobile Wholesalers advertised in magazines that it was selling late model autos for $595 to $995. What approximately 1,100 disappointed people got in return for their money was either a repainted and reconditioned taxi or nothing at all, netting the duo in the neighborhood of $400,000. All of the individuals were indicted in June 1967, totaling 519 counts, and plea deals were under consideration the following spring, pending a trial. At the time, Berman operated an art gallery in fashionable Millburn, New Jersey, with a partner, Marilyn

Pivnick, and a few part-time employees, including Major Coxson and Renwick Mitchell.

On the morning of 12 April 1968, Mitchell reported finding Richard Berman dead, wearing a sports jacket and slacks, slumped against a wall in his second floor art gallery office, shot once in the back of the head. Pivnick, clad in a black and white check suit, was face down at the foot of the stairs leading to the office, lifeless, shot at point-blank range in the forehead. Authorities speculated that she surprised whoever killed her. Given the numerous possible motives for the killing of a large-scale con artist, investigators were burdened with a multitude of possibilities. Berman was considered an important witness in the fraud case. For his part, Coxson told authorities he was in New York City with a gallery truck at the time. Though Coxson's criminal history was non-violent, investigators believed he was behind the murders because the victims would have been witnesses against him. The homicide investigations would go on for years, while Coxson kept hustling on both sides of the law throughout.

One of The Maje's pursuits was the 1970 opening of the Rolls Royce Supper Club. Coxson had partnered with buddy Stanley Branche in the upscale Center City bar, which was scheduled to open that summer on Watts Street, just off Broad. Branche, the civil rights entrepreneur, was a proponent of the era's government programs that infused massive amounts of dollars into any number of urban self-help and "community development" initiatives, which placed him at odds with Coxson who, despite his exploits, never asked for a handout. As Coxson explained, "The Negro has it made today. He can get all the money he wants as long as he's Black ... But there was no federal money to fool around with when I started out." Furthermore, as he joked with a beer salesman who popped into the budding Rolls Royce lounge, "I know how you and I can make a lot of money ... We'll go to one of these big bank guys and these civic leaders and we'll tell them that if they give you and me a certain amount of dollars we can control all the gang killing and nonsense ... I'll go over there and start talking and by next Monday we should have a million dollars promised to us to spend for the rest of the summer. I'm not kidding. I could do that." Coxson concluded by cracking himself up and saying, "Only thing I'm telling you right now is that I'm taking my $300,000 and getting out right away!"

The Maje planned on targeting a white clientele for the Rolls Royce, knowing that prominent African-Americans would also converge on the high-end establishment simply because of his name and reputation. In the lead-up to the grand opening, Coxson frantically toiled on the property himself to get it ready, one day falling off a ladder, breaking his foot. His main girl, Lois Luby, took him to the hospital in style in one of his Rolls Royces, so hospital staff were somewhat stunned when he used a Department of Public Assistance card to pay for his medical bills – vintage Coxson.

The injury didn't affect the grand opening bash, which headlined Muhammad Ali, Playboy club opener Harry Katz and city councilman Thomas Foglietta amid the prerequisite over-the-top Coxson antics. A blonde in a mini skirt unveiled a street sign outside for Rolls Royce Lane as a rock band played in the middle of Watts Street, topped off by go-go dancers doing their thing on the roof. Coxson blocked Watts Street by parking three Rolls Royces in the middle of the street outside the bar, and had women plying the crowd of 200-300, inside and outside, with champagne. The Rolls Royce itself was classic Coxson, from its fancy velvety walls with *fleur-de-lis* designs (gold and black at the bar, red and black in the dining area), the black chairs rimmed in bright red velvet, and the large chandelier inside, to its big neon and aluminum sign, white-trimmed blue canopy scripted with the letters *RR*, and the carpeted sidewalk outdoors.

Never one to forego free advertising, Coxson granted an interview for a feature story in *Philadelphia Magazine*. As he was being interviewed, his pal and partner Branche joked, "You know what they're gonna call you in that article, Major? They're gonna call you 'The Black Angelo Bruno'" – a reference to the city's leading Cosa Nostra don. In fact the article was mostly favorable, and concluded, "Major Coxson is *the* black entrepreneur in Philadelphia, undoubtedly the most active and probably one of the most successful businessmen in town. There's just no counting the deals he's been in, is in and will be in. He buys and sells cars and real estate at a feverish pace, owns dozens of commercial and residential properties and has operated businesses in fields as diverse as fried chicken and cemeteries."

True to form, among the personalities soon frequenting the Rolls Royce was Angelo Bruno himself, a friend of Coxson's, along with Muhammad Ali and Councilman Foglietta. "Some people can't believe that two black cats could open a place like this and make it go," commented Stanley Branche. "They say there's Mafia money behind us ... Everybody asks where we got the money. There's an FBI agent around here all the time. The other day he walked out on his tab. The next time he does that, I'm going to send the bill to J. Edgar Hoover."

Coxson would sell the lounge in less than two years to Philadelphia's most famous showgirl, Lillian Reis. The Maje was thought to have interests in several other establishments, though with the mysterious and self-promoting Coxson nothing was ever certain. Not everyone was enamored with his antics. An article in a local black magazine, *Philly Talk*, brusquely assessed Coxson as a "Hershey bar dipped in a vat of cyanide." The article explained that he was a "man who at heart is so soft and mushy he verges on the obscene and yet, by turns, a man who is so outwardly cold and calculating in financial dealings that people have been known to check the fillings in their teeth when he walks away from them."

Various criminal investigations were ongoing into Coxson's activities, and he turned himself in for the Bronx fraud case in December 1970, posted bail and was released. He stayed in the limelight and kept plenty busy with a variety of dubious pursuits, many of which caught the attention of federal authorities. Authorities were primarily occupied with income tax evasion issues, considering that Coxson could not entirely account for an ostentatious lifestyle that included a custom-built home, then valued at over $200,000, and eleven high-end cars. Coxson cherished his cars most among his luxuries, and his fleet included Rolls Royces, Lincoln Continentals, Jaguars, a Mercedes 350, a Maserati and others, many of them customized. His Mark IV, for instance, could be started by remote control, and others had items like sunroofs, color televisions, phones, leather upholstery, and bulletproof glass. Even his two relatively pedestrian Volkswagens had been augmented with Rolls Royce grilles. Each of his rides was housed in a large, carpeted garage. "Some people like horses," said Coxson. "I happen to like cars, the biggest and the best. I take care of them."

His home was all Maje too. Coxson lived on a wooded four-acre lot in the cushy Charleston Riding section of Cherry Hill, New Jersey, where his house sat on a knoll, his driveway ran for blocks, and his closest neighbor was a football field away. The home at 1146A Barbara Drive could not be seen from the street, and the driveway was marked by a mailbox that read, "M.B.C. 1146A." Cherry Hill was a popular, upscale suburban community that lured many Philadelphians away from the city. The drive from Coxson's home to Center City, which took him through Camden and across the Delaware River on the Ben Franklin Bridge, took about twenty-five minutes. Coxson's circular fieldstone and brick-faced home featured a sunken living room, carpeted in plush lime green, with a fieldstone fireplace and an all-glass ceiling that stood thirty feet above the floor. Some of the bedrooms upstairs had balconies overlooking the room, and Coxson's bedroom was highlighted by mirrored walls, plush red carpet, and a large circular waterbed, supposedly worth $3,000, with a fitted black velvet spread. He often entertained guests at lavish parties on his property, which included a large, well-stocked bar, a swimming pool and a whirlpool, even though Coxson himself didn't drink or swim.

In March 1972, the IRS "perfected a federal tax lien" on two of Coxson's cars, eventually seizing them in lieu of Coxson's "tax deficiency" just weeks before Ali-Quarry II in Las Vegas. Coxson owed $135,000 in back taxes, and the Feds had taken his prized Mark IV and his Cadillac limo. He responded by purchasing a tandem bicycle, placing his chauffeur on the front seat pedaling while he rode on the back waving to prospective voters. Coxson's friends did him one better by placing a horde of expensive cars in front of his Camden residence/office and offering him choices as replacements, including Muhammad Ali's donated silver Rolls Royce. "There were so many my wife could pick one to match the color of her outfit each day," bragged Coxson. The boxing star and The Maje became good friends in the summer of 1968, when Ali was in Philadelphia helping raise funds for the ill-fated Black Coalition, and for a time in 1969 Coxson was Ali's agent. In Philadelphia, Coxson's friends and associates included a remarkable mix of career criminals, con artists, politicians and assorted miscreants, and his drug connections were second to none, as evidenced by the IRS investigation.

On May 26, the Internal Revenue Service's Philadelphia regional office compiled a "List of Targets for Investigations" that contained twenty-one names, including Black Mafia affiliates Coxson, John Watson, Vernon Earl Walden, Carl Banks, Robert Bolar and Leroy Griffin. Each had substantial narcotics networks that were used, directed and extorted by the Black Mafia, and the syndicate's hierarchy would have a variety of relationships with these distributors over time. Coxson was preeminent, though Watson, Walden and Banks were also important in their own ways. John Stanley "Stan The Man" Watson owned Philly Groove Records, and employed the Black Mafia's Bo Baynes from January 1968 until June 1971. Baynes's stated position at Philly Groove was "road manager or promoter," and a PPD OCU report states, "Reliable sources claim that Baynes did work for Watson. However, his position with Watson was that of an enforcer. Baynes' primary mission was to intimidate disc jockeys to push certain records."

The report continues, "One of the groups managed by Watson was the 'Delphonics' and several years ago they had a million dollar seller ["La La Means I Love You"]. Due to the success of their hit they became very popular and received a lot of Night Club bookings. The Delphonics felt they no longer needed Watson's help and started collecting the monies for appearances themselves and therefore cutting Watson out of lucrative fees. In this instance Baynes supposedly talked to the Delphonics and straightened the problem for Watson."

A major heroin dealer in Cincinnati named Alexander Randolph, *aka* Dickie Diamond, *aka* Mr. Wiggles, promoted the Delphonics. Diamond owned a New Jersey-based concert promotion company called Capital City Attractions. He promoted such acts as the Jackson Five, Sly and the Family Stone, and the Moments up and down the East Coast. While on tour, he dealt narcotics and laundered the money through his box-office receipts.

Vernon Earl Walden was a big-time dealer who trafficked narcotics with the Black Mafia's Larris "Tank" Frazier. The IRS considered the thirty-five-year-old Walden one of the biggest narcotics dealers in the Philadelphia area, and estimated his extensive West Philadelphia operation netted more than $1 million a year. Walden was indicted by a federal grand jury in November 1972 for evading income taxes in 1970 and 1971. The IRS was quick to note that despite having no record of employment, "Earl the Pearl" Walden was "living high." The IRS seized two of his properties and a 1973 Lincoln Continental Mark IV. Walden took to the media to plead his case: "They didn't concern themselves when I was in the ghetto without shoes.

When a black man has a house and a car, they get concerned." At the time, he had a history of fourteen arrests, and he was later convicted for his role in a massive heroin ring.

Carl Banks was a lieutenant in Walden's organization with a history of five arrests, including the conviction for willful killing in 1965, for which he received a three-year suspended sentence. In December the IRS seized his home as well, just as he was awaiting trial for weapons and narcotics offenses.

Major Coxson's influence on the Black Mafia was manifold. He provided the group with quality narcotics suppliers, financiers, money launderers and other connections on 52nd Street. The Maje also partnered with, and ultimately tutored, them in numerous financial scams. In December 1972, for example, Coxson and gang devised a scheme involving a bogus firm called Pyramid Enterprises Inc. Black Mafia members such as Merrill Ferguson (who was also Brother Lt. in Temple 12), Edgar Rice and Lonnie Anderson led numerous others in the scams emanating from Pyramid Enterprises. Pyramid, unlike other Black Mafia frauds, was not formally incorporated. The basic scam consisted of applying for numerous credit cards in the fictitious names of employees of the non-existent company. The Black Mafia got around the fact that Pyramid Enterprises was a fantasy by providing credit companies with the same two phone numbers for the firm, each of which directed the calls to a home on Clearview Street. Whoever answered the phone at the Clearview "office" of Pyramid would refer to a typed list of "employee" names, job titles, and salaries and produce this information for any credit companies calling to verify the data on the credit card applications. One Pyramid employee was supposedly making $25,000 per year as a "traffic manager" and another was comically earning $46,000 as a "credit manager." The applications were numerous and went out to companies such as Korvette's, American Express, Diner's Club, Sun Oil, TWA, and Gulf Oil, with most being approved.

The Black Mafia frequently used the credit cards to rent cars for a variety of business-related purposes. The group recognized that law enforcement was confiscating automobiles used in the narcotics trade, and thus the rentals became a perfect solution to the tactic. Police had a difficult time confiscating a rental car for a variety of reasons, such as legal and ownership questions. Another standard practice that soon became a money-making machine for the Black Mafia was to rent cars using the bogus credit cards and simply never return them. A massive black market in autos originated through the credit card frauds. At some point that December, the Black Mafia also commandeered their second (known) community development organization, Community Urban Development (CUD). The takeover came to light a year later.

In the meantime, several agencies were tracking New York City's Frank

Matthews throughout the country, resulting in his arrest in January 1973 in Las Vegas. The Black Mafia's chief supplier of narcotics was charged with a variety of offenses stemming from a conspiracy to possess and distribute $1.6 million worth of cocaine and heroin. Concurrently, the Internal Revenue Service filed a claim against Matthews for $7,009,165 in taxes due for the year 1972.

Matthews's network was based in the Bedford-Stuyvesant section of Brooklyn, New York, and he distributed in such cities as Boston, New York, Philadelphia, Baltimore, Washington and Miami. If convicted, he faced more than fifty years in prison, and his $5 million bail reflected his significance. However, his bail was soon reduced to $2.5 million and then, against sound advice, a federal judge finally lowered it to $325,000. The day the bail was last reduced, the twenty-nine-year-old Matthews posted $100,000 in cash, and was released. He later jumped bail, failing to appear in Brooklyn federal court, and the DEA announced a reward of $20,000 for information relating to his whereabouts, then one of the two highest rewards ever offered. Matthews has not been seen since. Various reports state that he had stashed between $15 million and $20 million overseas, possibly in Algeria. His organization was large enough to continue operating, albeit at a diminished capacity, for a few years after its namesake was out of the picture. Its suppression eventually forced the Black Mafia to find other sources of narcotics.

Back in Philadelphia, the Pyramid Enterprises frauds were gaining steam, and the Black Mafia pulled a similar scam using the federally funded Safe Streets office in fraudulently obtaining another credit card. Lonnie Anderson, like Sam Christian the embodiment of Superfly on the street, mailed an application to Diner's Club using the alias Frank Stewart, claiming to be employed by Safe Streets, Inc., the organization started back in 1969 by District Attorney Arlen Specter.

One of the two Safe Streets field offices was initially run by Clarence Fowler, a Fruit of Islam Captain in Temple 12, who was imprisoned in 1970 for the murder of Rev. Clarence Smith. Law enforcement intelligence described Fowler as a Black Mafia power broker within Holmesburg Prison who orchestrated crimes from inside the walls. One informant said Fowler had influence "on all the shit that goes down in Holmesburg. Nothing goes down without his say-so." Fowler's cellmate was Darrell Jackson, a co-defendant with Black Mafia heavy John Clark in a 1971 bank robbery. Clark, like Merrill Ferguson, was another Brother Lieutenant in Temple 12. Fowler was in frequent contact with Black Mafia members as they rotated in and out of the prison, and was tight with Jeremiah Shabazz.

The revelations that John Clark's wife worked with, and that Lonnie Anderson was exploiting, Safe Streets were no coincidence. Of course, no one named Frank Stewart worked – or ever worked – at Safe Streets, and nor had Lonnie Anderson. Nevertheless, when a credit manager from

Diner's Club contacted Safe Streets to confirm Frank Stewart's employment status, a receptionist verified the information. Federal investigators discovered that the receptionist at the time was the wife of Brother Lieutenant Clark. After the group opened a bank account in the name of Pyramid Enterprises, one of the first checks it cut was to Temple 12. Other checks were cut to Black Mafia actors such as Wilson X. Spann, Roger Miller and Edgar Rice. Spann was a friend of Major Coxson's and a manager of soul music groups, and his address was listed on one of the bogus credit applications. Miller was a funny-money legend in the making, and Rice was a brutal street enforcer on the verge of infamy.

Amid all the scheming and scamming, the one thing that set the Black Mafia apart from the very beginning was always latent: their extreme, explosive, uncontrollable violence. It went to the dark heart of who they were. And at the same time Brother Lieutenant John Clark and his Black Mafia brethren were making a mockery of the day's "community development" initiatives, and exploiting their heavy-hitting political and civil rights connections, they were plotting one of the most diabolical crimes in U.S. history.

CHAPTER 7 ★
THE SEED OF THE HYPOCRITE

ERNEST MCGHEE played drums with some of the greatest jazz artists of the Twentieth Century, yet gave it up to follow his religious calling. Born in the steel town of Gary, Indiana, in 1922, he left Purdue University to study at the Conservatory of Music in Chicago and wound up at the City College of New York in 1948 after a stint in the Army. He filled the next three years drumming with the likes of Charlie Parker, Max Roach and Billie Holliday.

In 1951, McGhee joined the Nation of Islam's mosque in Harlem. His background and oratorical skills quickly gained him influence. Malcolm X was particularly impressed, and recommended him to Elijah Muhammad. Ernest "2X" McGhee subsequently went to Chicago and served as the NOI's national secretary from 1954-1957. However, in 1957 he was demoted, apparently for his increasingly orthodox Islamic beliefs and for some bitter disputes with Elijah Muhammad, and returned to New York City, where he turned to the Sunni branch of Islam. He changed his name to Hamaas Abdul Khaalis and studied and practiced a strand of Sunni Islam founded by Abu Hanafa before his death in 767; its followers were called Hanafi Muslims. Khaalis, as the Khalifa, or guide, opened the Hanafi Midh-Hab center in Harlem in a rundown building.

The operation was modest at best until a towering twenty-four year-old UCLA product and National Basketball Association rookie named Lew Alcindor became Khaalis's most famous convert. Alcindor, then with the Milwaukee Bucks, changed his name to Kareem Abdul-Jabbar in 1970. His conversion generated similar controversy to the firestorm that broke when Muhammad Ali had converted to the Nation of Islam. Ali had, in fact, tried to recruit Abdul-Jabbar. "They visited me," said the basketball star. "I was taken to dinner by one of their ministers and Cassius Clay." His use of Ali's former name – something Ali hated – was not inconsequential, and signified the bitter divisions within America's various Muslim sects. "I'll call him Cassius Clay or Cassius X," said Abdul-Jabbar in a harsh tone, "but not by the name of the prophet. He is not a Muslim."

Abdul-Jabbar embraced Khaalis and the Hanafis and rejected Ali and the Nation. "My own decision wasn't influenced by Ali," he said later. "I knew a lot of people who were in the Nation, and it just didn't appeal to me. I thought that what Malcolm [X, following his trip to Mecca and subsequent flight from the NOI] was talking about was a much purer ideal. I never met Malcolm; his autobiography was what turned me around." Unlike his Black Muslim counterparts, Hamaas Abdul Khaalis did not believe in segregation, and strikingly wore the American flag proudly on his lapel and displayed it in front of his home.

From 1967 to 1970, Khaalis was director of community outreach for the New York Urban League's street academy. When the program lost its funding, Khaalis was laid off and he moved with some of his most ardent followers to Washington, D.C. In 1971, Abdul-Jabbar purchased a home in the Capitol at 7700 16th St. NW for $78,000, and donated it to Khaalis and the Hanafis. Khaalis moved into the grandiose, three-story brick and field-stone mansion, which was located in a quiet upper-class, largely African-American, neighborhood called the Gold Coast, and the site doubled as Hanafi headquarters. The Khaalis family and their loyal followers kept to themselves, and neighbors remarked on the manicured headquarter property. One said the place was immaculate, and "if they [care] for the inside the way they do the outside, it must be clean as hell. They out there every day with brooms and brushes." Just as in New York, Khaalis proudly displayed the stars and stripes on the property. "I teach Islam is for everyone, not just for blacks," he explained. "That's why the American Flag is out front. I'm not going back to Africa."

By the end of 1972, Khaalis was leading approximately 1,000 members of the sect, and turned his attention – and vitriol – toward his old arch-enemy, Elijah Muhammad. He crafted a damning letter and sent it to fifty-seven NOI mosques across the country. On January 5, 1973, he sent a second, three-page letter to NOI ministers denouncing the Black Muslims and Elijah Muhammad as "false prophets", and, to put it mildly, called into question many of their beliefs. Most damning of all, in the opening paragraph Khaalis called Elijah Muhammad a "lying deceiver." Among other digs at the movement and its leader, he purposely misspelled Muhammad's last name as "Mukammad" and provided a footnote to its translation: "sad, grieved and blackened; to be laden with sin; sorrow-bound because of evil committed through ignorance (error)."

Khaalis also wrote, "Everyone of us were better off from a psychological point of view, before we heard or learned anything about Elijah Mukammad's temples with their lying masters of deceit ... Elijah Mukammad ... should have studied his lessons much closer than he did. For he is the perpetrator of the Fard man myth or lie. We warn all of you the nearness of the day of resurrection ... and the penalty which will be put upon those, who have set up an equal with almighty Allah." Just before his signature, Khaalis wrote, "Out of fear of knowing Allah will punish those of us, who know the truth, and do not attempt to remove falsehood from among his creatures. We do not want your money, your followers, or your false teachings, as you are." In the postscript, Khaalis noted, "As long as you are deaf, dumb, and blind … you will hear from us."

No one knows precisely what response Hamaas Abdul Khaalis was attempting to elicit from Elijah Muhammad or his followers, but he would not have to wait long to find out. Philadelphia's Temple 12 was on the Khaalis mailing list, and within days of the second letter's arrival, Ron Harvey was convening a meeting of Black Mafia leaders, most notably John W. Clark, in his West Philadelphia home and contemplating an assault – physical, not rhetorical – on the Hanafi leader. After meeting sporadically for a few days, they agreed to recruit a squad and make a trip to D.C. Though Harvey had the most frightening reputation, Clark would orchestrate the trip and subsequent events.

On January 12, several Black Mafia affiliates traveled to D.C. to scout the Khaalis home and map out escape routes. The team was satisfied with its "findings": no outside security, numerous main streets and nearby highways to escape via, and the home sat on a corner, making it accessible from several directions. On the morning of January 17, John Clark placed a call to another Black Mafia member, and told him, "Bring your shoes," code to gather the rest of the crew and to bring their guns to his home. The Black Mafia was about to venture south on Interstate 95 on a mission of vengeance.

Ronald Harvey, John W. Clark, James "Bubbles" Price (aka James 77X), John Griffin (Omar Jamal), Theodore Moody, William Christian, and Jerome (5X) Sinclair traveled in two cars from Philadelphia to D.C. That night the crew had difficulty finding a hotel room because it was inauguration week for President Richard Nixon's second term. After five unsuccessful attempts, they found lodging in the Downtown Motel. Clark and Harvey registered two rooms and the group convened a meeting in one to go over their plan for the following day. The seven Black Mafia affiliates stayed the night and were joined the following morning by their own Thomas Clinton, who had taken an early train from Philadelphia. After having breakfast together, the gangsters set their plan in motion.

John Clark phoned the home of Hamaas Abdul Khaalis, posing as someone named "Tommy Jones," to inquire about stopping by to purchase some of Hamaas's writings, namely a pamphlet titled Look and See. Amina, the Hanafi leader's twenty-two-year-old daughter, answered the phone and told "Tommy" the writings were indeed available, at which point Clark asked when he could stop over to pick them up. Amina handed the phone to her twenty-five-year-old brother Daud, who told the caller to stop over between one-thirty and two o'clock in the afternoon. Their fifty-one-year-old father was not at home to field the call; he was spending the day visiting friends, but the caller had not asked for him specifically. The Khalifa's first wife, Khadyja, was also out that day, shopping with one of the Hanafi followers, a man named Abdul Nur. There were, however, several of the Khalifa's family members at home, including Amina and Daud, their ten-year-old brother, Rahman Uddein, and Hamaas's second wife, twenty-six-year-old Bibi Khaalis (Islamic law permitted four wives). Four children under the age of twenty-two months lived with Khaalis, and they were all home as well.

"Tommy Jones" knocked at the door right at two o'clock as scheduled. Meanwhile, a group of at least three men convened in a nearby back alley, arousing the suspicion of neighbors who were unaccustomed to such activity in the pristine neighborhood. Amina Khaalis was in the kitchen, playing with her stepmother's son Abdullah, aged two, and went to look out a window to see who it was. She saw two neatly dressed men, and noted that they had cigarettes tucked behind their ears – very unusual for Muslims, she thought. She summoned Daud to answer the door, because their religious tenets dictated women did not open doors to strangers, and returned to the kitchen. Daud cracked the door open, leaving the chain-linked lock fastened, and discussed the purchase with the men. They requested only one copy of *Look and See*, and gave Daud more than the $1 cost of the pamphlet. Daud closed the door and went in the house to get change. When he returned, he again opened the door with the chain fastened, and this time discovered there were three men, the latest claiming to be a repairman. Daud told the latter individual to go to the back door, and as he stepped away from the door, the others approached, supposedly to get their change. At this point, the "repairman" changed course, turning abruptly around and approaching the door with the others. As Daud extended the change, John Clark put a gun to his face and told him to move away from the door. The threesome forced the door open and stormed into the home, with one shouting, "This is a stickup."

One of the intruders ordered Amina and Abdullah out of the kitchen into the dining room, where another had Daud on the ground with a gun pressed against his head. The three were soon ushered into the living room, where they were placed on their stomachs and bound hand and foot with clothing tossed over their heads. Another knock on the door came, and more men came in, a total of eight.

"Who else is in the house?" asked John Clark.

Daud replied there was a woman on the second floor, with three children in the room next to her, and a boy on the third floor. Clark promptly ordered his crew to find the other Hanafis, and the intruders methodically made their way through the home, looking for them while simultaneously rummaging for valuables. Clark next asked Daud and Amina where the money was stashed. He and his Black Mafia cohorts were convinced that a large cache of money must be somewhere in the ostentatious home, especially considering the group's ties to the wealthy Kareem Abdul-Jabbar. When Daud and Amina insisted there was no money, Clark became indignant: "Come on, in this big-ass house you have to have some kind of money in here!" Frustrated, he ordered all the hostages taken into the basement.

As the crowd assembled near the laundry room, one of the assailants informed Clark they had seen a locked closet in a bedroom. Hoping to find the much anticipated cash bonanza, Clark demanded the key. Daud told him it was on the chain around his neck, and his captors whisked him upstairs. The Black Mafia crew got into the closet, only to realize Amina and Daud had told the truth about there being no money. It was now obvious the robbery element of their mission was going to bear little fruit, and vengeance would have to suffice. Daud was taken into a prayer room on the third floor, forced to kneel, and summarily shot three times in the head at point-blank range.

Meanwhile, an increasingly enraged John Clark asked Amina, "Why did [Hamaas] write those letters? Shouldn't he have known better than to write those letters to the Honorable Elijah Muhammad? Why didn't you try to stop him? You should have expected this. Didn't you know this was going to happen?!"

"My father knows what is best," responded Amina. "It's his job."

"Well," said Clark, "you come upstairs with me."

She was taken to the third floor, ordered to kneel in Daud's closet, and as Clark proclaimed, "This is best for you," Amina was shot in the head. Remarkably, she survived, slumped on the closet floor. She witnessed her young brother Rahman being brought into the room and placed on Daud's bed. He pleaded with the madmen, "I'll do anything you say. Just don't hurt me." A Black Mafia hit man holding a gun to Rahman's head replied, "Alright," before pulling the trigger twice and ending the boy's life.

One of the gang realized Amina was still breathing. He went into the closet and shot her twice more in the head. Through the ringing in her ears, Amina heard the clicks of the gun jamming as the gunmen attempted to pump yet more lead into her skull. Though shot at least three times in the head, she would not lose consciousness throughout her ordeal. The ammunition in the gun was old and had lost some of its energy, and when the bullets came in contact with her skull, they flattened, unable to penetrate. This would be a crucial mistake on the Black Mafia's part, because it would leave a surviving witness to the hell.

A few blocks away, Khadyja Khaalis was in the Giant grocery store checkout line when she realized she didn't have any money. Her companion, Hanafi follower Abdul Nur, graciously offered to take the quick drive back to her home to retrieve some cash while she waited in the store. As he pulled up to the residence, he didn't notice anything odd, but the assassins inside noted his arrival and waited for him. As Nur opened the front door, three Black Mafia associates jumped him and bound and gagged him like the others. They carried him upstairs to Rahman's room, where he was shot twice in the right temple. The second bullet pierced his brain, causing him to vomit, and as the murderers walked down the stairs they casually discussed if this meant he had just eaten.

The whirlwind of horror accelerated as Ron Harvey ordered two hit squad members to fill an upstairs bathtub with water. The babies were next on his murderous checklist, and he wanted them drowned. James Price, apparently making a distinction between the killing of adults and children, raised an objection and asked why they would need to do that since none of the remaining children – infants who ranged from nine days old to twenty-two months of age – could identify the attackers. He had, he said, joined in for a robbery heist and perhaps an assault on Hamaas Abdul Khaalis, not the killing of little children. After caustically warning Price about his lack of respect, Ronald Harvey told him the children were to die because "the seed of the hypocrite is in them."

As the upstairs bathtub was filling, the rest of the crew went to the basement to slaughter the remaining adult, the Khalifa's young wife, Bibi, who mercifully could not have imagined what plans Ron Harvey had for her three babies. Bibi, bound and gagged, was shot eight times, with one of the rounds lodging behind an eye. Incredibly, like Amina, she survived, though she would be partially blinded and paralyzed for life. Bibi was left in the basement in a pool of blood as the intruders made their way up to the bathroom, where three of the infants had been taken. Each screaming child was placed in the tub. They shook violently, convulsing, as their assassins held them under the water, assuring they would not breathe again. The other baby was drowned in the basement sink. Three of the four infants were Khaalis's children, born to Bibi, and the fourth, nine-day-old Khadyja Tasibur, was his granddaughter, born to Amina.

The death tally stood at seven, though as far as Clark, Harvey and gang knew, it was nine, and all that was left to do now was wait for their ultimate target, Khaalis, to come home to his execution. During his basement interrogation of Amina, Clark had sarcastically asked, "When is this Mr. Hamaas going to be home? I want to meet this Mr. Hamaas," and he learned the Khalifa was supposed to return by five o'clock. He told the Black Mafia crew they'd wait for the "head dude" to return, and then execute him.

While her family was being slaughtered, Khadyja Khaalis was waiting in the store for Abdul Nur to return with her money. The trip should have taken no more than ten minutes. Impatient and perturbed, she called home, got a busy signal, and left her groceries behind to go to the house her husband was visiting. When she explained the curious circumstances to him, they rushed back to their home and discovered Nur's car parked in front. They found the front door locked, and just as they rang the doorbell, Khadyja saw an unfamiliar face through a nearby window.

"Who is it?" called Hamaas Khaalis. "Who is it?"

"It's Tommy," shouted back Ron Harvey.

The Black Mafia crew fidgeted inside the home. Khaalis didn't know any "Tommy" and yelled to Khadyja for her to go next door and call the police. Sensing something wrong, he approached the front door again. Ron Harvey opened it and tried to pull him inside. Khaalis, a strong man in his own right, successfully tore himself from Harvey's grip, and Harvey turned and fled through the home toward the back door. The rest of the crew also ran frantically out the back, perhaps thinking Khaalis had brought police back with him. Khaalis jumped into his car in an effort to track some of the intruders down, at this point having no idea what horror awaited his return. He almost caught up with one of the assailants, and was shot at in the process. He soon lost track of all the intruders and turned back.

The Black Mafia crew split up, finding different means of getting back to Philadelphia. A few made their way to a bus stop, while others went to Union Station to catch a train. Two flew home. Their mission was almost a total failure: their nemesis, the Khalifa, had escaped their wrath; they left a vast trail of evidence and a witness, and they brought little fortune back from the robbery. Their tally was about $1,000 from people inside the home, which they divvied up by donating $200 to Temple 12 and keeping $100 each for themselves.

Hamaas Abdul Khaalis returned to his street to find numerous police officials assessing the scene. He got his first sense of the carnage when he saw Amina sitting on the front steps wiping blood from her head wounds. She told police the assailants were "Elijah's people," explaining, "They aren't true Muslims and they are afraid we'll expose them."

Police had already scoured the house for suspects and were the first ones to see what mayhem the Black Mafia squad had left. Officers found trails and pools of blood throughout the home, on rugs, furniture and walls. The scene was so overwhelming that some turned away to prevent themselves from vomiting. One officer dutifully reported finding two babies and a doll in the upstairs bathtub. He was mistaken; the "doll" was in fact the nine-day-old child, Tasibur.

Police opted to use the basement as a staging area to process the vast crime scene, partly because it was where they found Bibi and Amina when they entered the home. There a detective went into the bathroom to wash his hands, only to discover another infant in the sink.

Amina Khaalis would recover fully from her wounds, but her step-mother was not so fortunate. Bibi Khaalis suffered brain damage and was left paralyzed on her right side, blind in the right eye, and unable to speak. One of Khaalis's followers grappled with the cruelty of the event: "A baby nine days old? Most people are afraid to hold a baby that young. But here you got somebody that took that baby in they arms and drowned it?" Bemused by the depravity of it, he declared, "These people is fiends, man."

The Hanafi massacre was the largest mass murder in Washington's history, and remains one of the most infamous crimes in U.S. history. Kareem Abdul-Jabbar, who was in Milwaukee that day, expressed the sentiments of many when he said he "couldn't understand the violence at all ... I can think of only crazy people, lunatics, who would do it." The basketball star immediately received a police escort because authorities believed his life was in danger. He flew into Washington to participate in the ritual washing of the bodies before burial, where, according to Hamaas Abdul Khaalis, a group of Black Muslims had gathered outside, and "were jumping up and down and rejoicing." Abdul-Jabbar spoke frankly with the press about the dispute between the Hanafis and the Nation of Islam. "Elijah Poole [Muhammad] has taken certain tenets, certain demonology that he's made up ... he's just made things up," he said. "If I am going to be a member of Elijah Poole's thing, I wouldn't be an American. And this is my country, my people have shed our blood here. I don't want a separate nation. The things this country stands for are all in accord with Islam."

Hamaas Abdul Khaalis soon accused Muhammad Ali of sharing the blame for the killings because Ali was a Black Muslim and helped finance the Nation of Islam. "They hate us because we are color blind," he added. "Poole [Elijah Muhammad], Clay [Muhammad Ali] ... and every one of [Muhammad's] ministers are spreading this poison that only the white man is the devil." Ali flatly denied the Black Muslims had anything to do with the murders, telling the media, "We are the most peaceable people in the world. We don't go killing babies." But Khaalis himself went on several national television and radio programs, including NBC's *Today* show, making his case against the Black Muslim movement. The NOI denied his accusations, and on January 28, the national spokesman and minister of Harlem's Temple 7, Louis Farrakhan, addressed over 1,000 people in the mosque and thousands via closed-circuit television. Of the Hanafi-Black Muslim dispute, Farrakhan publicly said, "They know us and we know them. They tolerate us and we tolerate them." Years later, however, Farrakhan reflected on his absolute allegiance to The Messenger during these hairy times and stated, "I loved Elijah Muhammad enough that if you attacked him, I would kill you. Yesterday, today and tomorrow."

The official publication of the Nation, *Muhammad Speaks*, took a vitriolic tone in 1973, calling Hamaas Abdul Khaalis an "Uncle Tom" who "would sell out his own brother for the favor of the devil" and accusing Khaalis of accepting substantial sums of money from white people "to gain enough nerve to appear on television and tell these outrageous lies against Messenger Muhammad and the Nation of Islam." Khaalis kept on, using the press to get his message out, stating that he learned from serving under Elijah Muhammad that The Messenger was a "mean, cowardly man ... and an arch-deceiver." Furthermore, he said, the Black Muslims "try to say ...

the white man is the devil. Do they expect me to allow them to pass that off as truth? What were the men who killed my babies – black angels?"

In addition to the pieces of evidence collected in the murder house, authorities found helpful information outside the residence. When the Black Mafia squad fled, they made quite a scene running through people's yards and in the streets. Many neighbors told police what they had seen, including a man later identified as Theodore Moody fleeing with a blue suitcase in his hands. A thorough search produced pieces of evidence on nearby lawns, including a .38 caliber pistol and the blue suitcase. The suitcase held a treasure trove of incriminating items: a box of shotgun shells, a brown paper bag, two sawed-off shotguns, a copy of the *Philadelphia Daily News*, credit cards belonging to a man named Willie Horton, and the shopping list Abdul Nur had with him in the grocery store. Furthermore, police found a receipt with the writing "Received for Brother Lieutenant John 38X" along the escape path.

The box of shotgun shells belonged to Daud, and had been taken from inside the Hanafi residence. The brown paper bag had John Clark's finger-prints on it, and a palm print taken from the newspaper was identified as coming from the left hand of James Price. Police were able to trace the pistol to a rape and robbery that took place at a North Philadelphia party on January 6, 1973. Five gunmen had robbed ten guests of $800 in cash and jewelry, and raped two women inside a home in the area of 7th and York. Hanafi murder suspect Theodore Moody was one of the perpetrators.

The pistol had been stolen from a person named Eugene White, and a man named John Taliaferro was arrested in that case. Washington D.C. Metropolitan police traveled to Philadelphia and interviewed him in late January about the Hanafi slayings. Taliaferro's lawyer, Black Mafia attorney Barry Denker, stated that while his client was a member of Temple 12, Taliaferro had no knowledge of the Hanafi sect or of the ideological dispute between the groups. This was a significant development though, and would fit in with others in the case. When police investigated Willie Horton, they discovered he had been robbed in December and had credit cards stolen. They traced use of his cards to a tuxedo rental in a shopping center just outside Philadelphia, where John Clark, *aka* Brother Lieutenant John 38X of Temple 12, had rented a brown tux to be picked up on December 29 and worn on New Year's Eve. Thomas Clinton rented a tux at the same time, forging the signature of a man named John Wright. The Horton credit card was also used to pay for the motel room in Washington, D.C. the evening before the killings.

The motel stay wound up providing several other items of note to inves-tigators. Phone records from Clark's Philadelphia home revealed calls made to the Downtown Motel on January 17 and 18. A call from the motel was placed to William Christian's Philadelphia home as well. Other calls had been made between a pay phone just outside the motel and the Philadelphia homes of James Price and John Clark. When the Black Mafia held their hotel room meeting on the eve of the murders, a maid who wanted to provide them with fresh towels had interrupted them. William Christian opened the door just enough to receive the towels, and the maid caught a glimpse of him. Ron Harvey's palm print was also found in the room. Investigators developed other compelling circumstantial evidence, much of it related to the items left behind by the crew.

Police discovered that one of the cars used to travel from Philadelphia to Washington, namely Thomas Clinton's gray 1969 Cadillac, blew a hose and forced the crew to stop in Aberdeen, Maryland. They used another stolen credit card to have it fixed. The Exxon credit card was issued to a Lorraine Goode, and John Clark was found to have forged her name on the receipt for gas and other services on several occasions during their excursion. The Exxon card had been pilfered from Goode's mailbox in Philadelphia. Theodore Moody had purchased a used Chrysler on January 16, and Goode's Exxon credit card was used to fuel this car in the days hence also. A mechanic testified the four African-American male occupants were accompanied by at least two other black males in another American model car, and they all headed south on I-95 (in the direction of the District of Columbia) when they left the station. Investigators also discovered numerous phone calls had been placed between the homes of several Black Mafia members and pay phones throughout the area surrounding the Hanafi residence. For instance, calls were placed to and from John Clark's home and a pay phone in the basement of Washington D.C.'s Union Station in the late afternoon of January 18, and one was placed from a pay phone at the Little Tavern to the home of James Price. A bold Metro P.D. detective who briefly infiltrated Temple 12 in Philadelphia gleaned some additional information.

As authorities discovered the multidimensional links to Philadelphia, two U.S. attorneys from Washington and five Metro P.D. detectives set up shop there. The investigation was a coordinated effort between the Philadelphia and D.C. police departments, the FBI and the U.S. Postal Service. There was a significant sidebar to the Hanafi case in that, during the course of the massive, multi-state investigation, authorities stumbled upon extensive credit card schemes, thefts of postal money orders and a network of stolen cars. The Black Mafia's white-collar crimes were now on the FBI's radar screen, and would be dealt with in time.

Though there was clearly a solid circumstantial case against most of the assailants, the most damning evidence came from one of the Black Mafia's own, James Price, who gave a detailed sworn statement. Price confessed in late June, was placed into protective custody on June 22, and was moved to Washington and gave a formal statement on July 3.

The other seven defendants were indicted on August 15, even though Thomas Clinton had in the interim died of leukemia. Minister Jeremiah

Shabazz was asked if rumors were true that all the Hanafi murder suspects were members of his mosque. He responded by saying he wanted "no part in this thing. It will be said they are Black Muslims anyway. Anything I say will prejudice the case against them." In January 1974, national spokesman Minister Louis Farrakhan said that "no sane Muslim would commit such crimes," and claimed the murderers were paid federal agents attempting to discredit the Nation of Islam.

The trial began in February 1974, with Ronald Harvey absent – he was still a fugitive. Concerned about security in light of the Black Mafia's history and the warring factions of Muslims and others, officials had a special courtroom constructed, complete with bullet-proof glass and metal detectors. U.S. marshals frisked everyone as they entered the courtroom. The trial of the five in custody would be lengthy and complex; the Government rested its case on the trial's forty-ninth day, after 135 witnesses had been produced and 510 exhibits of evidence presented. It included a couple of emotional exchanges between the Khaalis family and the defendants. At one point Khaalis described himself to the prosecutor as "the man who defends the faith. The man who knows tricksters and murderers and gangsters that deviate on Islam." Then he turned to the accused men and yelled, "You killed my babies. You killed my babies and shot my women. They killed them."

Khaalis was escorted, and eventually banned, from the courtroom, and fined $750 for contempt of court. His daughter Amina had referred to the Black Mafia defendants as "part of Elijah Poole's cutthroat gang," while Khadiya Khaalis, Hamaas's first wife, was ordered to cease calling the defendants "murderers", at which point she left the courtroom in disgust. She stated, "If I can't be heard – or my family in regards to this – there is no sense in us being here at all."

The emotional trial concluded after thirteen weeks on May 17, 1974. The all-African-American jury deliberated for a day and a half before reaching a verdict of guilty against John Clark, Theodore Moody, William Christian and John Griffin. Judge Braman termed the crime "a holocaust," and on July 10 sentenced the Black Mafia killers to 140-year prison terms. Jerome Sinclair was acquitted, however, when the Government conceded that it had no evidence against him because of the "refusal of a key witness to testify." The sole evidence against Sinclair was the word of James Price, who had stated it was Sinclair who first knocked on the Khaalis door and was the one who drew water in the upstairs bathtub.

Ron Harvey was also caught and brought to justice. Judge Braman later granted John Griffin a retrial because Amina Khaalis, the key witness against him, confused him with Harvey with Griffin as the one who took her child's life during Harvey's trial in November 1974. Harvey was convicted, however, and thus the Government had successfully prosecuted four of the eight suspected assassins and sentenced them to life terms in prison. Of the remaining four, Clinton was dead, Sinclair was exonerated, Price still faced a trial despite his dealings with the Government, and Griffin faced a retrial. Hamaas Abdul Khaalis and his followers, however, were incensed at what they viewed as injustice. The prosecution deal with Price, the overturning of Griffin's conviction, the outright acquittal of Jerome Sinclair, and, most damning of all, the failure to impose sentences of death for those convicted, drove Khaalis to madness, as history would soon witness.

★

In the immediate aftermath of the January 1973 Hanafi murders, multiple law enforcement investigations and media inquiries were born. As Hamaas Abdul Khaalis absorbed the gravity of his losses and outsiders pieced together the multifarious story lines, the Black Mafia marched on. In fact, four of the Hanafi suspects were soon creating news again.

The twin terrors of Philadelphia: Sam Christian (left) and Ron Harvey (right) were the two most important figures in the early days of the Black Mafia.

An historic photo of many members and associates together at the "Black Mafia Ball" in December 1973: 1. William Roy Hoskins; 2. Ricardo McKendrick; 3. Timothy "Tino" Graves; 4. Clarence "Geech" Starks; 5. Robert "Hasty" Smith; 6. James Fox; 7. Gary "Opie" Williams; 8. Russell Barnes; 9. Frederick Armour; 10. Lonnie Dawson; 11. George "Pie" Sampson; 12. Barthaniel "Black Bart" Thornton; 13. Gene Hearn; 14. Dave Anderson; 15. Joseph "Jo Jo" Rhone; 16. Bill "Cadillac Billy" Smith; 17. Larris "Tank" Frazier; 18. Larry "Large" Starks; 19. William "Skinny Terry" Jefferson; 20. Gregory "Shank" Hill.

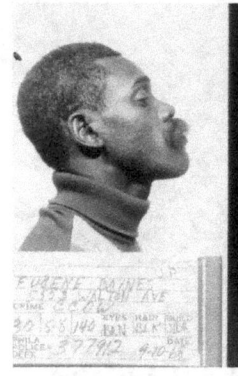

Eugene "Bo" Baynes

Robert "Bop Daddy" Fairbanks

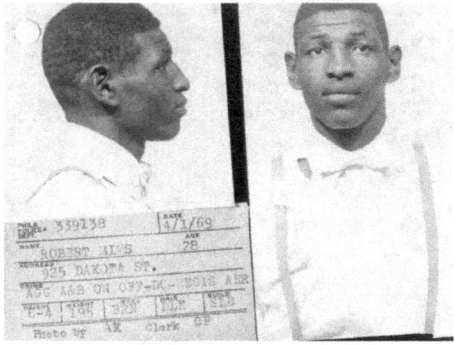

Robert "Nudie" Mims

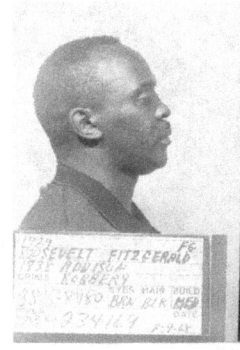

Donnie Day

Roosevelt "Spooks" Fitzgerald

The early Black Mafia elite. Along with Sam Christian and Ron Harvey, these men were named in police files as founders of the group.

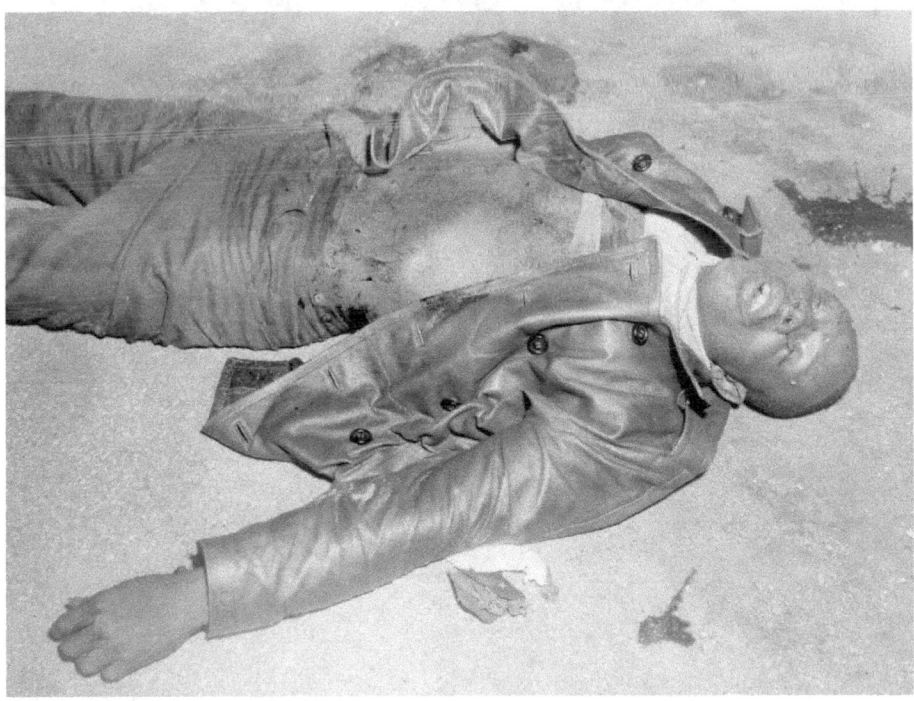

Another early Black Mafia figure, the youthful Nathaniel "Rock and Roll" Williams. Known on the streets as "Death Struck" for his fearlessness, he made the mistake of sticking up a craps game frequented by his fellow gangsters. He wound up shot dead (below), his body dumped on the highway.

Jeremiah Shabazz, leader of Nation of Islam Temple 12, confidante of Muhammad Ali and a highly influential figure in the black Philly underworld. Inset: Surveillance photo of the mosque on Susquehanna Avenue that became a headquarters for many of the syndicate's toughest enforcers.

Club owner Gus Lacy and civil rights activist Stanley Branche were power brokers within Philadelphia's black community, and were part of the milieu in which the Black Mafia flourished.

James Fox was a leader of the 20th and Carpenter Streets gang who was targeted by his former friends when he switched allegiance to the Black Mafia.

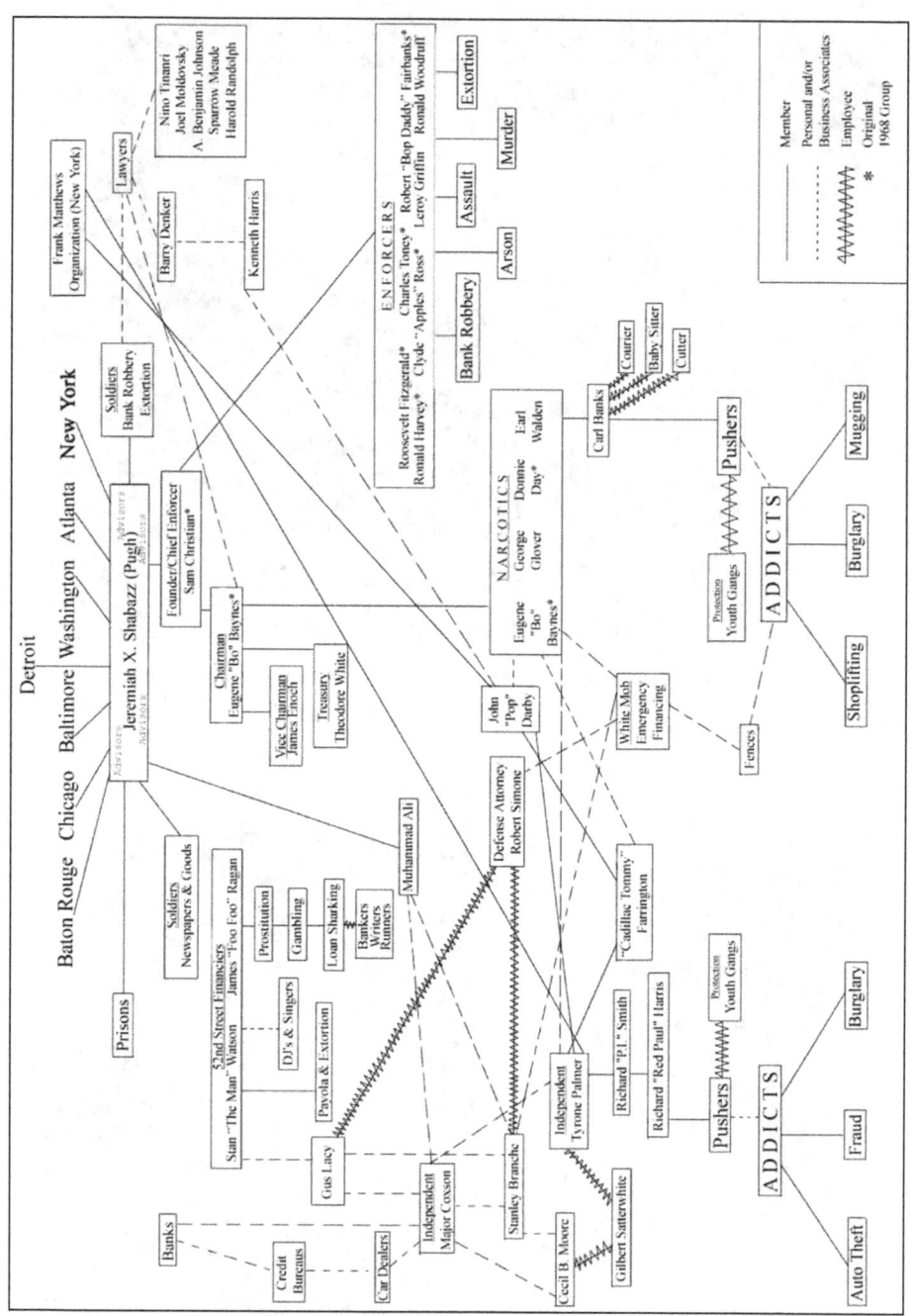

Organizational chart of the Black Mafia circa 1973, compiled by reporter Jim Nicholson and adopted by law enforcement. It shows the group's links with drug suppliers such as New York's Frank Matthews, with lawyers, financiers and political fixers, and with the Black Muslims.

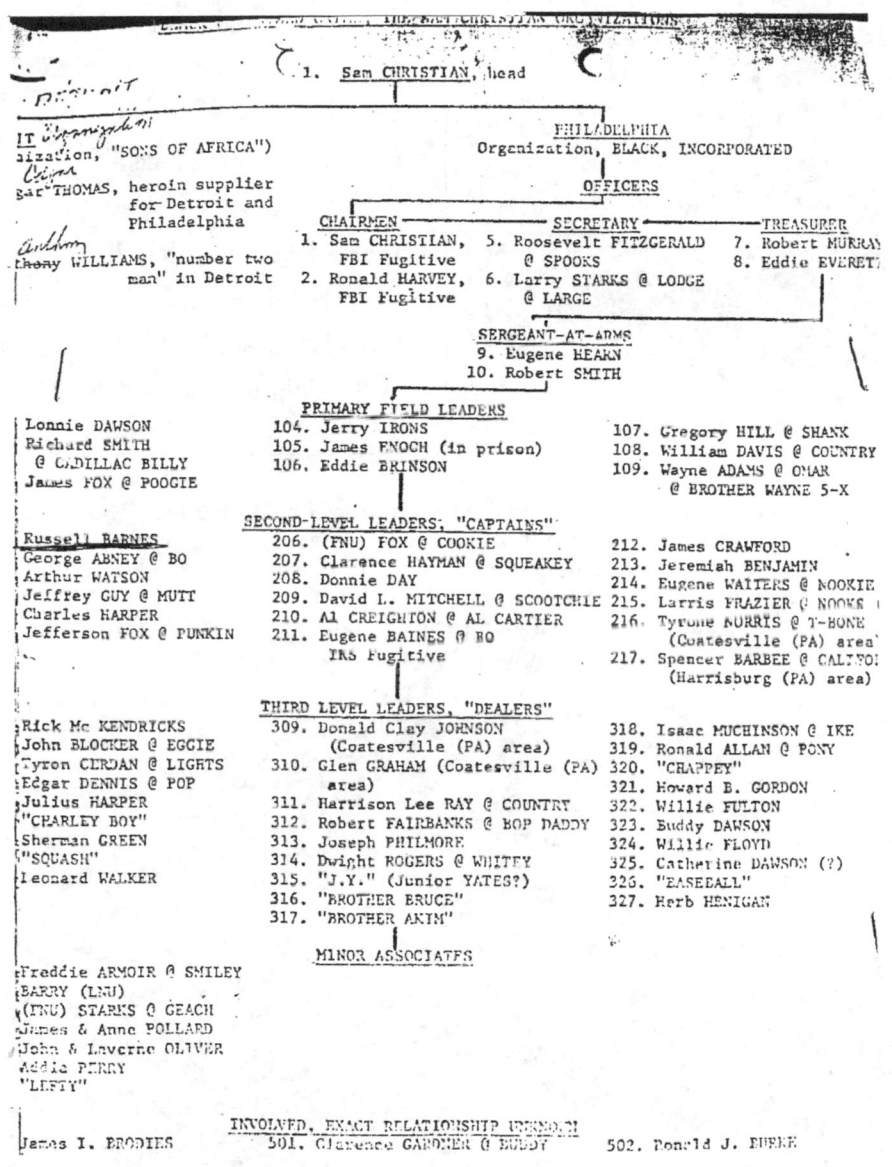

An Organized Crime Strike Force chart showing their take on the membership and structure of the Black Mafia

ATTENTION!

BLACK B. INC. INTENDS TO BETTER OUR COMMUNITY BY:

1. STOPPING ALL GANG WARFARE
2. STOPPING BURGLARIES
3. STOPPING ALL MUGGINGS
4. STOPPING RAPES
5. STOPPING DRUG TRAFFIC
6. STOPPING GRAFFITTI
7. STOPPING ROBBERIES
8. CLEANING UP OUR COMMUNITY

FOR INFORMATION CONTACT: BLACK B. INC.
1443 SOUTH ST · KI-5-1386 or KI-5-1439

Black Brothers, Incorporated operated from an office on South Street (above left), ostensibly as a community organization devoted to reducing gang activity and youth crime. Despite its strident literature, however (poster, above right), it was in truth a front for some of the worst criminals in the city. The sharply dressed founders at its grand opening included (below, from left) David Mitchell, Lonnie Dawson, Frederick "Smiley" Armour, James Fox and Gene Hearn.

CHAPTER 8

IS ERNIE HOME?

ERNEST KELLY, Senior was a forty-seven-year-old tavern owner who doubled as a smalltime numbers writer. Slightly built at five feet nine and 135 lbs, he wore large eyeglasses typical of the times. Ernie, as he was known, owned two bars, including a favorite Black Mafia haunt, Ernie's Club Paree, at 18th and Cumberland in North Philadelphia. He also had an impressive arrest record, complete with pinches for illegal lottery violations and crimes of violence. He should have known better when, in conversation with a few Black Mafia members in his club in early 1973, he made the mistake of mentioning how profitable his business had become.

Around midday on February 8, John Clark, William Christian, Thomas Clinton, Richard Dabney and John Griffin traveled to Kelly's home in the West Oak Lane section of the city. Ernie was home with his mother, his wife Thelma, aged forty-seven, and three little grandchildren, who all lived together. Dabney, heavyset and dressed in a blue suit with a pink shirt, and Clark, wearing a plaid overcoat, rang Kelly's doorbell.

"Who is it?" asked Thelma, via the home's intercom system.

"It's Lefty," responded a voice. "Is Ernie home?"

Thelma called for her husband, and told him someone named Lefty wanted him. Thelma, dressed only in underwear covered by a bathrobe, and her three grandchildren went upstairs, joining her mother-in-law, who was in her bedroom, and Ernie went to answer the door. He recognized Dabney from the Paree, but didn't recall his name. He invited Dabney and Clark inside, and Dabney proceeded to ask him for a job. Kelly said he would need to confer with his son, Ernest Kelly, Jr., and told Dabney to meet him at Club Paree at two o'clock.

As he got up to show the pair to the door, Clark put a gun to his head.

"I'm the police," said Clark. "Be quiet if you don't want to get your head blowed off. Give us all the money in the house or everybody in the house dies."

Kelly was taken into the basement, at which point the doorbell rang again. Thelma again asked who it was over the intercom, but before any response could be offered, Ernie was ordered to open the door, and William

Christian, Clinton and Griffin entered. Kelly's assailants placed an object over his head and then asked him where they could find money in the home. After Kelly told them about $800 stashed in a bedroom pillowcase, Dabney became enraged and demanded $100,000 or he'd kill them. Kelly pleaded that he could not get that kind of money, and was immediately pistol-whipped, kicked, grabbed by the testicles, and interrogated about his bank accounts.

While Ernie was being beaten, his wife was being assaulted upstairs. Two men stormed into the main bedroom, with one putting a gun in Thelma Kelly's face and pushing her onto the bed. They tied her hands and feet together, and put her face down into a pillow. They also herded the children together, placing a coat or something similar over them so they couldn't see. After the assailants had ransacked the home and come across a key to a safety deposit box, they returned to the bedroom, where one of them sat on the bed beside Thelma and told her they were going to take her someplace to get money. She was untied and ordered to get dressed, then a sweater was placed over her head and she was taken to the basement, where she heard Ernie describing the assets in his safety deposit box. They questioned her about the bank accounts and deposit box too.

The first plot hatched by the crew involved taking two cars to Kelly's bank, the Continental Bank at Broad Street and Nedro Avenue, to empty the contents of the safety deposit box. Ernie and a couple of his captors would be in one car, with his grandchildren and the remaining men in the other, and if anything went wrong they would kill the children. Considering what had been done to the Hanafi babies by some of these very men, this was no hyperbole – in fact, one of the guns used in the Hanafi murders was being used in the Kelly household. Dabney and Clark decided instead to accompany Ernest Kelly to the bank by themselves. Dabney retrieved Kelly's coat, hat and shoes for him, and before leaving the home, charged Christian, Clinton and Griffin with holding the family hostage. After getting Kelly's phone number, Clark made it clear that if anything went wrong at the bank, he would call the house and order everyone to be killed. Clark and Dabney then made Kelly drive them in his car to the bank, with Dabney riding shotgun. Thelma Kelly was taken to the first floor of the home and made to sit on the living room couch. At one point, John Griffin pressed a gun against her head and reminded her, "If things don't work out right, we will kill the little bastards."

Ernie Kelly pulled his black 1972 Cadillac into the parking lot of Gino's, a fast food restaurant, at Old York Road and Nedro Avenue. As he and Dabney walked the short distance to the bank, Clark positioned himself at a phone booth in front of Gino's and waited. He left Kelly's car running in the parking lot for their departure. Kelly and Dabney entered the bank and began walking toward the desk to sign the requisite card for the deposit box. The two walked past a line of patrons awaiting tellers, and Kelly recognized one of them as a police officer he knew. The off-duty officer was waiting in line to cash a check, and tried talking to Kelly, who only nodded nervously in return. Just as the officer sensed something was wrong, Ernie Kelly spun around, yelling, "Buddy, I'm being held up! They have my family tied up at my home. There's another man in Gino's."

Kelly then shoved Dabney and darted for the exit door. In his haste, he frantically tried to open the door outward – it was designed to be pulled inward – and wound up crashing through the glass to escape. Outside he ran northbound on Broad Street, eventually finding refuge in the 35th Police District at Champlost Avenue, two blocks away. Meanwhile, Dabney fled the bank across the street near Gino's, running west on Nedro into an alley, where he reached into his pants pocket as he turned toward the off-duty officer and a bank security guard who had given chase. The cop was carrying a revolver and shot at Dabney three times. The security guard also unloaded three shots from his pistol, but all six shots missed their target. After another brief chase, the officer caught up with Dabney and arrested him.

Kelly, his face bleeding heavily from the cuts sustained crashing through the glass door, hysterically explained the hostage situation to a sergeant in the lobby of the 35th District. The supervisor ordered officers in the control room to get Kelly to a hospital, and jumped into his patrol car headed to Kemble Avenue. On the way, he broadcast the details over police radio and requested help to meet him at the Kelly home. The sergeant soon reached the home, and with backup arriving he knocked on the door.

Inside the home, the intruders peeked out a window and saw police. Chaos broke out. Thomas Clinton hurried Thelma Kelly into the kitchen, while Christian and Griffin ran around trying to figure out what to do. Clinton told Thelma to use the intercom and tell the police on the doorstep that everything was fine. She complied, and the sergeant responded by telling her to open the door. Thomas Clinton took the sweater off her head, put a gun in her right side and told her, "We're going to the front door and tell them everything's alright."

As she walked toward the front door, Thelma saw John Griffin and William Christian wearing her husband's bathrobes, each running into the basement. One also sported one of Thelma's wigs and a scarf, in a poor effort at disguise. Thelma Kelly opened the door with Thomas Clinton immediately canted behind her right side, and saw two officers on the steps. Another sergeant had arrived with backup, and the house was surrounded. Thelma quickly pulled away from Clinton and made a dash between the officers, shouting, "My kids are tied up!"

A police supervisor swiftly subdued Clinton and placed him in handcuffs. One sergeant stayed with him as the other entered the home, going to the second floor. He saw Ernie Kelly's seventy-one year-old mother, Harriet

Spencer, lying unharmed in a rear bedroom, and next discovered Kelly's grandchildren, Barry, age four, Troy, five, and Felicia, just five months, in the front bedroom, bound hand and foot with stockings.

While one sergeant was upstairs, the other handed his "pinch" over to a police officer who had arrived with his wagon partner. One officer stayed with Clinton in the living room as his partner and a supervisor began searching the first floor and basement. They discovered John Griffin in the basement's bathroom where, comically, he pretended to be the legitimate occupant of the house, stating, "What are you doing? I live here." The responding officers were not impressed, and arrested him. While an officer guarded Griffin, the sergeant continued the search, making his way to the rear of the basement, where he found William Christian hiding behind the home's gas burner.

Four of the five conspirators were now under arrest, leaving John Clark as the only one who got away. He had fled his position at Gino's, leaving their getaway car running in the restaurant's parking lot. Clark was eventually arrested on March 16. Police also found a small notebook on Christian that listed names, phone numbers and random notes about members of Temple 12. The document would come in handy as law enforcement grappled with this secretive syndicate.

In March 1973, Clark began his fifteen-year sentence for the 1971 Southeastern National Bank robbery. Indictments were returned in the Kelly case in August 1973, though Christian and Griffin remained fugitives until arrested in Jacksonville, Florida on October 2. They were taken without incident, though one of them had a loaded .38 caliber pistol in his possession. FBI agents had tracked the pair down in an apartment complex. Christian was living under the name William Cotton, and had a social security card, Florida driver's license and checking account all in that name. He worked at the Jacksonville shipyard as "Thomas Jones." Richard Dabney was put on trial in May of 1974 for the previous year's robbery and kidnapping of Ernie Kelly and his family. A jury convicted Dabney, and Ernie and Thelma Kelly were next scheduled to testify in the trial for the remaining defendants, John Clark, William Christian and John Griffin, slated for mid-October.

The Kellys were at home the Monday evening of the week prior, when the phone rang.

"You're testifying against the brothers," the caller admonished.

"I have to," said Kelly.

"Well, you're dead, your family's dead, and the FBI won't be able to save you," said the anonymous voice. "We'll get you one by one, day by day."

Kelly immediately called a U.S. marshal, who took the family to a motel within fifteen minutes. The threats were enough to dissuade him from testifying, and the following day he informed the court of his decision and of his predicament. Kelly made it clear that if the threats had been aimed simply at him, he would have been willing to go through with the trial, adding, "We fear for the survival of our sons and our grandchildren and Thelma's mother and father and my mother. He said our family, and that takes in everyone."

U.S. District Judge Herbert A. Fogel was outraged, called the threat a "monstrous travesty" and ordered around-the-clock protection for Kelly's entire family. The judge added that it was "a sad day in this country" when "people who have testimony are threatened." After U.S. marshals placed their family in protective custody, Ernie and Thelma again reconsidered, and decided to testify. Marshals were in place to guard the courtroom as the trial convened, and Thelma Kelly was the first to take the stand, breaking down in tears several times as she recounted the horror in her home back in February 1973. Ernie Kelly testified next, despite the threats, and each defendant was eventually found guilty, adding time to the sentences being served for the Hanafi murders.

★

If the Black Mafia was concerned about the publicity they were getting following the Club Harlem, Hanafi and Kelly incidents, or about the heat law enforcement was beginning to apply by the spring of '73, no one noticed. That year saw the group soar within the Philadelphia underworld, and the Black Mafia would reach their zenith within the next year. But they were now under the watchful eyes of federal and city investigators, and perhaps more perilously for them, had been targeted by the Philadelphia Police Department's hyper-aggressive Highway Patrol (HP). In time, these developments would crush the syndicate.

For now, however, results were mixed. In March 1973, James Enoch was found guilty of committing perjury regarding testimony under oath before a grand jury investigating narcotics traffic in Pennsylvania. On Friday, May 18, at 7:20 P.M., two HP officers were conducting surveillance at 20th and Carpenter when they observed Frederick Armour and Lonnie Dawson in a parked white over white Cadillac. Armour got out of the car and walked in the officers' direction, and the cops stopped him for questioning. They patted him down and found a loaded .38 caliber Smith & Wesson inside his coat. As Armour was being handcuffed, Dawson emerged from the car yelling at the police and demanding an explanation. As he ranted, one of the cops checked the Vehicle Identification Number to see if the car was stolen. Then the officer looked inside and saw a loaded .38 caliber Colt pistol lying on the driver's seat. Armour said he was carrying the gun for protection because he "had a problem with a guy," but was arrested for weapons violations. It turned out he also had a tiny foil packet on him, thought by police to be heroin, and an ornamental spoon in the shape of a female figurine. A test of the substance showed it was actually amphetamine, and Armour was charged for possessing a controlled substance. At the time, "speedballing" – the mixing of amphetamine and heroin (speedballs) to use intravenously – was popular in some sections of society.

Around this time, a meeting was held at the Mount Airy Lodge in the Pocono Mountains, a resort area 115 miles northwest of Philadelphia. Big-time New York drug dealers had called the conclave of delegates from Philadelphia, New Jersey, New York and Pennsylvania. A couple of federal agencies were tipped off, but in an example of the poor coordination over the Black Mafia, each agency thought the other had personnel on site and no investigation was conducted. Meanwhile, Russell Barnes and Larry Starks roamed the Philly streets corner by corner, recruiting gangs throughout African-American sections of the city. From 1968 to 1973, the Black Mafia had worked on and off with several of the city's larger and more influential gangs. As their power increased, however, their reliance on these gangs lessened, but the independence of some gangs continued to cost the Black Mafia business.

Their nemesis was the heavy-handed 20th and Carpenter Street gang, which had run its lucrative South Philadelphia territory for years. The gang was very skeptical about any proposed compromise with the Black mafia, but feared it would not win a battle with them, especially now that they were aligned with the Black Muslims. So the 20th and Carpenter crew became the first such group to accept the Black Mafia's terms, particularly the loss of territory and the payment of a "street tax." Once this gang was in the fold, the Black Mafia was able to enlist the services of others from around the city, primarily in South and West Philadelphia. Six of the gangs totaled approximately 150 members. The 20th and Carpenter crew, with the backing of Barnes and Starks, victimized any gangs not in compliance. The Black Mafia ranks grew significantly, prompting one federal agent to remark, "The big car and fancy clothes look good to these kids on the corner. They should be with us when we go to their fancy apartments with thousands of dollars worth of clothes and shoes in the closet and there he is laying on the floor, on his expensive rug, with half his head blown away. This superfly thing is what you call, 'temporary stardom.'"

Authorities heard hints of the Black Mafia's involvement with numerous shakedowns, organized extortions and robberies, as well as homicides. On May 29, two people were executed inside the Inn Tower Motor Hotel at Broad and Huntingdon Streets in North Philadelphia. A maid found Leroy Jackson and Denise Walter, both twenty-five years old, bound hand and foot with neckties and shot in the head – a hallmark of the Black Mafia. Police were left to speculate about motive, and a few discoveries pointed to drugs. Glassine bags containing what was thought to be heroin were found in the room, and Jackson's history of arrests including a 1970 collar for narcotics. Some police theorized a drug deal had gone bad, and that Major Coxson had ordered the hit on Jackson.

★

In stark contrast to his sinister, ultra-violent Black Mafia associates, Major Coxson was out kicking off his mayoral campaign at the biggest nightclub in the South Jersey area, the Latin Casino in Cherry Hill. The 2,300 guests, fronted by Muhammad Ali, were treated to full-course steak dinners as they enjoyed live performances by the Supremes and the Temptations. In 1973, Camden had a population just over 100,000, and bore the typical urban burdens. It had the second-highest crime rate in the United States (Newark had the highest). Coxson was supposedly sparked into running for mayor in 1972 by the Camden administration's rejection of his proposal for a multi-million dollar housing project. At the time, he didn't have a Camden residence, and thus bought a rundown house at 414 Cooper Street. Part of the renovation included redecorating the house to incorporate a gold-carpeted campaign office, painting the house white, and installing an Astroturf lawn. Coxson then had business cards printed calling it the White House, and used the gimmick throughout the campaign. This was part of his larger plan. "What I'm gonna do is become Mayor ... then Governor of New Jersey and in twelve years I'm gonna be the first black President of the United States," he declared.

The Maje, as was his custom, entertained some interesting people in the White House, including criminal confederates Alzie "Count" Kelly and Renwick Mitchell. Mitchell had worked for Muhammad Ali as a chauffeur and bodyguard, while federal informants described Kelly as a drug courier for Coxson. Two other notorious personalities visited Coxson in his Camden office – John Berkery and James "Reggie" Edgehill. Berkery was a member of Philadelphia's K&A Gang and an associate of many of the city's organized crime figures. Edgehill owned the Jamaica Hotel and other properties in Atlantic City, and knew his share of underworld types. Comically, Coxson's White House was located next door to the Camden regional office of the FBI, allowing Coxson to ask, "If I'm doing all of these bad things, why would I move next door to the FBI? They know everything I'm doing."

Only Jeremiah Shabazz was more significant to the Black Mafia's criminal enterprises than Coxson. Where Shabazz afforded the Black Mafia more street presence, mosques as sanctuaries, meeting spots and warehouses, prison networks and a veil of legitimacy, Coxson afforded the group with countless illicit opportunities. In fact, for years several Black Muslims, including Muhammad Ali, courted Coxson to join their ranks, to no avail. Though founders Sam Christian, Ron Harvey and Nudie Mims provided the muscle and the rep, it was Coxson who provided the multifarious connections necessary for big-time underworld success. The Maje was the hub of a wheel with spokes emanating out to legitimate business people, quasi-legitimate sharpers like himself, non-violent hustlers, and outright violent predators, providing opportunities for all who were a part of the wheel though otherwise independent of the other spokes. Such inter-relationships didn't depend on Coxson, but he played a vital role in launching deals and introducing players to other players. He was the archi-tect of several financial scams involving the Black Mafia, and he mentored several members on pursuits such as credit card frauds, check scams, fencing stolen goods, and the laundering of money.

Coxson also provided the Black Mafia with a guise of legitimacy in some quarters, and in others he helped the group fill neighborhoods with racial pride, particularly when he mocked the establishment for repeatedly focusing on his criminal background, "If I wanted to do wrong, I would take the FBI, the Secret Service, the Philadelphia Police Department, the State Police and everybody else, and I'd keep them *all* busy," he said. "I think I'm capable of doing that. I'd keep them busy *and* confused. *Really confused.*"

Adding to the confusion so treasured by Coxson (as a shield against prosecution), for much of his life The Maje was, as one journalist put it, "a grade-A stool pigeon." Coxson traded so many "live bodies to the law" in order to stay on the street that one Assistant District Attorney built his reputation on the cases Coxson gave him. In an effort to describe The Maje, considering how frantic and variegated his life was, Stanley Branche simply said he was "a thousand guys, a thousand guys." Such words were music to Coxson's ears. "There has to be mystery," he loved to say. "I make myself mysterious." As he campaigned for mayor, Coxson played to his supporters. "I'm no priest, but I'm not the devil either," he said. "In New Jersey, most office holders start as politicians and wind up being arrested. I thought I'd reverse the trend."

Coxson's public relations acumen was perhaps best exhibited by the largely favorable treatment he received in the press. Influential columnist Chuck Stone wrote, "He's a black Horatio Alger, a poor boy who climbed out of the coal mines in Uniontown, Pa., and built a financial empire from a small car-washing business." Stone summed up Coxson's run for mayor of Camden by saying, "He's no angel. But then again, angels are rare these days in politics."

Coxson did not exemplify the day's tough and edgy Superfly image as the Black Mafia did, but he was still flashy as hell in his own way. His cars and his homes were gaudy, and his dress was always sharp – Pierre Cardin and Geoffrey Beene suits, alligator shoes, and the omnipresent wide-brimmed Stetson hat – whether he was outside or inside. Coxson frequently made a show of traveling with his chauffeur, Quinzelle Champagne, at the wheel of his flashy rides, and made a point of being seen with Muhammad Ali.

His political competitors predictably made his dubious background an issue, but these were complex times when it came to race and social class, and Coxson exploited the era's emotions magnificently. A *New York Times* reporter covering the race summed up the paradox: "Though he says he is "retired" and cites no visible means of support, his obvious affluence makes him a hero to those who admire the use of wit to beat the system. People he does not know honk when they meet his cars. They wave from the sidewalks when he goes by."

As a Coxson supporter said at the time, "They call [Coxson] a hustler and con man, but ghetto folk identify with brothers and sisters who've been in the stir and come back stronger than ever." The Maje's close relationship with Ali didn't hurt his campaign either. One observer said, "To Ali, the Major's a God. He can do no wrong." Coxson was fond of saying, "Muhammad Ali will add a real punch to the campaign." People in the South Jersey area knew that Coxson had sold two of his properties, one in the Overbrook section of Philadelphia and one in Cherry Hill, to the boxer. When he sold his Spanish style home on Winding Drive in Cherry Hill to Ali, Coxson simply moved a few blocks away and the two became neighbors. The grand opening of a hardware store in the Germantown section of Philadelphia featured Ali and "the incomparable Major Coxan [sic]."

Ali mugged for the cameras with Coxson at ringside before his bout with Ken Norton in San Diego, and told the assembled media that Coxson was his "unpaid financial adviser." Six days before the May 8 election, Ali joined Major Coxson at his "victory" party, once again at the Latin Casino. The crowd was a bit smaller, around 1,500 diners, than for the kickoff dinner, but the meal and atmosphere were the same. Totie Fields and Billy Eckstine performed on stage. Coxson said he was holding the victory party early because he simply wouldn't have time for fun after the election because he'd be consumed with correcting Camden's numerous ills. In fact, Coxson knew he had little chance of winning the election, and went on to lose the mayoral race to Angelo Errichetti in a landslide, despite heavy financing from the Black Mafia and entrepreneurs along Philadelphia's 52nd Street Strip.

And behind the façade of Coxson's failed bid for mayor of Camden, New Jersey, an important business deal was about to go south – literally and figuratively.

CHAPTER 9 ★
BROKEN PROMISES

ONE MILLION DOLLARS: that was the estimated street value of a single heroin shipment – the latest in a series – sent by the the Italian Mob in New York to the Black Mafia in Philly. It was authorised, law enforcement officers later heard, by Carlo Gambino himself, perhaps the most powerful Cosa Nostra boss in the land, and its intended recipient was Bo Baynes. It never reached him. In transit, the shipment was intercepted by some foolhardy black independents, identified by police as Philadelphians Hilton Stroud and Walter Tillman. They effectively signed their own death warrants.

The Italians naturally wanted to recover the heroin, if not to gain retribution, and sought help. Enter The Maje. Major Coxson brokered a deal by which he would receive $300,000 from Gambino and his associates simply for producing the names and whereabouts of the hijackers. Coxson then went to his Black Mafia associates and subcontracted the job for $200,000 – and things went wrong from there. Apparently there was a miscommunication, because in the early hours of May 1, Black Mafia enforcers tracked down Stroud and Tillman and promptly executed them on an isolated Camden street. The Italian mobsters were furious, realizing they would recoup neither the large cache of heroin nor the profits from its sale. They also didn't appreciate the publicity they were now getting, and refused to pay Coxson for his services. That created a big problem for The Maje, because the Black Mafia fully expected the $200,000 for services rendered, however untidily.

Coxson spent weeks greasing his pals around Philadelphia, trying in vain to come up with the cash. He knew the Black Mafia's history and that no matter who he was or what he represented to others, to them he was just another expendable confederate if he came up short. The Black Mafia no longer needed Coxson for his NYC drug contacts, since they had developed their own, while his mentoring skills in white-collar crimes had already been learned and applied with some success. Lastly, with the backing of Jeremiah Shabazz and the Nation of Islam, which reached farther and higher than any of Coxson's networks, the Black Mafia no longer viewed his connections as indispensable. The clock was ticking on Major Coxson's life.

Despite his problems, nothing seemed odd about Coxson's demeanor or activities during the first week of June. On Tuesday, June 5, he traveled to Philadelphia to gather information about the person who had stolen a pair of coachlights from his White House in Camden the night before. Coxson drove himself in his black and silver Rolls, the one upholstered with blue velvet in the back seat and blue leather in the front, along with a telephone. He parked right in front of City Hall around noon, and enjoyed the company of passersby who wanted to ogle his car, with its license tag MBC-1. Coxson hung out for about half an hour, speaking with his friend Cecil Moore and others. He left the city with no apparent leads concerning the light theft and returned to New Jersey.

Two days later, he returned to Philly, and attended a noontime affair at the Sheraton Hotel, and afterward spent time with Muhammad Ali, entertaining the public at 16th and Chestnut. The two were spotted by the media, and by law enforcement officers conducting surveillance, hanging around Coxson's Rolls Royce around 2 P.M. Later that evening, Coxson visited close friends Stanley Branche and Gus Lacy at their Advance Security office. According to Branche, they sat in his office from eight o'clock to eleven o'clock. "We were just three guys sitting around talking ... just like we always do," he said. No one who spoke with him or who observed him that week sensed anything peculiar; The Maje was being himself, publicly joking with his closest friends – Ali, Moore, Branche and Lacy – as was his custom. It is questionable if this was all an act or if Coxson thought for some reason that his failed deal with the Black Mafia was behind him. Whatever his mindset, the Black Mafia had not forgotten about their money, as Coxson was about to realize.

The forty-three year-old Maje lived in Cherry Hill with his common-law wife, thirty-something Lois Robinson Luby, and her three children, Lita, who was fifteen, Toro, fourteen, and Lex, thirteen. About five hours after Coxson bade farewell to his friends Branche and Lacy, he was at home when a honking horn shook him out of his sleep. Coxson put on a red bathrobe and descended the stairs from his bedroom to answer the door, where he saw a few familiar faces. Sam Christian, Ron Harvey and two of their strongarm men wanted to talk – and more. Lex, upstairs, was woken by the car horn, but went back to sleep after he heard Coxson let the men in and speak with them. The next thing Lex knew, he was being assaulted, gagged and bound with neckties hand and foot, and left on his bed. While guarded in his room, he heard cries from elsewhere in the home, including his brother Toro screaming downstairs in the living room. He also heard one of the intruders say, "Let's get the hell out of here. There's no money here."

When his assailant left the bedroom, Lex got off the bed and backed up to a sliding glass window. With his hands tied behind him, he opened the door to the outside and, dressed only in his underwear, hopped for several hundred yards along a mini-bike trail through the woods. He tripped and fell several times in the darkness before arriving at the home of the Khalil family, directly behind the Coxson estate. He noticed the garage door open, hopped inside and began banging his head on the glass of the kitchen door, alerting the Khalils' dog, which began barking. Lex had just slipped the gag from his mouth when one of the Khalils came to the door to see what was bothering the dog.

"It's Lex," he shouted. "Let me in. My house is being robbed."

While Lex was fleeing, the Black Mafia rained down on Coxson and his family as payback for the broken deal months prior. When police arrived, they found all four occupants bound with neckties, their hands and feet behind them. Each had been shot. Major was dead, kneeling by his $3,000 waterbed, gagged and shot three times at close range in the back of the head. One bullet shattered when it broke through The Maje's skull, and the fragments lodged behind his left cheek and his left eye. Another stopped beneath his jaw, and the last came through the front of his neck. Lois had been shot in the head as she tried to flee their bedroom into a bathroom. She survived but was blinded. Lita was shot twice in the back of the head – parts of her skull littered the floor – and was barely alive when police found her in her bedroom. She died four days later. Police found Toro in the sunken living room, leaning on a chair, shot twice in the back of the head. Like Lois, he survived though blinded in his left eye.

Lex Coxson was placed under guard in an undisclosed motel, where he provided details to police. Lois Luby had overheard Coxson greet the persons at the door with the words, "Hi, Sam, c'mon in." Neighbors also offered what little insight they could. Police put out alerts to surrounding areas, but had little description beyond four black males, two wearing suits, driving a black Cadillac. Stating the obvious, Camden County Medical Investigator Thomas R. Daley termed Coxson's killing "an execution." Almost three decades later, *The Philadelphia Inquirer* placed the Coxson murder on its list of "violent crimes of the 20th century."

Not surprisingly, at death Coxson was the target of several criminal investigations, involving tax evasion, possession of stolen or counterfeit credit cards, narcotics trafficking, and involvement in a Pennsylvania-New Jersey car ring. According to one former U.S. Attorney, "We had Coxson under very active investigation. You might say we were just inches away from indicting him." Authorities also disclosed they were looking at Coxson's involvement as a drugs financier as early as 1971, when they placed a Black Mafia meeting under surveillance. The West Philadelphia conference was to be raided, but a legal technicality snuffed the effort. Yet after decades of grand-scale criminality, and despite the world in which he operated, Coxson's record did not list a single arrest involving violence or a weapon. Perhaps this is why popular syndicated columnist Claude Lewis remembers Coxson as a "lovable rogue."

In the days immediately following the murders, police were concerned for the safety of Coxson's close friend Muhammad Ali. An informant had claimed those who killed Coxson wanted to kill Ali because of what he knew regarding The Maje's involvement in the Philadelphia underworld. Ali dismissed the rumors by stating they were "probably [started by] some white man who doesn't like me because I got two Rolls Royces, a $200,000 house and I talk too much for a nigger." Incredibly, during interviews with reporters, the boxer tried to distance himself from his late friend, virtually disavowing knowing Coxson. "Coxson was a good associate of mine, not a true friend," he said. "The Koran preaches that only a Muslim can be true friends with another Muslim, and Coxson was not a Muslim."

Coxson's death caused some to cast a curious eye on Ali because of his close ties to The Maje and his vicious crowd. Indeed, an Ali biographer later criticized a book on the champ for providing little insight into the Ali-Coxson relationship: "Surely, no life of Ali is complete without a thorough investigation of the Philadelphia and Cherry Hill years, without a thorough investigation of the New York and Philadelphia mosques." Innuendo such as this has abounded ever since the Coxson slayings, with little, if any, comment on its validity. While Ali certainly traveled with an interesting crowd in Philadelphia and South Jersey, there is no suggestion, let alone evidence, of wrongdoing on his part. Examinations of surveillance records and other intelligence documents, many of which include analyses of Ali, do not reveal a single item implicating him in dubious activities.

A day after Coxson's murder, the *Philadelphia Bulletin* concisely and accurately summed up his life, stating The Maje was a "small man with a big, toothy grin who rose from poverty to riches under mysterious circumstances and adopted a flamboyant lifestyle that delighted his friends and confounded his enemies."

It was soon discovered that Coxson hoodwinked just about everyone when it came to his financial prowess. It turned out he did not own his Cherry Hill home or the White House in Camden, or the fleet of luxurious cars he so commonly flaunted. Rather, each property was rented, and the vast majority of his cars were leased. According to Gus Lacy, "It was an appearance, that's all it was. It was a day-to-day thing, but he put up a good front." Police estimated that 5,000 people filed past Coxson's ebony steel casket inside the Wayland Baptist Church at 25th Street and Columbia Avenue in North Philadelphia. One of the speakers that evening said Coxson was a financial genius whose accomplishments were debased by white society. His longtime friend Cecil Moore said, "His ingenuity was far superior to that of men with more formal training."

Years later, Gus Lacy offered his take on the Coxson murder, "I don't like to speak on it too much ... As they said [on the street], he was in 'violation' ... He made a promise he couldn't keep, and it got him killed."

★

Within weeks of the Coxson killings, Ron Harvey was subpoenaed to appear in a lineup in the grand jury proceeding for the Hanafi murders, and failed to show. Federal agents found him in Philadelphia, and placed him under surveillance for a few days. Harvey was ultimately arrested for contempt of court on June 28, at the wheel of his car in front of his South Philadelphia home. Camden authorities immediately revealed they had arrest warrants against him for the Coxson slayings and assaults, and filed a "detainer" to get him back when he was done in Washington. The Camden prosecutor admitted the warrants for Harvey had been signed the day after the Coxson killings, but that authorities didn't publicly disclose this fact out of fear that "Ronald 14X" would "go underground." Harvey listed his employment as "butcher-baker" for the Shabazz bakery at Carlisle and Susquehanna Sts. in North Philadelphia.

On July 3, Harvey was indicted on eleven counts arising out of the Coxson assaults. His wife, Lucinda, posted the requisite ten percent of his $165,000 bail in cash at Police Headquarters, but Harvey failed to appear for an extradition hearing on August 21. He fled just moments before he was to be indicted by a grand jury in Washington, D.C. for the Hanafi case, despite being tailed by FBI agents. The agents immediately put a call out for Harvey, and swept airports and train stations for probable escape routes, to no avail. Harvey surreptitiously left Philadelphia for Chicago, using the network of NOI mosques. He joined Robert "Nudie" Mims in the Windy City, where the latter was serving as Elijah Muhammad's bodyguard while hiding from the law for the Dubrow Furniture homicide. Sam Christian also fled the Philadelphia-South Jersey area following the Coxson murders, using the Black Muslim underground system, and ultimately wound up in Detroit.

Because of the infamy of their actions, their flight, and the use of a national, clandestine network to hide them, the two Black Mafia leaders made history by appearing on the FBI's "Ten Most Wanted" list in December 1973. Harvey and Christian were the 320th and 321st individuals to make the list, which dates back to 1950. Commenting on their inclusion, the FBI said they were members of an organization "which preys upon black communities and deals in murder, narcotics, extortion, the numbers racket and prostitution." Harvey's Most Wanted poster was headlined, "Wanted by the FBI: Interstate Flight – Murder; Conspiracy; Assault to Kill;

Armed Robbery; Armed Burglary." The Bureau's write-up focused on his role, in conjunction with six accomplices armed with pistols and sawed-off shotguns, in the Hanafi murders: "During this slaughter, four children were drowned and in an execution-style manner four adults and a nine-year-old child were shot at close range after they were tied and blindfolded. The nine-year-old and two of the adults were killed; however, the other two adults survived."

FBI agents arrested Harvey in Chicago on 27 March 1974. His bail this time was set at $5.5 million. He was tried for the Hanafi murders, and was convicted that November. On 7 January 1975, he was sentenced to 140 years, just as his co-conspirators had been months before. Harvey next went on trial in May of 1977 for the Coxson slayings. The main witnesses in the case, the two sons of Major Coxson's common-law wife, were placed under guard throughout the trial. They also each wore sunglasses and baggy clothes to hide their identities, prompting one observer to comment, "You can see these people are concerned." It was therefore not entirely surprising when the teenage boys testified they could not recall anything about the night of the murders. They stated they could not recall giving statements to police in 1973, and certainly could not identify their assailants at the time of trial some four years later. The prosecution thus relied on the photo identifications made by the boys immediately following the murders. On June 1, after two days of deliberation, a jury convicted Ronald Harvey for the murders of Major Coxson and Lita Luby, and he received two more life terms.

In a rare twist for law enforcement, a traditionally cumbersome profession marked by bureaucracy and political infighting, often at the expense of prudent analysis, authorities retroactively examined Harvey's history in the criminal justice system just after his stint on the Most Wanted list:

> The criminal record of Ronald Harvey, consists of 3 pages ... dating back to 1959, when he was 19 years of age, enumerating 17 arrests nearly all consisting of some form of violence ... This does NOT include the contacts he encountered with the police as a juvenile. Harvey has documented 18 separate home addresses, hidden in the shadow of six aliases, and culminated his career with a reputation, soon to be substantiated in a Court of Law, of a hired assassin. A full 9 ... arrests involved, among other charges, the carrying of concealed deadly weapons. He has assaulted arresting police officers, and engaged in running gun battles with police authorities to avoid arrest.
>
> In deadly contrast to the above narration of crime, is the pitiful record of conviction. Of the 17 arrests the subject has sustained a mere 3 convictions, one of which was for the insignificant charge of Disorderly Conduct. Ronald Harvey has spent a little over a year in

jail, and this was actually awaiting trial, and NOT the result of a formal sentence. However, the lack of convictions lie NOT with the Court System, but rather with the subject's ability to threaten and intimidate victims or witnesses, to such an extent they refuse to testify against him.

Major Coxson was Harvey's last killing; his days as a free man were over. He was sent to the federal prison in Atlanta, and in August 1977, he died of congestive heart failure in a hospital for federal prisoners in Springfield, Missouri, while a direct appeal from his conviction for the Hanafi slayings was pending before the District of Columbia Court of Appeals.

Sam Christian had not managed to stay at large for as long as Harvey. "Christian," stated his Most Wanted poster, "who is reputed to be a cold-blooded killer and a murderer for pay, is wanted for unlawful flight to avoid prosecution for armed robbery. He has been charged with the wounding of a New York City Police Department detective, and the murder of five individuals resulting from a shoot-out in an Atlantic City, New Jersey, nightclub during a robbery. He allegedly travels with two body-guards." The FBI noted that Christian was a "baker-salesman" for the Shabazz Bakery in North Philadelphia. By the time Samuel Richard Christian made their list, he had amassed an incredible record of arrests and aliases. He had been pinched thirty-three times and charged in seven murders, and used the following names, among others: Samuel Bay, Sam Bazahad, Richard Bey, Sulieman Bey, Samuel Beyah, Richard Carter, Richard S. Christian, and Sam Christie. One Philadelphia detective told an officer from another agency, "Listen to me, I know Sam Christian. If you see him on the street, you draw your gun as soon as you see him, because, if he sees you first and he even *suspects* that you are going to arrest him … he will walk up to you and shoot you dead."

Federal agents caught up with Sam Christian as he walked at night along the 3000 block of Detroit's Hazelwood Street on 11 December 1973, and arrested him without incident. Christian immediately put a contract on the life of the FBI agent who had tracked him from Philadelphia and who ultimately placed him under arrest. The agent received the appropriate protection, and was never threatened or harmed. Authorities were concerned about Christian's ability to flee, and thus a U.S. magistrate set bond at $1 million.

Christian was never convicted for the Coxson or Palmer murders; witnesses simply refused to testify against him. An example of the legalese contained in many Black Mafia rulings is found in the New Jersey Superior Court's dismissal of charges against Christian for the Fat Ty Palmer killing, where the court stated, "Two of the State's material witnesses in a companion case involving the same factual basis that gave rise to [the indictments against Christian] have recanted and now claim that they are unable to remember or to recall any of the events leading up to the incident that resulted in the above-captioned indictments. It is on this 20th day of August, 1974, ordered that [the indictments] be dismissed without prejudice."

One of the few cases against Christian not dismissed because of a lack of witnesses was the 1971 Harlem record store robbery in which an NYPD officer was shot. Following Christian's stint on the Most Wanted list and his subsequent arrest, he was extradited to New York and ultimately convicted by a jury of three counts of attempted murder of the officer, and related offenses. Christian would serve time until New York authorities paroled him in November of 1988. For now, at least, the most feared man in Philly was off the streets.

Sam Christian and Ron Harvey were the two most significant Black Mafia members, the group's founder-leader and chief enforcer, respectively. Imprisonment ended their decade long run of murder and mayhem, yet also provided opportunities for their understudies in the syndicate. One of their peers would now quickly take over the reigns.

★

Eugene Carl Baynes was born on 22 October 1938, in Philadelphia, and went to work as a street sweeper for the city in June 1961. In 1966 he worked briefly as an equipment operator, then as a bartender at the J & E Bar on Mantua Avenue. He became manager before leaving in September 1967 when the bar changed hands. Baynes then worked for John "Stan the Man" Watson at Philly Groove Records from January 1968 to June 1971. In November 1971, Baynes and his wife, Jacqueline, purchased a food store on S. 56th Street and ran it together as B & D Market, Inc. In April 1972, Baynes began operating Baynes Variety Store on Fairmount Avenue. Compared to the other founding Black Mafia members, Baynes was a modest character. Like Christian and Harvey, he drove a late model Cadillac, and was a Muslim with close ties to Minister Jeremiah. Unlike his buddies, his arrest record was tame, sporting only six arrests by 1972.

As June 1973 ended, the PPD OCU "received information that a group of black men [were] organizing under the name 'Black Incorporated.'" Authorities had no idea what "Black Incorporated" was or what it meant. Intelligence reports simply suggested the group was "supposed to take over the drug traffic in West Philadelphia" and that "Bo" Baynes was one of the group's leaders. Baynes inherited the Black Mafia mantel as the group was peaking, and his primary challenge was fending off the law enforcement push that was steadily building against the syndicate.

Immediately following the June 8 Coxson murders, Black Mafia activities kept going apace, with no discernible change in strategy. Law enforcement wondered whether this was attributable to ignorance or arrogance, with the good money on the latter. Addressing the string of audacious Black Mafia acts up to and including the Coxson incident, one FBI official at the time commented, "What has marked these people's activities is the wholesale disregard of human life … these guys kill the family, innocent bystanders, anyone. We're dealing with animals here."

Late in the afternoon of Monday, 18 June 1973, federal agents conducting surveillance at the intersection of 20th and Carpenter Streets saw James Fox talking to a group of men on the northeast corner. Fox walked over to a late model Cadillac, opened the trunk, pulled out a 9mm Browning automatic pistol and placed it in his waistband. As Fox walked away from the corner, he was arrested for violating the Uniform Firearms Act. A records check revealed that the weapon was one of fifty-seven guns stolen from a Pottstown store less than one month prior. Law enforcement thought the Black Mafia was behind this and several similar weapons heists, but no such cases were ever developed sufficiently to be charged.

On June 29, a mere three weeks after the Coxson killings, police found Charles Cooper, thirty-three, and Olga Leonard, eighteen, dead from gunshot wounds to the head in Cooper's apartment. The pair were estimated to have died in the apartment at 50th and Spruce Streets three days before they were discovered. Speculation centered on ties to Major Coxson; Cooper was a close friend and business partner of The Maje's. It was yet another suspected Black Mafia case left unsolved.

The law enforcement press on the street continued, regardless. On July 5, Highway Patrol officers pulled over a new white and blue Cadillac for rolling through a stop sign at 12th and Mt. Vernon Sts. The car was driven by Clarence "Squeaky" Hayman, with Lonnie Dawson in the passenger seat and Frederick "Smiley" Armour in the rear. As an officer checked the vehicle's serial number inside the car's windshield, Dawson conspicuously placed a loaded black Walther 9mm pistol on the car's floor. Dawson was arrested for the gun, while Hayman and Armour were let go following a brief investigation. Incidents like this were helping law enforcement to produce a picture of Black Mafia alliances, relationships and patterns of activity.

One of the many discoveries made in the course of their investigations was that Ronald Harvey and Roosevelt "Spooks" Fitzgerald, *aka* Roosevelt Bey, were partners in a sandwich shop. Your Brothers' Steak 'n' Take shop at Broad and South Sts. was a former White Tower, and one of several such Steak 'n' Take shops throughout African-American neighborhoods. This particular shop featured an outside decorated with two large, crude paintings of architectural domes befitting the Taj Mahal. The Steak 'n' Takes sold food prepared according to Black Muslim dietary laws, and were supplied by one of the two Shabazz Bakeries. Fitzgerald also ran the Steak 'n' Take at 1601 S. 24th St. in South Philadelphia, joining the majority of Black Mafia members who listed these locations as places of employment. Others listed themselves as salesmen for the NOI's newspaper, *Muhammad Speaks*, operating out of the city's mosques, and all of these locations of "employment" were placed under considerable surveillance by local and federal authorities. The net was tightening.

CHAPTER 10 ★

BLACK INK

I
F THE GROWING pressure from law enforcement wasn't bad enough for the Black Mafia, the media – led by one intuitive and ballsy investigative journalist – was finally piecing together their extraordinary story. Jim Nicholson was a very interesting character himself. He was born and raised in South Philadelphia, though his family in time moved around the country following his father, a career Marine. Nicholson returned to the Philadelphia area and graduated from high school in South Jersey in 1960, before heading to Mississippi for college, eventually graduating with a bachelor's degree in journalism from the University of Southern Mississippi. Like his father, he had the itch for military service, and served in the United States Marine Corps Reserve until his honorable discharge as a private first class in 1965. He returned to the Northeast just as the Black Mafia was forming, and his wild professional ride was about to begin.

Nicholson worked as a reporter for several newspapers, mostly in the Mid-Atlantic region, including stops at the *Philadelphia Daily News*, *Wilmington News-Journal*, *Baltimore News-American*, *Camden Courier-Post*, and the *Independent American* in New Orleans. In 1970, he began doing investigative work on the murder of United Mine Workers Union official Jock Yablonski, and traveled throughout the coal regions of Pennsylvania, Ohio, Virginia, Kentucky and Tennessee. His reporting on the murder in the *Philadelphia Inquirer* garnered a Pulitzer nomination, and Nicholson became a *de facto* investigative reporter for the *Inquirer*. On the heels of the successful Yablonski investigation, he looked into the shoddy construction of Veterans Stadium, resulting in a nine-part series in the *Inquirer* that won a Sigma Delta Chi (the Society of Professional Journalists) award for Greater Philadelphia, and another Pulitzer nomination. Nicholson next set his sights on a far more challenging project, namely documenting the vast narcotics traffic in Philadelphia. Heady from the success of his two large investigative projects, the twenty-eight-year-old Nicholson's hubris blinded him to what an unwieldy, overwhelming venture this would be.

Three prodigious investigative reporters, Don Barlett, Cliff Linedecker, and Hoag Levins, joined Jim Nicholson on the drug trade project in 1971. The group orchestrated street drug buys, mail order drug buys, and developed sources in the criminal justice system and on the street. Their investigation lasted a modest four or five months, and the results were not at all what was expected of the talented group, led by Nicholson. Tracked down more than thirty years later, Nicholson praised the hard and dedicated team, reserving criticism for himself. "The investigation was a failure. We could not show the network. I could not diagram the flow. I looked for 'Mister Big' and I found him. He was on every street corner and he was fifteen years old."

Despite generating some great street sources, they hadn't produced anything approaching award nominations, and Nicholson left Philadelphia burned out by the "disaster," as he called it. He spent the following year or so back in the South, working intermittently as a speechwriter, aide, tactician and grass-roots organizer in more than a dozen county, state and national campaigns for both political parties in Mississippi and Louisiana. But as Nicholson says, he quickly grew "tired of the sleight-of-hand carnival life of an iterant political campaign operative," and returned to Philadelphia. There he wrote stories for the *Philadelphia Inquirer's* TODAY magazine, a weekly pullout that was under a different administrative umbrella than the news division. Though it lacked the prestige of the news division of the *Inquirer*, TODAY afforded its writers greater latitude of style, substance and space, and permitted them to take more risks than ever would have been allowed over in "news." As Nicholson spent more time back in Philly, a question that had nagged him since the failed drug investigation attracted his attention more and more: What is the Black Mafia? *Is there a Black Mafia?*

One of the few important discoveries Nicholson had made two years prior was that there was "a largely unseen – certainly unpublicized – force moving through the African-American community that was both brutal and sinister." One of the female junkies interviewed in 1971 said it was called the "Black Mafia." A Gaudenzia (halfway) House counselor told the reporters that it was an organization composed of "men in dark suits" who moved legal and illicit things around the city. Though the anxious feeling had not left him from the embarrassment two years prior, Nicholson decided to follow up on the numerous leads he and his colleagues had developed, and took his case to the TODAY editor, Howard Coffin, who liked the concept of a crime-ring story and gave his approval as 1972 turned into 1973.

Nicholson began by canvassing the *Inquirer* building, seeking out beat writers who might have knowledge of, or street sources on, African-American racketeers, hustlers, robbery crews, organized drug rings and so on, perhaps acting in concert. If fellow reporters knew something, they didn't let on, and Nicholson went into the venture alone with no more information than he had two years earlier. Before hitting the street, he sought whatever the Philadelphia Police Department had on black groups that transcended gangs. Rather than wasting his time going from police district to police district, cop to cop, Nicholson thought it would be prudent to quiz the more sophisticated units of detectives specializing in gathering intelligence. This would require some great connections.

He went right to the top and called Mayor Frank Rizzo. Back in 1970, Nicholson had spent hours at the then-Police Commissioner's home and interviewed Rizzo while he watched himself on a national television special called *Super Chief*. The two hit it off, so much so that Rizzo offered Nicholson a position as public relations officer with the department. Nicholson politely declined, despite the offer of a substantial pay increase. Rizzo was apparently not offended by the rejection, because when Nicholson called him requesting help on the proposed Black Mafia project in 1973, Rizzo called Police Commissioner Joseph F. O'Neill and told him to give Nicholson access to pertinent information.

Commissioner O'Neill set Nicholson up with the Organized Crime Unit, which, ironically, had very little helpful information. Next was the Intelligence Unit, and for the first time, Jim Nicholson viewed formal documents marked "Black Mafia," consisting of folders and photos of the group's original 1968 members. However, beyond the photos and lengthy rap sheets overflowing with violent crimes, the Unit seemed to view the group as a bunch of street thugs no different than any of the dozens of street gangs in black Philadelphia at the time. The city's gang problem was almost exclusively an African-American phenomenon, and the gangs warred mostly over turf, though a few dabbled in illicit enterprises. Police estimated there were between 5,000 and 8,000 gang members in approximately 105 gangs, mostly located in West and North Philadelphia. As Nicholson recalls, there was nothing there that suggested an "organization that would inspire citywide intimidation in the African-American community," and he thus kept plugging away on the street, generating sources and bits of gossip.

The memory of the narcotics trafficking investigation lingered in his head as months wore on and the legwork seemed to produce little in return. "After months it still seemed I had a good, little story," he said. "But the vague outlines of a major syndicate seemed to be there. There was a small core of toughs who called themselves the Black Mafia. There did seem to be some Muslim converts in that group and the Muslims in Philly were shaping up as a powerful, almost intimidating force. Then there seemed to be some connection with the old Damon Runyonesque world of 52nd Street, which brought in the club owners, gamblers, sportsmen, drug dealers, politicians and local celebrities. A lot of pieces – colorful pieces – lying on the table but not a clear picture or clean fit."

Nicholson plugged along looking for something – anything – that would validate his informed suspicions that these groups were related. During the Yablonski murder investigation, he had gotten to know people inside Philadelphia's District Attorney's Office. He now went to them to see if they had anything related to his research. According to Nicholson, "The D.A.'s office didn't have anything about any 'Black Mafia,' but one of their reports – obviously drawn from an inside source – described a clandestine meeting in West Philly that was heavily attended. The names of some of the attendees and what was discussed was an indisputable intersection of the [renegade] Muslims, 52nd Street and the hardcore group known as the Black Mafia. That one document, of unquestioned validity, brought everyone together under one tent. Now, a lot of previously collected information, seemingly unconnected, made sense. *The Black Mafia was a major, well-organized crime syndicate, operating behind the impenetrable veil of the Nation of Islam.*"

As he was completing the draft of the explosive exposé, he made another visit to the Organized Crime Unit to run his findings by them. Though stunned – the Unit had nowhere near this comprehensive a picture of the Black Mafia at the time – a core group of detectives was impressed by his findings, and also fearful for Nicholson's well-being. An OCU memo dated July 27 states:

> On Wednesday, 7/18/73, James Nicholson, free-lance investigative reporter, currently working for the Philadelphia Inquirer, contacted ... the Organized Crime Unit, and informed the [Unit] of a story he was writing concerning the "Black Mafia" and their infiltration into organized crime. After reading excerpts of Mr. Nicholson's investigative report, [the OCU] advised him of possible threats and/or pressure as a result of this story being published. Mr. Nicholson was advised of the Phila. Police Department's concern for his safety and assured him of protection, if needed.

Following his visit to the OCU, Nicholson polished his manuscript, which relied on his remarkable assortment of sources. In addition to the Philadelphia Police Department's intelligence files, Nicholson used interviews and records in four states. Among those he interviewed were police, former policemen, city, state and federal officials, social workers, ex-junkies, ministers, attorneys, prison inmates and assorted "street" people. Of supreme importance, Nicholson had great sources in the African-American community.

On August 12, the cover of the *Philadelphia Inquirer*'s TODAY pullout section featured a 1969 black and white photo of Richard "Red Paul" Harris lying dead at the foot of a barstool, with the bright red headline "Philadelphia's Black Mafia." The nine-page article included a full complement of mug shots for the original 1968 members, and jumped in the reader's face, starting: "The Black Mafia is real. It is not a cop fantasy, newspaperman's pipe dream or movie myth. It is a black crime syndicate that has been growing unchecked in Philadelphia for the past five years. It has expanded and evolved into a powerful crime cartel with chains of command, enforcers, soldiers, financiers, regular business meetings and assigned territories. It specializes in narcotics, extortion and murder, with minor interests in loan sharking, numbers and prostitution. It has a war chest that bankrolls drugs and gambling and buys the best lawyers."

The TODAY exposé walked the reader through five years of the group's history, and included a flow chart of the relationships between individuals. Often used in organized crime investigations and trials, these charts provide a visual image of how things and people are connected, and the direction information or goods flow, person-to-person, network-to-network. No one had ever done this for the Black Mafia, and a vastly more detailed version of this chart soon became a centerpiece of Black Mafia files in law enforcement agencies throughout the area. In fact various agencies, beginning with Philadelphia's OCU, immediately contacted Nicholson and requested meetings to probe his knowledge of matters largely unfamiliar to them. The OCU was the lead investigative agency against the Black Mafia, and during their meeting following the TODAY article, the Unit asked that he forward any more discoveries to them, provided it did not violate agreements with his sources.

First and foremost a journalist, Nicholson debated the ethics of such a relationship, but opted to accept it largely because of his safety concerns. He sensed that the more people were looking into the Black Mafia, the less his life would be endangered. Being at the vanguard of the media's coverage was a rush, but it also brought hazards, and the free-lancing Nicholson had no physical or administrative protections during this perilous time. So when the FBI contacted him just after the OCU, he accepted their invitation as well. Within weeks of his August 12 piece, Nicholson was providing law enforcement with information never heard before, and was firming up previous analyses or disputing others.

Nicholson's solid reputation with "ordinary" folks, especially in the African-American community, placed him in a good position, however dangerous, in that he often gathered sensitive, dead-on information unavailable to authorities. In his exchange with the police, Nicholson provided leads about previously committed crimes and those still in the planning stages. His relationship with investigators would stay in place throughout the rise and fall of the Black Mafia, and served to fill a void in law enforcement's intelligence bank. Freelancer Nicholson's legwork and incisive analysis would have an impact beyond informing and entertaining an audience of *Philadelphia Inquirer* readers.

The publication also resulted in a rash of phone calls to the *Inquirer*, primarily from people offering information about the group. "After publication, the invisible barrier was broken," said Nicholson. "Everything subsequently started breaking loose on the information, law enforcement, media and political fronts." Better still, he added, "Informants, very good ones, came to me out of the woodwork that helped me to fine-tune the schematic of the Black Mafia." Just a few days after the TODAY piece ran, one caller reached Nicholson with hints of very sensitive information. He had been impressed by the degree of detail in the article, and couldn't believe someone outside the black community cared about the issue. The source provided information over the phone, but Nicholson wanted to meet him in person to vet the information and further develop the source's trust, against the advice of colleagues and friends who thought he was being set up by the Black Mafia – the information was *too* good. The source agreed to be interviewed in person, but would only meet in a predominantly white area or establishment out of concerns he'd be exposed as snitching on the syndicate. "[The] Melrose would be a hip place," he said.

The source thought the Melrose Diner, a well-known eatery in South Philadelphia, was ideal because the clientele was "predominantly white, very few black folk go in there, and the ones that go in there are mostly ordinary people." Nicholson agreed, and it was settled they would meet at ten o'clock on an early September morning. The reporter told the informant what to look for – he was five feet nine, 155 lbs, had dark hair, a thin moustache, and would be wearing a dark blue suit, blue shirt, and blue tie. Asked what he would be wearing, the source replied that he'd be in a yellow shirt.

"Watch that you're not followed tomorrow," Nicholson cautioned.

"No problem. I'll take a bus," was the reply.

The conversation ended with each telling the other to be careful, understanding how heavy this situation was. The meeting went off without a hitch, and Nicholson left with the impression the source had been waiting years for someone to expose the Black Mafia story. Their relationship would flourish and the source would routinely provide some of the most damning evidence against the group.

Nicholson's source pleaded with him to put a phone number in the newspaper so that victims could call and provide anonymous tips. Nicholson questioned why people with information on the Black Mafia wouldn't just call the police. Rather than stating the conventional wisdom that police were racially insensitive and abusive, the source mentioned the "word on the street": he claimed that, in addition to fearing the Black Mafia, these victimized African-American citizens firmly believed that police and government officials were on the take. To anyone in the areas being exploited by the Black Mafia, it was not possible to believe police had no knowledge of what was going on.

When the journalist pressed for examples, his source said he didn't have any proof of corruption, but cynically asked the reporter to use his street sense: Dandridge? Foglietta? Eddie Lee? 52nd Street's ties to Rizzo? *Think about it.* Nicholson would pursue these leads for years with no success, but the implication of the source's claims in the Fall of 1973 were significant regardless of their merits. It mattered little if the police, the courts and the city administration were not, in fact, protecting the Black Mafia, as long as competitors, and especially prospective victims and witnesses, *believed* they were.

Loaded with cutting-edge information in late August and throughout September 1973, Nicholson tried to get articles into the news division of the *Inquirer,* with little success. A single follow-up got into print but was heavily edited, and other articles never saw the light of day. There are several possible explanations for this: Nicholson was not on staff at the time, which posed a variety of administrative, if not territorial, problems; the staff and standards in "news" were different than on the TODAY side of the paper; editors may have been reluctant to get too heavily involved in the sensational, racially-tinged story. Whatever the reason, Nicholson's sources were frustrated at what they saw as a lost opportunity to capitalize on the first TODAY splash. Throughout the first two weeks of September 1973, community activists and their supporters in black Philadelphia phoned the *Inquirer*, unsuccessfully pleading with the editors to publish Nicholson's findings. Nicholson empathized with their frustration, since he, too, was taking great personal risks investigating the story, and was seeing few substantive results. When Nicholson briefly considered abandoning his research, an African-American community organizer implored him to continue because he was "doing a service to the black community." In the meantime, Police Commissioner O'Neill signed off on a permit for Nicholson to carry a firearm for his protection, since it mattered little to the Black Mafia that much of his work wasn't being printed – yet.

Nicholson found an outlet for his unpublished research when *Philadelphia Magazine* agreed to a cover story on the Black Mafia, comparing it with the Bruno Family, Philadelphia's Italian syndicate at the time. "Underground on the Brink of War" ran in the November 1973 issue, the cover depicting a bearded, superfly gangster, decked out in a brown full-length leather coat and a wide-brimmed hat, backed up against a salt-and-pepper-haired Italian mobster in a wide-collared black shirt covered with a bright red suit jacket. Their faces were serious, and each brandished a pistol. The cover and the related narrative were grabbers, and the story blew up. The flow of information from street sources to Jim Nicholson to the public and law enforcement continued unabated for several years, and directly affected the history of the Black Mafia and, by extension, the lives of entire communities.

In August 1973, Nicholson's work stood alone because no one in the media – and certainly no one in law enforcement – had put the seemingly disparate Black Mafia pieces together into a comprehensive mosaic. Law enforcement had investigated many crimes committed by members of the Black Mafia, but countless others were not reported, and those that were had been treated as independent, separate offenses. Where one agency or unit looked at low-level drug deals alone, another focused on bank robbery crews, and still others probed extortion gangs. Perhaps even more important than the lack of coordination and intelligence-sharing was the lack of imagination. Interviewed decades later, one member of the Organized Crime and Racketeering Strike Force in Philadelphia said the notion of African-American organized crime before 1972-3 "wasn't even on our radar screen."

There were reasons for this mindset. Philadelphia's OCU, in particular, was born as a unit (initially named InterSect) in the early 1960s as a response to an infamous 1957 meeting of numerous Italian mobsters in Apalachin, New York, by the New York State Police. Other urban police departments also created units with mandates to crush Italian-American organized crime, and allocated resources accordingly. In 1970, a "highly placed law enforcement official" in New York City stated that until the late 1960s, "when we went after organized crime, we only went after Italians." Thus, it is not surprising Philadelphia OCU's primary task was to investigate Italian-American mobsters. This mission kept attention and resources away from groups such as the Black Mafia, which was hitting its violent stride just a few years after the Unit's inception. This had ramifications on the street beyond the fact that Black Mafia affiliates were not being subjected to a coordinated investigation. Several informants voiced a sentiment common among citizens in Black Mafia-dominated territories where there was no comprehensive police response to the rampant extortion and other illicit activities. The sentiment was that the Black Mafia had corrupted law enforcement officials, and thus the group's "untouchable" reputation grew larger. Victims and witnesses generally feared testifying against the group because of its established penchant for brutalizing its enemies and detractors, and people were increasingly less likely to test the criminal justice system waters because of their belief in the corruption legend, misguided or not. The effect on the street was to permit the Black Mafia's reputation, and thus the related criminal activities dependent on intimidation, such as extortion, to flourish.

Once the OCU began investigating the Black Mafia in 1972-3, they still had problems bringing cases against members of the gang. This was partly attributable to the relative lack of black officers to work undercover, but, as described in an OCU memo, the main reason was because of the "extreme difficulties encountered in obtaining complainants [victims/witnesses] concerning this group." Numerous examples of victim and witness intimidation found their way into the files of local and federal law enforcement agencies in the Philadelphia-South Jersey area, and are backed up by others who eschewed reporting their harrowing tales to police. What is more complicated, though no less significant, is the role race played in the non-reporting phenomenon.

Race relations in Philadelphia in 1973 contributed to ambivalence, if not animosity, toward law enforcement and the criminal justice system in general. Ambivalence in black Philadelphia can be easily understood by looking at the many contemporary and historical examples of disadvantaged groups turning to organized crime and exploiting the vices to climb the socioeconomic ladder. As an authority on the subject has stated, "Poverty and powerlessness are at the root of both community acceptance of organized crime and the recruitment into its networks. Conditions of poverty also nurture community desires for the services organized criminal operations provide. Escapism accounts in part for both wide-spread drug use and numbers gambling; the resentment poverty and powerlessness brings in the subordinated population makes drugs and gambling attractive as mechanisms of rebellion. Organized crime is esteemed for the very reason that society outlaws it." It is thus not striking that in some cases, like other prominent organized criminals of other ethnic and racial backgrounds, black gangsters became community heroes who garnered "social honors." However, African-Americans so identified with criminal elements within their communities that they refused to assist authorities during investigations.

In the case of Philadelphia's Black Mafia, many community members possessed vital, often incriminating, information yet would not contact police. These people who opted not to contact authorities, and who were almost exclusively African-American, are a key part of the Black Mafia story, and were the ones who vaulted Jim Nicholson's path-breaking research beyond the realm of reporting and into public service. He fielded a steady stream of their calls and, when appropriate, passed on information to authorities. The "non-reporting" situation was found in other urban areas as well. A study of Harlem, New York, and Paterson, New Jersey, during roughly the same time period discovered antipathy toward "the system" as a key impediment to victim/witness participation in African-American communities. This was particularly true regarding criminals who doubled as, or associated with, black militants. As studies have commonly noted, "The black community ... sees the black crime activist as at once the victim and the protagonist of the white power structure. Patronage, acceptance and admiration toward black ... organized criminals define the attitudes of many of the blacks we spoke with ... The reasons are not difficult to find: black crime activists are 'making it' – in spite of and in conflict with an oppressive white establishment."

As if all of the above racial matters were not enough, there was also an unmistakable concern on the part of investigators to "get it right" before going public with any statements, and before arresting offenders. "It's a politically explosive subject," one police officer told Nicholson.

"Everybody's afraid people will think a racial issue is being created by [police] saying there is a Black Mafia." Similarly, an anonymous white politician stated, ""If we attack the [Black Mafia], people would think a racial issue was being created. The name itself [black] involves a substantial portion of this city's population. I don't believe the politicians will touch it because first, they don't have a feel for it and second, they will not move unless they are sure. And police can't really move until the politicians send down the word."

Authorities were afraid of unfavorable press stories and subsequent public criticism, which they considered inevitable if they began arresting large numbers of African-Americans. Additionally, prominent civil rights attorneys and activists entered the fray, and some of the city's black leaders claimed the Black Mafia was "a figment of the imagination of the white-controlled press." Nicholson, however, heard from street sources that the largely white establishment – government, law enforcement and media – had it all wrong, and one of them told him so as Nicholson grappled with the murky racial issue, "A lot of white people are probably layin' off of this. They afraid they gonna get some flak from the black community. Listen, if you never believe anything I say, believe this: *You will not get any flak whatsoever from the black community*, and if you do, it will be [from] a few hustling cats."

Jim Nicholson's articles greatly influenced public sentiment in favor of a criminal investigation of the group. In the weeks following his revelations, firebrand African-American activists issued denunciations of the Black Mafia, and other reporters put together stories on them. In particular, Tyree Johnson, a courageous *Daily News* reporter with numerous street contacts of his own and an expert on the black gang scene, picked up the story at the grassroots neighborhood level. Mike Leary, an enterprising reporter with the *Inquirer,* also broke several significant stories, relying mostly on quality sources in the federal government. Charles Searles, who owned and operated *Nite Life*, a black newspaper primarily distributed in South Philadelphia, also had quality street-level sources, and law enforcement routinely followed leads that first appeared in his *Nite Life* columns.

Interviews with several members of Philadelphia's criminal justice system cited Nicholson's seminal article "Philadelphia's Black Mafia" as one of the keys to obtaining public support for their investigations. While this, and subsequent related articles, did not entirely stop the charges of racism levied against authorities and the media, they largely ended the view of the gang Black Mafia as a figment or tool of the white establishment. This vital public support and subsequent political backing led to the prosecution of practically every living member of the organization. Thus, Jim Nicholson directly and indirectly helped vanquish the Black Mafia – directly as an intelligence gatherer for law enforcement, and indirectly by putting the stories into print and altering public opinion.

Nicholson's dedicated ethnographic work on the Black Mafia would span three years, ending in 1976, though he would report on this crowd for more than a decade. Years after the TODAY article ran, one of Nicholson's key sources called him to reflect back on those crazy times – on the streets of Philadelphia, where the Black Mafia terrorized citizens under the radar screen of law enforcement and the media, and in Nicholson's life, when he armed himself and met with people from all walks of life throughout Philadelphia and South Jersey, at all hours of the day and night, all the while shielding himself and his sources from the peril that awaited them if they were ever uncovered. The source was effusive in his gratitude, and summed up the episode by telling Nicholson "If you had never gotten that stuff in there, shit, I don't know what this neighborhood'd look like."

This was several years after the fact, however, and as summer turned to fall in 1973, the Black Mafia was still hitting its stride.

CHAPTER 11 ★

TO IMPROVE THE PLIGHT OF OUR BRETHREN

AS THE SUMMER of 1973 was ending, the Black Mafia legend was growing exponentially in Philadelphia's blighted neighborhoods in South, West, and North Philly. In particular, the murderous duo of Sam Christian and Ron Harvey cast a pall over many ghetto residents. It was an open question as to who was more feared, but it was Christian who inspired wannabe gangsters. One newspaper article got it right when it said, "To a lot of young bloods on 52nd Street or South Street, Sam Christian is Shaft, Superfly and Bad Leroy Jones rolled into one."

Christian and Harvey were on the run that summer following the Coxson murders but still featured highly on investigators' charts of the Black Mafia. According to one, the hierarchy at the time was as follows: chairman, Eugene "Bo" Baynes; vice chairman, James Enoch; chief enforcer, Sam Christian. Other enforcers included Harvey, Roosevelt Fitzgerald, Robert Fairbanks, Clyde Ross, Donald Day, Leroy Griffin, Charles Toney and Ronald Woodruff. The field lieutenants who controlled narcotics territories were John Darby, George Glover and Earl Walden.

Though Bo Baynes seemed to have taken over from Sam Christian following the Coxson murders in June, he had little time to enjoy his reign at the top. On August 16, he was indicted by a grand jury convened by the DEA on federal income tax charges of "willful failure" to file income tax returns for 1970 and 1971. The IRS wanted to make an event of arresting Baynes, and leaked word of the indictment to the press that morning while simultaneously announcing IRS agents had Baynes holed up in his house. An IRS official described Baynes as a "major drug dealer who directs the drug traffic in West Philadelphia." Knowing the Black Mafia's penchant for going underground, the agency asked reporters to hold off reporting the indictment until Baynes was in custody. As the day wore on with no updates on the situation at Baynes' residence, court reporters got frustrated and anxious. Finally, at 4:30 P.M. an IRS bulletin from the scene to the court reporters read, "Arrest is imminent. Arrest is imminent." Half an hour later, agents approached the home, only to find Baynes somehow gone. The search of the immediate area was not fruitful and was called off around 7:30 because, according to an IRS spokesman, "after dark, that neighborhood gets dangerous." The official also stated the obvious when he said, "[Baynes] must have gotten word that we were looking for him."

Despite being arrested on six previous occasions dating to 1958, Baynes had never spent time in prison. In an effort to keep that streak going, he went into hiding and was thought to be with his close friends and peers Christian and Harvey. This was speculation, however, and some even contemplated whether Baynes's intimate knowledge of the syndicate and Temple 12 posed such a threat to these groups that they would have liked him killed before he was picked up by authorities. "We're puzzled by Baynes' disappearance because he is only wanted for a misdemeanor," said an IRS official. "He may have been killed. We haven't overlooked that possibility, although it is more probable that he is with his friends."

While the Baynes fiasco unfolded, the City of Philadelphia hosted the annual Black Expo for the third consecutive year. The Expo was designed to help close the gap between the business community and the African-American community. Traditionally, it ran for three or four days and consisted of business seminars, voter education and registration, entertainment and exhibits of black culture and art. When the city first hosted the event in 1971, it featured a political education seminar with a panel that included Common Pleas Court Judge Robert N.C. Nix, Jr.; civil rights activist and lawyer Cecil B. Moore; and the soon-to-be Clerk of Quarter Sessions, Eddie Lee. Perhaps not coincidentally, all three had close ties to the Black Muslim movement. The 1972 Black Expo, sponsored by an organization named Urban Priorities, had twice as many display booths as the year before. Thus, expectations were high when Mayor Frank Rizzo signed a proclamation designating the week of August 15 as "Black Expo '73" week. The public face of the event was Expo, Inc. chairman Dr. Stanley Johnson, and the ostensible beneficiaries of the Expo's proceeds were the United Negro College Fund, Philadelphia Association for Retarded Children, sickle-cell anemia research, the Mary Robinson Multiple Sclerosis Helping Hand Society, and the Nation of Islam Educational Fund. The scheduled acts for the five-day fair included Aretha Franklin, Nina Simone, Roberta Flack, James Brown, and Carlos Santana.

Behind the scenes of the Black Expo operations, various tidbits trickled in to the Philadelphia Police Department that Black Mafia elements of Temple 12 were planning a takeover of the event. One memo stated, "Information further states that Jim BLOCKER and Donald "Ducky" BERTZ (sic), black businessmen presently in charge of the EXPO, will be moved out by the Muslims and other black businessmen are being told to donate money and maintain booths at the EXPO." Ducky Birts (misspelled in the memo) was the head of Urban Priorities, which had run the Expo the previous year. The source of the suspicion was a legendary West Philadelphia con artist named Stanley A. Culbreth, who had supposedly been hired as an organizer for Black Expo '73.

Stan "the Man" Culbreth, a Black Muslim, was a former nightclub operator and record store owner with a record of twenty-four arrests, mostly for thefts, forgeries and frauds, though at least one of his convictions was for armed robbery. The Black Mafia's John Griffin has called him "a very gifted brother with the gift of gab." In 1972, as head of the local chapter of the Southern Christian Leadership Conference (SLSC), Culbreth organized a $100 per plate dinner, supposedly to benefit sickle cell anemia research. When none of the proceeds from the event made it to the Sickle Cell Anemia Foundation, the national SLSC body revoked the local chapter's charter. One informant said Culbreth orchestrated the charity scam because he was long overdue on payments to loansharks from Philly's Italian mob.

In the run-up to Black Expo '73, evidence mounted that Culbreth was a front for the Black Mafia, which planned an extortion bonanza by forcing businesses to rent booths at the event. One of the more striking discoveries involved the Pyramid Enterprises credit card scam. The Black Mafia's Merrill Ferguson, using one of his aliases, Robert Jones, rented several cars and hotel rooms at the Holiday Inn on City Line Avenue. Ferguson was wanted at the time, and posters with his picture had been disseminated throughout the area. A clerk recognized Ferguson and contacted police, but when police arrived at the hotel, Ferguson was not in the room he had rented. Significantly, however, Stanley Culbreth was there – in the company of three Black Mafia members. Law enforcement also received information regarding entertainment for the Black Expo: "Isaac Hayes, a black singer, was informed by the Muslims that, if he should come to Philadelphia, he would be killed. The reason for this threat is to enable the Muslims to bring in their own entertainers to perform at the EXPO."

Black Expo '73 started on August 15 as planned, though in no time controversy erupted when Aretha Franklin didn't show, as promised. Nina Simone and Roberta Flack were also no-shows, bringing Culbreth's role under public scrutiny when numerous complaints came in to the fraud division of the District Attorney's Office, and lawsuits were filed. Left out of the public discussion was the Black Mafia/Black Muslim backdrop. It was later discovered that two of the listed charities supposedly to receive proceeds from Black Expo '73 did not exist, and others had not given permission for their names to be used.

★

Reports kept pouring in about the Black Mafia's vast extortion networks, and police were left to wonder how many thefts, shakedowns, robberies and more were not being reported. Investigators privately expressed fascination at the group's impressive rise in the underworld. One report said that four men visited Eddie Simons' variety store at 16th and Federal Streets on August 24, and collected their weekly $300 "assessment." Simons had a modest numbers operation on the side and could not go to the authorities. Most of the numbers writers under the umbrella of the Black Mafia were themselves black, but as the syndicate grew, its leaders looked beyond their own race for extortion opportunities and crossed into rival's territories. Philadelphia's Italian-American mobsters were soon faced with an impending turf war.

Throughout their rise in black Philadelphia, the Black Mafia largely avoided any conflicts with the Bruno crime family. They did deal with each other sporadically, and Black Mafia ties to people like Gus Lacy, Stanley Branche, and especially Major Coxson provided key connections to the Italian mob and meant both crime syndicates co-existed amicably. Lacy, Branche and Coxson were all very active in the Philly nightlife and underworld scenes, white and black, and had very close relationships with Cosa Nostra types. Beyond the club scene, Coxson routinely cut illicit deals with the Bruno crowd, while Branche and Lacy lent their services as "investigators" to high-profile lawyer Robert Simone for mob-related cases.

One such instance was the June 1972 "dispute" between Leon Altemose, a non-union builder, and the Philadelphia Area Building and Construction Trades and Council. Altemose was constructing a large project including a Sheraton Hotel just outside Philadelphia. Over 1,000 union men, led by Roofers Union Local 30 president John McCullough and Council president Thomas McGrann, picketed the site. At the time of the protest, John McCullough was under investigation by the FBI and the Department of Labor for actions he and other Local 30 officials had taken the previous year involving a roofing job at the Teamster's Health and Welfare Building in Center City, where a contractor from Troy, New York, refused to hire a Local 30 laborer. McCullough and several others visited the job site, resulting in two supervisors being assaulted by Roofer's Union goons and sent to the hospital and the job site being shut down for a time.

The Altemose picketing turned quickly to vandalism, and before long sections of the partially developed hotel were damaged and construction equipment was on fire. McCullough contacted Simone to defend twenty-three union members charged in the incident, and Simone enlisted two other high-profile defense attorneys as co-counsel, Cecil B. Moore and Charles Peruto, Sr. In addition to being a skilled lawyer, Moore, of course, was very close friends with Major Coxson, Stanley Branche and Gus Lacy. He was selected in part because a main defendant in the case was a black member of Local 332, whose membership was predominantly African-

American. Charles Peruto was among the few peers to Simone when it came to high-profile mob attorneys. Branche and Lacy served as investigators for the Simone-led defense team.

Roofers Union Local 30 was a notoriously corrupt, abusive and violent organization, and John McCullough was a *de facto* organized crime figure with none of the appearance of a stereotypical *mafioso*. Two of his closest associates, in addition to his drinking buddy Simone and several Bruno family members, were Frank "The Irishman" Sheeran and John Carlyle Berkery. Sheeran was a longtime Teamster who started working as a trucker in 1947 out of Philadelphia's Local 107. He next worked as an organizer for Local 299 in Detroit just before his friend, International Brotherhood of Teamsters leader Jimmy Hoffa, gave him a local of his own in Wilmington, Delaware. Sheeran's best friend was upstate Pennsylvania crime boss Russell Bufalino, who was tight with Philly mob boss Angelo Bruno. Thus, when a massive gathering of rival Local 107 factions threatened to turn violent in September 1967, Sheeran picked up the phone and called Bruno to ask for "some Italian muscle." Bruno readily agreed to help out, but the men he sent, including Joseph "Chickie" Ciancaglini and Rocco Turra, could not stop the shooting that ensued (assuming they didn't start it themselves). It ended with Ciancaglini surviving a shot to the stomach, and a rival Local 107 member dying of his wounds. Sheeran was arrested and charged for pointing the man out and ordering him shot, but charges were later dropped. He was out of jail in time to join the many well-wishers at the Frank Sheeran Appreciation Night on October 1974, honoring him as the Teamsters "Man of the Year." The evening was put together by John McCullough and held at the Latin Casino in Cherry Hill, New Jersey, the venue for Major Coxson's campaign events. Joining Sheeran on the dais were Philadelphia Mayor Frank Rizzo, Jimmy Hoffa, John McCullough, Cecil Moore, and former Philadelphia District Attorney F. Emmett Fitzpatrick. The front table had Russell Bufalino seated with Angelo Bruno, and assorted mobsters populated the surrounding tables. The popular Italian singer Jerry Vale entertained this fascinating mixture of personalities. Sheeran would gain infamy the following year when he was tied to the mysterious July 1975 disappearance of Jimmy Hoffa.

John McCullough's pal John Berkery headed the K & A gang, which was essentially a burglary ring centered at Kensington and Allegheny Avenues, in a rough, largely white, working class section of the city. Berkery was closely aligned with assorted mobsters and several Local 30 heavyweights. In August 1959, he was named in a heist in the coal region of Pottsville, Pennsylvania. Berkery, Ralph Staino, Jr., and Robert Poulson allegedly broke into the home of coal baron John Rich and stole $500,000 in cash and jewels. Authorities believed Staino's girlfriend, showgirl Lillian Reis, was provided with information about the safe's contents and passed it along to Staino and gang. Soon after the burglary, Reis purchased the Celebrity Room nightclub, and it was alleged she did so with proceeds from the heist. It was suspected Poulson was soon diming out his partners, and that two brothers with information on Berkery's activities named Vincent and Richard Blaney were also cooperating with authorities. After Poulson was beaten, stabbed, and shot the following summer, he recanted his statement to police. Next, on 23 August 1960, the lifeless, swollen body of Vincent Blaney was pulled out of the Atlantic Ocean just outside Margate, New Jersey. He had been shot in the head, wrapped in chains and dumped in the ocean. His brother, Richard, decided to testify for the government, and was largely responsible when Staino, Berkery, and Poulson were convicted in the summer of 1961. Weeks afterward, on July 27, Richard Blaney was blown to pieces when he started his car and it exploded in front of his Philadelphia home. Soon afterward, Lillian Reis was tried for plotting the heist; the trial resulted in a hung jury. She was retried in 1964, and found guilty of conspiracy, but her lawyer, Robert Simone, successfully argued her appeal the following year. Due in part to the defense's inability to cross-examine statements of the deceased Blaney brothers, over time Berkery, Reis, and Staino would all be released from prison and exonerated on charges stemming from the now-legendary burglary.

Lillian Reis went on to purchase the Rolls Royce Lounge from Major Coxson and Stanley Branche in 1971. Staino was arrested with Black Mafia member Alfred "Sonny" Viner in September 1972 by the Secret Service for possessing and dealing in counterfeit Federal Reserve notes. Their arrests followed a probe by the Justice Department's Organized Crime and Racketeering Section involving intercepted phone conversations and surveillance at Viner's pad in the notorious, narcotics-infested West Village Apartments on West Conshohocken Avenue, where Major Coxson also rented a place. John Berkery was back on the street in time to hang out at Coxson's "White House" in Camden during The Maje's failed run for mayor in early 1973. This amorphous mix of Italian mobsters, union racketeers from Locals 30 and 332, and related hoods would deal on and off with Black Mafia figures for the next thirty years.

From the early days of the Black Mafia, the group's relationship with the Bruno family offered each organization certain benefits. For the Black Mafia, there was financing, while for the Bruno crowd it was the safety net of narcotics if one of their shipments or stashes was co-opted. All organized crime groups have a vested interest in avoiding warfare on the streets, since it brings unwanted attention to, and heat on, their activities. The Bruno crowd's turf in South Philadelphia stretched from Broad Street east to the Delaware River waterfront, a vast and densely populated area with a variety of ethnic enclaves. Its identity, however, was shaped mostly by the Italian immigrants who made it their new home, and as far as the underworld was concerned this territory was not in play – it belonged to the Bruno Family.

The west side of Broad Street was more complicated territorially, because of the lack of a more or less uniform identity. A large black ghetto sprawled from Broad Street to 26th Street, bordered roughly on the north by South Street and on the south by Federal Street. Immediately south of the blighted area was another Italian enclave, and other ethnic neighborhoods dotted the area. Predictably, the Black Mafia extorted black numbers bankers first and foremost, but also white numbers bankers who worked in predominantly African-American areas. Among the former, their targets included infamous figures such as Carl Robinson and Caesar Nelson. In addition to being "taxed," Robinson was taken at gunpoint to his home and relieved of $30,000 just before he was about to start a prison stay. As the Black Mafia grew in size and stature in the early 1970s, they kept extending their extortion networks, making territorial skirmishes with the Bruno family likely, especially in the disputed turf west of Broad Street in South Philly.

Through the spring of 1973, numbers operations west of Broad Street had loosely-held ties to the Bruno crowd. Such operations were using Italian mobsters to handle bets too large for their own rackets, and would also use the Italian syndicate to help with various financing issues. In the summer of 1973, the Black Mafia began making inroads into these numbers rackets. Two independents, Joseph "Pepe" Fannelli, a sixty-one-year-old writer, and one of his workers, a man named Lombardi, were severely beaten and robbed of $1,800 after they picked up their daily take. Fanelli and his partner, Ralph Patrone, had made the mistake of operating west of Broad Street on the Black Mafia's turf after refusing to pay their street tax. Fanelli and Patrone refused to cooperate with authorities, and it is unknown how the event affected their business. Interestingly, Patrone and other Italian-American racketeers were soon after arrested with a lower level Black Mafia drug dealer named Donald "Chips" Woodruff. Woodruff had an apartment at the infamous West Village apartment complex and was tight with major Black Mafia dealers Bo Abney and Leroy "Chinaman" Griffin.

Two other major independent numbers writers, "Black Pat" Monzelli and James "Jimmy" Singleton, were soon visited. In late summer 1973, Monzelli, whose nickname came from his predominantly black clientele, sat at the bar of the Caravan Hotel at 15th and Catherine Streets, which he used as the main drop for his numbers operation. He was approached by Black Mafia emissaries who informed him that he was expected to pay a street tax. Monzelli soon disclosed to OCU detectives that he was told to pay $700 per week, but refused to confirm he made the payments or to cooperate with authorities by identifying who had approached him. One of Jimmy Singleton's underlings told the OCU that he too had been approached by the Black Mafia, but couldn't disclose the details of the discussions until he checked with Singleton. "It was apparent that [he] was deeply concerned and fearful of the 'Black Mafia,'" summed up an OCU debriefing report of the interview. Singleton was beaten by a Black Mafia crew for not accepting their conditions, and moved his operation to New Jersey. As detectives investigated, they discovered Black Mafia-inspired intimidation had spread throughout the numbers underworld: "It was determined by talking to various people, both white and Negro, that they are in great fear for their lives, and, therefore, are very reluctant to give anyone information unless recommended by their peers."

Philadelphia detectives also questioned Frank "Chickie" Narducci, then one of the "fast rising and most powerful men in the [Bruno Family]" and a veteran loanshark and gambler. Asked about the Black Mafia beatings and the territorial dispute, Narducci told authorities, "If you shoot two niggers, the rest will learn," and assured authorities he would handle anything which concerned him. According to reporter Jim Nicholson's sources, Monzelli eventually went back to his Italian mob backers, including Joseph D'Amato, detailing the threats and demands. While the white mob did not exert control over Monzelli, one of the group's members still exploded with rage. "You pay them one goddamn dime and there'll be six dead niggers on your doorstep the next morning," he said. Disregarding the bravado, Monzelli paid the Black Mafia off big, to the tune of $1,000 per week on some occasions. In return, the Black Mafia informed numbers writers on the east side of the Schuylkill River to Broad Street they were now working for Black Pat. One of Monzelli's closest associates was interviewed a few months later and said Black Pat was "doing better now than ever in his life," making upwards of $5,000 a day with Black Mafia backing.

★

Notwithstanding the headline-grabbing, violence-laden news coverage the Black Mafia was generating, especially after the Hanafi and Coxson murders, and the commensurate rise in law enforcement activity against them, the brazen group was crafting another "community development" scam throughout the summer of 1973. The Black Mafia sent invitations out to the *Daily News* and the city's leading African-American newspaper, the *Philadelphia Tribune*, to cover the grand opening of Black Brothers, Inc. The ceremony was set for October 1 at the group's headquarters, 1443 South Street. The press release explained that Black Brothers, Inc. was interested in suppressing gang activity and youth crime in South Philadelphia's African-American neighborhoods, so *Daily News* managing editor Dave Lawrence dispatched the paper's gang reporter, Tyree Johnson, to the event. When Johnson arrived, the flashy dress and the sparkling late-model

Cadillacs immediately struck him. The Black Brothers officers on display for the media wore expensive suits and sharp hats, and had a decidedly different aura about them than typical social workers or community organizers.

The headquarters, essentially one large office, was a former rummage shop, and the group had put $1,000 into renovating it. Unlike the CYCD operation, in which they paid the City of Philadelphia only $1 per year rent, the group was paying $75 per month on this property, yet one news reporter described the storefront office as "scruffy." The windows were covered with posters warning drug dealers and thieves to leave the neighborhood and telling gang members to abandon their weapons. A sign hung over the office's front door that read, "Black 'B' Inc., Community Action Group." Above the front door a sign read, "Through These Doors Walk the Finest People."

Tyree Johnson noted Tom Foglietta's presence at the grand opening. Foglietta had been a key proponent, along with Judge Paul Dandridge, of the Council for Youth and Community Development, the earlier iteration of Black Brothers, Inc. The key link between the two organizations was James Fox, a leader in both groups who was once thought of as an up-and-comer in the political world by Foglietta, and community organizer and quasi-hustler Jimmie Lester. By the time Black Brothers, Inc. was being put in motion during the summer of 1973, however, Lester had gotten wind of the Black Mafia's plan and opted out of the impending scam. Apparently, word had not yet spread to Foglietta and Dandridge, who also served as an advisor to the group. Dandridge, of course, was an overseer of the Safe Streets, Inc. program that also had ties to the Black Mafia. He and Foglietta supported the CYCD starting back in 1970, with the assistance of a man named Ken Brown, who had a complicated and significant relationship with the Black Mafia's James Fox. Fox's girlfriend was Tamara Robinson, sister of Charles and Donald Robinson, each of whom had their battles with the Black Mafia. Tamara Robinson rented an apartment just outside the city in Upper Darby, under the name of Mrs. Ken Brown, and Fox "often resided there," according to intelligence documents. The documents continue, "this apartment is actually leased for Fox by Ken Brown, who is a court stenographer for Judge Julian L. King, Common Pleas Court. Information further states that James Fox has a .38 revolver and, possibly, a machine gun inside this apartment." Another memo stated that Brown "does not have a criminal record, however, he is friendly with some members of the Black Mafia." Despite his ties to James Fox and perhaps other Black Mafia associates, Ken Brown was apparently not the target of further investigation. The Robinson family interactions with James Fox and the Black Mafia hierarchy, however, would soon come into play. For now, getting the Black Brothers, Inc. con off and running commanded Fox's attention.

Tyree Johnson returned from the Black Brothers, Inc. ceremony to the *Daily News* offices and wrote a mostly favorable article, "5 Black Gangs Now War on Trash," on the group and its stated goals. He generously quoted noteworthy gangsters – and Black Brothers officers – James Fox, Lonnie Dawson and Eugene Hearn. "Black, Inc., a community group of 50 young black men, wants to clean up South Philadelphia's gangs, crime and trash," Johnson wrote. "The group said its main objective was to stop the gang killings." He quoted Fox, the "secretary of the group," as saying, "We are doing this today to show there is pride in our neighborhood," and Dawson, the "treasurer," as saying, "We were aware that our younger brothers were being neglected." Johnson's article also featured Black Brothers officers David "Scoogie" Mitchell and Frederick "Smiley" Armour. Larris "Tank" Frazier was the formally listed incorporator on the group's non-profit, tax-exempt state charter.

Each of the officers publicly associated with Black Brothers, Inc. was in his mid- or late-twenties, and had an impressive arrest record (they averaged seven arrests each). All six officers had arrests for crimes of violence, five had been arrested for weapons offenses, and five had arrests for narcotics offenses. On many occasions, charges were dropped or the Black Mafia members were found not guilty in court. In fact, at least three of the Black Brothers officers, Mitchell, Dawson, and Frazier, had appeared before Judge Dandridge's court on drug charges, and in each instance had been exonerated. Some law enforcement officers have always looked at this with a raised eyebrow, though there have been no formal allegations of impropriety on Dandridge's part. In addition to his involvement with Safe Streets, Inc., the Council for Youth and Community Development, and Black Brothers, Inc., Judge Dandridge was involved in several progressive programs or initiatives concerning criminal justice issues such as juvenile corrections and drug rehabilitation.

On two occasions in the summer of 1971, however, Dandridge caused the Philadelphia Police Department and D.A. Specter grief. First, he criticized Philadelphia's elite Highway Patrol Unit for damaging police-community relations in black neighborhoods. He said that HP officers were unnecessarily frisking and harassing people, and were causing fear in the community. Weeks later, Judge Dandridge was speaking at Temple University about drug abuse, drug dealing and gang violence when he proposed legalizing heroin sales to addicts at a price of ten cents per bag. "Drugs are taking over the gangs in Philadelphia and are a predominant factor in the gang structure," argued Dandridge, and he suggested that community centers should be used to distribute the drugs. Needless to say, a large segment of the law enforcement community reacted with indignation. The legalization suggestion, in particular, started a media firestorm and Specter had to work hard to suppress the controversy. He said Dandridge's proposal would "sell [heroin addicts] down the river," and the matter never evolved beyond public debate.

The judge was again the source of controversy in late 1972. On December 6, he was honored at a testimonial dinner, and accepted a "gift" of $23,500 during the event. The dinner was organized by two defense attorneys who then argued at least fifty-four cases in Dandridge's court between the time of the dinner and early 1974. As a result, the State Supreme Court's Judicial Inquiry and Review Board took up the matter, and concluded, "The acceptance of the said proceeds by Judge Dandridge for his own personal use gave the appearance of impropriety and was improper." The court ordered Dandridge to turn the funds raised over to the State.

At the time of the Black Brothers incorporation, all of the group's officers were known Black Mafia members, and under law enforcement scrutiny. Tank Frazier was the active target of several OCU and DEA investigations for dealing large quantities of heroin, cocaine and marijuana. Fittingly, Nino V. Tinari, a high-profile defense attorney with several Black Mafia clients, served as the Black Brothers, Inc. counsel. Outside of the self-perpetuating "community development" movement, reaction to the Black Brothers incorporation was indignant. Residents and law officers were incredulous that violent career criminals were being accepted – in fact, *courted* – by segments of the establishment. They did not grasp or appreciate, or had forgotten, the era's fading political philosophy, begun almost a decade earlier, regarding anti-gang and community initiatives. The extensive criminal backgrounds of Black Mafia members did not disqualify them from membership in Black Brothers, Inc. To the contrary, *that was the idea*. The gangsters were simply taking what the establishment was looking to provide. As social commentator Tom Wolfe has critically said of these programs, "The idea that the real leadership in the ghetto might be with the *gangs* hung on with the poverty-youth-welfare establishment. It was considered a very sophisticated insight. The youth gangs weren't petty criminals ... they were 'social bandits,' primitive revolutionaries ... It was a truly adventurous and experimental approach ... From the beginning, the poverty program was aimed at helping ghetto people rise up against their oppressors."

The phrase "community organizing," according to Wolfe, became code for "'power to the people,' the term for finding the real leaders of the ghetto and helping them to organize the poor." African-American criminals abused these government "community development/organizing" programs on numerous occasions throughout the U.S. The most notorious example was Chicago's infamous Black P. Stone Nation, which received a $937,000 grant from the Federal Office of Economic Opportunity supposedly to help gang members find jobs. Wolfe could just as easily have been discussing Philadelphia's Black Mafia when he wrote that "the police would argue that in giving all that money to gangs like the [Black P. Stone] Nation the poverty bureaucrats were financing criminal elements and helping to destroy the community. The poverty bureaucrats would argue that they were doing just the opposite. They were bringing the gangs into the system."

In the case of the Black Mafia, the problem with government officials lending support to the syndicate's "anti-gang" front group was that it confused and intimidated people. Many assumed the syndicate had paid off the authorities, since it was difficult for citizens to grasp violent cons being openly embraced by these officials. It mattered little to the victimized black community that the Black Mafia's political connections in the criminal justice system were part of a legitimate, though failing, progressive reform effort. Witnesses and victims in Black Mafia cases, already fearful of testifying against this vicious cast of characters, were further dissuaded from cooperating with police, and the result was the strengthening of the syndicate's extortion enterprise.

According to the Black Mafia's own records, the group first thought of opening another community center at their 20 May 1972, meeting. The minutes of that meeting state, "the Chairman spoke about hooking up something along the lines of the Help Organization. We may even call our organization Help." In fact, several intelligence records indicate that many in the group referred to it as "Black Help, Inc." when they were promoting their activities, even after the formal name became Black Brothers, Inc. (or Black B., Inc., for short). As stated on the formal incorporation documents, the purpose of Black Brothers, Inc. was: "To promote general welfare and improve conditions of our community and to improve the plight of our brethren as a whole by collecting money through sponsoring shows, dances, cabarets, acceptance of donations. Said money to be utilized to clean up the community – to stop gang warfare through better human relations – stop violent crime in the black community – stop drug traffic and malicious graffiti – and to stop any and all activities that do not benefit the community. If this corporation is dissolved, assets will be distributed to other non-profit organizations."

Ironically, the Black Mafia likely played a role in the reduction of gang violence by taking over territories previously controlled by street gangs. Confiscated documents reveal that the group had access to grant writers, perhaps best illustrated by a set of guidelines they used to apply for funding. A federal task force looking into Black Mafia activities noted, "Black, Inc. is attempting to obtain [U.S. Department of Housing and Urban Development] funding 'to help to start new businesses and fight gang warfare in the Black community in Philadelphia, Pennsylvania.'"

It is not clear, however, what "community development" monies Black Brothers, Inc. received, either from public or private funding streams. There is general consensus among street and law enforcement sources, including some who investigated the links between influential public officials and the Black Mafia, that councilman Foglietta and Judge Dandridge were each duped into believing the organization was a bona fide self-help group. The incorporation of Black Brothers, Inc. by leaders of the Black Mafia was probably best explained by a combination of factors, notably a lack of oversight, and the social and political climates of the times.

The structure of Black Brothers, Inc. was a mirror image of the Black Mafia's. It had a board, a set of officers, and a cadre of youths active at the bottom of the hierarchical chart. The stated roles for each set of individuals differed from those of the Black Mafia. The board of Black Brothers, Inc. was ostensibly to organize community functions and to help youths get jobs, while the officers were to promote a cleaner neighborhood. The youths were to assist the group's leaders in getting gang members to join "Black B." or "Black, Inc." in the hope of curbing ghetto violence. Part of the dilemma for law enforcement and for citizens was distinguishing theory from reality. While the leaders of Black, Inc. did, in fact, organize social functions for youths, heavily promoted with posters throughout South Philadelphia, they used these gatherings to sell narcotics and to raise funds for their own purposes. Additionally, Black, Inc. employed many youths in their narcotics and extortion rackets. They were outfitted in black shirts bearing the organization's name, further confusing observers.

Copying a 1970 Safe Streets, Inc. initiative, officers distributed trashcans in the community, with "Black, Inc." painted on them, resulting in favorable media coverage. However, distribution was limited to businesses that paid off the Black Mafia. Stickers were distributed to homeowners that read, "Warning! Burglars Beware! This House Protected by BLACK, INC." These, too, only went to people who had paid off. The Black Mafia also went door-to-door handing out leaflets promoting the good work of Black Brothers, Inc. throughout their territories. The group successfully manipulated their extensive extortion racket into a public relations coup.

Within weeks of the Black Brothers, Inc. grand opening, three Black Mafia members were arrested for running numbers. The threesome had more than $5,000 in cash confiscated, in addition to number-writing slips and a tablet marked with "Black Help, Inc" in handwriting. Two of the three said they worked for the group, and soon after, informants described a stockpile of weapons in the basement of the group's South Street office. Word on the street was that Black Brothers, Inc. extortion targets were being selected by the Black Mafia's William "Country" Davis. In no time, police confiscated a document that listed Herschell "Jolly Green Giant" Williams as the Black Brothers, Inc. "sergeant-at-arms," further illustrating the absolute Black Mafia influence over the supposed community development organization.

Following reporter Tyree Johnson's initial encounter, his sources began detailing the true activities of the group, and from that point forward his articles were critical of the role Black Brothers, Inc. was playing in the community. In fact, when his article ran on October 2, he received calls that very day explaining whom the Black Brothers "employees" really were. As Johnson took calls and processed the revelations, the Black Mafia was back at work for real – terrorizing people on the streets of Philadelphia.

CHAPTER 12

CADILLAC TOMMY AND THE MOZ

N EW YORK DRUG kingpin Frank Matthews used a number of independent narcotics dealers to put his product on the streets of Philadelphia. In addition to Fat Ty Palmer, who was assassinated by a Black Mafia hit squad, and Pop Darby, he used "Cadillac Tommy" Farrington. Matthews and Farrington were both born in Durham, North Carolina, where they became lifelong friends, the relationship continuing when one moved to Philly and the other New York. Farrington, who became closely aligned with several Black Mafia heavyweights, was first arrested was for burglary at age fifteen and his sheet grew over the next twenty years, with offenses ranging from possession of narcotics to weapons violations, rape and murder. Some of these cases were dismissed, though he was sentenced to serve twenty days to a year for the rape.

By 1973, the thirty-four-year-old Farrington had become a major player in the Philly drug scene, and was out on bail for a 1971 murder. He got his heroin shipments directly from the Matthews organization, the most important drug trafficking network in the U.S. at the time. Cadillac Tommy's supply was more constant than rival dealers, and could easily be upgraded in quantity because of Matthews's substantial networks. Thus, like Major Coxson, Palmer, and Darby, he was a key intermediary between the Black Mafia and international drug dealers in New York City. Farrington's rise in the underworld was inextricably linked to that of the Black Mafia. Tall, stylish and sporting a well-groomed goatee, he displayed his status by driving around in his sparkling white 1973 Cadillac Fleetwood.

All was not well between him and his associates, however. Cadillac Tommy had recently not been paying enough protection money to the Black Mafia, an oversight they took very seriously. Lonnie Dawson and James Fox visited him late in the afternoon on October 2, and Dawson ended the conversation by saying, "We will see you tonight between eight-thirty and nine o'clock." Cadillac Tommy wound up inside Ernie's Club Paree – owned by extortion victim Ernest Kelly [see Chapter 8] – around nine that evening. The club was in a residential neighborhood.

Farrington was styling as usual in a dark brown outfit that included pants, a silk shirt, and a jacket with a belt in the back. He completed the look with high brown boots that zippered up the side. After accepting a drink from a female regular at the bar, he next ordered a quart of Budweiser for himself. In the meantime, he fielded at least two calls on the bar's phone. It was a warm evening for October, and had just stopped raining when Farrington took his quart of Bud outside, where he joined James Johns and Alfred Moore. The trio stood talking on the sidewalk outside the bar's front door at the point of the street corner, under a large, neon "ERNIE'S CLUB PAREE" sign.

Suddenly a black male ran eastbound on Cumberland and across the street toward them from behind. The man knocked Johns hard to the ground and turned toward Farrington. Without saying a word, he pulled a gun and started shooting. Johns and Moore ran a short distance south on 18th, and heard the sound of a .38 caliber handgun being unloaded into Farrington at close range. They turned to see him clutch his head and fall to the ground, as the gunman continued shooting. The assailant got off five shots, striking Farrington with four of them: one in the head which fractured his skull and lacerated his brain, two in his back and one in his right hand. The shooter fled, again on foot, westbound on Cumberland as Johns and Moore rushed back to Farrington.

The handful of patrons inside Ernie's had ducked for cover when the shots rang out, with a few hiding in the bathrooms. As they came out of the bar afterwards, they saw the riddled body of Cadillac Tommy lying face down in a large pool of blood. His loaded .380 semi-automatic Harrington & Richardson had been of no help; it lay under the front passenger seat of his prized Caddy, parked beside him when he was slain. A police wagon took Farrington to Temple University hospital, where he was pronounced dead. When his body was taken to the medical examiner for autopsy, it was noted that Farrington had an empty holster strapped to his left ankle. It is unclear if a weapon should have been in the holster and Farrington had mistakenly left himself unarmed, or if he simply didn't have time to reach it during the ambush and someone took it from his body before police arrived.

A few days later, Yvonne Farrington went to a local funeral home to oversee arrangements. She was presented with a small, manila envelope addressed to her that had been slipped under the door. "Evon," it read, "You only have one chance to survive. Tommy owes us two years money which adds up to $25,000. We know you have all the money. We will not hurt you unless you don't do as told. You can not run or hide. If you tell police, we have men in dept. who will tell us. If you tell someone or try to trap us, we will kill your hole family. We will call you at this no. at phone on Belmont Av. at [illegible] ROAD (pay phone). Your home phone tapped. We will not boter you when you pay us. One slip up and youre dead. We will get you – XX." It is not known if anything ever came of the threats, or if Yvonne gave in to the demands.

It emerged that in the months leading to his death, Cadillac Tommy had received threats from the Black Mafia for not paying, or at least not paying enough, protection money. He sensed life was becoming more perilous in the days leading up to his death, and went so far as to tell those close to him that if anything happened to him, to "hold 'Country' responsible." Country was the street name for Black Mafia field leader William Davis.

Country was no stranger to police, having been arrested at least seventeen times. One of his primary duties for the Black Mafia was to identify extortion targets, including businesses as well as individuals. One year earlier, he had been pulled over by police for a traffic violation that resulted in an arrest for weapons violations. Country was in possession of two loaded – and stolen – handguns, including one that was part of a shipment supposedly lifted from a platform of a Philadelphia freight company; three cartons of handguns being housed for shipping to a Norristown gun shop had been reported missing in March 1972. The Black Mafia was thought to have a role in the job, and the discovery of Davis with one of the guns furthered that suspicion. Following that arrest, Davis listed his occupation as "part time bartender" at Ernie's Club Paree. Philadelphia Police investigated his possible role in Farrington's murder to no avail, and he was never charged with the homicide.

Federal agencies had a different perspective on the death of Cadillac Tommy. In 1974, the Office of Drug Abuse Law Enforcement (ODALE) Task Force compiled a report that assessed drug trafficking in the Philadelphia-South Jersey area. The dossier was an extensive assemblage of disparate FBI and DEA reports and intelligence data on drug dealers, their subordinates and associates, and was broken down by major organizations: the George Abney organization, the Reginald Cole organization, the Larris Frazier organization, and so on. Though the death of Farrington was not of central concern to the ODALE task force, the report contained several informant reports about the murder. The consensus emerging from the informant accounts was that Farrington was shot to death by "Black Charlie" Russell, contracted by George "Bo" Abney, a low-level Black Mafia affiliate. The reports suggested the killing was a territorial dispute, and that after Farrington's death, Abney took over his turf. DEA intelligence reports indicated a marked increase in Abney's trips to New York City and in the quantities of narcotics he was dealing. Soon after the murder, Bo Abney was seen in a late model Cadillac with Black Mafia leaders Lonnie Dawson, Eugene Hearn and Gregory Trice. Their new partnership would be tested within months. The ODALE Task Force review of the Farrington murder does not include a single mention of anyone named William Davis or "Country." The Philadelphia Police Department considers the murder of Thomas Farrington an unsolved case, and no one has ever been charged.

★

When Johnny Clark (no relation to the John W. Clark involved in the Hanafi murders and the Kelly robbery) agreed to join the start-up of Community Urban Development (CUD) back in April of 1972, he believed it would be a legit body specializing in low-cost home repair. Johnny Clark thought his background as a general contractor in Camden, New Jersey, would serve the progressive, grassroots group well. In no time, however, funds were pilfered and used for illegitimate expenses, causing Clark to buy tools with his own money to work on the group's projects. He quickly realized that a shadow crowd of people from Philadelphia's Temple 12 were co-opting the organization, namely Black Mafia hoodlums who, to put it mildly, were not committed to the cause. Clark was not alone, as law enforcement authorities also discovered that CUD was essentially a "non-existent company."

While not one of the incorporators, George McAllister served as secretary and treasurer to CUD. In December 1972, he withdrew all of its money without the permission or knowledge of other officers, and CUD ceased operations with Johnny Clark and McAllister on bad terms. Sometime in mid-October 1973, CUD incorporator John Roberts and McAllister, each of whom were Black Muslims, attempted to get together with Clark again for the purpose of re-starting CUD, and also tried to recruit him into the mosque. When Clark rebuffed them, he became a liability to the Black Mafia, and by extension to Temple 12, because he possessed incriminating CUD documents.

McAllister set up another meeting with Johnny Clark, for 5:30 P.M. on 29 October 1973, causing consternation among Clark's intimates, who couldn't believe he was entertaining the advances of this crowd. Clark, for his part, was clearly intimidated, but the prospect of flat-out ignoring the criminal subgroup of the Black Muslims – or worse, reporting the situation to the authorities – was even scarier, and so he split the difference by exchanging "ideas" with them on occasion without taking any real action. For all the adjectives used to describe the Black Mafia, "deliberative" and "patient" were not among them, and Clark would have to make a decision soon.

McAllister showed up at Johnny Clark's South Camden row house in the 500 block of Division Street as scheduled, and the two had a short conversation that ended with Clark refusing an invitation to go with McAllister to another meeting. It didn't take long for McAllister to return to Clark's door, this time with Black Mafia friends Edgar Rice and trigger-man Lucius Jones. Jones wore a brown suit and Rice a gray one, with the latter carrying a briefcase, and thus their appearance belied their background – and their intentions. McAllister led the duo into Clark's house and immediately demanded the lucrative and incriminating "silver seal and original papers" for CUD. When Clark told them he did not have the sensitive materials, two men drew guns and approached him. Indignant at Clark's refusal to play along, the gangsters gave him a last chance to come clean, with one adding, "Why don't you join the Moz?" Moz was street lingo for the Black Muslims.

Angered by Clark's response and seeming disrespect, Lucius Jones shot him in the chest and head as his wife, Debra, and his two-year-old son Johnny Boy looked on. Debra whisked little Johnny Boy upstairs, after which two of the men in Clark's dining room leaned over his body and stuffed newspapers underneath him. Lucius Jones went upstairs to get Debra, followed by McAllister. They grilled Debra about the location of the much sought-after documents but she too insisted she did not know where they were. Aggravated, McAllister took Johnny Boy out of her arms and left the house, leaving Jones to escort Debra downstairs, while telling her that the house was on fire. The boy and Debra were paraded past Johnny Clark, whose body was on the floor between the dining room and the kitchen, covered with miscellaneous articles of clothing and fully engulfed in flames. She couldn't believe her eyes; as she later said, "Johnny's hair was sizzling." Debra fought with her assailant, screaming and calling out her husband's name, at which Jones said, "I ought to shoot you, too, right here." Terrified, she grabbed her coat and went outside into a waiting car, where McAllister sat in the back seat with Johnny Boy. They drove her to the Marriott on Philadelphia's City Line Avenue, where Jones and Rice got out of the car and left McAllister with a standing order: "We don't want to see her again."

Perhaps because he had a romantic interest in Debra, McAllister decided not to kill her or Johnny Boy, opting instead to travel to an apartment in Harrisburg. All the while, Debra and McAllister exchanged concerns – McAllister threatened to kill her and her son if she ever talked to anyone about her husband's murder, while she vowed to keep her mouth shut if McAllister would let them go. He relented at 6 A.M. the next morning and drove her to a train station, and she traveled back to Philadelphia to stay with a relative.

Firefighters arrived at approximately 11 P.M. to find what they thought was a pile of discarded clothes on fire. It was the smoldering body of Johnny Clark. Despite the efforts of police and fire officers and emergency room staff, Clark died in the hospital in the morning hours of October 30. When Camden police and fire officials eventually tracked down Debra Clark in Philadelphia, she initially lied. In time, however, she relented, pressured by authorities in Camden and Philadelphia and perhaps still fearful of the Black Mafia, and the subsequent investigation resulted in convictions for the three men who entered her home that day, and for a fourth, Eugene Coffer, who aided the conspiracy.

The Clark inquiry had other bad consequences for the Black Mafia. It furthered inter-agency cooperation between the Philadelphia and Camden Police Departments, and added to a growing body of intelligence on the group. For instance, authorities noted that Rice and his wife operated a candy store in West Philadelphia, and that he was also planning to open another store next to Foo-Foo Ragan's shop at 52nd and Locust. In addition to numerous bars and speakeasies, law enforcement was convinced the Black Mafia was adding more generic fronts to its enterprise. Agencies also discovered that Rice didn't own a car, and in fact used Bo Baynes's ride or, more commonly, rental cars obtained through stolen credit cards.

*

As the Black Mafia enjoyed the ever-increasing profits from their drug and extortion rackets, the 20th and Carpenter Gang regretted the deal they had brokered in May. The gang began operating independently again in late 1973, led by Donald Robinson and Elliott Burton, who were apparently willing to risk battle with their erstwhile partners. Over the next few months, Philadelphians witnessed some of the most violent street warfare in the city's history, including the remarkable sight of teenage gang members on bikes shooting at well-dressed men in Cadillacs. The strife included several firebombings, and on one occasion the target was the Black Brothers, Inc. headquarters in South Street. The 20th and Carpenter crew was far outnumbered, though, and eventually the group forfeited whatever territory it still claimed back to the Black Mafia.

*

On the street, some informants and other sources started to use used different terminology to describe the Black Mafia. By November 1973, a name commonly heard was "The Family." These sources referred to members and associates as "Part I" and to troops – gang members and drug runners – as "Part II." Yet others called the drug runners and other low-ranking affiliates The Little Brothers, mid-level members such as enforcers, The Brothers, and Black Mafia leaders, The Big Brothers. There were criteria for graduating from one rank to another, and to become anything but a Little Brother, members had to become Black Muslims. The lowest rank, regardless of what it was called, served as a training ground for officers and leaders. The syndicate also used the Black Muslim-controlled prison system to recruit and train.

Among the panoply of names for the group were Black Mafia, Black Brothers, Inc. and derivations such as Black B. Inc., Black B., and Black

Inc., and The Family. Just as Italian-American crime groups came to be known under a variety of terms such as the Mafia, La Cosa Nostra, and The Mob, people in the community got the picture when any of the Black Mafia terms was used.

There was an interesting paradox regarding the numerous, multi-jurisdictional, multi-agency investigations into Black Mafia activities. Dating back to when the Philadelphia Police Department's OCU began investigating the Black Mafia in April 1972, a vast pool of intelligence had accumulated detailing things like the group's structure, activities and *modus operandi*. Nevertheless, despite the amount and quality of the information, agencies still had problems bringing cases. According to an OCU memo, this was because of the lack of witnesses or victims prepared to testify. As one source in the Philadelphia District Attorney's office said regarding a grand jury inquiry into Black Mafia-dominated narcotics trafficking, "When I got into this ... investigation, I soon realized that normal investigative techniques would not work here. The targets were not white-collar workers where, if indicted, would be around for the trial, and witnesses take the stand, and so on. It soon became apparent that we could not secure or protect witnesses. Their identity would surface as soon as the presentment was made [a public record] and basically they were afraid to testify. We could have put the witnesses into protective custody, but you would then have the situation of the pusher making bail and being free on the streets and our witness being the one in jail. And if you let your witness go back on the street with the defendant you had to ask yourself, 'How long will it be before he is reached ... with either money or a knife?' We began using black witnesses mostly for search and seizure warrants after that. On the basis of his testimony before a grand jury [with his name protected under the secret informant clause] as an informant, and with information we developed, we could search a suspect's home or business. But even then, I would practically have to get down on my knees and beg a witness to go before the grand jury and give him all kinds of assurances about his identity being protected."

Examples of victim and witness intimidation are found in abundance throughout Philadelphia Police Department intelligence files. The Department theoretically scored a large victory when, after a series of arrests, they confiscated what came to be known as the "Black Mafia notebook." There were several occasions on which arrests took place and critical notes and the minutes of Black Mafia meetings were confiscated. It is not clear precisely when the Black Mafia notebook was confiscated, though it appears to have occurred in late 1973. It was literally a copybook, the type most often associated with grade school children, and was replete with names, dates, and figures relating to vast extortion networks. The targets included small legitimate business owners, quasi-legitimate businessmen such as bar owners who were complicit in vice activities, drug dealers and numbers writers and runners. OCU detectives were assigned to interview those listed in the notebook as current or prospective targets. Though police gathered other, independent evidence that showed the notebook was accurate, they still could not persuade individuals to come forward to testify.

The standard procedure for extortion included a preliminary, unannounced visit by a goon crew during which a "request" would be made for a "donation" to a front organization or to Temple 12. The visit typically ended with the target being told the weekly fee and the date the first payment was expected. Threats were not explicitly uttered or even implied in most of these visits, but if a target failed to pay when the group returned, violence and/or vandalism would eventually ensue. One typical case occurred on Poplar Street in October 1973. A Black Mafia crew had visited the target five or six weeks earlier and asked for a contribution to Black Inc. of $100 per week. When they returned to collect, the target refused to pay and was shot in front of his property, though he survived.

The Philadelphia Police Department was having such a difficult time getting citizens to cooperate in Black Mafia investigations that the OCU enlisted the services of other agencies and began a series of meetings in order to create a strategy which would not require witnesses to eviscerate the group. One outcome was the decision to focus on the group's possession of weapons. The ATF representative on the Strike Force noted that "most of the members of the (Black Mafia) probably had felony convictions and since federal law forbids their owning a firearm of any type; arrest and prosecution by ATF through the Strike Force would be a very effective way of resolving the problems [the Black Mafia] presents to the public."

Though any number of law enforcement officials were tracking Black Mafia members down and arresting them, one in particular was giving them fits. Philadelphia Highway Patrol officer John D'Amico was more than a nuisance with his car stops, street-corner "interviews," gun pinches, narcotics collars, street-level intelligence collection and subsequent convictions. In late November, the Black Mafia had a discussion in their South Street headquarters, and the leadership decided action was needed. A consensus was reached at the meeting: they would kill a Philadelphia Highway Patrol officer. Word of the contract got back to authorities from a disgruntled Black Mafia affiliate, and D'Amico, his wife, and his daughter were guarded around-the-clock for at least four months by the department's stakeout (SWAT) unit. D'Amico was fired at twice during that time, but the shots missed him each time. One of these events took place as D'Amico and his partner Frederick Morse were driving past 20th and Fitzwater Streets in South Philadelphia.

Meanwhile, the Black Mafia began making plans for New Year's Eve. Members visited an After Six shop and used stolen credit cards and bogus identifications to rent thirty tuxedos for the grand evening. The rental agency was no doubt relieved when no threats or extortion demands transpired; the tough-looking customers didn't even ask for donations to Temple 12 or Black Brothers, Inc., as was their custom. As if to demonstrate their arrogance had no limits, the group was preparing for its very own Black Mafia Ball, to be held at the Sheldron Ballroom at Broad Street and Cheltenham Avenue.

The ball was attended by all of the Black Mafia leaders, each decked out in their tuxes and rapping about their various cons and acts of intimidation. Unbeknown to the gangsters, police had an informant at the affair who was making mental notes of the conversations. During one discussion, several Black Mafia leaders decided to lure Highway Patrol officer D'Amico to the Black Brothers, Inc. headquarters and kill him on May Day, 1974. All of this got back to police, who simply could not believe the balls this crowd of hoods possessed.

Perhaps the Black Mafia Ball and the contract on D'Amico should not have been surprising. After all, despite the murders and other high-profile crimes, the group had just incorporated a community organization complete with an office and press conference to boot, placed a contract on a cop, and had made efforts to fulfill it. The City of Philadelphia was effectively experiencing gangster hubris on steroids.

As these sensational events were transpiring, the ODALE task force was analyzing the area's drug market for 1972-3. It concluded there were "several black independent wholesale distributing organizations which were highly active" during this period. The report noted that black wholesale distributing organizations were "becoming increasingly more sophisticated in their operations. White suppliers have gradually become phased out or virtually non-existent during this era in black communities." Further, it stated that 1972-73 was

> Marked by increased violence, murder, extortion and coercion amongst the participants of narcotic distribution. This has apparently "spilled" over or encroached into legitimate areas where the same tactics are being used. Toward the end of the period surveyed one witnessed the emergence of BLACK, INC., where most black organizations selling narcotics in the Philadelphia, Pennsylvania area either sell narcotics belonging to BLACK, INC., or pay tribale (sic) to conduct business independent of the organization. This leads to the inevitable conclusion that if continued unchecked in the near future, BLACK, INC., will control all of the drug selling in black areas.

In a brief departure to the sober analysis in the rest of the roughly 100-page report, the Task Force noted, "Practically all suppliers included in the top echelon own either a Cadillac or/and a Lincoln Continental, which could indicate a status symbol in the traffic to mark his station."

As 1973 came to an end, Sam Christian was in prison, and Nudie Mims, Ron Harvey and Bo Baynes were in hiding, on the run from local and federal authorities, and Major Coxson was no longer around to help finesse deals between the Italian families in New York and Philly, nor to orchestrate financial scams and to poke fun at the establishment in the media. These events marked the first time since the syndicate's inception that such a mix of leadership and muscle had been removed from the group's hierarchy. To add insult to injury, one very brave man was about to declare war on the Black Mafia.

CHAPTER 13 ★
INVESTIGATE CONTENTS OF BLANKET

T HE BLACK MAFIA had begun to feel pressure after Jim Nicholson's splashes in the *Inquirer* and *Philadelphia Magazine*, and as the law officers slowly awoke to the group's actions in late 1973. To make matters worse, another storm was brewing against them, in the shape of Reverend Muhammad Kenyatta. Kenyatta was born Donald Brooks Jackson in Chester, PA, in 1944, and was drawn to the church at an early age. Like many parts of Philadelphia, Chester was a tough town and the young Jackson often found himself in fights. His mother and the church eventually convinced him that all those days suspended from school were unnecessary, and that he could more convincingly win fights with his mouth if only he would devote his energies appropriately. He reformed, began preaching at the age of fourteen, and was soon billed as the "Boy Wonder Preacher." Jackson later said that he and others close to him expected him to become "some kind of Negro leader."

The following year, he joined the Chester branch of the NAACP, but quickly became frustrated with what he considered a lax attitude, and left after two meetings. He attended nearby Lincoln University for a year, where he was an honors student. Jackson quickly established himself as the campus radical, before running out of money. His next experience emboldened him as an activist for life.

Jacskon spent sixteen months in the Air Force, which included, "experiences like painting yellow lines on asphalt in 110-degree sun while the white GIs watched from a shack with the fans going." He protested zealously, and soon found himself arrested trying to get a cup of coffee in Oklahoma, where he was stationed. Jackson was charged with mutiny and treason, and a career and a cause were born. "The movement seemed some thing I could plug into. I felt more at home on a picket line than I did clapping and praying." Ironically, it was the Chester branch of the NAACP that got him out of the jam, and honorably discharged, by contacting a congressman on his behalf.

As he made a name for himself locally and nationally as a firebrand civil rights activist, Jackson caught the attention of the FBI and of his competitors, in particular, through his efforts over voter registration and related activities at Tougaloo College, near Jackson, Mississippi. It was around this time that Donald Jackson abandoned his "slave" name in favor of Muhammad Kenyatta, representing two of his heroes – Elijah Muhammad and Jomo Kenyatta, President of Kenya. In the latter part of 1967, the FBI put his name on its "Rabble Rouser List" because of his actions at Tougaloo. The agency employed a variety of tactics against Kenyatta, including intercepts of his phone calls and mail correspondence, and produced false documents and engaged in other counterintelligence measures to disrupt his activities through 1969.

Kenyatta left Mississippi for Pennsylvania, where his flamboyant style soon jarred with notorious figures in the area such as Stanley Branche. The former head of the Chester NAACP sneered that Kenyatta Muhammad was a phony name to begin with: "Muhammad is Muslim and Kenyatta is pagan. So, how can a man with a name like that be for real?" Within a few years, Branche's connections in the African-American underworld would be a target for Kenyatta's return fire. In the meantime, Kenyatta became director of the Black Economic Development Conference (BEDC), which espoused and advanced a variety of inner-city causes. The BEDC operated out of a spartan storefront office in North Philadelphia at 10th and Somerset Streets. It was plastered with posters touting self-help and empowerment. Kenyatta was often in the news and commonly a source of controversy. Nothing, however, compared to what he was about to get into.

On 3 January 1974, the BEDC board of directors held a press conference, one of many it had convened over the years. This time, Kenyatta eschewed the usual topics for a more specific concern. As the *Philadelphia Inquirer* wrote the following day, he effectively "declared war on the Black Mafia." Kenyatta said that much of the criminal activity in black neighborhoods was "caused by the heroin traffic" which itself was "spawned by the mobsters of black organized crime called the Black Mafia." As he decried the lack of substantive police action against the syndicate, he noted, "The black community has known of its existence for some time. The [Black Mafia] have been shaking down small stores and businessmen ... Even churches have been given blood letters." Kenyatta was referring to extortion letters the Black Mafia sent to ministers demanding money, most of which were never reported to police.

As part of his call to action, Kenyatta asked ministers to publicly denounce members of their congregations who were engaged in the drug trade. He said this was a particular issue for Black Muslims, since many Black Mafia members were part of the Mosque. Kenyatta also called on Mayor Rizzo and Police Commissioner O'Neill to work with the BEDC in dismantling the Black Mafia, stating, "We're asking them to do this because a lot of public officials fear they might be labeled 'racist' if they crack down on the black criminal."

It was a courageous outburst, and was backed up by others. At another BEDC event, board member Rev. Wyncliffe Jangdharrie explained that when Jimmie Lester, a civic leader and early advocate of Black Brothers, Inc., "found out that Sam Christian and his group were dope pushers and planned to use Black B. Incorporated to distribute narcotics, he quit." After further stating that "a state representative and several city councilmen were instrumental in starting this organization, and a couple are still involved," Jangdharrie called on people to contact their local politicians.

In time, Kenyatta and Jangdharrie would become marked men for their outspoken efforts against the Black Mafia. For now, the syndicate was still preoccupied with sporadic internecine warfare involving 20th and Carpenter Street gang members. Clarence Starks and an accomplice walked up to Jeremiah Middleton, aged sixteen, as he waited for his school bus at the corner of 19th and Carpenter on a January morning. After a brief exchange of words, the two men opened fired on Middleton, who ran but tripped over a step. As he lay on the ground, Starks pumped bullets into him. Middleton was hit six times in the head, chest, and back, and died shortly afterwards. A little more than an hour later, police stopped a car driven by Black Mafia member Terry Mills. Gregory Trice and Starks, who was in the back seat, were with him. As the officer asked some routine questions, he saw Starks take a .32 caliber Smith & Wesson from his waistband and place it under the front seat. The gun was loaded. All three were taken into custody, where Starks denied shooting Middleton but admitted he was a member of Black Brothers, Inc. He also told police that Black B. was warring with the 20th and Carpenter Gang over territory and membership issues.

Another Black Mafia member taking advantage of the era's community development push was Lonnie Anderson. In addition to abusing the Safe Streets, Inc. office, he had become adept at crafting credit card scams, and ran a related car theft ring. He was also scheduled to testify before the grand jury in Washington, D.C. investigating the Hanafi killings. That investigation was, obviously, preoccupied with the murder case, but had uncovered all sorts of criminal activities relating to Philadelphia's Temple 12. The hit squad's use of stolen and fraudulent credit cards turned investigators on to the Pyramid Enterprises scam because one of Pyramid's "employees" was Hanafi murderer William Christian. Another area of interest to the D.C. grand jury was the exploitation of federal Safe Streets funding. For instance, it was suspected that Philadelphia's Safe Streets funds were funneled into Major Coxson's failed run for Mayor of Camden, New Jersey. Thus, it was anticipated that Lonnie Anderson's testimony regarding his alias Frank Stewart's "job" at Safe Streets would provide insights into the con.

He never got to testify before the D.C. grand jury. On January 10, Anderson was shot and killed by a major national heroin trafficker named Felix Mike in Mike's Philadelphia apartment. Mike argued that he shot Anderson in self-defense when the two argued over Mike refusing to pay $50 per week in protection money to Philadelphia's Black Muslims, and was later acquitted of murder.

Due in part to the massive investigation emanating out of Washington regarding the Hanafi murders, the Safe Streets abuses, and the increasing number of Black Brothers disclosures, the Black Mafia was getting attention at the highest levels of the Philadelphia Police Department, as an internal memo illustrates:

> On Tuesday, 1/29/74, a meeting was held in the Police Commissioner's Office concerning Black Inc., and the question was raised as to the identity of the person who drew up the formal papers for the Council for Youth and Community Development Inc. Information was received by the Organized Crime Unit that James T. Giles, an attorney-at-law with offices in the Fidelity Building, was the author of the legal papers for the youth council.

Giles was a rising attorney who had become the first black associate at the prominent Philadelphia law firm of Pepper, Hamilton and Scheetz, and later the firm's first black partner. He had partnered with Judge Paul Dandridge on other community initiatives including the Safe Streets program and the Philadelphia Tutorial Project. Police had no reason to suspect Giles of inappropriate actions, and there is no evidence any further inquiry took place. The investigators did take note, however, of the significant political players who at one time or another supported the group, most notably Judge Dandridge and Tom Foglietta.

On February 1, the OCU received credible information that at least twelve teenage gang members had not attended school for over three months after finding out that enforcers Larry Starks and Russell Barnes had been ordered to find the remaining 20th and Carpenter members, perhaps numbering fifty, and kill them. Beyond the territorial disputes with the gang, the Black Mafia no doubt wanted to expand the size of their extortion zone. At the time, federal law enforcement agencies estimated the proceeds from heroin netted the group $50,000 per week, while extortion brought in another $40,000.

★

Almost immediately after Bo Abney took over Cadillac Tommy Farrington's drug territory in October 1973, DEA and FBI reports began noting that the Black Mafia had put a contract on Abney's life. Though he lived the high life, with an impressive wardrobe and the requisite late model Cadillac, a green Eldorado with a white top and sliding roof, Abney would have little time to enjoy the benefits afforded a big-time drug dealer. Like Farrington, he was not paying a large enough percentage of his profits back to the Black Mafia to suit them, and apparently hadn't learned from Farrington's death. Bo was thus at considerable risk, given the Black Mafia's propensity for violence when a target didn't own up to his obligations, however irrational the target may have thought they were.

In December, the Jolly Green Giant, Herschell Williams, approached Abney and told him there was a contract out on his life. Abney also discovered that "Country [William Davis], [James] Fox and Lonnie [Dawson]" had something to do with the contract. He said it concerned Black Inc., and that he would take care of the matter himself. Abney visited William Davis at Ernie's Club Paree, and left with the impression things had been ironed out. In fact, word on the street was that the Black Mafia's Donnie Day approached Abney and told him, "It's better to give up some money than your life." Abney was not persuaded, and perhaps planned to rely upon his mettle. Abney was a sturdy 5'9" and 200 lbs., was always armed, and was an intimidating force. He had been arrested many times for crimes of violence. None of this impressed the Black Mafia, which wanted the $25,000 he owed them – or else.

Just before 7:30 on the morning of February 20, a teenage girl was on her way to Olney High School when she saw what looked like a body lying in the street and quickly returned home to tell her mother what she had seen. After her mother called Philadelphia Police, a call went out over police radio: "Nineteen hundred Willard Street, man lying on the highway." Police arrived to discover a body up against the curb. What they had not expected was the condition of the corpse, which was covered with a gold bed sheet, lying stomach down, hog-tied with its hands and feet behind its back with white and gold metal clothes hangers. The body was dressed in blue jeans, blue socks, green nylon underwear, a gold colored t-shirt and a blue long sleeve shirt with orange, light blue and white circles. Strewn nearby were a black left shoe, a brown leather cap, and a three-quarter-length tan coat with a brown fur collar. Missing, however, was the body's head.

As police cordoned off the street and began processing the crime scene and canvassing the area for interviews, another discovery was being made three miles south, near Center City. A boy waiting for a school bus noticed something on the steps of the boarded up Wanda Inn Bar. At 8:23, police radio dispatched another call: "Investigate contents of blanket on corner." In minutes, officers were setting up another crime scene following the gruesome discovery of Bo Abney's head, severed at the neck, inside two gold pillowcases. A medical examiner later determined that Abney had been alive when his head was cut off.

Police received information from numerous sources that the Black Mafia was behind the murder, and there was general agreement the motive was his wanton disregard of the syndicate's extortion demands. Two informants made reference to the Nation of Islam when suggesting motives, including one who claimed Abney was killed "because he cursed Elijah Muhammad, and because he wouldn't pay the Muslims for protection. They would ask him for a donation and he would say, 'Fuck Elijah!' But they didn't care about that. They killed him because he wouldn't get up the money." The other source said it was the work of the Black Mafia or the Black Muslims. When pressed why she thought this, the police source said, "Because they are the only ones crazy enough to do something like that. Bo was a member of the [Black Mafia] and he was a Muslim, he got his 'X.'"

Authorities were also interested in links to Black Muslims because they had been notified of two beheadings in Newark, New Jersey, in October 1973. These were thought to be indirectly linked to the Hanafi murders and internal disputes within the NOI. Federal informants had the most interesting take on the slaying, stating that Abney was approached by the Black Mafia when Ronald Harvey was trying to post bail following his 1973 arrest. Bo Abney refused to put up the money, the sources said, resulting in the contract on him. *Daily News* reporter Tyree Johnson heard that Abney was actually drowned by Black Inc. men before he was decapitated. Other intelligence sources said that Black Mafia chieftains Russell Barnes and Ricardo McKendrick were the ones who killed Abney. Word on the street put Barnes and McKendrick at a Black Inc. meeting volunteering to pick up the contract on Abney, and later attempting to drown him in a bathtub. Abney was apparently too strong for the duo, and they were forced to take other measures. Somehow, they wound up sawing off his head. There is no way to vet the numerous theories. Philadelphia Police never charged anyone with Abney's murder, and the case is still unsolved.

After Bo Abney's head and body were found, the stories ran wild throughout the city, and especially in black neighborhoods. Hours after the discoveries, 20th and Carpenter Street Gang leader Donald Robinson received a phone call with a simple message, "You're next," which he fully understood. Robinson opted to go on the offensive. That evening, James Fox was shot in the back and seriously wounded, but survived to remain an influential force in the underworld. Donald Robinson and two other gang members were suspected, and Robinson would get his comeuppance later.

Incredibly, the very next day brought the Black Mafia still more notoriety. On February 21, syndicate members were making a routine visit to an extortion target to collect their protection money. This time, the target was Ulysses J. Rice, owner of Nookie's Tavern on Wister Street in West Philadelphia. Rice had been paying the Black Mafia for only a few months. In December of 1973, Alonzo Robinson, whom Rice knew, visited the tavern on several occasions to hawk Black Muslim pies, orange juice, fish, and *Muhammad Speaks*. On December 8, Robinson ("Brother Alonzo") and Merrill Ferguson came to the tavern and told Rice to have $200 ready for them later that day, supposedly in support of the NOI's Founder's Day. Robinson, Ferguson and Donald 13X Abney returned to Nookie's Tavern on the 11th and Rice paid them $150. Robinson and Abney came back on the 18th and told Rice he was to begin making payments of $200 per week since, if he could pay "taxes to the white man and the government," he could pay taxes to them. Rice didn't have long to process this arrangement, because on the following day Larry Starks came up to him in a movie theater and said there had been a change; the Black Mafia had decided that he would have to give $1,500 per week, but that Starks had it reduced to $500. Ulysses Rice was terrified by the rapid developments, and hid in his apartment for much of the next two months. On February 19, he was back at Nookie's Tavern when Starks entered and asked for $500 "to get the Black Mafia brothers out of jail." Starks told Rice to have the money by 8:45 on the night of the twenty-first, when he would come to pick it up.

As scheduled, Larry Starks, then perhaps *the* leader of the Black Mafia, popped into Nookie's Tavern, this time in the company of his cousin, Clarence Starks, who was out on $25,000 bail for the January 25 murder of Jeremiah Middleton. Just after Ulysses Rice paid Larry Starks the $500 tribute, FBI agents popped up, yelling, "FBI, freeze!" A Black Mafia associate lingering in the tavern named Deramos Knowles lunged at one agent with a knife and was hit with double-o buckshot from a sawed-off shotgun the agent hid beneath his coat. The Black Mafia extortion crew didn't know that Rice had gone to the FBI after the February 19 visit by Larry Starks. The Feds had provided him with a tape recorder and $500 in marked bills. On the twenty-first, he hid the tape recorder on his body and it was on throughout the entire conversation with Starks. Alonzo Robinson, Merrill Ferguson, Larry Starks, and Clarence Starks were arrested for extortion. Deramos Knowles sustained injuries to his back and shoulder but survived the FBI shooting.

The Black Mafia responded in typical fashion. Ulysses Rice's family received threats immediately following the arrests. The Philadelphia Police Department learned "that Rice had been recognized by members of Black Inc. at an unknown motel in the King of Prussia area where the FBI had made accommodations for the subject's protection." The FBI also received credible information that if Black, Inc. couldn't "get to Rice, they would seek retaliation against Rice's son as a result of [Rice's] complaining to law enforcement authorities concerning 'the shakedown reported to the FBI'." Local and federal authorities took the threats seriously and detailed officers to several locations throughout the region and took other security precautions. On February 25, the Philadelphia office of the FBI "received an anonymous telephone call, on their switchboard, asking for [the agent who shot Deramos Knowles during the sting operation]." When the caller was told that he was not in the office, the caller said, "Give (him) the following message – he's going to get his fucking head blown off."

Events came fast and furious, and on March 6 the *Daily News* devoted a vat of ink to the ongoing "bloody struggle for power" over "South Philadelphia turf" between the syndicate and the 20th and Carpenter Streets gang, then estimated as having between 100 and 200 members. Tyree Johnson was at it again, picking apart the criminal conspiracies emanating from Black Brothers, Inc. He had obtained a copy of the minutes from a December 30 meeting, which included a statement that Black Brothers was "out to control everything in the black community." Roosevelt "Spooks" Fitzgerald, a Black Mafia founder and high-ranking Black Muslim, was listed as the head of BBI, and the minutes referred to him as "General Overseer" and "First in chain of command." This was news to BBI attorney Nino Tinari, who claimed, "I've never heard of him."

Fitzgerald, *aka* Roosevelt Bey, had the usual lengthy arrest record, dating back to 1949, including charges for narcotics and burglary. Following him on the list of officers were Arthur Watson (*aka* Brother A), Eugene Hearn, and James Fox. Lonnie Dawson was listed as "town inforcer (sic)." Watson was a fugitive for the May 1973 murders of two independents who stole the large drug shipment destined for Bo Baynes, and Fitzgerald, Hearn and Fox were Black Mafia mainstays.

As luck would have it, the FBI had Watson under surveillance when Johnson's article ran. The bureau found Brother A living in a Philadelphia apartment under the name Robert Nedd, and prepared to raid his pad. On March 7, Watson and fellow Black Mafia member Timothy "Tino" Graves were in the apartment when the phone rang. After Watson hung up, he told Graves, "You had better leave right now. I think the law is out there." Graves headed toward the hallway but FBI agents fired a shot through the apartment door, and others lobbed tear gas canisters into the rear of the apartment. Staring into the barrels of numerous shotguns, Graves and Watson gave up. Police found a loaded .45 caliber pistol, two rifles and two sawed-off shotguns in the apartment. In addition to the charge of "unauthorized flight to avoid prosecution" for the murder cases, Watson was charged with conspiracy to distribute heroin. Tino Graves was charged with harboring a federal fugitive.

While tracking down Watson, the authorities had uncovered his close relationship with Sam Christian and Ron Harvey. In fact, Watson supposedly employed Harvey as a truck driver in a dry cleaning business at some point. Graves insisted during interrogation that he was not a member of Black Brothers, Inc., but said he could understand why people thought he was since he often drove kids from his neighborhood to the Black Inc. dances. He also denied being one of the Black Mafia members who put the contract on Highway Patrol officer D'Amico's head, stating, "The business about me and Russell Barnes having a contract out on a cop is a lot of bull. I think it was made up by those young dudes [20th and Carpenter Gang] to bring heat on Black Incorporated."

By now it was clear to anyone who cared that Black Brothers, Inc. was nothing like what was presented to the public back in October 1973. Reforming gangs, if it ever was the mission, had taken a back seat to extortion rackets. One BBI member had even been picked up by police in the course of his extortion stops, and had $4,000 in his pockets. Gang members who truly reformed or who agreed to pay a percentage of their ill-gotten gains to the Black Mafia – in the name of Black Brothers, Inc. – were steamed. "They tried to take us over and use us," said one gang member. "We did the hard work and they drove the Cadillacs."

With uncanny timing, the day after Tyree Johnson's two exposés on the South Philly power struggle saw another chapter in the war. BBI secretary David "Scoogie" Mitchell was in a convertible with the Black Mafia's Albert Ross, John Yates (a hit man according to federal authorities) and Charles Lark as it approached Kimball Street on 20th Street at 4:30 in the afternoon. As they stopped behind a truck, a hail of shots were fired at the car from nearby rooftops, striking three of the occupants. Only Mitchell escaped the ambush unharmed – Lark was hit in the back of the head, Yates was hit in the face and back, and Ross was hit in the leg. Mitchell was rattled so much by the assassination attempt that he told the media he was considering leaving the city because he was "scared to death I'll be killed."

A little more than two weeks later, on March 26, Tyree Johnson found himself part of the Black Mafia story firsthand. Johnson was assigned to cover the story of a baby girl found in a trash can in the back of a lot in North Philadelphia. As he sat at a red light on the way to the crime scene, he saw a very large man running after a tan-colored Cadillac, firing shots at it from a large gun. As the car successfully sped away, the large man turned to see Johnson in his car. Rather than expressing shock or concern that there was a witness to the shooting, the man defiantly held the gun in the air before grabbing it by the butt, sticking it in his pants and slowly walking away. The reporter had just witnessed Black Mafia hit man Herschell Williams, the Jolly Green Giant, miss his target, and had to make a difficult decision: report the incident or not? He, perhaps more than anyone, knew the perils of going against the Black Mafia in court. Despite this, he reported the shooting to police when he arrived at the scene of the morbid baby discovery, which was just around the corner. Police quickly went to the sight of the Williams shooting, and arrested the Jolly Green Giant without incident.

In the days following, word on the street spread that Tyree Johnson's life was in danger. The DEA contacted the *Daily News*, which promptly purchased Johnson a snub-nosed .38 caliber gun called "The Bodyguard." Because of the exigent circumstances, Johnson's license to carry permit was approved in a day, and he was also given police protection for a time. Interestingly, Johnson received a phone call from Stanley Branche telling him not to worry about the threats. He survived the tumultuous times without incident, and the Black Mafia continued to get hammered in the press.

On April 4, the front page of the *Philadelphia Inquirer* headlined, "Police Say 'Black B' Is Front for Drug Dealers". The story, by Mike Leary, who had quality federal sources, detailed the many criminal connections to the supposed community development group. Some of the revelations included the following: the FBI estimated the Black Mafia controlled eighty per cent of the city's heroin sales in the city; the group's extortion take for one set of targets (apparently in South Philadelphia) was estimated at $15,000 a month, based on records seized by authorities; and, depending on how the numbers were tabulated, the Black Mafia membership numbered in the hundreds. The public was also told that proceeds from the Black Mafia extortion network were being sent to the Nation of Islam headquarters in Chicago. The discovery was made by federal authorities in Washington, D.C. who obtained copies of Mosque donation slips in the course of investigating the Hanafi murders. One federal investigator said, "They can always say that the money is a donation from pious Muslims, but look who the money comes from – pious Muslims like Ronald Harvey, Sam Christian, and Nudie Mims."

Even drug dealers got ink, including one who was quoted as saying, "They want it all – all the heroin traffic. If a dude crosses them too much, they gonna take him away from here." He also said, the Black Mafia "got more pieces [guns] than anybody in town. They be their own little army." Another dealer said, "They be big, very big, and they be getting bigger … Gonna take an army to stop those dudes cause they ain't your ordinary, low-life sort of crook." Community activist and Black Mafia nemesis Muhammad Kenyatta said, "Black Mafia, Black B, the name is the same, but a lot of the members overlap. They are vicious, cold-blooded vermin who prey on their brothers in the black community." *The Evening Bulletin* ran a story the same day that stated Black Brothers, Inc. sent "support payments" to Sam Christian and Ronald Harvey while they were on the FBI's Most Wanted list, hiding from authorities.

The media spotlight stayed bright as Kenyatta held another press

Dubrow's furniture store (above) had not suffered a robbery for fifty years until a Black Mafia team came calling, shooting and pistol-whipping staff and setting the building and an employee on fire.

Police Commissioner Frank Rizzo (right), here in conversation with District Attorney Arlen Specter, called the Dubrow's attack "the most vicious I have ever come across."

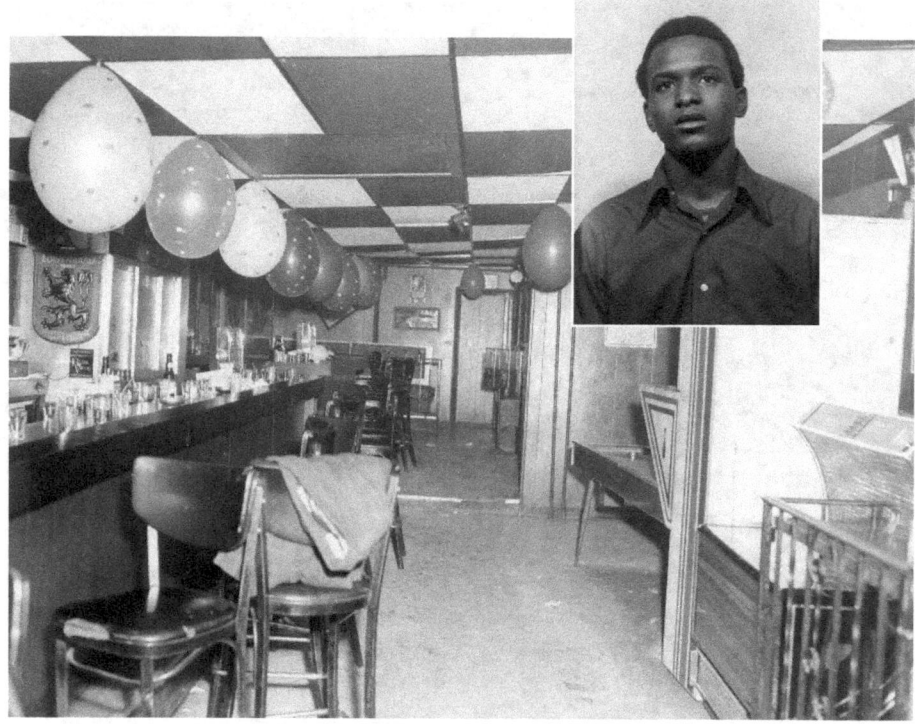

The Black Mafia went looking for Wardell Green at a birthday party in the Reynolds Wrap Lounge (above) after a petty argument. Green (inset) was executed inside the packed bar. Self-confessed contract killer Russell Barnes (below left) was later charged, but the only witness against him, Wardell's sister Velma, was murdered as she answered her door just days before his trial was to begin (below right).

The outrageous Major Benjamin Coxson outside his futuristic house with his chauffeur, Quinzelle Champagne. A wheeler-dealer extraordinaire, Coxson had his fingers in just about every criminal pie in the city.

Boxing legend Muhammad Ali, pictured in Philadelphia, was the Black Muslim's most high-profile convert, and was also close to controversial figures such as Jeremiah Shabazz and the criminal Major Coxson.

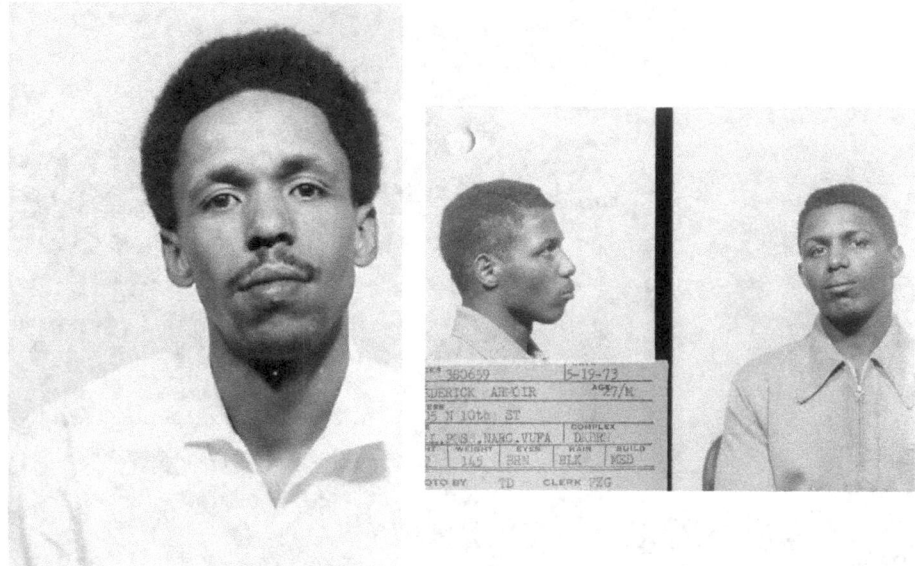

Larris "Tank" Frazier (above left) clashed with Frederick "Smiley" Armour (above right) when his former partner encroached on his drug turf in the notorious Richard Allen Homes housing project. Frazier gunned down his fellow Black Brothers, Inc. officer in the street below.

One of the most cold-blooded crimes in U.S. history was the slaughter of two adults and five children in a house in Washington, D.C., owned by basketball great Kareem Abdul-Jabbar, in 1973. The murder squad responsible included:

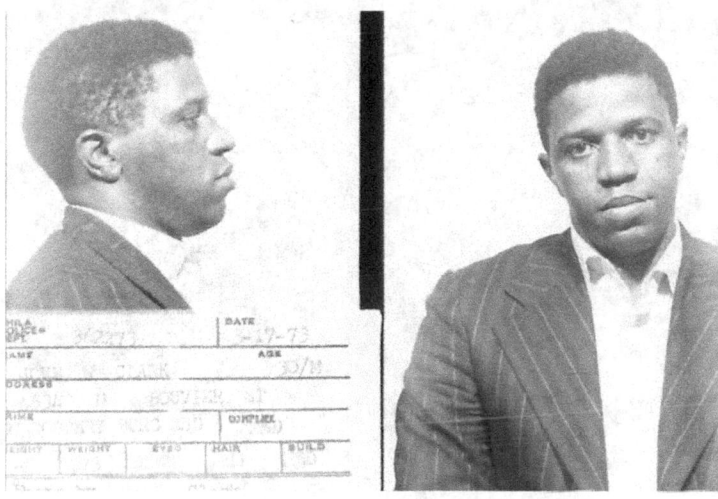

John Clark

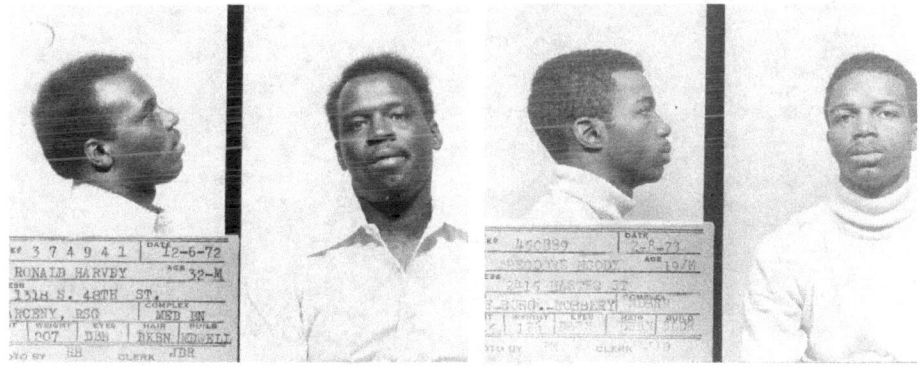

Ron Harvey   Theodore Moody

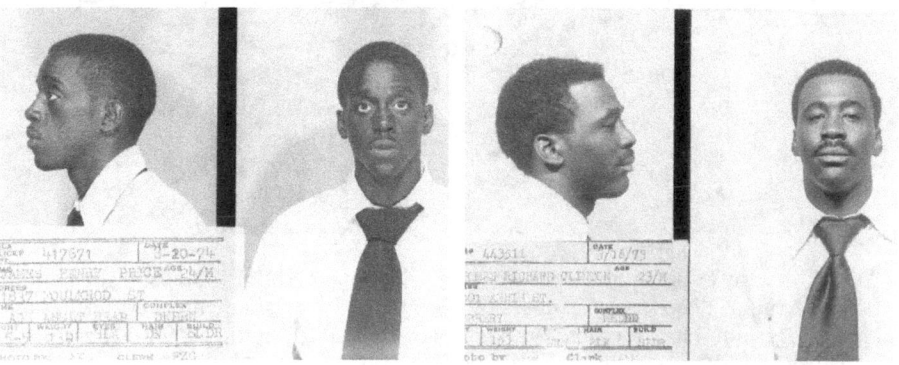

James Price   Thomas Clinton

"You killed my babies and shot my women!" Hamaas Abdul Khaalis, leader of the Hanafi Mulims, lost seven members of his family in a massacre after criticizing the Nation of Islam. He is pictured on bail awaiting trial for taking 149 hostages in an armed siege in Washington, D.C., in 1977, in protest at the killings.

Ernest Kelly, owner of Ernie's Club Paree, a Black Mafia hangout, testified against the syndicate after an extortion attempt. His son and daughter-in-law were later murdered.

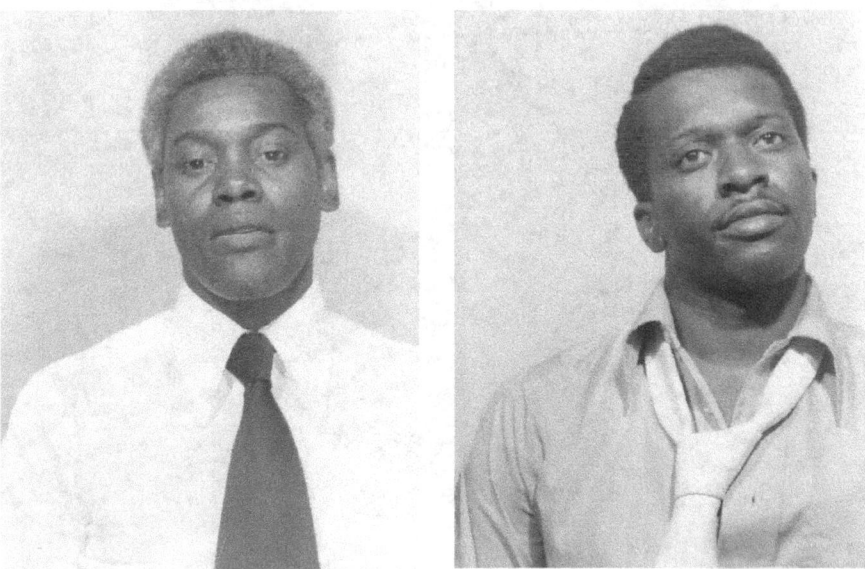

Eugene "Bo" Baynes (left) was acting head of the Black Mafia until he was jailed. Lonnie Dawson's (right) reign as leader was also brief, cut short when he was given a life term for murder in 1975. His influence was just as great in prison.

Investigative reporter Jim Nicholson was the first journalist to lift the lid on the Black Mafia. His cover stories for *Philadelphia Magazine* and *TODAY* revealed a vicious, insidious syndicate that was unknown to the wider population

conference on April 11, this time to sharpen his criticism of Jeremiah Shabazz. According to the activist, Shabazz offered him $30,000 for "information about police action against the Black Mafia." Kenyatta said that on January 9, just days after his first barnburner press conference, he visited Shabazz at Temple 12 seeking the Black Muslim leader's support against the syndicate. Shabazz not only spurned the offer, he took to the offensive, publicly referring to Kenyatta's efforts as "Uncle Tomming for the white man." Asked if this was a matter of conflicting religious ideology, Kenyatta, a Baptist minister, said, "I'm not attacking the Nation of Islam and I'm not saying all Muslims are in the Black Mafia, but many of the city's Black Mafia leaders hold prominent positions in the mosque here and Minister Shabazz has said nothing about it."

Kenyatta pointed to the likes of James Fox, Eugene Hearn and Roosevelt Fitzgerald, who were active in Mosque 12. Fitzgerald at the time was captain of Shabazz's Fruit of Islam, and thought by many to be running the Black Mafia since the arrests of Sam Christian and Bo Baynes. Though Kenyatta focused most of his attention on its drug networks, the syndicate maintained its extortion of businesses and illicit entrepreneurs. Police stymied part of the racket when they arrested several men for trafficking untaxed cigarettes on April 15. They discovered the group was purchasing "nakeds," or cigarettes bearing no tax stamp, from North Carolina and affixing a stamp on them in Philadelphia. The network was using more than 130 vending machines throughout the city to distribute the black market products, and the Black Mafia was taking a percentage.

The withering attacks from law enforcement and the media seemed to have some effect when lawyer Nino Tinari announced on April 17 that Black Brothers, Inc. was disbanding. Tinari said the group had, "taken down their sign. They've abandoned their headquarters and I'll file for a dissolution of their state charter." He also said the founders were "totally disappointed because no other community group would join them in the effort to stop the gang problem," before adding that police harassment and a bad press also contributed to the downfall of BBI. While it was true the group abandoned its headquarters and would no longer exploit the community development funding, the names Black Brothers, Black B., and, most commonly, Black Inc. would be used on the street and in prisons when referring to this cast of characters for decades to come. For example, when IRS agents finally caught acting Black Mafia head Bo Baynes after a nine-month manhunt by multiple federal and local agencies, the headline in the newspaper was "Nab Fugitive 'Black Brother.'"

It was during a court proceeding involving Baynes that a federal judge offered a succinct and damning critique of BBI's poisonous effect on the community: "This conspiracy, in which you are named as the highest-ranking member, held itself out to the community to be a legitimate organization towards self-improvement for Blacks. The criminal activities of this group did irreparable damage to the community and to the respect of law, especially to Black youths, for whom as self-claimed Black leaders, you and your co-conspirators set forth an insidious example, and to whom, you and your co-conspirators sold heroin."

CHAPTER 14 ★
THEY WERE MISUSING ISLAM

EVENTS FORCED JEREMIAH Shabazz, reluctantly, into the limelight. The private, soft-spoken Shabazz was compelled to take the microphone to counter the bad publicity Philadelphia's Black Muslims were receiving. Throughout the spring and summer, he became a quote machine for the press, with most of his rhetoric aimed at Muhammad Kenyatta's charges against the Black Mafia, and against the media's treatment of Muslims. He held a press conference in the days following Kenyatta's accusations about his alliance with the syndicate. "I am not now, nor have I ever been, connected with any crime or drug-related activities," he declared. To emphasise his point, Shabazz disseminated a press release that stated: there is no Black Mafia, the Nation of Islam in Philadelphia did not control any so-called Black Mafia, and the Temple 12 administration was not engaged in any dope or crime activities, nor did it condone or encourage crime. He denied offering Muhammad Kenyatta money for his silence and ever threatening his life. He also complained of media bias against the Nation, stating, "The press only prints a criminal's religious affiliation when he is a Black Muslim ... Everybody knows that most of the criminals are Christians, not Muslims." He added, "Through the teachings of the Honorable Elijah Muhammad, we are taking people off dope, stopping our people from robbing, stealing and hating one another."

Shabazz even granted interviews, something he rarely did. He was asked on public television by a panel of three black journalists if he knew what his followers did outside the temple. "Arresting criminals is not the job of the minister," he replied, "it's the responsibility of the police." He told the panel, "Muslims do many positive things and are the only blacks who are independent of the white man." Repeating a theme often espoused by NOI leaders, that was at least partly based in fact, he said there was a conspiracy in Philadelphia and across the United States to crush and discredit "the works and progress of the Honorable Elijah Muhammad and his followers."

In another interview, asked if Temple 12 collected tithes, he responded, "We're not a church. In our religion every Muslim is urged to give as much as he or she can give." Questioned whether temples were responsible for keeping track of how members make a living, Shabazz said, "No, we don't have any investigative staff. There is no religious group that I know of that has an investigating arm that goes around checking on members to see how they make a living." He went on, "Our ranks are infested with rats and spies and agents provocateurs from the federal, state and local governments. The Honorable Elijah Muhammad warned us that the white man would not allow a religious movement like this to grow and flourish in America unless he had agents and spies among us to report to him our every move."

★

Philadelphia police and other law enforcement authorities amassed evidence against the Black Mafia throughout 1974. With each successful prosecution, getting witnesses to testify became less important. This was because authorities were increasing their intelligence base with the assistance of informants, wiretap and other surveillance efforts, and, perhaps most importantly, documents confiscated during arrests. In August 1974, Philadelphia police executed a search warrant at Black Mafia member George Sampson's home. They found two shotguns, a pistol, twenty-five bags of heroin, and $1,500 in cash. There was added significance to the arrest, and successful prosecution, of Sampson. In addition to the guns and drugs, officers found numbers slips tallying $105,708. They also confiscated several ledgers listing extortion targets and the prices they were paying to the Black Mafia. Many of the targets were prominent numbers bankers.

Daily News reporter Tyree Johnson thought it would be newsworthy to attend a Black Muslim rally inside Temple 12, at 13th and Susquehanna Streets. A few things he witnessed fascinated him. When he entered the temple, he was seated by none other than James Fox. As he sat in one of the armless wooden chairs, he looked around to see approximately 200 people filling the building. Men and women were separated, with women in flowing white robes. On stage were members of the Fruit of Islam flanking their leader, Minister Jeremiah Shabazz, who wore a suit and a bow tie. Shabazz was known outside the mosque as a soft-spoken but articulate orator. Johnson was therefore stunned to see him work the crowd into a frenzy with a stirring talk in the fashion of a fire and brimstone preacher.

At some point, Shabazz recognized Johnson in the crowd. He pointed down at him and announced, "There is one of the people in the media vilifying Black Muslims." In no time, Eugene Hearn, dressed in his FOI uniform, was escorting the reporter from the temple. Shabazz and his Black Mafia henchmen may have sensed the impact Johnson and others were having in the court of public opinion, and had to know they were helping law enforcement with each published article.

*

Following his unsuccessful hit attempt on James Fox, 20th and Carpenter leader Donald Robinson effectively went into hiding. He spent the rest of 1974 staying indoors at night because he could not recognize cars well enough to stay on the street, and cleared furniture from his living room, which had become a target for drive-by shootings. Robinson also at some point decided to become an informant against the Black Mafia, and provided tidbits to Muhammad Kenyatta, who would pass them along to the press and law enforcement as he deemed appropriate. Perhaps the Black Mafia caught wind of this, because by September it was common knowledge that Kenyatta had a price on his head.

In response, Kenyatta altered his routines and made sure his .38 was tucked under his shirt wherever he went. "I don't feel too nervous about the present situation after ten years of the FBI tapping my phone and following me, after living through Klan shootouts and fighting Mississippi bigots," he told one reporter. "After all, the Black Mafia is as American as Gerald Ford. But it is painful for me to speak out against other black folks." Making the point that he and his followers were no pushovers, he added, "We will not sit by and watch someone harm us. We will not try to stop a bullet with a prayer book. We intend to take whatever steps necessary to defend ourselves. Anything that happens to one of us will cause a response from all of us."

Kenyatta's daring actions prompted one columnist to question if he had a death wish. "Why are you challenging the Black Mafia if you fear for your life?" asked one reporter. Kenyatta responded, "Because they're there. They are child killers and somebody has got to put a stop to their activities. Sure, I would rather that someone else did it, but we can't wait for others to stop them. It's our responsibility and our obligation to save the children, so we're doing what we can." He was speaking literally, in reference to the Hanafi murders, and figuratively, of the deleterious effects narcotics were having in the black community. According to him, "Professional adult criminals, especially heroin and cocaine racketeers, have unleashed a reign of terror in ghetto neighborhoods."

Kenyatta kept on all the while receiving clandestine help and information from Donald Robinson. Robinson's older brother was also fighting the Black Mafia behind the scenes. Shortly after Charles "Mickey" Robinson founded the Council for Youth and Community Development in 1970, he left Philadelphia to attend Utah State College. Returning less than a year later, he found the CYCD co-opted by the crowd from Temple 12. Fellow CYCD incorporators James Fox and Russell Barnes were dealing drugs and shaking people down with new pals like Sam Christian and Ron Harvey. As far as Robinson was concerned, "They were misusing Islam." Mickey Robinson opted out and had an acrimonious relationship with James Fox for the next few years.

Donald Robinson and his gang still intermittently battled with the Black Mafia too. As their conflict escalated at certain points throughout 1973-74, the car belonging to Mickey Robinson's mother was firebombed and his wife was shot, leaving her paralyzed from the waist down. In March 1974, Mickey Robinson voluntarily went to the Philadelphia DEA office to offer his services in crushing the Black Mafia. He told them he had two motives: he was concerned for his family's safety after Fox had intimidated members of his family, particularly his mother; and he wanted to help control the drug traffic, which he considered to be a threat to young African-Americans. A court later said that Robinson was also bothered that Fox was manipulating "several youth organizations, in which both men had been involved, by using them as a base for the narcotics trade." Investigators were delighted; they finally had a chance to crack the syndicate wide open. Intimidation had stalled most investigations, and these failures were only adding to the Black Mafia's street rep, resulting in yet more extortion and terror.

Mickey Robinson soon began immersing himself in the Black Mafia's vast drug network. Intelligence generated from his efforts and elsewhere provided the legal basis for getting wiretaps on phones. The best information was gleaned from twenty days of intercepts beginning on 15 May 1974. The DEA arrangement with Robinson also involved a series of telephone calls made by him, in the presence of agents, that were monitored and recorded. Robinson talked on the phone about drug trafficking with a host of Black Mafia men, including James Fox, Russell Barnes, Barthaniel Thornton, Ferris Foster, and Herschel Williams. In one taped conversation, Fox told Robinson, "We get the B's [bundles of heroin] because we wholesale." Following some of the conversations, narcotics buys were made by Robinson from Williams, Thornton and Foster, who were Fox's associates.

The investigation went on for months before a federal grand jury indicted Black Mafia leaders Eugene "Bo" Baynes, James Fox, Eugene Hearn, Russell Barnes, and four other affiliates on 11 September 1974 for their involvement in a "massive drug distribution ring" selling heroin and cocaine. DEA intelligence estimated that, from 1972 through 1974, the Black Mafia accounted "for over 60% of the heroin distribution in Philadelphia." Additionally, the DEA concluded the Black Mafia ring "controlled virtually all of the heroin traffic in South and West Philadelphia," made considerable inroads into the North Philadelphia market, and that independent traffickers "either paid tribute to [the Black Mafia] for the right to sell heroin or they met a violent end."

Agents of the DEA and the Bureau of Alcohol, Tobacco and Firearms, joined by Philadelphia police and members of the Justice Department's organized crime and racketeering strike force, arrested sixteen Black Mafia members, including Baynes, Fox, Barnes and Hearn, in early morning raids on September 16. The sweep was hailed by DEA chief John R. Bartels, Jr.

as "the breakup of Philadelphia's infamous Black Mafia, an all-black crime syndicate dealing in narcotics, gun trafficking and murder." DEA regional director Arthur Lewis said the group also passed counterfeit money. The following day saw the arrest of more conspirators, including BBI runner and leader Clarence "Squeaky" Hayman, who was arrested for gun trafficking. The raids uncovered a large quantity of heroin. Another series of arrests were made on September 23. Following his arrest, Russell Barnes confessed to being a contract killer for the Black Mafia.

The arrests resulted in three trials. The first ended with the conviction of Herschell Williams, who received a sentence of six months in prison and eight years of parole probation. The third trial was the main show, with the Black Mafia leadership – Bo Baynes, James Fox, Russell Barnes, Eugene Hearn – and four others facing serious prison terms. The lively trial lasted three weeks, included some great exchanges between the prosecution and defense teams, and featured Robinson's testimony and the revelations on the taped conversations. During one recess outside the courtroom, Russell Barnes approached reporter Tyree Johnson and caustically accused him of "working with the devil." Two of the defendants pleaded guilty before the major trial, and a jury found the others each guilty on 1 February 1975 of engaging in a conspiracy to distribute heroin.

As the sentencing phase began, the testy and hyperbolic rants from prosecutors and defense attorneys continued, including one exchange between the Assistant U.S. Attorney for the Strike Force, David J. McKeon, and Eugene Hearn's attorney, the high-profile Nino Tinari. Tinari told the court that Hearn had "come upon religion" and should thus have been spared a lengthy sentence. McKeon retorted, "Rather than spreading religion, he's spreading the destruction of society." Bo Baynes had already been sentenced to four months' imprisonment in October 1974 for providing false statements to the Internal Revenue Service, and on March 25, he and Fox were sentenced to twenty-seven and thirty years, respectively. Barnes was sentenced to twenty-one years, and Hearn to fifteen. Charles "Mickey" Robinson entered the federal witness protection program, received a new name and was relocated to Arizona with his wife and family.

There was also a strong rumor that Charles Robinson was not the only one talking to the cops. In October 1974, Tyree Johnson ran a story in the *Daily News* that stated Black Mafia founding member Roosevelt "Spooks" Fitzgerald, who often used his Muslim last name Bey, was "a key government witness" against the recently arrested mobsters. Reliable sources told him that Fitzgerald was stripped of his leadership at the temple when suspicions arose that he was informing. The sources said "Fitzgerald, his wife and six children" were "under heavy government guard in another city." If true, this was a coup for law enforcement, since Fitzgerald was close to the two most significant players: he was a close associate of Sam Christian, and a confidant of Jeremiah Shabazz, at one point heading the FOI guard in

Temple 12. Fitzgerald contacted the *Daily News* the day the story ran, stating, "I've never done anything like that, and I never will." He confirmed he had been demoted within Temple 12 and that he had not attended in months, but declined to say why. Beyond the accusation in Johnson's article, there has never been any evidence of cooperation between Fitzgerald and law enforcement.

During the course of its six-month investigation, the DEA had discovered the Black Mafia was importing heroin, cocaine and marijuana from Jamaica. For years, it was assumed their heroin arrived primarily from New York and the cocaine from Atlanta. The change may have been due to events in New York, namely the suppression of the Frank Matthews network. It was yet another example of how confounded law enforcement was when it came to this supposedly new phenomenon of African-American organized crime. There was little, if any, coordinated effort between regional offices of federal agencies when it came to groups like Philadelphia's Black Mafia. Their missions were still dominated by a focus on Italian-American organized crime.

The successful prosecution of the Black Mafia elite was noteworthy for many reasons. The cases were developed by the region's D.O.J. organized crime and racketeering strike force, which used details from a key informant – who went into the federal witness protection program – to help form the legal basis for court-authorized wiretaps. The strike force concept, an outgrowth of the 1967 Task Force on Organized Crime, was just coming into its own, and wiretaps for non-national security matters were made possible by the Omnibus Crime Control and Safe Streets Act of 1968. Lastly, the federal witness protection program was an element of the 1970 Organized Crime Control Act. Collectively, the legislative efforts against organized crime spawned in the late 1960s provided an array of new tools and resources to combat organized crime. These would be refined and implemented on a grand scale nationwide, with great success from the mid-1970s onwards. One could reasonably argue the Black Mafia came onto the racketeering scene at the worst time, since they missed most of the organized crime heyday that followed World War II and ran through the early 1970s. Law enforcement was primed to vanquish entire syndicates in major U.S. cities, and to greatly reduce the importance of others for good.

The Black Mafia were also paying the price for crafting their organization exclusively as a "power syndicate." Academics use this term when referring to crime organizations that offer few, if any, goods or services the public desires, such as prostitution, gambling, and black market products. Power syndicates simply extort illicit entrepreneurs, shake down and rob other individuals and businesses – and make a lot of enemies. Philadelphia's Black Mafia brought nothing but mayhem and fear to the ghetto, all the while draining blighted African-American neighborhoods of what little capital resided there. Even if one were to consider the dumping of massive quantities of heroin and cocaine into these communities as providing a wanted commodity, drug supply is not tolerated as much by the criminal justice system or the community as are other rackets. In sum, the Black Mafia had plenty of people, not to mention law enforcement agencies, constantly pressing for their demise.

When the Black Mafia was predominantly extorting drug dealers rather than taking part in the trade itself, this was prudent, because it largely spared them from prosecution. Prosecuting cases involving the extortion of drug peddlers is problematic because the dealers are properly apprehensive about taking their case to the authorities. In the rare event a drug dealer approached law enforcement to file a criminal complaint alleging extortion of their illicit trade, something made possible by the 1970 RICO statute, prosecutors typically force the victim to admit to their crimes. Prosecutors are always wary of putting a dubious complainant or witness on the stand, let alone one susceptible to having his or her credibility destroyed if their dubious backgrounds are disclosed at trial. Therefore prosecution teams almost always insist on a vigorous vetting. There is also a great reluctance to grant such persons immunity because their offenses are considered far more damaging to society than those of, say, a numbers writer. Not only does society treat drug dealing as a serious offense, the narcotics trade often involves violence and therefore many drug dealers have histories that preclude a U.S. Attorney, for example, from providing immunity from prosecution for those offenses. This process collectively trends heavily against drug dealers becoming complainants in extortion cases. In fact, it would take a remarkable set of circumstances to have a drug dealer come forward as a viable prosecution witness, and these cases are thus very rare.

The Black Mafia leadership made a fatal, though predictable, mistake when they leapt into the narcotics trade. Dissatisfied with merely taxing the trade and taking a percentage, they got greedy and commandeered the majority of the heroin market and a large percentage of the cocaine market. Now law enforcement was no longer burdened with developing witnesses or victims who were shaken down, or worse, and getting them confident enough to testify. Furthermore, criminal sanctions have always been stringent for narcotics offenses.

DEA head Arthur Lewis credibly claimed the successful prosecutions of Baynes, Fox, Barnes, Hearn and Co. "crippled the very top leadership" of the Black Mafia, and said the cases were bound to have national implications, considering the syndicate's lofty spot in the drug trade. The successful prosecutions augmented the guilty verdicts against the Hanafi killers in May 1974 in Washington, and the collective effect was a body blow to the Black Mafia. These two cases were in addition those successfully pressed against Sam Christian and Ron Harvey in the previous year, and by late 1974 the vast majority of the heavy-hitting Black Mafia founders were either dead or in prison.

However, there were still significant men on the street, notably Roosevelt Fitzgerald and Larry Starks. Law enforcement intelligence got mixed messages on which of the two, if either, was heading the new iteration of the Black Mafia following the massive arrests. Needless to say, the blitzkrieg of arrests vaulted the group – again – into the news, and ingrained them into the city's psyche. When the Ernest Kelly robbery and kidnapping trial took place in October, and the threats to his family continued, the public became more outraged. For many organized crime groups, this much "heat" would be too much to withstand, but the Black Mafia was still a viable crime outfit, however withered, as plenty of victims –and witnesses – would soon discover.

CHAPTER 15

CELL BLOCK D AND THE HOODLUM MOSQUE

WHILE THE AUTHORITIES were building a case against the Black Mafia, one of the syndicate's own was playing a risky game of cat and mouse with his compatriots and the federal government. In May 1973, Charles "Bubbles" Price, *aka* James 77X, was arrested in Philadelphia on a firearms charge. On June 7, Amina Khaalis identified him as one of the killers in the Hanafi massacre. In addition to weapons and multiple murder charges, Price faced charges on several Philadelphia offenses, including robberies and a murder. He was in a jam. So, throughout May and June, Price met clandestinely with federal prosecutors in motels in remote areas of Pennsylvania and Maryland to vet a possible deal. Finally, on June 21, Price and his wife Josephine met prosecutors to discuss a formal agreement to testify for the government. The following day, he was placed in protective custody and transferred from Philadelphia to Washington, D.C.

On July 3, James Price gave a scintillating, forty-five-page, handwritten confession that spelled out his involvement in the Hanafi massacre. The lengthy and detailed statement also identified the seven men who joined in the slaughter, along with their explicit roles. Perhaps most importantly, the statement was said to have named whoever gave the orders to kill Hamaas Abdul Khaalis in the first place. Price affirmed his confession before the Hanafi grand jury on July 5, and in return, federal authorities promised him a variety of goodies if he repeated the assertions at trial, including a substantially reduced sentence and protection for him, Josephine ("Sister Josephine" to most), and their children. Price's court-appointed defense attorneys, however, were never convinced he would go through with his promise to testify and proceeded under the assumption that he would need a defense. Thus, they "maintained the secrecy of Price's status – in order not to jeopardize either his life or the future performance of his plea bargain." Though there was a lot of circumstantial evidence, it was Price's confession that solidified the case against the eight conspirators, resulting in indictments being returned by the grand jury on August 5.

Almost immediately after cutting a deal with the Government, Price and his wife became displeased with various aspects of their pact, and quarrelled with the U.S. attorneys who had brokered the agreement. Sister Josephine was never sold on the idea, especially the need to relocate under new names, and her close relationship with Jeremiah Shabazz didn't make matters easier. She worked in a Shabazz bakery and was firmly established in the local Black Muslim community.

James Price was primarily concerned about safety for himself and his family. When he agreed to cooperate with the Feds, he was placed in different institutions to his co-defendants. This troubled Price greatly because he thought it would alert them to his role as a witness, and he pleaded to be put in a prison with them. His fears were soon aggravated by a leak to the press.

Though the Hanafi charges were addressed in his deal with the FBI, Price still faced numerous charges in Philadelphia. When federal authorities contacted the Philadelphia District Attorney's Office to give Price immunity against the local charges, they were unexpectedly rebuffed. Even worse for Price, someone in the D.A.'s Office leaked word of Price's cooperation in the Hanafi case to the Philadelphia press, resulting in articles published in August 1973 discussing his role as a cooperating witness. Though Price was segregated and, theoretically, safe in prison, Sister Josephine and his kids were living an otherwise regular life in Philadelphia – and thus were at risk – as word spread about his duplicity. Price begged to be housed with his "Black Muslim brothers" so that he could explain to them in person that the news articles were wrong and that he was not an informer. Prosecutors and prison officials at first rejected his proposals, but gave in when he consented to signing a waiver effectively acknowledging the dangerous game he was playing by re-entering the general prison population.

Price's decision was unbelievably risky. From November 1973, he roomed on several occasions with different co-defendants. On the outside, his family was intermittently under protection as Josephine wavered back and forth between accepting security and remaining in the neighborhood. In December, at Price's request, he was transferred to Philadelphia's Detention Center, where Theodore Moody was housed and where Price shared a cell with John Clark before each man was brought back to the D.C. area for the Hanafi trial in February 1974.

On the first day of the trial, one of Price's defense attorneys walked into the D.C. Superior Courthouse in the company of another defendant's attorney. When Price's lawyer started toward the prosecutor's office instead of toward the courtroom, the other lawyer said, "We're supposed to go this way." Price's attorney confirmed for the first time what the Black Mafia defense team had suspected for months when he responded, "Sorry, I'm going the other way." It was official: Price was cooperating with the Government. Price had, in fact, been severed from the trial on February 6 and would face his own trial.

The Black Mafia defense team asked the judge to throw the case out because there had been an "enemy in their camp," since Price was often incarcerated with his co-defendants. The judge, however, accepted the Government's word that Price provided no information about the defense team's strategy during his plea negotiations. Predictably, the revelations startled and enraged the Black Mafia defendants, and security precautions were heightened further still. U.S. Marshals guarded the judge and prosecutors, and police minded Price's attorneys, one of whom slept with a shotgun under his bed. Josephine Price and her kids were still in harm's way in Philadelphia, however. She received threatening phone calls and her children were taken to a Black Muslim mosque for "safekeeping."

Next, James Price was "visited" in prison by an attorney named David Pasha. Pasha told authorities he was Josephine Price's attorney and that he wanted to visit her husband and serve as his counsel too. The day after their meeting, Pasha filed a motion on Price's behalf that stated, among other things, that Price denied having ever given a statement and claimed to have no knowledge, whatsoever, of the facts in the indictments against him or the other defendants. Furthermore, the motion stated that Price wanted to replace his two court-appointed attorneys with Pasha as his sole counsel. As the judge considered the motion, it was disclosed that Pasha was, in fact, the Minister of Cincinnati's Temple 5 and also worked out of Philadelphia's Temple 12 on occasion. There was no David Pasha listed as a member of any bar, and the court learned that this was because Pasha was licensed under his "slave" name, David Bradley. Elijah Muhammad had given him the name Pasha. Furthermore, Pasha had previously "represented" Ron Harvey, one of the men against whom Price had testified. The Government concluded this was a blatant NOI effort to intimidate Price and obstruct justice. The judge ruled against allowing Pasha to represent Price, though he did acquiesce and appointed new counsel.

Price's decisions were no doubt influenced by a not-so-veiled threat sent to him over the public airwaves the day he first met with David Pasha. During a national radio broadcast titled "The Opponents of Muhammad," a rising NOI Minister named Louis X. Farrakhan declared, "Let this be a warning to the opponents of Muhammad. Let this be a warning to those of you who would be used as an instrument of a wicked government against … our rise … Be careful, because when the Government is tired of using you … they're going to dump you back in the laps of your people. And though Elijah Muhammad is a merciful man and will say, 'Come in,' and forgive you, yet in the ranks of black people today there are younger men and women rising up who have no forgiveness in them for traitors and stool pigeons … And they will execute you, as soon as your identity is known. Be careful because nothing shall prevent the rise of the messiah, the Nation of Islam and the black man the world over."

When Price was called to testify on April 17, he refused and was held in contempt of court. The case against Jerome Sinclair was substantially weakened because it relied heavily on Price's statement. With the prosecution's plan to use Price's testimony to tie Sinclair to the other defendants thwarted, the trial judge acquitted Sinclair of all charges. However, the four other defendants were found guilty, partly as a result of Price's earlier sworn testimony, and received *de facto* life terms in prison. It was difficult to gauge the Black Mafia's reaction to Price's role in the prosecution, however, because following the trial he was still often housed with his co-defendants. In June 1974, Price wound up in Philadelphia's Black Muslim-dominated Holmesburg Prison, formerly run by the Black Mafia's Clarence Fowler.

Fowler had been transferred from Holmesburg Prison to the State Correctional Institution at Graterford in October 1973. His leadership role in Holmesburg's Black Muslim cellblock D was replaced by Hanafi murderer and Brother Lieutenant John Clark, who ran the block with a man named Theodore X. Brown. Brown was also a lieutenant in the NOI and therefore was in constant contact with Black Mafia members in the prison. While in Holmesburg, Brown wanted to end discussions that were critical of Elijah Muhammad and the Nation. A Hanafi Muslim prisoner named Samuel Molten, an outspoken critic of the Black Muslims, was undeterred – if not emboldened – by the experience of Hamaas Abdul Khaalis, and kept bashing The Messenger. In response, Theodore X. Brown, along with three other inmates, plotted his murder. On 17 August 1973, the NOI crew used a sharpened screwdriver to stab Molten up to fifty-four times.

When James Price was transferred to Holmesburg, he requested to be placed in D block. In addition to serving as a refuge for Black Muslims, D block was a maximum security area of the prison, meaning that inmates there were not permitted to leave it, and other inmates were not permitted to enter it without an institutional escort. Four of the Black Mafia Hanafi murderers Price had testified against were on the block at that time: John Clark, Theodore Moody, William Christian and John Griffin. All four were in Holmesburg awaiting trials for murders unrelated to the Hanafi case. Strangely, Moody and Price were cellmates, even though there were thirty-seven vacant cells in D block. Price was in Holmesburg awaiting the myriad of local charges against him, while his trial for the Hanafi murders was scheduled for February 1975. He was also due to appear before the D.C. grand jury looking into crimes emanating from the Hanafi murders, and he was expected to be pressed on who ordered the murders.

The morning of Sunday, 29 December 1974 started as usual for the forty-nine inmates of Holmesburg's cellblock D. James Price and his Black Muslim brothers generally woke before 8 A.M., mopped their cells, and found their way to the exercise yard for "yard out." Typically, they would play basketball, run, box and march, and the Black Muslim ministers would often demand turnouts for more formal routines. On this particular morning, after assembling in formation, the Black Muslims ran laps while singing and chanting in cadence. At about 8:30 that morning, a non-Muslim inmate named Calvin Hunter was transferred into D block for disciplinary reasons, and was not permitted to join the others outside in the yard. Hunter was among the four or five people left in the cellblock, including a few guards, when he heard a commotion approaching his cell, number 453, at around 9 A.M. It was otherwise very quiet inside with everyone else out in the yard, so Hunter got up off his bunk and went to the edge of his cell to see what was coming down the block.

Theodore Moody, John Griffin and Theodore Brown were tussling with James Price and escorting him down the block as if they were in a football huddle, with Price in the middle. Soon after the four men passed Hunter's cell, he heard the sounds of a scuffle, a metal bed frame screeching against the floor, and the loud cries of James Price.

"Help! They're killing me!"

Price's yelps bounced off the concrete walls and floors of the cellblock, but no help came. The screaming of words quickly turned to high-pitched shrieks as Price was brutally assaulted. In moments, the screams and screeches from cell number 457 ended. As the three henchmen paraded back past Hunter's cell, he called to John Griffin, "Hey, Griff, what's all that noise?"

Griffin tersely replied, "Nothing that concerns you," and kept walking.

The rest of the day went on as usual, according to the three guards assigned to D block. Following yard out, the inmates returned for lunch when one of the guards brought the food cart back to the block around noon. Most went to the showers in preparation for the 1 P.M. temple service. After the one-hour service, many D block residents went to watch the Los Angeles Rams play the Minnesota Vikings on television. At 3 P.M. the guards changed shift, and five minutes later a guard who had just come on duty was making the usual rounds when he found the body of James Price in the unoccupied, unlocked cell 457, hanging by seven intertwined strands of white cloth from a ventilation grate. A pool of blood was on the floor directly beneath him. Price was in prison garb: blue denim-type jacket and pants, gray sweatshirt, thermal underwear, white wool socks with orange and black piping, and brown high-top boots. The guard felt his body; it was cold and already somewhat stiff. Price had been dead for several hours. The guard flagged down a colleague and they cut the body down from the grate.

Price had been badly beaten about the face, and his testicles were crushed and filled with blood. This accounted for the cries heard early in the assault. The chilling shrieking Calvin Hunter heard, it turned out, was

Price having a knife or other sharp metal object inserted into his rectum. The formal cause of death, however, was strangulation. Three strands of black shoelaces taken from high-top boots were braided together and used to kill Price.

Before Price's body was discovered, Calvin Hunter sat down and wrote to someone outside the prison expressing his angst over what he saw and heard, and about the fact that the murderers knew he was the only witness. The letter, dated "Morning 10:am, 12-29-74", reads in part (in Hunter's exact words):

> Today, I got into a arguement with a guard and now I have to have what they call a special hearing. The only bad thing about it they transferred me to "D" Block where they keep all the "Black Muslims" and I heard this man hollaring help there trying to kill me! in the back, and now they just took someone out in the back cell and it could be they killed him this morning. I seen two of them back there, but got to stop now because I'm scare now because I don't want no part of this because you know what happens to people that tell on Muslims … My nerves are shot …

In fact, Hunter spoke with the authorities that afternoon and was immediately put in secure custody. Calvin Hunter was eventually transferred to another facility, and was the lead witness against the three murderers, who were each convicted of first-degree murder.

The fact that no prison guards responded to James Price's dying screams raised suspicions of complicity. "For the guards to say they weren't in on the crime or knew nothing about what was going on defies logic," said one prosecutor. No guards were ever prosecuted, but three were sanctioned, though not for failing to hear the screams, see the assassins, or discover his bludgeoned body hanging in a cell for hours. Rather, they were suspended for failing to lock unoccupied cells. Price's wife, Josephine, unsuccessfully sued the city for creating "an unsafe environment" and failing "to properly guard" him.

James Price was actually the second government witness in the Hanafi case to die prematurely. In September 1974, a Black Muslim named Marvin Greer was found dead a few months after he had testified that Theodore Moody had used his identification to buy the car for him to travel to the Khaalis home. Greer had a history of drug use, so when he was found with a single puncture mark in his arm, the authorities speculated his death was a simple overdose. Nevertheless, a probe into his death commenced because of his role in the Hanafi case, but no evidence was found of murder.

The remarkable trail of death that began with the January 1973 Hanafi murders in Washington and wended its bloody way through Holmesburg Prison did not end there. Shortly after Calvin Hunter had testified against

Price's three assailants, he was placed on six years' probation. Before being released from prison, a judge implored Hunter to take the state's offer of protection because of the "reputation of the Black Muslims," but Hunter refused, prompting the judge to say that by going back on the street, Hunter was effectively signing his own death warrant. Sure enough, Calvin Hunter was found dead inside his North Philadelphia home in late April 1975. His body was on the bathroom floor with fresh needle marks in it, suggesting that Hunter, who had a long history of drug abuse, had shot up one too many times. Though there was justifiable suspicion about his death so soon after returning to the street, police determined he died of an accidental heroin overdose.

Throughout all of these events, the question remained: who ordered the Hanafi murders? Was it simply John Clark, or Ron Harvey, acting alone, or were they under orders from above. Speculation, of course, focused on Elijah Muhammad and Jeremiah Shabazz. The two were close, longtime friends, and it was not a stretch of the imagination that if one wanted something done, the other would gladly oblige. Hamaas Abdul Khaalis always believed the order originated with Elijah Muhammad in Chicago, but, like everyone else who made such educated guesses, Khaalis didn't have a single piece of hard evidence. News accounts of James Price's detailed confession intimated that he named Jeremiah Shabazz as the one who ordered the killings, but his confession has never been seen by the public. As a federal prosecutor said following the string of related deaths, "The investigation really died with Price. Now, we'll probably never be able to prove who ordered the deaths."

★

The January 1975 issue of *Philadelphia Magazine* placed Bo Baynes on its list of "75 people to watch in 1975." Yet Baynes's associates faced torrid times. The Black Mafia, now led by Lonnie Dawson, was still adjusting to the new order following the massive arrests in late 1974 when word broke out of New York about the Frank Matthews organization. Two factors had contributed to a fundamental shift in the international traffic in narcotics in the early 1970s: the Turkish Government began limiting the production of opium in 1968, and banned opium poppy growing entirely on 30 June 1972; and the French Government suppressed heroin production in Marseilles, putting an end to the infamous French Connection. This hit the Frank Matthews organization just as it began crumbling following Matthews's arrest in January 1973. These events altered the heroin market in the U.S., and soon "H" was coming in not from Europe but from Mexico. The Black Mafia adapted by splitting time between making their traditional runs to New York and sending couriers out West.

Another series of arrests effectively ended the Matthews organization for good in January 1975. John Darby, along with numerous remaining members of the group, was indicted by a Brooklyn federal grand jury for "conspiring between September, 1968, and January, 1975, to import into the United States, and to distribute and possess with intent to distribute, substantial quantities of heroin and cocaine" in the black communities of Philadelphia, Boston, New York, Newark and Baltimore. Federal officials called the group the largest in the country selling predominantly to African-Americans. The Government considered Darby a "key lieutenant" in the Matthews mob, who "supervised the distribution of narcotics in Pennsylvania." The Darby connection was vital to Black Mafia markets, and thus the New York case forced what remained of the syndicate to shop elsewhere again. In no time, the majority of heroin was coming in from Los Angeles, and one of the main architects of the deals was the Black Mafia's Robert Blair. According to a DEA spokesman, the product was Mexican brown heroin, and "contrary to popular belief" it was being used just as much as it was in 1970 during the drug's heyday.

Following the grand-scale prosecutions of Black Mafia members in late 1974, and after the massive case in New York City involving Philadelphia suppliers from the Matthews organization, another blow to the group occurred when the Honorable Elijah Muhammad died on 25 February 1975. In Muhammad's last years, his control over the national chain of mosques had waned considerably, allowing Philadelphia's Black Mafia to enjoy relative freedom. The NOI leadership, however, kept watch and simmered. The regional Department of Justice Strike Force received intelligence as far back as September 1973 that the "Black Muslim headquarters in Chicago was considering wiping out the Philadelphia Muslim Mosque because of the great deal of bad publicity they had brought upon the Muslims." One of reporter Jim Nicholson's sources told him that "Chicago" was not upset over commission of the high-profile crimes such as the Hanafi and Coxson murders, "but rather the sin of getting caught." Following the death of Elijah Muhammad, the Black Muslim movement fragmented. The Messenger had handpicked his successor before he died, his forty-two-year-old son, Wallace D. Muhammad, who began a series of reforms called the "Second Resurrection." He transformed the Nation religiously, organizationally, and politically.

The reforms were more in line with the teachings of Malcolm X, who, following a pilgrimage to Mecca, had split from the NOI because he favored incorporating all ethnic groups into the Mosque. "What was taught yesterday was yesterday's message," said one of Wallace's spokesmen. "Now we are evolving where the Nation will be open to anyone regardless of race, color or creed. There will be no such category as a white or black Muslim. All will be Muslims. All will be the children of God." Wallace Muhammad disbanded the Fruit of Islam and eventually changed the name of the sect to the World Community of Al-Islam in the West. "In the old days, we had to appeal to the Superfly mentality," said the editor of *Muhammad Speaks*. "The message had to be very dramatic. You couldn't just tell the people we were recruiting that they should pray five times a day to Mecca. That would have been too austere."

The Second Resurrection reforms swept through Philadelphia, where the local temple was referred to nationally as the "Hoodlum Mosque." Philadelphia's Black Muslim population fell precipitously. One writer concluded, "Apparently, after years of being told by the late Elijah Muhammad that 'all' whites couldn't be trusted and were the source of their degradation, many members dropped out rather than accept the possibility of sitting next to a white in the temple." Most importantly, Jeremiah Shabazz was put on notice that the days of criminality and attendant publicity must end or his rule over Temple 12 would be abruptly terminated.

The war of words between Philadelphia's Black Muslims and the media continued when the *Philadelphia Inquirer's* TODAY magazine permitted a member of Temple 12 to write the cover story of its April 27 issue. Sterling X. Hobbs wrote a tribute entitled "The Young Muslims" featuring the education programs and other positive community efforts espoused by Minister Jeremiah Shabazz and his followers. Incredibly, days after his story appeared, Hobbs killed a liquor store clerk in Delaware during the commission of a robbery. Nevertheless, the Hobbs piece drew the following letter to the paper's editor.

I read your article about the Black Muslims with great interest because I am black, and live in a part of the city where the Muslims are quite strong. I believe the author was quite correct when he said the daily media have only told one side of the Muslim story – the bad side. The same is also true, though, of the media's handling of all poor and powerless minorities. The author, though, makes the same mistake by going to the other extreme. By presenting the Muslims as a group of honest, dedicated persons deeply concerned about the uplifting of the black community, he may be fooling the white readers of the *Inquirer*, but those of us who have to live in the same community with them know that the author is 'jiving,' to put it mildly. The Black Mafia has a record of terror, drug-trafficking and assassination in our community that is unmatched anywhere west of Vietnam; the fact that the Black Mafia is made up entirely of Muslims, with the tacit approval of the Muslim leadership, is well known by anyone in the black community with two eyes and a brain, as well as by all law enforcement personnel. All of the Black Mafia leaders who were recently sentenced to long terms in federal court here for running the heroin game in North and South Philly admitted they were Muslims, as were dozens of others, and every person in North Philly over the age of 10 knows that this blood money is used to fuel all the lucrative Muslim enterprises. If you call this black pride, then we are all living in a lunatic asylum. Please don't use my name. I don't want to end up like Bubbles Price and Calvin Hunter (two men who died after crossing paths with the Black Muslims).

★

Herschell Williams was out on bail for the March 1974 shooting witnessed by Tyree Johnson when he was arrested on April 30, along with syndicate members Donnie Day and Nathaniel Pittman, for attempting to extort $10,000 from the owner of the Dreamland Café in Lawnside, New Jersey. A few weeks earlier, Williams and four other Black Mafia members had been seen with Dreamland's doorman, Franklin Robinson, just before he was found dead of an overdose in a vacant North Philadelphia lot. It was the latest black eye for Temple 12, but fortunately for Jeremiah Shabazz, only local media covered the story. Shabazz knew that Wallace D. Muhammad and the new leadership in Chicago were closely monitoring events out of No. 12. He had an opportunity to demonstrate his influence in the prison system on May 20, when Philadelphia's Superintendent of Prisons, Louis Aytch, called upon him to end a hunger strike in Holmesburg Prison. A third of the prison's inmates, all Black Muslims, were taking part in a hunger strike following the disciplining of an inmate. Shabazz successfully ended the dispute, but had little time to enjoy the favorable publicity.

Minister Jeremiah and his Temple 12 followers were again the focus of media disdain in the June 5 issue of *New York Magazine*. The magazine's feature story dealt with the crime epidemic in black communities, and included the following analysis of the Philadelphia situation: "It is no secret that if there is any [Black Muslim] temple that has all but gone out of control, it's Philadelphia. Some Muslim sources refer to it as the 'hit mosque.' It is one temple where the rehabilitation of Muslim converts seems to have failed miserably. Philadelphia gang members, long considered the most vicious gang-bangers in the country, have put an X behind their names and have hidden behind the shield of the Nation while pursuing their former trades."

While Shabazz fretted over the likely response from headquarters in Chicago, the Black Mafia suffered another significant loss. By the summer of 1975, Jerome Barnes had lost some of his reputation on the street to the younger guns in the group. Nevertheless, the founding Black Mafia member and enforcer still oversaw numbers and narcotics rackets in South and West Philly. He was standing at the corner of 13th and Kater Streets in his South Philly territory late in the evening of June 15 when a man walked up behind him and pumped a single bullet into the back of his head. Barnes died three days later, just as authorities were piecing together the case and trying to identify the shooter. Given the numerous enemies he had created over the years, the possibilities were many. For the past decade, Black Mafia members had weathered street warfare with much success. It was therefore noteworthy that someone took the liberty of killing one of the group's founders so blatantly. Police received information that a man named Harold Williams had been repeatedly shaken down by Barnes and was exacting revenge for the show of disrespect. Though Williams was charged with murder, a jury acquitted him after his defense attorney successfully argued, "Everybody in the neighborhood wanted to kill this man because of the type of individual he was." The attorney also introduced Barnes' lengthy criminal record into evidence, including the fact that he had been charged in three murder cases and cleared each time when witnesses were too afraid to testify. The Black Mafia infrastructure soon took another hit weeks later, when Philadelphia's NOI leader received unexpected news.

CHAPTER 16 ★
THE JOLLY GREEN GIANT

NO DOUBT AS a response to the criminal activities mentioned in the June *New York* article, and the media coverage of them, Temple 12 leader Jeremiah Shabazz was "promoted" by Wallace D. Muhammad to Eastern Regional Minister for the Nation of Islam on 1 July 1975. Shabazz was now in theory in charge of all temples in New York, Philadelphia, Harrisburg, Atlantic City (NJ) and other smaller cities in the area, and split his time between New York and Philadelphia. Black Muslim insiders, however, considered the move an effort to reduce his influence in the gangster-plagued Temple 12. An FBI teletype dated July 2 noted that informants told their handlers in the Bureau the move was "to break up Black Mafia group in Phila. This is not considered promotion for Pugh [Shabazz]." Within weeks, the FBI office in Chicago noted that an informant "stated Wallace Muhammad is desiring to rid the NOI of criminal elements using the NOI as a shield and hopes to re-emphasize religion and economic endeavors therein."

A short while later, the Black Mafia lost one its better minds when Black Brothers, Inc. secretary David "Scoogie" Mitchell was killed. Unusually, Mitchell's death, on July 28, was unrelated to his involvement with the Black Mafia. Rather, he was shot by his brother during an argument. Meanwhile, if Shabazz was surprised by his "promotion" within the NOI following Wallace Muhammad's edicts about criminality and bad publicity, he had to be shell-shocked when he saw the *Philadelphia Inquirer's* front page of 24 August 1975.

Philadelphia's main newspaper featured a heavy-hitting article titled, "Now the Black Mafia Bilks Banks." The lengthy piece was again written by Mike Leary, who had been tracking Black Mafia developments for almost two years. He examined the syndicate's multifarious white-collar crime operations, which included credit card and checking scams. Though some of the scams had started years before, authorities were just beginning to penetrate their complexities. Leary focused on one involving "the Muslim-run Crescent Furniture Co." Just like the Pyramid Enterprises scam from a few years prior, Crescent was used as a dummy corporation that "employed" Black Mafia members as "outside salesmen." They used this employment status to open bank accounts under aliases. The Crescent scandal was more complex than the Pyramid con, and operated out of Merrill Ferguson's home. The conspiracy began in late 1973 with Black Mafia characters opening numerous checking accounts at different banks. They were shrewd enough to open so-called "cashmatic" accounts, so that when their checks started bouncing, rather than getting flagged right away, the overcharges would simply get registered as loans to the account holder. It worked like a charm.

Next came an ingenious scam. Burglars stole corporate checks belonging to a number of corporations – along with the rubber stamps that company treasurers used to endorse checks – from an office building in West Philadelphia. Even more impressively, the checks were only taken from the backs of check pads, so that the thefts would go unnoticed until after they had been misused. Crescent was but one of the "companies" in the scam and, remarkably, Pyramid Enterprises was also used again. There were many scams taking place, including depositing the stolen corporate checks into the bogus personal accounts the members had set up, which were then used to cut personal checks for a variety of purposes.

The Black Mafia, led mostly by a heroin dealer and Temple 12 member named Thomas Trotter, continued renting cars and not returning them, and purchased any number of niceties befitting the big-time hustlers they were. Trotter, like many of his brethren, enjoyed the fruits of his labor only so long, and authorities never got to interview him about his crimes. On 27 October 1974, he was found with a .9mm bullet in his head, dumped in a bushy, weed-covered area in the rear of the 6500 block of Cherokee Street. The case was never solved.

The Crescent Furniture-induced scams kept bubbling to the surface throughout 1975, resulting in more arrests, more revelations, and inducing Leary to write the article. Some, including Minister Shabazz, claimed the article was, at a minimum, inflammatory because of language such as "Muslim-run." On August 28, between 800 and 1,000 Muslims and their supporters picketed the offices of the *Philadelphia Inquirer* in response to the article. Shabazz said the reference to the Black Mafia as "Black Muslim-dominated" sparked the protest. This was curious, however, since the paper had used exactly the same phrase in an article more than a year earlier without incident. It was possible Shabazz knew the unflattering publicity would not be tolerated by Wallace Muhammad and therefore went into damage-control mode. He demanded that the *Inquirer* retract the article, give the Black Muslims equal space for rebuttal, and end "religious persecution against the Muslims." Incredibly, three of the participants in the rally were facing lengthy prison sentences. Donald Abney and Alonzo Robinson (*aka* Lorenzo Taylor) were out on bail while appealing their federal court convictions on the Nookie's Tavern case, and each was in his blue FOI uniform as he marched. Sterling X. Hobbs was also in the crowd, despite being wanted in Delaware at the time for the May 5 murder of the liquor store clerk.

Upstairs in the *Inquirer* offices, Leary stood beside other reporters and editors, peering out the windows at the large crowd below. One editor leaned over to him and quietly said, "I hope you're right." Gene Roberts, the paper's editor, said the surreal scene was reminiscent of mobster Joe Colombo's Italian pride rallies in New York City. Roberts eventually met with Shabazz, who also demanded that the newspaper stop referring to him as the "Godfather of the Black Mafia." Shabazz and his followers made no claims regarding the factual merits of the article, and indeed refused to go over the allegations in the piece. "We don't have to answer to lies and half-truths," said Shabazz. The Black Muslim leader did, however, offer the assembled press a great quote: "There is no such animal as the 'Black Mafia,' and there is no connection with this animal and the Nation of Islam."

Chuck Stone, a prolific social commentator who wrote for the *Daily News*, also took exception to the *Inquirer* article's angle, and wrote a column titled, "Christians, Jews, Muslims and Crime." He labeled the Leary article "ethnic tar-brushing," and specifically criticized what he considered the story's "shaky three-part thesis" that the Black Mafia existed, that it was controlled by the Black Muslims, and that Muslims appeared to be disproportionately responsible for organized crime within the black community compared to black Christians, black agnostics or black atheists. Stone summed up his criticism stating, "You came away with the fleeting, but nagging impression that the Nation of Islam is master-minding the Black Mafia's operations which, in turn, control black organized crime." Stone interviewed Shabazz, who said, "We realize there are good and bad people everywhere. We admit we have a few strays, but no more than any other religion." The Nation of Islam minister also said, "We'll match our record for taking people off dope with any agency in America."

Tyree Johnson couldn't believe his eyes when Stone's column ran on September 3. He immediately approached Stone in the *Daily News* office and told his more acclaimed colleague – the only other African-American newsman at the paper – that he was being duped, like so many others when it came to Shabazz, Temple 12, and the Black Mafia. In an impressive display of professionalism and humility, Stone offered his valued column space the following week to Johnson to give his more informed perspective. On September 10, Stone wrote, "Here are the views of a young and upcoming brother in whose integrity I have unshakable respect. Furthermore, he is together." Tyree Johnson's portion of the column methodically walked the reader through the numerous, irrefutable ties of

Black Mafia chieftains who held high-ranking positions within the NOI, such as Sam Christian, Ron Harvey, Robert Mims, James Fox and Eugene Hearn. He summed up his detailed analysis by writing, "Minister Jeremiah Shabazz, eastern regional representative of the Nation of Islam, has denied there is any such 'animal' as the Black Mafia or that it has any connection to his Temple. But for too long, the stories I've done on the group's killings, extorting and terror have led me back to 1319 Susquehanna Ave., the Nation's [Philadelphia] headquarters ... Some might justify Muslim involvement in crime as one means of scaling the American success ladder. All ethnic groups, according to that theory, have had their mafias. But these mafias have always victimized the poor – especially the black poor – to fuel their successes."

More salvoes were fired by Rev. Muhammad Kenyatta, who wrote two huge op-ed pieces that ran in the *Inquirer* and *Daily News* respectively in successive weeks in late September. Shabazz was left to wonder how Wallace Muhammad was reacting to the overwhelming amount of negative publicity Temple 12 was enduring.

★

As a youth, Herschell Williams was a member of North Philadelphia's DeMarcos gang, and spent his life in and out of reform schools and jails. He survived several stabbings and a shooting, graduated to more serious crimes, and eventually landed in Graterford Prison at the age of nineteen on a burglary conviction. By then, he was six-and-a-half feet tall and was nicknamed the "Jolly Green Giant." His two-year stint in prison ended in 1971, and he vowed to become a community anti-gang organizer. He was soon back to his old warring ways, however, and was arrested in February 1972 for carrying a shotgun when police responded to an altercation at a bar.

At some point afterward, Williams became a strong-arm man and drug dealer for the Black Mafia. He was one their members who took frequent trips to California to pick up Mexican heroin for distribution in Philadelphia, and spent a brief time in prison in 1974 for selling the product. Following the sweeping arrests of Black Mafia men in September '74, Williams was left to deal most often with syndicate leader Lonnie Dawson and Robert Blair. He lived with his wife and two children at Bayard Street in a quiet neighborhood in the Mount Airy section of the city. As his family and neighbors said, it was as if he lived two lives – one with his family in serene Mount Airy, and the other in the ultra-violent black underworld.

At 10:15 A.M. on 5 November 1975, Roy Hoskins drove a borrowed 1975 Cadillac over to Lonnie Dawson's house, and picked him up. Next they collected Joseph "Jo Jo" Rhone, then headed to their Black Mafia colleague Herschell Williams's house, arriving just after noon. With Dawson behind the wheel, the three-man Black Mafia crew first parked at the top of Williams's street, three doors away from his home. Ten minutes or so later, Dawson sat in the car alone as Hoskins and Rhone paced along the sidewalks nearby. Neighbors were curious about the two men, who had no apparent business or reason to be walking about their properties. Hoskins particularly stood out, as he was dressed all in brown –pants, jacket, shoes, and wide-brimmed hat – and wearing sunglasses. He was also carrying a yellow bucket and a handkerchief. Rhone was more nondescript, and the only thing of note was that he wore a jeff cap. At least two neighbors called police to report suspicious persons, and patrol cars were dispatched.

At 12:30, Herschell Williams walked out of his home and down his walkway toward the street with his two kids, Keesha, aged four, and Herschell, Jr., aged two. His attention was on his children and he didn't notice the men, even though Hoskins waved a handkerchief in the air frantically, facing toward the top of the street, where Rhone had settled himself. Just after Williams placed his children into his late model Cadillac, Hoskins and Rhone ambushed him. They pumped a total of twelve shots into him, six fired from within eighteen inches, hitting him in the head, face, chest and back. Williams died from multiple wounds as his children looked on a few feet away.

Dawson pulled up and the two killers hopped in before speeding from the scene. Police arrived just moments after, and within minutes a description of the getaway car was broadcast over police radio. About twenty minutes after the murder, police spotted the Cadillac on the Schuylkill Expressway and pulled it over. All three men were arrested and a search of the car found a hidden compartment that held two guns, though not the ones used in the hit. Two revolvers used to kill Williams were fished out of a sewer near the crime scene.

When the three were brought in to the Police Administration Building, home of the Homicide Unit, Dawson told police that the Williams assault was "to get him back in line with the dope business." According to the Government, Williams was murdered over a $2,000 cocaine debt relating to his involvement in Black Brothers, Inc., an organization "which engaged in the illegal distribution of drugs." Federal authorities later developed intelligence suggesting the Jolly Green Giant was killed after a dispute with Robert Blair. According to police, Hoskins attacked Detective Michael Chitwood when the two were in an interrogation room. Hoskins was subdued by another detective who hit and handcuffed him when he was on top of Chitwood on the floor. According to Hoskins, he was beaten with a nightstick during the interrogation. That evening, his attorney, Barry Denker, contacted Common Pleas Judge Paul Dandridge for permission to get Hoskins into a hospital. Hoskins was charged with assaulting a police officer, though he later sued the city and settled for $21,000. The events surrounding the Hoskins-Chitwood altercation would later play a role in court.

At Williams's funeral, the former enforcer was dressed from head to toe in green – shoes, socks, tie, and "hit man" gloves. A green hat sat on top of his coffin, which was surrounded by green and white flowers, as mourners, many dressed in green, stopped to pay their respects. In their eulogy for Williams, his family described how he gave up church, school and a government employment program for "clothes, money and cars." The family added, "He wasn't all bad, and many good things could be said about [Herschell], but we will have to live with the old saying, 'Live a violent life. Die a violent death.'"

*

Herschell Williams' sister, Rene, was also caught up in the Black Mafia mess. She was an alibi witness for the Hoskins defense, claiming she saw him in a different section of the city at the time of the murder. She said he was at the Unusual Gift Store, which was owned by a fringe drug conspirator named Elaine Vineyard. To complicate matters more, Rene Williams's common-law husband was Robert "Phil" Blair, a major Black Mafia drug dealer who used Vineyard's residence as a stash house. Blair had a history of almost forty arrests, for offenses ranging from robbery and weapons violations to burglary and narcotics offenses. Blair, like Herschell Williams, made numerous trips to California to pick up Mexican heroin for the Philadelphia market, and was making headlines of his own in the Fall of 1975. However, it was Blair's white-collar criminality, not his drug dealing, that brought him most unwanted attention.

Robert G. Blair's financial shenanigans went back at least to 1969, when he fraudulently manipulated the values of Western Union money orders. At the time, he was president of Shur Kleen Co., Inc., a small, essentially defunct dry cleaning store on West Allegheny Avenue. Blair's scheme was sophomoric and easily detected. He deposited $350 to start a checking account for Shur Kleen in the Girard Trust Bank in August 1969, identifying himself as "Fred Blair." He proceeded to send Western Union money orders to Shur Kleen from different fictitious people in the amounts of $10, $10.10, $10.05 and $20, and then altered the orders so that each would state they were valued at $20,000. Almost immediately after depositing the inflated money orders into Girard Trust, Blair siphoned the money out. Within seven days, he had withdrawn $67,000. Police discovered that Blair was the owner of Shur-Kleen but that a fire had destroyed it months earlier. When he was arrested, he told police he always wanted to be a bank troubleshooter. Comically, he said that while he was in prison in 1967 and 1968, he thoroughly studied banking procedures so that he could lend his expertise to banks and advise them on how to detect and avoid frauds.

Robert Blair was convicted of "causing altered securities to be transported in interstate commerce," and served part of his prison sentence in the New Castle County Correctional Institution, where his misfortunes continued – a fellow inmate stabbed him with a knife. Blair was later paroled, went home to Philadelphia, and operated something called Step Ahead Enterprises with Elaine Vineyard. At the time, Blair was also using the name Robert Bartee, and maintained a second residence in Baltimore.

At some point, using the name Phil Blair, he phoned a corporate lawyer in California named Alan Wellman and asked him if he could sell a $50,000 U.S. Treasury bill. In December 1974, Blair traveled to meet with Wellman in his California home and asked him to negotiate the Treasury bill. Blair trafficked in narcotics throughout California and was frequently in the area. For a fee of $500, Wellman, a tax law specialist, agreed. However, when he attempted to cash the note in Los Angeles, Lloyd's Bank told him it was stolen. The note was discovered missing from the First Pennsylvania Bank in Philadelphia. Blair was indicted by a federal grand jury for selling or receiving and concealing a stolen U.S. Treasury bill, and released on $5,000 bail. His trial was scheduled for January 1976. Alan Wellman would be the prosecution's only witness. If convicted, Blair faced another twenty years in prison – in addition to the time remaining to be served on his parole term from the 1969 stolen federal securities case.

Blair and a companion took a TWA flight from Baltimore to San Francisco on 11 December 1975, and stayed for a few days with a third confederate at a Hyatt hotel in nearby Oakland. Late in the afternoon on the fourteenth, a call was placed from their room to a residence in the San Fernando Valley area of Los Angeles. Soon after, the three men flew to L.A. Their rented white Ford Thunderbird pulled into an Encino motel parking lot at about nine o'clock, and Blair went in to ask for directions to Scadlock Lane. The owner illustrated the way on two maps in the motel office, and Blair realized he was a mere three miles away from his destination.

Alan and Renate Wellman were out dining with a friend that evening, and were dropped off at their San Fernando Valley home by mid-evening. As they settled in for the night, the phone rang, just as it had some four hours earlier, and the caller once again was Robert Blair. It is not clear what the Wellmans thought of these conversations, or if they even knew the caller on each occasion was Blair, the man against whom Alan was scheduled to testify in mere weeks, but the calls did not stop the couple from changing into their bathrobes and getting ready for bed. At some point in the next two hours, Alan and Renate were shot, execution-style, with a Colt Cobra .38 handgun.

Neighbors saw two-thirds of the hit squad leaving the Wellman porch at approximately eleven o'clock. The crew drove to the Los Angeles

Marriott, booked a room under the name of Robert Bartee and stayed the evening. All three flew from L.A. to Baltimore on a TWA flight the next morning. As they arrived back on the East Coast, the Wellmans's six year-old daughter was making the grim discovery of her slain parents lying face down on the floor, dressed in their robes, with pillows over their heads. The gun used in the killings lay on the floor in the front room of the house.

★

Law enforcement agencies were routinely getting information from street sources and from inside prisons that founding Black Mafia members Nudie Mims and Sam Christian were attempting to maintain control in the hopes of getting out of prison and staking their claim to the group's old rackets. Each held hopes of appealing their convictions and returning to the streets to reclaim their lofty status in the Philadelphia underworld. Organized crime experts believed the Black Mafia wanted Mims back on the street in 1975 because he was intelligent and a great organizer. Considering the syndicate's problems, the return of Mims would have been key. The autumn 1975 appeal of his conviction for the 1971 Dubrow case was vital to the group's continued success.

Mims's appeal rested primarily on the identification made of him during his trial by the key witness, Dubrow's Furniture Store greeter Louis Gruby. When asked during the first trial to identify Mims in the courtroom, Gruby initially identified another man. The trial judge, Paul M. Chalfin, allowed the prosecutor to direct Gruby to rethink his choice, after which Gruby picked Mims, who was subsequently convicted and sentenced to life in prison. A prominent defense lawyer named Louis Lipschitz filed the appeal for Mims rather than Mims's usual attorney, Barry Denker. This curiosity wasn't lost on interested observers, who knew that Lipschitz and Judge Chalfin were former law partners and that Chalfin would be hearing the appeal. In an apparent effort to quash allegations of impropriety and conflicts of interest, Chalfin appointed two other judges, Edward Blake and Robert Williams, to hear the appeal with him. In January 1976, the three Common Pleas Court judges met to consider the merits of the case. From here things quickly got interesting – and deadly.

The day after the three-judge panel met about the Mims appeal, Assistant District Attorney Frank DeSimone was at the Spectrum watching the Philadelphia Flyers thump the Atlanta Flames in the National Hockey League. DeSimone, who had successfully prosecuted Nudie Mims months prior, was walking inside the arena when, out of the blue, he was approached by Barry Denker. As if this wasn't strange enough, Denker asked DeSimone, "Would you be opposed to bail for Mims, if he could get it?" DeSimone was incredulous since, as far as he knew, the panel considering the appeal had not made a decision yet. Furthermore, he told Denker that as far as he was concerned Mims was a convicted murderer, and thus he would absolutely not agree to bail. DeSimone left flustered, and it also struck him as odd that Denker was interceding on behalf of Mims, since it was assumed Denker was out of the picture in favor of Louis Lipschitz.

Two days later, Lipschitz visited Nudie Mims in Holmesburg Prison. It is widely assumed that Lipschitz expressed optimism about the pending appeals decision. Similarly, one police informant said that Barry Denker told several Black Mafia members that Mims was getting a new trial and that "the only thing that could convict Mims was another identification by Mr. Gruby." Mims knew or, just as importantly, believed that there was only one thing – one person – standing between him and freedom: sixty-seven year-old Louis Gruby.

Louis Gruby and his wife of many years, sixty-three-year-old Yetta, had lived rough lives. Louis was orphaned at age three and raised in a New York orphanage. Yetta Posner was born in Poland, and her mother brought her to Ellis Island when she was seven years old. When mother and daughter arrived, they could not locate her father, and speculated that he might have wound up in England during the exodus. Yetta would never see him again. Although only five feet tall, Louis Gruby eventually became a career Army man, specializing in counterintelligence, and married Yetta. They and their four children finally settled in Philadelphia, where Louis conducted security clearances for civilian and military personnel until he retired in 1962. He next bounced around a handful of jobs such as security manager of a department store, salesman for a men's clothing store, and assistant manager of a Radio Shack. It wasn't until he landed the job at Dubrow's on South Street that he settled down.

Gruby retired from Dubrow's a year or so after the terrifying attack, and had settled into a routine with his wife in their home of twenty years. They lived in a modest, ranch-style, semi-detached house in the quiet, upper-middle-class Rhawnhurst section of Northeast Philadelphia. Louis followed hobbies such as gardening and photography, but his passion was collecting stamps. Neither he nor Yetta had a driver's license, and the couple relied on neighbors and family members to get around, which they did infrequently anyway. The two were homebodies who enjoyed the company of their family and neighbors. Yetta was the caretaker of the neighborhood, offering to help out those who were sick or otherwise in need.

Despite the seemingly pleasant retiree life the Grubys led, the specter of danger arising from Louis' testimony against Nudie Mims never left their minds. Neighbors and relatives described Louis as security-minded, and his involvement in the Dubrow's event only heightened his anxieties. He put inside lights on timers, so that it appeared someone was always home. He had a routine for turning lights on outside each night and had multiple locks on the doors. The elderly couple never answered the door without first peering out the windows, even if they were expecting the company of neighbors or even their own children or grandchildren. Such was life after Louis made the courageous decision, against his wife's wishes, to testify against one of the most feared men in Philadelphia.

Several hours after defense attorney Lipschitz met with Nudie Mims inside Holmesburg Prison, an oil truck parked on the 1900 block of Pratt Street in the Frankford section of the city. As the oil deliveryman and his partner stood in the street, a new, light-colored Cadillac with a dark top pulled up beside them. A tall, middle-aged black man, dressed sharply in a gray suit, stepped out from the driver's side, approached the deliveryman and asked him for directions to Faunce Street. Armed with the information, the suited man got back in his car to join his passenger, who had remained in his seat during the brief exchange.

At 2:30 the next morning, John Gallagher and his wife arrived at their home on the 2100 block of Faunce Street, in a lily-white section of Northeast Philly, and noticed their neighbor's lights on. Though this was curious, Gallagher excused it as a oversight; perhaps his neighbor, who was also a close friend, had gone to his son's home for the weekend and left the lights on. The next morning, Gallagher awoke to discover the lights still on, and noted they were also on later that day. Concerned, he called his neighbor's children to see if they had heard from their parents. When it was discovered no one had heard or spoken to them since late afternoon the day before, the neighbor's son said he'd be right over to make sure things were okay.

When he arrived, he went up to the house and immediately noticed something odd – the front door was open. His security-conscious parents would *never* have left the door open. He entered the home, stepping across the threshold right into the living room and quickly saw his parents, clearly lifeless, on the sofa. Michael Gruby went back outside to catch his breath, trembling as he took in what he had seen, and was met by John Gallagher. He blurted out that his parents were dead, and Gallagher ran back to his house, phoned police and hastily returned. The two men ventured inside the home. It appeared undisturbed, other than for a multi-colored afghan that was lying out of place in the middle of the floor. Gallagher turned off the television and the knob fell off the set onto the floor, where he left it as he and Michael focused their attention on the bodies.

Louis and Yetta were slumped, seated next to each other on the sofa, with Yetta slightly under Louis' right shoulder and arm. Each was fully clothed, and Louis was wearing slippers, while Yetta's slip-ons were next to her feet on the floor. Louis's black plastic eyeglasses were on the floor at his feet, folded with the lenses down against the carpet. Yetta's silver-metallic eyeglasses sat just beside her on the sofa. Each of the bodies had pillows behind the lower back. Michael noticed what looked like a bullet hole behind Yetta's left ear, and similarly found that Louis had apparently been shot in the head and neck.

As the two men waited for police to arrive, Michael spoke of his family's omnipresent fear of reprisal for the Dubrow's case. One prosecutor during the trial had said the tiny Gruby was "David" fighting "Goliath" in the shape of the 6'3" Nudie Mims. Michael Gruby recalled how prosecutors had escorted his father to the courtroom out of concerns for his safety, and how officials would meet with Louis in clandestine locations instead of in police or prosecutor's facilities when they prepared for the trial.

Detectives and investigators from the Medical Examiner's office noted that Louis had been shot twice: once in his left temple and once in the left side of his neck. Each shot was fired from within six inches. There was also gunpowder residue on the folded cuff of Louis Gruby's sweater's left arm, prompting the medical examiner to conclude that Louis likely tried to defend himself against the shot that wound up in his neck. Louis's head tilted to the left after the shooting, spilling his blood onto the glass coffee table at that end of the sofa. His body and clothing were also soaked in blood. A bullet was later removed from his neck, and another was taken out of his head. Yetta was shot once behind her left ear, and evidence suggested the gun was pressed against her head when it was fired. The .38 caliber bullet fragmented when it hit her skull, and two parts were later recovered from inside her head during the autopsy. The multi-colored afghan strewn on the floor was ashen from gunpowder residue, suggesting it may have been on the sofa when the Grubys were shot. Police quickly surmised this was a planned execution mainly because an extensive search of the home found nothing disturbed or taken. Even the jewelry worn by Louis and Yetta remained on them.

The killings were the first violent crimes in that quiet neighborhood in several years. Police officials grasped the significance of the murders, and Police Commissioner Joseph O'Neill made a rare appearance at a crime scene. In addition to the standard crime scene collection of evidence, dozens of police officers were bussed to the area to search for clues and to canvass the area for possible witnesses. Meanwhile, A.D.A. Frank Desimone was down at the New Jersey shore for the weekend and saw the news on television. When he returned to work on Monday, he visited the office of Judge Edward Blake, one of the three judges considering the Mims appeal. One of Blake's staffers informed DeSimone that the judges' opinion had been completed and they intended to give Mims a new trial. DeSimone next spoke with Judge Blake personally, and the judge reiterated the position of the panel – Robert Mims was getting a new trial. Unbeknown to DeSimone at the time, there had been speculation about the panel's decision passing around the Mims defense team for days. The prosecutor suddenly grasped that the dastardly scenario may have been unfolding when Barry Denker had approached him back on January 22 to ask about Mims's bail prospects. For unknown reasons, though likely as a result of the Gruby assassinations, the three-judge panel ultimately denied Mims a new trial.

As police got more into the investigation, they noted the remarkable similarities between the December 1975 Wellman slayings and the Gruby murders just one month later: no evidence of burglary or robbery; no signs of a violent confrontation; indications of outright assassination; and victims who were scheduled to testify against Black Mafia heavies. "Death Squad Sought," splashed the cover of the *Philadelphia Daily News*. The feature article said, "Police are working on a theory that both couples were slain by a Philadelphia-based hit squad whose targets are important witnesses against Black Mafia members throughout the country."

In fact, police would never solve the Gruby case, despite some detailed information provided by informants. The leading theory, according to the Philadelphia Police Department and the FBI, involves a corrupt police officer and a Black Mafia up-and-comer, and generally goes like this. The Grubys were duped into believing the men at their door were police officers, hence there was no indication of forced entry or any struggle. Informants told authorities that a corrupt police officer named Frederick Morse had co-opted police intelligence files and was helping the Black Mafia thwart cases against the syndicate's members. Morse, ironically, was a partner of the Black Mafia's nemesis, Highway Patrol Officer John D'Amico. Like D'Amico, Morse was a decorated cop. At some point, he and D'Amico ceased being partners, and Morse became close with the Black Mafia crowd he formerly investigated and often put in prison. There was considerable speculation about Morse's role in Temple 12, and some informants referred to him as Frederick Ali. He was one of the lead suspects in the Gruby murders, along with Black Mafia upstart Robert Blair, who was attempting to fill the void left by the arrests of syndicate leaders in 1973 and 1974.

Variations of the story have Morse and Blair visiting the Grubys in the company of one or two other men. One informant said the duo traveled in two cars with Daniel Roy and a big-time drug dealer named Leroy "Bubbles" Johnson. Law enforcement officials never charged any of these men with the Gruby murders, though this was only a temporary solace for Morse and Blair. The Organized Crime Strike Force in Philadelphia picked up discussions of drug dealers on wiretaps discussing Frederick Morse as a cop on the take, and he was ultimately arrested along with four other dealers as part of a nine-month DEA investigation. The group dealt with Black Mafia leader Larry Starks, and with old-timer Alfred "Sonny" Viner. After he was kicked off the police department, Morse pleaded guilty to conspiracy in the distribution of cocaine and heroin and was sentenced to five years in federal prison.

As January 1976 came to an end, Robert Blair was still on the street despite the suspicions of many regarding his involvement in at least two murders. But the more he bragged to his confederates about his ability to avoid prison, the more he put himself in law enforcement's crosshairs, and informants were describing his increased importance in the Black Mafia enterprise.

CHAPTER 17 ★

THE KHALIFA'S REVENGE

WHILE THE AUTHORITIES were untangling the vague details of the Gruby murders, a Black Muslim tribunal convened in Chicago and found Minister Jeremiah Shabazz guilty of violating Islamic law. The council, which did not divulge the specifics of its ruling, reduced his rank from minister to soldier, the lowest rank in the sect. The Nation leadership no doubt heard the same things that sources were telling law enforcement agencies, including the FBI, which noted, "Informants in Philadelphia have reported [Shabazz] as being in charge of narcotics traffic handled by NOI members and involved in killings by NOI members. None of this can be proved in a court of law."

Reporter Jim Nicholson's street sources told him that the Gruby murders were the last straw. Even though there were no hard links – at least publicly – to Nudie Mims or any other Temple 12 members, the media storm that ensued compelled Chicago to pull the plug on Shabazz once and for all. In response, Shabazz abruptly left Wallace D. Muhammad's Nation of Islam – or was privately forced out, depending on who is telling the story – and was out of Temple 12 by the second week of February 1976. The formerly influential minister hooked up with his longtime friend Muhammad Ali and became part of the superstar's entourage.

Shabazz later admitted, "Some of the alleged Black Mafia members came out of my temple, but I would no more accept responsibility than the Catholic priests would accept responsibility for the Mafia." Despite the constant inferences and allegations, Jeremiah Shabazz was never arrested during his tenure in Philadelphia. Apparently, the closest he ever came was in 1974, when ODALE records indicate he was formally investigated for tax fraud, but no charges were ever filed. It was also intimated that James Price told authorities it was Shabazz who ordered the 1973 Hanafi assault, but no evidence was ever produced that remotely backed up this assertion.

Now that Shabazz's lengthy, controversial reign over Philadelphia's temple, Temple 12, had finally come to an end, the Black Mafia would have to adapt. For the first time in years, the syndicate's members were left without a refuge, and could not use the veil of religion so forcefully to fend off accusations of illicit activity. When Elijah Muhammad died, his son Wallace's "Second Resurrection" reforms caused serious organizational problems for the Black Mafia. They were robbed of an infrastructure that provided, among other necessities for a criminal enterprise, places to hide throughout the country, to launder money, and to serve as commercial fronts for rackets. Now, with Shabazz, their powerful, politically connected leader ousted, grand-scale racketeering was suddenly more problematic.

Those Black Mafia members who had served as the enforcement arm of the Black Muslims now found themselves without the prominent backing they had enjoyed under Shabazz's watch. The connections they had developed over the past decade would be exploited in other ways, however, especially in the ever-profitable, if chaotic, drug market. The Black Mafia had also become a fixture within the Muslim prison networks, using them to provide protection, goods and services on both sides of the prison walls.

Beginning with the September 1974 arrests, the Black Mafia had suffered a crushing eighteen months, ending with the expulsion of Shabazz from Temple 12. Law enforcers had clearly made up for their late start, and were discovering how to employ the tools first made available in the late 1960s and early 1970s. Black Brothers, Inc. had dissolved, along with their other community fronts, costing the group revenues and cover. The 20th and Carpenter Streets gang routinely fought the Black Mafia in the street, and provided intelligence to the police. Daring and outspoken community activists pressed on against them, aided by the media's bright and damaging spotlight. And the Nation of Islam was in the midst of historic reform.

For many organized crime groups, the collective effect would have greatly diminished their vitality, if not ended them outright, and as spring arrived, black Philadelphia was no doubt cautiously optimistic that the threat posed by the Black Mafia was eviscerated. The initial signs, however, were mixed. The group's formal hierarchical structure was no longer maintained, nor were the semi-regular meetings which had been convened for over five years. Remaining affiliates continued their operations and still used the group's name, but their influence had dissipated. For a group predicated upon power and fear, the results were predictable. Some affiliates began operating more independently, fearful of further prosecutions if they remained intact, and rival dealers began staking their own territories in parts of the city. This period was marked by sporadic Black Mafia activity and uneasiness, as law enforcement and the community tried to get a feel for what the new arrangements would be.

A seemingly inconsequential sale was completed in March, when the NOI purchased St. Thomas More High School from the Archdiocese of Philadelphia. The property, a three-story brick building with eighteen classrooms, a cafeteria, a basement gymnasium and an auditorium, sat on Wyalusing Avenue in West Philadelphia and was renamed Sister Clara

Muhammad School after the wife of the late Elijah Muhammad. It also housed a mosque. The transaction, $80,000 in cash with no mortgage, showed how strong the Black Muslim interest was. The sale made headlines because of its racial overtones, and because the Archdiocese was criticized for dealing with an organization aligned with a crime syndicate. The controversy over the new Black Muslim institution soon faded, but would return to the spotlight in a big way. For the moment, law enforcement agencies were content to conduct surveillance of the mosque at certain dates in April and May 1976. Nothing of note was recorded.

Lonnie Dawson and Roy Hoskins were tried separately for the November 1975 murder of Herschell Williams in the spring of 1976, and both trials resulted in convictions and life sentences for the defendants. Their co-defendant, Jo Jo Rhone, was still a fugitive after jumping bail, though he had not left the area entirely, as James "Monk" Hadley discovered. In the early hours of April 11, Hadley had words with Rhone and the Black Mafia's Daniel Roy inside Sherman's Bar at 20th and Pierce Streets in South Philadelphia. The three men stepped outside, with Rhone walking to his home across 20th Street. As Hadley and Roy continued the verbal exchange, Rhone stepped out of his home and fired shots diagonally across the street. Hadley tried to run but was struck twice in the back and once in the shoulder, and collapsed a short distance away, where he died. Rhone fled the area again, and would successfully elude police for years.

*

From the moment police learned of the December 1975 murders of Alan and Renate Wellman, particularly considering that the condition of their house was wholly inconsistent with a burglary or robbery, all attention focused on Robert Blair as the "doer." With no witnesses to the slayings, pinning the hits on Blair would require a lot of circumstantial evidence. The ever-accommodating Black Mafia kingpin left a remarkable trail of credit card charges and phone calls, providing investigators a veritable roadmap to his murderous plan. Furthermore, Blair was a self-avowed drug dealer, and Elaine Vineyard's home was a trafficking hotspot. Thus it was not a total surprise when police found a large quantity of narcotics in Vineyard's home. They also found an incriminating letter written by Blair concerning the Wellman killings.

Blair was arrested in the Philadelphia area in May 1976 for violating the conditions of his parole from the 1970 conviction – he was not permitted to leave the state. While he was incarcerated, police finished developing the murder case against him, resulting in charges filed on May 17. Blair was indicted yet again as he awaited trial, this time by a federal grand jury, on charges of conspiring to defraud an insurance company by falsely reporting that insured cars had been stolen. Blair was one of five people named in the indictment, including his girlfriend – and the late Jolly Green Giant's sister – Rene Williams. Though Blair had wiped out the sole witness against him in the stolen $50,000 Treasury bill case – the charges were dropped within a month of Alan Wellman's murder – he was eventually convicted by a jury on two counts of first-degree murder for the Wellman executions.

Just as Blair was being processed in the criminal justice system, the Philadelphia Police Department's Organized Crime Unit was assessing what was left of the tattered Black Mafia. A memo dated May 10 listed fifteen "subjects who are active in the 'Black Mafia' and are closely associated with the 'Black Muslims'." It added, "These subjects are also involved in drug trafficking," and said they included high-ranking members Roosevelt Fitzgerald, Daniel Roy, Joseph Rhone, and Walter Hudgins.

Lonnie Dawson, Roy Hoskins and Robert Blair were the latest in a long string of influential Black Mafia members taken off the street. With each prison sentence, the group's influence waned. This particularly hit their extortion networks, and the once all-encompassing syndicate became ever more dependent on the drug trade. The group did, however, maintain a powerful presence in the prison system, especially in Philadelphia-area institutions. The Detention Center (DC) and Holmesburg Prison sat within the city limits, while the State Correctional Institution at Graterford Prison was forty miles away in Montgomery County. The DC was a facility designed to house offenders and suspects for short terms while awaiting trials and, along with Holmesburg, often handled temporary stays for inmates who were brought to Philadelphia for court proceedings from other prisons. Consequently, if Black Mafia convicts were doing time in federal prisons elsewhere in the country, they would often be housed in the DC or Holmesburg while awaiting local trials and appeals.

All three facilities had substantial Black Muslim populations, and the Black Mafia held a special status within them. Though the syndicate's drug territories were maintained by the members and associates who remained on the street, a great many deals were being orchestrated from behind prison walls. Even within prisons, the Black Mafia manipulated the system to broker any number of deals, including operating markets in drugs, prostitution and other goods and services. Informants disclosed the different means used to bring contraband into the prisons, and they almost exclusively centered on Black Muslim visitations. On some occasions there would be a "drop" of products that would be retrieved by an inmate or a corrupted guard. According to the informants, Black Muslim women would often be used to conceal items under their robes when visiting the prisons. Corrupt guards were compensated either with cash, drugs or women supplied by the syndicate, and the payoffs took place in and out of prison.

Nudie Mims was committed to Graterford in May 1976 for the Dubrow's Furniture Store attack. When he arrived, Clarence Fowler, the former Temple 12 FOI captain convicted of the 1970 murder of Reverend Clarence Smith, was on his way out. He had spent the early portion of his prison term in Holmesburg, running the Black Muslim-dominated cellblock before being transferred to Graterford in October 1973. His stay lasted until a divided Pennsylvania Supreme Court overturned his conviction in January 1976 and ordered a new trial. The court held that a "suggestive pre-trial identification procedure" had been used against him; police had repeatedly and inappropriately shown the witness, Reverend Smith's daughter Beulah, photographs of Fowler, thus influencing her eventual identification of him. According to law enforcement officials, Beulah Hopewell was reluctant to participate in a re-trial, fearing for her safety. In the time that had passed since her identification of Fowler in 1970, the Black Mafia had become known for killing witnesses and it was rumored one of the group's founding members threatened her or her family. Regardless of the merits of such speculation, law enforcement could not produce any new evidence as of April 1976, and Fowler was not tried again for the murder. The Pennsylvania Department of Corrections released him on July 21, and he returned to civilian life at the age of thirty-eight as Shamsud-din Ali – "the sun and light of the faith."

Shamsud-din Ali believed police coerced the witness who testified against him, and proclaimed that he held no animosity toward his accuser. His perspective on prison life was philosophical: "It was a knowledgeable experience and a blessing in disguise. No man wants hardship, but when he sees it is part of growth and development then he realizes it to be a blessing."

Ali was in prison during the Second Resurrection, and had not witnessed the effects of Wallace D. Muhammad's reforms. Upon his release, he took over from Shabazz as head of Temple 12, and was announced by Wallace as the spiritual leader of Muslims in the Greater Philadelphia area. In one of his first interviews as the new head of Temple 12, Ali was asked about the history of the temple and the Black Mafia. He stated that "criminal elements" probably exist within all religious groups, adding that he would work hard to project a better image of Temple 12 in the eyes of the black community. The soft-spoken, articulate Ali was not kidding, and began forming alliances with numerous influential community, business and political leaders.

His experience as a power broker, honed in prison, would be a valuable asset, and like Shabazz before him, he would confuse the public with differing visions as to whether he was a law-abiding, peaceful man who used religion as a tool for the advancement of the underserved population, or a career con who used the religious veil of Islam to shield himself from prosecution as he orchestrated drug and extortion rackets, while keeping his own hands out of the nasty businesses.

As Shamsud-din settled into power at Temple 12, the Black Mafia's discordant relationship with street gangs came to light again. At some point following the 1973-74 street war with the Black Mafia, the 20th and Carpenter gang developed internal problems when some members went over to the Black Mafia. The gang's leaders, Donald Robinson and Elliott Burton, each charged the other with trying to lead the gang back into the Black Mafia. In January 1977, the internal strife flared up as some members aligned themselves – again – with the Black Mafia. On January 23, Donald Robinson, the brother of informant Mickey Robinson, died in a shootout with renegade gang members who went with the Black Mafia.

The Black Mafia dispatched their new recruits to take over extorting protection money from a numbers operator at 16th and South Sts. who had long paid off the 20th and Carpenter crowd. The episode renewed fears that they were regenerating. Despite the notable decrease in street activity, information still trickled in suggesting that whatever remnants of the syndicate remained were still engaged in drug trafficking and the extortion of drug dealers. Word on the street was that several imprisoned Black Mafia leaders were biding their time, waiting to return to their old territories. Though incarcerated, they were maintaining their networks in South and West Philadelphia as they appealed their respective cases and petitioned for parole.

★

In March 1977, the convicted Hanafi killers were dispersed throughout the prison system. Theodore Moody was in Graterford, John Clark and William Christian were in the federal penitentiaries at Lewisburg and Marion, Illinois, respectively, and Ronald Harvey was in the Camden City-Council Building's sixth-floor jail awaiting trial for the Coxson slayings. John Griffin's retrial on the murder charges was pending, and he was in Holmesburg awaiting trial for murdering informer James Price in that very institution. Though charges against Jerome Sinclair had been dismissed for the Hanafi slayings, he was incarcerated at Huntington serving a sentence for aggravated robbery. Yet on March 9, corrections officials scrambled to identify the whereabouts of the above Black Mafia members to immediately place each one under protective custody. For a change, *they* might be the hunted rather than the hunters. Hanafi leader Hamaas Abdul Khaalis had finally lost it, and was publicly calling for a war with the Black Mafia hit squad.

Theodore Moody was placed in isolation at Graterford, and then transferred to an undisclosed facility. John Griffin was placed in isolation in Holmesburg, and, according to the Camden County sheriff, Ron Harvey was "very much contained and isolated" in their county jail. A Bureau of Corrections spokesman told the media he could not provide details regarding Moody and Sinclair: "I can't tell you where they are. They are trying not to let that get out for security purposes. I really can't tell you any more. Just that steps have been taken to ensure their safety." The Black Mafia members were provided with few specifics as to why they were being protected, but at least one knew exactly what was going on. In Camden, Ronald Harvey sat in an isolation cell listening to radio broadcasts chronicling the extraordinary events that were unfolding in Washington, D.C.

Khalifa Hamaas Abdul Khaalis and six of his followers drove a U-Haul truck loaded with weapons and ammunition to the national headquarters of B'nai B'rith, the international Jewish humanitarian organization, which sat six blocks northwest of the White House. At approximately 11:15 A.M., the heavily armed men stormed into the lobby, attacking some of its occupants and announcing they were taking over the building. As a few Hanafis held people at gunpoint in the lobby, others returned to the truck and emptied more weapons from it. They next went through the building collecting people floor by floor, shooting, pistol-whipping and assaulting some as they were taken hostage. One of the victims had his hand severed between the thumb and finger with a machete, and was then shot when he attempted to flee. At one point, the hostages were forced to lie face down on the floor but ran out of space, and were thus forced to stack themselves on top of each other.

Khaalis instructed his followers to take all the hostages to the eighth floor, where he gave them a semi-formal address about a "holy war" begun years before. "I am Khalifa Hamaas Abdul Khaalis ... I want to remind you all of a terrible deed which happened to me and my family, something which you in this room did not show any compassion concerning when it occurred, and I am out for justice in this matter ... Be prepared to die because many of you will die and heads will be blown, brains will be blown out and heads will roll! ... In a holy war there are no innocent victims. Men, women, and children die in holy wars, and if you have any sense you will pray to your God and be prepared to die."

He said he blamed the Jews for the fact that the Hanafi slayers were not dead, because the Jews controlled the banks, the newspapers and the media. Khaalis expressed delight there were 103 hostages because he had prayed to Allah for 100, and informed the hostages that he and his men "had all prayed to Allah before they came, that all said goodbye to their family. They were prepared to die ... " He told the herded hostages, "This is only the beginning of an operation which will cause those who have ignored my plight up until this point to sit up and take notice ... This is only the beginning and you will be hearing of other things to come."

His comments soon made sense. At about 11:30, three Hanafis wielding guns, knives and a machete stormed the Islamic Center on Embassy Row. They first assaulted three women in the center's office, and then took eleven people hostage, binding them hand and foot. The center's director, Dr. Mohammad Rauf, was returning from midday prayers when someone grabbed him by the shirt collar and placed a rifle against his back. The attack on the Islamic Center was apparently because of a comment made by Rauf back in 1973 immediately following the murders; he had described the Hanafis' knowledge of Islam as "superficial." Khaalis spoke over the phone from B'Nai B'rith to Rauf in the Islamic Center and accused him of "playing a game" against him. He also chastised Rauf for "supporting the X's" – Khaalis's way of referring to the Black Muslims.

At 2:40 P.M., two Hanafis armed with a shotgun, knives and a machete stormed the D.C. City Council chambers in the District Building, less than two blocks from the White House. The men went directly to the fifth floor, where the City Council and Mayor's offices were located, stepped into a corridor and opened fire. One fired a shotgun with double-O buckshot, killing Maurice Williams, a reporter on a local radio station, and wounding City Councilman Marion Barry in the chest. Another Hanafi fired a shotgun at Robert Pierce, a law student and City Council intern, as he lay on the floor with his hands tied behind his back. Barry would recover fully from his wounds, but Pierce was paralyzed for life. Within twenty minutes, the two Hanafis had taken fifteen hostages, including a security guard, each placed face down on the floor and bound with venetian blind cords, phone cords and masking tape. A total of twelve Hanafis, led by Khaalis, held at least 129 hostages in the three buildings.

Khaalis, and especially his daughter Amina, had weathered the burden, sorrow and frustration of multiple criminal trials, appeals, administrative delays and media coverage throughout 1973-6. Adding to the anguish of lost, maimed, and traumatized loved ones was the acquittal of one defendant (Jerome Sinclair) and the overturning of another's conviction (John Griffin, who was awaiting retrial). Intermittently throughout late 1976 and early 1977, Hamaas Abdul Khaalis expressed disgust with what he viewed as outrageously lenient treatment of his family's assailants, for even those convicted had not received the ultimate sentence of death. It was of no consequence to Hamaas that the death penalty was not an option at the time. As a sign of their bitter disdain for society's reaction to the 1973 killings, Khaalis and his followers became more militant, conducting daily military drills, which caught the attention of neighbors in their bucolic, affluent neighborhood.

In the B'Nai B'rith headquarters, Khaalis and his men had the largest group of hostages, including press officer Hank Siegel. One particularly tense moment occurred when Khaalis called Siegel over and ordered a guard to point a rifle at his head. "The elevator is coming up," said Khaalis. "If there's a cop on it, he's dead and you're dead." He also threatened to cut off Siegel's head. The elevator was empty, and Siegel survived without further incident, though he did witness Khaalis pistol-whip a hostage whose hands were tied behind his back and who lost consciousness. Khaalis ordered a follower to tie the unconscious man's bound hands to his ankles.

The Khalifa and his followers were surprised to discover African-Americans working for the Jewish group. Siegel watched as one black man was stabbed "because he was working for Jews." Throughout the ordeal, Khaalis and his cohorts repeatedly threatened to kill hostages by beheading if their demands were not met, often stating, "Blood will flow, heads will roll, people will die." When police appealed to his sense of decency and pleaded with him to surrender peacefully, Khaalis responded that no one had cared when his babies were killed.

The events were directly attributable to the 1973 killings at the hands of the Black Mafia. Hamaas and his followers were distraught over what they deemed unsatisfactory punishments for the Hanafi killers. Amina Khaalis, Hamaas's daughter, said the family was satisfied with the police investigation, but not with the judge who tried the case. The family believed Judge Leonard Braman's Jewish background played a role because it contributed to Khaalis's contempt-of-court charge, and to the resolution of the case. Thus, for the first of his three demands for releasing the hostages, Khaalis demanded authorities turn over the 1973 killers from Philadelphia's Temple 12 to him, personally. He also demanded the court pay him back $750 for the contempt fine he received during the trials in 1974. His third demand was that the recently released film *Mohammad, Message of God* stop being shown. The group considered the film to be sacrilegious.

During the siege, Khaalis demanded, "First thing, I want the killers of my babies ... I want to see them right here. I want to see how tough they are. I want the one who killed Malcolm [X] too." He also insisted that Wallace Muhammad, Wallace's brother Herbert, and Jeremiah Shabazz appear before him at the B'nai B'rith center to apologize for their involvement in the 1973 massacre. Next, he complained about "Jewish judges" letting criminals go free. One of his cohorts stated "Zionest Jews" were behind the Black Muslims. Khaalis frequently ranted at Jewish hostages, calling one woman "a stinking Jew bitch" and yelling at others, "Yehoudis, get the hell out of America! Trying to take over the damned world!"

He also granted several interviews with the media, in one explaining that, in court, the convicted men were laughing, jesting and making fun. "The Cassius Clay gang was laughing when we were bringing out the biers of our little babies and children," he said. In another interview he demanded, "I want those that walked into my house. I want them! Are you listening? It has not even begun. We've been nice so far. We have some more wild men out there, in the name of Allah, for their faith, wild in the way of faith because they believe it to the death. You just tell Cassius Clay and Wallace X and Herbert that they got to report here in Washington, D.C., because people's lives depend upon it. I want them to come here. They're not big people. They're roaches and rats and gangsters. I want them here. I want the killers here!"

Following more than a day of heightened tensions and assaults, the ambassadors to the U.S. from Egypt, Iran, and Pakistan were called upon to meet with Khaalis to resolve the situation. They sat down with Khaalis, discussed the Qur'an with him, and following these discussions Hamaas and the other Hanafis surrendered in the early hours of March 11.

Police recovered a remarkable amount of weaponry. In addition to items found on and around the Hanafis, such as shotguns, knives, machetes, a curved sword, a bayonet, chains, and a throwing star, they found twenty firearms, including carbines, shotguns, rifles with mounted telescopic sights, revolvers, and semi-automatic pistols, 8,700 rounds of live ammo, three axes or hatchets, twelve folding knives and razors, nineteen fixed-blade knives, eight machetes, a crossbow with arrows, a blackjack, throwing stars, and garrotes. Before the thirty-nine-hour assault and hostage crisis ended, Hamaas Abdul Khaalis and his followers had killed one person and wounded over forty others, some severely.

At trial, the Khalifa admitted many of the allegations against him. He was outspoken in his rationale for the assaults and testified that he was disappointed that no city official was caught in the District Building. "The attacks were partly to demonstrate the insensitivity that we received when my family was slaughtered," he said. "When the most heinous, most brutal-izing crime was committed here in this city, not one councilman, not one church leader, not one civil leader said one word."

He and his followers were convicted for assorted offenses stemming from the siege. For his part, Hamaas Abdul Khaalis was sentenced to a prison term of forty-one to 123 years for kidnapping and murder.

CHAPTER 18 ★

SQUEAKY, TANK AND SMILEY

D EA INTELLIGENCE SUGGESTED that for the Black Mafia, some old habits died hard. In 1977, one dealer told federal authorities that he was giving $2000 a week to the Masjid, Shamsud-din Ali's mosque. That October, founding Black Mafia member Grady Dyches was shot and killed during a dispute in a North Philadelphia speakeasy, apparently over drugs. Robert A. Johnson, *aka* Fattah Alim Samed, a member of the mosque and a lifelong friend of Grady's, pleaded guilty to the murder. At the time of his death, Dyches had been arrested more than thirty times.

In November, a DEA source was asked to describe the relationship between Shamsud-din Ali and activities on the street. The source said, "Those heavy into drug dealing are told not to have any overt contact with the mosque, though we have found there are members with continued loyalties." There were rumors the syndicate's traditional extortion racket was up and running again – and perhaps had never stopped. Such innuendo seemed to gain legitimacy when two underlings named Sylvester White and Wayne Adams were involved in a "Wild West" shootout on December 12. White was shot twelve times – in the chest, stomach, arms, hands, and shoulders – and died, while Adams survived despite being hit seven times in the chest, stomach and buttocks.

Investigators theorized that White's murder could be traced back to events in October 1976, when an internecine drug war was brewing. At the time, a charter member of Black Brothers, Inc. named Alfred Clark was operating a North Philadelphia drug network. Clark and his right-hand man, Major George Tillery, were in dispute with a West Philadelphia group over a hijacked shipment of methamphetamine. The acrimony culminated in an incident on October 20, with one of the rivals, Joseph Hollis, hitting Clark in the face with a gun and questioning his credentials as a "real gangster." Sylvester White invited the rival factions to a "peace meeting" inside a North Philly pool hall, a meeting attended by Clark, Tillery, White, Hollis, and one of his men, John "Ya" Pickens. Another of Clark's men, Emmanuel Claitt, guarded the door of the pool hall to prevent anyone else from entering, and the hall's manager, William Franklin, was also there.

As soon as the parties were inside, Clark expressed his displeasure over the disrespect shown him days before by Hollis.

"You shouldn't have hit me with that gun," he said.

"Ain't no big thing," retorted Hollis. "You can't do nothin' about it."

Tillery and Franklin, standing behind a nearby pool table, promptly reached under the table, grabbed .38 caliber revolvers, and took out Hollis in a hail of gunfire. Pickens promptly yelled at White, "Sylvester, you motherfucker, you set us up!" and he, too, was shot. He survived a chest wound and later refused to cooperate with the police.

The December 1977 killing of White piqued the interest of authorities because he was a drug dealer and a "very important man" in Shamsud-din Ali's Masjid. One of White's relatives said that whenever people asked White how he could afford his two late-model Lincoln Continentals and costly Malvern home without ever having a job, he would say, "I work for the mosque."

Fears of a Black Mafia revival were heightened that month when South Philadelphia experienced four firebombings in five days. It was surmised they were related to a drug war, which was partially correct. In fact, they were part of a plan hatched at a meeting of Black Mafia members inside Holmesburg Prison to revive their old protection racket. The meeting took place in the latter part of 1977, and one of the attendees was Clarence "Squeaky" Hayman, a former Lieutenant in Temple 12 who had ascended from runner to main player. This was not the first meeting of minds in Holmesburg, as an informant had detailed a meeting in the prison between inmates and visitors one year earlier involving heavyweights Russell Barnes, Lonnie Dawson, Robert Mims, William Hoskins, Ricardo McKendrick, Robert Blair, Larry Starks and Clarence Hayman. The plan was for Hayman to start a war between rival drug gangs in the hopes of creating chaos on the street, after which the Hayman-led remnants of the Black Mafia would offer to settle the dispute and make them a cohesive organization – for a price. The big picture was for Hayman to lay the groundwork for Sam Christian, who was thought to be near a release from prison. "It's been in the planning awhile," said one informant. "They miss the big money, the big cars. They trying to get things lined up and have everything in place to go when Sam gets out. They gotta have a leader." Hayman overestimated his clout on the street, and the firebombings made him a marked man. He was forced to lay low for a while as both sides in the drug war pursued him.

Another Black Mafia member was having his own problems. Robert "Bop Daddy" Fairbanks had slowly divorced himself from the syndicate's activities and was an independent numbers writer by 1977. On one occasion that year, two other independents kidnapped Fairbanks and drove him to Camden before robbing him and demanding protection payments. The forty-year-old former enforcer must have noted the irony, especially when he was robbed again weeks later. Remarkably, Fairbanks took his case to authorities, who prosecuted the two-man extortion crew. During the trial, the prosecution had to concede that Fairbanks was "not a pillar of the community," but was a victim nonetheless. Flippant reports of the Black Mafia's demise, however, were put to rest a few months later when the syndicate's penchant for exacting revenge on informants and witnesses was shown yet again.

Ernest Kelly, Jr., who, along with his wife, Shirley, operated his father's Club Paree, was thirty-four-years old in 1978. He left Shirley, who was four years his junior, at the couple's home on Dorset Steet in West Mt. Airy the afternoon of February 14. When he returned at 5 A.M. the next day, he found her lying in a pool of blood in the living room, bound hand and foot with a blue and white cord, stabbed with a kitchen knife eleven times and shot four times. She was fully clothed, and an autopsy revealed there was no evidence of a sexual assault and that she died of strangulation.

The *Daily News* immediately made the connection: "Alleged Muslim Threat Eyed in Slaying," read the headline. The article stated that Shirley Kelly "was the victim of a vendetta promised against her father-in-law in a kidnapping case involving three convicted Black Muslim mass murderers, detectives believe." Indeed, police still view Shirley Kelly's brutal slaying as payback for the testimony of Ernie Kelly against the Black Mafia in 1974, and the case remains unsolved.

On the heels of the Sylvester White incident, the Shirley Kelly murder was apparently the trigger for Imam Wallace D. Muhammad to take action. He was apparently serious about his Second Resurrection reforms, beginning with the expulsion of criminal elements from the sect. Muhammad had changed the sect's name from the Nation of Islam to the World Community of Al-Islam in the West in November 1976, and again in April 1978 to the American Muslim Mission (AMM). Mosques were now called masjids. The reforms were considered radical to many, and two factions split from the larger Muslim community. Louis Farrakhan and Silis Muhammad each left Wallace D. Muhammad and created their own sects to re-form the Nation of Islam as it was under Elijah Muhammad, with an emphasis on racial pride. Silis created the Lost-Found Nation of Islam (LFNOI), and moved to Atlanta, Georgia, while Farrakhan re-founded the NOI in Chicago. Most of Elijah Muhammad's followers went with Farrakhan, though former Temple 12 Minister Jeremiah Shabazz aligned himself with Silis Muhammad.

In April 1978, the Philadelphia Masjid, headed by Shamsud-din Ali, was placed on suspension for ninety days in response to reports of "an old element operating" in the local Muslim community. According to Imam Muhammad's chief secretary and spokesman, the Imam "received reports of problem people from the old days in the Masjid there in Philly ... and the [Imam] put the whole community on a ninety-day suspension." The suspension, the equivalent of a temporary excommunication, was lifted on June 25.

On July 24, an extortion victim named Barry Wright became "fed up" with being hassled by Squeaky Hayman, and pulled a gun on him. Hayman fled on foot, but was not fast enough to lose his pursuer, who shot him near the pumps of a gas station at 9th Street and Rising Sun Avenue. After Hayman collapsed, the extortion target stood over the once feared Black Mafia runner and fired two more shots – one into Hayman's eye and another into his head.

Around this time, former Temple 12 leader Jeremiah Shabazz returned to Philadelphia in the company of Muhammad Ali. Shabazz had personally solicited Ali to make the trip so the two could stump for incumbent U.S. Representative Robert N.C. Nix. It was a gathering of old friends, reprising an earlier time in the city's history. Shabazz, of course, had served on the Black Coalition board of directors with Rep. Nix's son, Pennsylvania State Supreme Court Justice Robert N.C. Nix, Jr., in 1968, and the two were friends. Another longtime friend, Cecil Moore, joined them at the fundraiser. The timing of the get-together was ironic, because the law enforcement community and the media had just turned its eye back on the role of Philadelphia's main mosque in response to the Kelly and Hayman killings, with the Black Mafia again in the spotlight.

The focus of interest this time was Shamsud-din Ali's role as Imam of Philadelphia's Masjid. He hosted services on Sundays at the Islamic school at 47th Street and Wyalusing Avenue, the property purchased by the NOI two years before. Procedures had changed since the days of Temple 12 in that worshippers were no longer frisked, but were required to pass through a metal detector, and bags were still searched. Asked about the role of Shabazz in the Philadelphia Masjid, Imam Shamsud-din Ali said, "He has not attended the masjids here. I don't know his position in the community … Certainly, we leave open to him if he ever wants to become a member here … He is not an influence here or any other place in the World Community of Islam that I know of. At this point, he is really a man who is employed by Muhammad Ali."

Clarence Hayman, once a lieutenant under Shabazz in Temple 12, had been one of the few significant players not stuck in prison, and after his death, Black Mafia activities were seemingly modest for a time until an old street rivalry made the news. William Johnson was a former member of South Philadelphia's 21st and Pierce Streets gang, one of the gangs that were put under the thumb of the Black Mafia. Johnson was now a numbers writer, and Daniel Roy paid him a visit to demand protection money. Roy, who was long considered one of the syndicate's musclemen as opposed to an organizer, entered the Silver Dollar Bar on Tasker Street on February 24 to straighten out Johnson. The two were in the pool room section of the bar when Roy began shooting Johnson, hitting him eight times in the neck, chest, and back. He collapsed and died in front of the men's room.

Several weeks later, another Black Mafia street tough was taken off the street – for good. Alfred Clark had avoided murder convictions on two occasions, once in 1974 for the death of an eighteen-year-old girl and again in 1976 for the deaths of a man and a woman. After the jury in the second trial announced its not guilty verdict, the presiding judge told Clark, "You bear a charmed life. I hope you realize how the law has protected you." Unfortunately for Clark, the law was not on the street to protect him on 9 April 1979, when he got out of his car in front of the Philadelphia Masjid at 47th Street and Wyalusing Avenue. As he approached the mosque, a man in a gold and black dashiki walked up to him carrying a box of books. The man quickly dropped the box of books and fired five shots at Clark before running away. The bullets tore into Clark's chest, back and neck, and he died within minutes.

As the 1970s came to a close, several imprisoned Black Mafia leaders were due to come up for parole, and others were at various stages of the appeals process. In June 1979, the Supreme Court of Pennsylvania granted retrials to Roy Hoskins and Lonnie Dawson. In Dawson's case, the court ruled that the voluntary nature of his inculpatory statement, following the police skirmish with Hoskins, was not properly vetted in the initial trial. It granted him a retrial because the prosecution erred by questioning Hoskins about his involvement in Black Muslim Temple 12 in his initial trial. In Hoskins's case, the court said, "We cannot ignore the fact that certain adherents of the Muslim faith known as the 'Black Muslims' have been the subject of widespread unfavorable publicity, primarily because of some of its follower's involvement in criminal activity." Thus, the court argued, injecting this discussion served to prejudice the jury against Hoskins unless the prosecution could demonstrate the relevancy of that line of questioning. It overturned the conviction, stating, "At no time ... was any effort made by the assistant district attorney to show the relevance of the cross-examination questions concerning 'drug trafficking' and the 'Muslim' religion." Thus, Dawson and Hoskins were each released, pending retrial. They wasted no time in getting back to business. Dawson and Hoskins approached BBI founder Larris "Tank" Frazier about taking over the remaining Black Mafia narcotics territories. Frazier reluctantly agreed, and the old crew formed anew.

Meanwhile, Shamsud-din Ali's efforts to take his sect mainstream continued, and on 4 July 1979, his Masjid sponsored a walkathon to demonstrate unity between races and religions. In a sight unthinkable just years prior, about 600 of Ali's followers walked from the Art Museum down the Benjamin Franklin Parkway to JFK Plaza, in the company of representatives from the city's Board of Rabbis, the Metropolitan Christian Council, the Catholic Diocese and the African Methodist Episcopal

Conference. The Philadelphia rally was one of many coordinated throughout the country to commemorate Wallace D. Muhammad's vision of the "New World Patriotism." Red, white and blue banners adorned the crowd during the event, which ended with a brief rally at which Shamsuddin Ali proclaimed, "God did not create division among the races, man did. This fact has to be made known. We all share a common existence. Our duty is to make the American promise a reality." Federal and local law enforcement officials who were convinced Ali was back in the old Black Mafia business of shaking down drug dealers were left to watch as his influence flourished, and the public's impressions of the Imam crystallized.

★

The 1980s got off to a rough start for Philadelphia's underworld when Angelo Bruno, the longtime leader of the city's Italian-American crime family, was slain, on 21 March 1980. Bruno had headed the family from 1958, and his death sparked an intense war within the Philadelphia Mob that lasted more than five years. Before it was over, twenty-eight members or associates had been killed, and several high-ranking members were cooperating with the Government, some as informants. Like the large 1974 Black Mafia case, the Bruno cases demonstrated that authorities were honing their investigative and prosecutorial skills with the new organized crime-fighting tools. Their expertise coalesced nicely with the growing number of gangsters wishing to cooperate out of fear for their lives, and the combination was devastating to Philadelphia's gangsters.

The parallels between the two groups' circumstances were striking, because the devastating mix of internecine violence and grand-scale prosecutions had inexorably altered each group, and each would make efforts to regenerate, without much success. Philadelphians probably didn't realize it, but they were witnessing the end of organized crime's salad days. The 1980s Bruno war would affect members of the Black Mafia in a variety of ways, but in the spring of 1980 the old heads were still trying to get things going again. In May 1980, the Pennsylvania State Supreme Court granted Nudie Mims a new trial for the murder of Dubrow's janitor Alton Barker. Mims was freed on $300,000 bail, and went right back into the drug trade.

Meanwhile, one of the group's adversaries was reminded of an old warning. On the first Friday of June, 1980, Ernie Kelly lent his rented maroon and white 1980 Chrysler LeBaron to his twenty-nine-year-old son, Barry. He knew something was wrong when he hadn't seen his son by Monday, and reported the car stolen. It had been approximately five years since his family's robbery/kidnapping case was tried in court, and two years after the vicious murder of his daughter-in-law, Shirley, and grim possibilities were on everyone's minds.

On Thursday, June 12, Ernie received an anonymous phone call akin to the threatening calls he had received years earlier. This time the caller directed Ernie to 23rd and Diamond Streets, where he could find his LeBaron. He didn't have keys for the car, but traveled to the location and discovered it just where the anonymous voice claimed. He approached cautiously, and was overwhelmed by a strong odor. He called a locksmith, who arrived and opened the locked trunk. In it, they found the badly decomposed body of Barry Kelly, who had been severely beaten about the head. Barry was fully clothed, and police ruled out robbery as a possible motive. While the case has never been solved, the Black Mafia is believed to have been responsible.

In mid-June, founding BBI officers Frederick "Smiley" Armour and Tank Frazier clashed over an all-important North Philadelphia drug territory. Richard Allen Homes was a dilapidated public housing project. It was once accurately described in a Philadelphia Police Department press release: "Historically, the Richard Allen Homes Housing Project has been a hotbed of illicit narcotic trafficking, where drug-related crimes and violence have created intolerable living conditions for the residents. Indeed, violence is not an uncommon companion of the trafficking activities. Drug trafficking related shootings, beating and stabbings, many of which are committed in broad daylight, are not unusual."

A prosecutor pointed to the bleak conditions in the project as a way of demonstrating just how much Tank Frazier stood out – "you can't even get the water to run, and rats and roaches, he's over here dressed like he's out of *Gentleman's Quarterly*, pinstripes ... " Richard Allen was Frazier's primary drug territory, and when Frederick Armour encroached on his turf, the two exchanged harsh words. By the first week of July, they were still at odds, and Armour wound up assaulting the smaller Frazier on back-to back days. Frazier responded by telling others, "Ain't no motherfucker coming down here and take things from me ... I am going to show that motherfucker that he ain't bad. He thinks he is Jesse James but I am going to fix him." On July 6, Frazier called some "Muslim brothers" to help him kill Armour. The following day, Frazier told Armour he had a job for him and invited him to meet. Frazier told associates he was going to make an example of Armour, saying that if he let one guy "get away with taking his shit that they would all do the same."

As Frederick Armour pulled up on his bicycle – bikes were best for getting through the housing projects and selling drugs – Frazier was hiding in a doorway. A female associate of his tried to coax Armour inside, but the drug dealer said he couldn't leave his business or his bike, and flashed a large amount of money in the air. Just after Armour shook the green bills, Frazier popped out into the open and shot him in the head. Part of Armour's head was ripped off, and he collapsed off the bike, lifeless. At least one other man proceeded to shoot Armour as he lay on the ground. An observer who understood the bigger picture said, "The killing of Smiley was not done of course on a dark night in a dark alley somewhere, which it probably could have been done. You don't make an example of somebody by murdering them in a dark alley when only two of you are there. What kind of impression does that make? You do it in front of other people to make an example."

Homicide detectives investigated the Armour homicide throughout July and August, and Frazier stayed busy hustling all the while. On August 25, he sold five bags of heroin to an informant who was wearing a mini-tape recorder. Frazier happened to frisk the man and found the wire. At gunpoint, he took back the heroin and stripped the recorder off the informant. Frazier let the man go but placed a contract on his life. When detectives went on the street to arrest him on August 30, they predictably found the stylish drug dealer at work in Richard Allen Homes. Dressed in a beige suit and wearing alligator shoes, he saw police walking his way and quickly ditched the product he was selling. Police easily caught up with him, and retrieved thirteen packets of heroin he had been carrying. Frazier was convicted of murder and heroin trafficking. DEA informants detailed his *modus operandi*, including his use of two units in the Richard Allen Homes that he rented for the purpose of selling drugs.

The Black Mafia had long valued the Richard Allen Homes projects as a narcotics territory, and it was *the* place serious drug dealers in Philadelphia plied their trade. Such kingpins as Fat Ty Palmer, Palmer's protégé Roland "Pops" Bartlett, John Darby, Reginald Cole and Robert Bolar all "ran" Richard Allen at some point in the 1960s or 1970s, and each worked with or on behalf of the Black Mafia. Interestingly, among some observers, Larris Frazier and his crowd were referred to as the Richard Allen Mafia ("RAM" for short) instead of the Black Mafia. The confusion was no doubt due to the significant decrease in membership and street status of the original Black Mafia. Said one federal source in September 1980, "If we don't put our finger on the pulse now, it could jump off into a Black Mafia type situation." At the time the nomenclature seemed inconsequential, and operationally it was, although as later iterations of the group used the name it gained its own cache. In time, RAM would have fewer ties to the Black Mafia, despite the lineage of the name.

The death of one BBI founder, Armour, at the hands of another, Frazier, was remarkable. To gain a sense of the Black Mafia scene at this point in time, it is worth looking back to 1 October 1973, when they opened their Black Brothers, Inc. headquarters on South Street. A photographer, Bill Peronneau, took what is now a historic photo that appeared with Tyree Johnson's coverage of the event. It shows BBI leaders David Mitchell, Lonnie Dawson, Frederick Armour, James Fox and Eugene Hearn. Left out were the group's listed incorporator, Larris Frazier, and its sergeant-at-arms, Herschell Williams.

The bogus community development group's hierarchy had experienced a destructive eight-year stretch, much of it their own doing. As of July 1980, the status of the seven BBI leaders was as follows: Mitchell was shot dead in 1975 by his brother; Dawson was out on bail awaiting re-trial for the shooting death of Williams in 1975; Armour was shot to death by Frazier; and Fox and Hearn were in federal prison for narcotics trafficking and related offenses.

Fox and Hearn were each petitioning for parole, with the former ultimately getting rejected and the latter being released from prison later in 1980. Hearn, who was now also using his Muslim name, Fareed Ahmed, served only five years of his fifteen-year sentence. Fox's parole application failed after a U.S. Attorney explained to the board, "Fox was the second in command in a large scale heroin distribution ring operating in Philadelphia. Intercepted conversations and subsequent purchases of heroin by a government informant showed that Fox was the overall coordinator for the distribution of heroin. Drug Enforcement Intelligence information indicates that this group, calling itself the Black Mafia, accounted for over sixty per cent of the heroin distribution in Philadelphia."

CHAPTER 19 ★
THE INSIDERS

L AWRENCE SIMONS GOT out of jail in February 1981, and went to work at an AM-PM mini-market at Broad Street and Lehigh Avenue in the heart of North Philadelphia. The mini-market was one of two owned and operated by Lonnie Dawson, aka Abdul Salim, and Roy Hoskins, *aka* Muhammad Waliyud-Din, who had purchased them after their release from prison. Simons, who had no known prior connections to the Black Mafia, began working in the mob's heroin, cocaine and methamphetamine operation. He did not know that the FBI and the DEA were already deep into an investigation of the Dawson-led network. It was no surprise to federal authorities that Dawson and Hoskins leaped back into the drug trade and exploited their Black Mafia connections and street reps. The pair should have known that law enforcement would be watching and that they were operating on borrowed time. In March 1981, DEA agents witnessed Dawson in Wilmington, Delaware, picking up two fifty-five-gallon drums containing methylamine, an essential ingredient for the manufacture of methamphetamine.

Something interesting happened the following month that was a hint of things to come between mobster Raymond "Long John" Martorano and the Black Mafia. Martorano was suspected of arranging the December 1980 slaying of Roofers Local 30 head John McCullough, another of the early casualties of the mob war. It was widely assumed that Martorano and Albert Daidone had recruited a man named Willard Moran to kill McCullough, one of the late Angelo Bruno's chief associates, because he was trying to organize an Atlantic City bartenders' union to rival Local 33, of which Daidone was vice president. Moran and an accomplice, Howard Dale Young, were arrested within months of the hit. In April 1981, Moran spoke with Martorano about his concern that Young would cooperate with the prosecution, to which Martorano responded, "Don't worry about Howard Dale Young, because when [he] gets over to Philadelphia, I'm a large contributor to the Black Muslims." Few knew at the time, however, precisely to what, or to whom, Martorano was referring.

When federal authorities began their pursuit of Dawson in February, Philadelphia narcotics officers were also developing intelligence on Nudie Mims. The investigation resulted in a search warrant being issued for Mims's Northeast Philadelphia apartment. On May 13, police executed the warrant, and discovered two ounces of cocaine, estimated to be worth between $2,000-5,000 on the street, a Thompson submachine gun, an Israeli Army Uzi submachine gun, strainers, scales and other drug-related equipment.

Around this time, Dawson and Hoskins approached Lawrence Simons with a $10,000 offer to kill Robert Brown, the witness largely responsible for their first conviction in the Williams murder case. Simons accepted the assignment, though the deal would later fall through. Shortly after, Lonnie Dawson scheduled a meeting with Frank "Frankie Flowers" D'Alfonso, a principal member of the Bruno crime family. In June, the two underworld figures met inside a West Philadelphia bar to address brewing territorial disputes between the Black Mafia and the Bruno family. D'Alfonso arrived at the meeting in a light blue Lincoln Town Car along with two bodyguards. Dawson traveled to the meeting with Simons and John "Ya" Pickens, who each stayed outside with the other body-guards while Dawson spoke with D'Alfonso. The meeting ended amicably, and Dawson soon dealt in significant quantities with Philadelphia's Italian mobsters.

By August, federal agencies were listening to phone conversations, augmenting their vast intelligence on the drug trafficking already gleaned from informants and surveillance. Largely as a result of the wiretaps, authorities executed search warrants in September 1981 at two cutting houses overseen by Dawson and Hoskins. These spots were under the immediate supervision of a Dawson lieutenant named Michael Johnson. Officers confiscated large quantities of heroin, drug paraphernalia, and cutting agents used to stretch heroin. They estimated the Dawson-led syndicate was selling 200 pounds of methamphetamine per week, in addition to smaller quantities of heroin and cocaine. Each pound of meth was worth $10,000 wholesale, and the heroin sales were only slightly less in value.

Federal agents were soon treated to a comical sight, considering the gravity of the violent world in which Dawson operated. Dawson, who was flying back from Florida, was overheard on a wiretap asking to be picked up at the Eastern Airlines terminal at Philadelphia International Airport. In response, an FBI agent went to the airport at the given time to conduct surveillance. He witnessed Dawson, the Black Mafia kingpin who was part of the hit squad that killed the Jolly Green Giant, at the terminal in the company of children wearing Mickey Mouse hats.

No doubt as a result of the significant investigative actions and findings, low-ranking runner Lawrence Simons became a confidential informant in early 1982. Simons was also facing charges for an unrelated 1975 murder, and agreed to develop intelligence on other cases. He walked investigators back to the start of his involvement in the network one year earlier, and detailed the Dawson-Hoskins plot to kill Robert Brown. In addition to providing historical background, he continued to work with Dawson and Hoskins, often wearing a wire. Through February 1982, Simons routinely purchased drugs from Dawson, and he also worked in Dawson's AM-PM mini-market. On the night of April 4, Simons and Dawson went to Gus Lacy's bar, Mr. Silk's Third Base, as federal agents conducted surveillance and listened in – Simons was wired for sound. Just after Simons and Dawson left the bar in the company of two other dealers, James Watts and Robert Hardwick, the two federal agents approached their informant to talk. They unwittingly let Dawson witness the conversation, thus disclosing Simons' undercover role as a cooperating informer.

Later that morning, around 4 A.M., Simons was driving alone in his car on I-95 near Chester, just south of Philadelphia, when a car containing Dawson and Robert Hardwick came up behind him. Dawson and Hardwick flashed their headlights to get Simons to pull over, but he knew better and tried to speed away. A wild chase ensued, with Dawson and Hardwick shooting out of their car windows at Simons as they sped after him. They lost control of their car and crashed into a utility pole, allowing Simons to get away in his bullet-ridden vehicle.

Dawson and Hardwick fled to a nearby Howard Johnson's restaurant, where Dawson called Hoskins. Dawson told him, "We, by some kind of fate, ran into that lame, right, on the expressway." He added that he "went through about four or five one-way streets ... we moved on him, gave him all we had, right? ... but it didn't get him, right? We ran into a tree." Dawson then told Hoskins to report the car stolen, which he did minutes later. The FBI had tapped Hoskins's phone long before these unexpected events, and got to listen as this conversation took place. Thus, the agents were listening live to a discussion about an attempted hit on their witness that had transpired just moments before.

Dawson next called a woman and told her to meet him at the Airport Sheraton Hilton, and also to bring a "hit," meaning a gun. About half an hour later, the woman showed up as instructed with a .25 caliber automatic pistol in her purse. FBI agents arrived at the hotel, found Dawson and Hardwick trying to hide in the rear seat of the woman's car, and arrested them. Hoskins was also soon caught. Informant Simons then disclosed that Lonnie Dawson had obtained meth from another dealer out of a second floor cash register inside Silky's. On April 9, officers executing a search warrant found methamphetamine on the upper floors of the bar. A federal grand jury handed down indictments against Dawson, Hoskins and others. Simons joined the witness protection program and was relocated.

Almost immediately after arriving in the city's Detention Center, Lonnie Dawson forced the leader of the Center's American Muslim Mission (AMM) to step down, and assumed his role. He also commandeered a top position on the prison's betterment committee, whose members were elected by inmates, and brokered deals with other influential inmates. In no time, his network included guards who were given favors in and out of the prison in return for cooperation. His network of guards was supposedly so complex he had to keep records of which were involved in certain transactions. According to inmates and guards, Dawson was able to get inmates transferred to his cellblock in order to do business with them. He used his position on the betterment committee to effect the transfers by filing complaints or doing favors for guards. Dawson also took care of "problem" inmates for the guards on his payroll. One prison guard commented, "If you have a problem with a guy, you'd say, 'Lonnie, why don't you talk sense to the guy?' And he'll talk to him." On the outside, in addition to the financial payoffs, he provided sex for guards with several women in South Philadelphia. Dawson was also meeting regularly with Afghan heroin smugglers inside the prison, and dictated trafficking in areas of North Philadelphia and in the Germantown and Mount Airy sections of the city.

Also in the prison was Raymond Martorano. On the outside, the two had met often to negotiate the purchase of P2P, the key chemical in the manufacture of methamphetamine, commonly known on the street as "speed." They now ran a heroin business together out of the Detention Center. Dawson and Martorano had so corrupted guards within the institution that even if they were housed in separate areas, guards would arrange phone calls between them. The inner workings of the drug network included paying off guards in advance of strip searches or court appearances. Drugs were hidden in places such as lighting fixtures, mattresses, cracks in ceilings and walls, and in rolls of toilet paper. Guards who were not complicit still kept any knowledge of the corruption to themselves. "You knew who was doing it, but you looked the other way," said one. "If I did [reveal it], I'd be walking down the [cell] block and get a shank in my back."

Nudie Mims was conducting similar business from his cell in Graterford Prison, and concentrated his efforts on North Philadelphia. The FBI monitored calls between Mims, Dawson, Martorano and others in the network for some time. Mims, as the prison's AMM head, was permitted to receive visitors at his prison office and chapel, and was very influential in the prison culture. At some point in 1982, George "Cowboy" Martorano, Raymond's son, visited Mims under the guise of donating boxing equipment to the AMM. Like his father, George was a major narcotics dealer. Following the meeting, the FBI monitored phone calls to Dawson and Mims that focused on the quantities of heroin they wanted from the younger

Martorano. George Martorano also told an undercover FBI agent, during another monitored conversation, that he controlled "all of North Philly," because two groups of Black Muslims worked with him. Mims and Dawson, of course, orchestrated the two groups. Mims and Dawson separately said they could each sell two kilograms a month – about $400,000 worth of heroin.

George Martorano's intermediary in the deals was a twenty-five year-old drug dealer and former boxer named Michael "Blood" Youngblood. Not long before the Martorano–Black Mafia pact, Youngblood was arrested twice for dealing methamphetamines in unrelated cases. When asked about his occupation, he claimed to be a roofer, a job he obtained through his uncle who was a business agent with Roofers Union Local 30. Youngblood was also familiar with Local 30 because he boxed for years at a club run by union heavy Stephen Traitz. When Youngblood pleaded guilty in 1982 to the methamphetamine charges, he received a suspended sentence in one case and was sentenced to five years probation in the other by a judge who, interestingly enough, was later removed from the bench for accepting cash gifts from Traitz. Just after he was sentenced to probation, Youngblood began distributing cocaine for Martorano. In fact, it was Youngblood who placed the phone call to Nudie Mims inside Graterford that was monitored by the FBI. Unbeknown to Youngblood and Martorano, the phone call was made in the midst of an FBI sting operation at the lush Bellevue Stratford Hotel, where the duo thought they were meeting with a drug pilot and his lawyer – they were actually undercover agents. While the foursome was in the room, Youngblood called Mims to discuss how much heroin his group was going to be able to sell in Philadelphia each month and the appropriate price.

Dawson's trial for the April 1982 indictment lasted almost three weeks before the jury returned its verdict on 29 October 1982. The trial included the emotional testimony of Robert Brown, one of the witnesses against Dawson in the Herschell Williams case. Dawson, of course, then approached underling Lawrence Simons with an offer to kill Brown for his incriminating testimony. When Brown testified, he broke down in tears and said, "I'm just so scared. I was scared and I'm still scared. I don't want to be here. I'm frightened to be here to testify." After giving his evidence, he added, "I was so scared I didn't even want to look at them."

Lonnie Dawson and Roy Hoskins were convicted on multiple drug-related charges, including possessing and distributing heroin, cocaine and methamphetamine, and for engaging in a continuing criminal enterprise. They were sentenced to 134 and 126 years, respectively, and fined a total of $440,000. Federal law enforcement officials claimed the sentences Dawson and Hoskins received were the harshest ever imposed by a federal

THE INSIDERS / 219

judge in the Philadelphia area for drug offenses, and were believed to be the stiffest for any federal offense in the area. The DEA agent in charge, Norton J. Wilder, said, "It's a milestone getting them out of the community, especially the black community."

There was perhaps a wider importance to the case. It was the first joint FBI-DEA drug probe in the Philadelphia area. Rudolph Giulani, then-Associate Attorney General of the United States, stated it was "a perfect example of what can be accomplished by cooperation" between the DEA and FBI. Yet as he remained in the Detention Center while awaiting a variety of legal proceedings, Dawson maintained his networks inside and outside the walls.

Philadelphia was one of twelve regions in the country to establish a U.S. Organized Crime Drug Task Force in June 1983, and the latest anti-crime investment would soon pay dividends. The task force was staffed with seven prosecutors who coordinated with the FBI, DEA, IRS, ATF and the U.S. Customs Service. One of the techniques employed by the new crew was actually an old, though rarely used, law – a 1970 statute that permitted the federal government to seize the assets of convicted drug dealers. Thus, one component of the new strategy was to ask for high bail, and if the defendant could post the bail, the prosecutors demanded to know the source of the funds. Often this would result in asset forfeiture. In June and August 1983, Philadelphia D.A. Edward Rendell indicted the primary suppliers to the Black Mafia's drug network. The main figure was Albert "Sid" Butts, the conduit for heroin brought to Philadelphia from a wholesaler in Harlem, New York. Eleven of Lonnie Dawson's conspirators were indicted for operating a heroin and meth distribution network in the Philadelphia region. The indictments were the outgrowth of the massive investigation begun in early 1981 that included information provided by Lawrence Simons, FBI and DEA surveillance and wiretaps. The effort consumed more than fifty federal agents and Philadelphia police officers. Eleven defendants were convicted, and then sentenced in November of 1983, prompting DEA Special Agent Nick Broughton to proclaim that the combined efforts of the DEA, FBI and the PPD Narcotics Unit had "put a stop to the effectiveness of the [Black Mafia]. I think we put a pretty good dent in it." This was, however, not the end of the group's activities. Remnants continued on, many from inside prison walls, seeking out new partners and networks.

As the Dawson-led conspiracies were being unraveled and exposed to the public, Gene Hearn became the focus of controversy in Philadelphia's mayoral race when it was discovered he volunteered for Mayor Wilson Goode's campaign staff as a fundraiser. Goode's political opponent used the opportunity of a televised debate to charge, "Wittingly or unwittingly, Mr. Goode and his campaign have developed a relationship with a convicted heroin dealer – Eugene Hearn, who was identified by the

Philadelphia Daily News as a kingpin in the heroin traffic in Philadelphia. He has raised money for Mr. Goode, and his organization ... has supported Mr. Goode." Goode successfully dodged the issue by claiming he had no knowledge of Hearn's past because he only knew him by his Muslim name, Fareed Ahmed, even though "Eugene Hearn" appeared on a donor's list. Just months prior, Hearn was providing large amounts of heroin to Lonnie Dawson, who then put it on the street. At the time, Hearn listed himself as the founder of the community development group called the Southwest Center City Civic Association. The Association had received $10,000 in city funds for a Summer Youth Program after the 1983 primary. It was just the latest in a series of politically sensitive matters involving Black Mafia members, and such instances would arise from time to time for years to come.

Meanwhile, the Afghans who had visited Lonnie Dawson in jail were caught on December 7 smuggling a quarter-pound of high-grade heroin into the city after the FBI monitored calls between Dawson and his associates. Times had changed and law enforcement was now familiar with the Black Mafia's trade emanating from area prisons. The Philadelphia Police Department and the DEA worked in concert to suppress the network, specifically its trafficking in Richard Allen Homes. In February 1984, Police Commissioner Gregore Sambor "announced that a federal grand jury [had] returned seventeen indictments charging twenty-eight individuals with various violations of the Federal narcotics laws, specifically conspiracy and the distribution of controlled substances, including heroin, cocaine, and methamphetamine." Reginald Cole, Robert Bolar, and Willie Rispers, three major traffickers who had long worked in concert with the Black Mafia, were among the indicted. By this time, some observers were increasingly, though loosely, referring to this group of individuals as the Richard Allen Mafia (RAM).

Other FBI-led investigations focused on drug trafficking in Philadelphia-area prisons. The Bureau got one of the corrupt prison guards, Kevin Pearson, to cooperate, and he described the network in detail. Pearson was a key link in trafficking at all three Philadelphia correctional facilities – the Detention Center, Holmesburg Prison and the House of Corrections – and was a courier for George Martorano. Among other revelations, Pearson admitted receiving $6,000, a car and a half-kilogram of cocaine in exchange for testimony favorable to Raymond Martorano.

On March 8, Pearson received a death threat from an anonymous phone caller, which he suspected was a prisoner. Eight days later, he gave the latest in a series of briefings on the Philadelphia prisons drug network. By that time, Pearson had agreed to testify against at least two other guards. This would not come to pass, however, because Pearson shot himself in his left temple with a rifle in his North Philadelphia home just hours after his last meeting with the FBI. Now without their key source, the Feds discontinued their probe in June, though the prison system undertook its own investigation. Lonnie Dawson was removed from his positions of power in the Detention Center sometime in December 1984, and placed on administrative segregation before eventually being sent to federal prison in Marion, Illinois.

CHAPTER 20

GET DOWN OR LAY DOWN

D URING THE FBI's large-scale probe into the Black Mafia narcotics network led by Lonnie Dawson, two prominent Black Muslim personalities became part of the investigation because of court-authorized wiretaps: former Temple 12 ministers Jeremiah Shabazz and Shamsud-din Ali. Though neither man was convicted as part of the Dawson investigation, the revelations placed each Muslim leader under increased FBI scrutiny. The Bureau expanded investigations into the activities of Shabazz in New York and of Ali in Philadelphia. Concerning Shabazz, the FBI wrote:

> During 1981-1982, [name redacted by FBI] along with Shabazz were intercepted during FBI/DEA Title III's [wiretaps] in [Philadelphia] case ... which had targeted Philadelphia's Black Mafia and its involvement with heroin trafficking. Insufficient evidence was developed re: Shabazz and [name redacted] to indict them though it was apparent they were involved in narcotics trafficking. FBI/DEA did indict and convict 27 other subjects for narcotics trafficking."

While the narcotics trafficking and money laundering were being investigated, the FBI also took note of Shabazz's business activities. "It was revealed that during late 1981-1982 [name redacted by the FBI] and Jeremiah Shabazz were in partnerships in the fight promotion business in the New York area and had maintained an office there," noted the Bureau. "Shabazz is known by the FBI to have close contacts with the top people involved in professional boxing including [redacted] and [redacted] along with close relationships with numerous black entertainers involved in the music industry."

When Shabazz left his position in the NOI in 1976, he became part of Muhammad Ali's entourage. Ironically, though it was their allegiance to the NOI under Elijah Muhammad that brought the two men together, after The Messenger's death the two friends adopted different religious paths.

Muhammad Ali went with Wallace Muhammad, while Jeremiah Shabazz followed Silis Muhammad in the Lost-Found Nation of Islam. Their differences apparently had no effect on their friendship, and the two spoke openly of their decisions.

"Wallace changed the direction of the Nation," said the boxer. "He'd learned from his studies that his father wasn't teaching true Islam, and Wallace taught us the true meaning of the Qur'an. He showed that color don't matter. He taught that we're responsible for our own lives and it's no good to blame our problems on other people. And that sounded right to me, so I followed Wallace, but not everyone in the Nation felt that way. Some of the ministers didn't like what he was teaching. Jeremiah Shabazz didn't like it. Louis Farrakhan didn't like it either. They believed Elijah was a prophet ... But I've changed what I believe, and what I believe in now is true Islam."

Jeremiah Shabazz, indeed, thought Elijah Muhammad "had the best program for black people," and didn't mince words when he addressed the subject. "Ali changed all right, and so did the Nation," he said. "There's been a metamorphosis, and I don't like it ... What I truly regret is, because of our discipline at the time and because of our respect for Elijah Muhammad, we didn't oppose Wallace. We accepted him; and another reason for that actually was our fear and dislike of the white man. We didn't want to show the white man that we were divided. We wanted to appear united as far as the enemy was concerned."

Though Muhammad Ali's public presence started to diminish in the early 1980s, Shabazz remained a part of the boxing legend's inner circle. Remarkably, considering the acrimonious relationship between Ali and fight promoter Don King, Shabazz began working for King at some point prior to 1984. The FBI summed up the situation: "Jeremiah Shabazz is a major black organized crime figure in the Philadelphia area who associates with both black OC figures and Philadelphia's LCN [La Cosa Nostra]. In addition, he maintains a high profile in the Philadelphia area through his image as a religious leader and through his contact with Don King Productions and major entertainment stars, when in fact, he is a narcotics trafficker who utilizes both his religious background and business associates as a cover for his illegal activities."

Even though the spotlight was no longer as bright on Ali or Shabazz, a series of FBI teletype messages in early 1984 illustrates the Bureau's opinion of, and continued interest in, Shabazz. Though it had been almost a decade since Wallace Muhammad ended Shabazz's reign over Philadelphia's crime-riddled Temple 12, it is clear the FBI and the DEA believed he had simply moved his illicit operations to New York City. An FBI teletype dated 9 January 1984, described Shabazz as a "large cocaine dealer in the Philadelphia area" who traveled "back and forth between NY and Philadelphia by train" with an unnamed cocaine supplier. A follow-up teletype sent on January 13 elaborated, "Shabazz is a long-time Philadelphia black organized crime figure who has been the subject of numerous FBI investigations in the past. Jeremiah Shabazz is known for his association with Black Mafia narcotics dealers and Shabazz's forte in the past has been his ability to obtain kilo quantities of heroin and cocaine for the Black Mafia in Philadelphia. He is also active as the 'front man' in numerous Black Mafia businesses, particularly fight promotions and entertainment promotions. Past investigations of Shabazz have shown he has numerous contacts throughout the East Coast particularly in New York, Washington, D.C., Atlanta, Ga., Miami, Fl., and the Bahamas."

On February 17, yet another teletype stated that Shabazz was a "known heroin trafficker which coincides with information received from the DEA that Jeremiah Shabazz is a documented heroin trafficker." By March 1984, agents were requesting permission to use electronic devices to monitor private conversations between "Shabazz and others in a narcotics investigation." Furthermore, the agents planned to use undercover agents to purchase fifteen to twenty kilos of cocaine from a dealer for the purpose of getting introduced to Shabazz so that an undercover could attempt to buy heroin from him.

By mid-March, the investigation had bloomed into a major operation targeting "heroin/cocaine dealers within the Black Muslims." The plan was to orchestrate an initial $30,000 buy to produce the "primary narcotics connection" – Jeremiah Shabazz. There were many prongs to the investigation, including cocaine trafficking and money laundering in California, cocaine trafficking in Miami and Newark, and heroin trafficking and money laundering in New York. As early as 3 May 1984, the FBI was exploring Shabazz's ties to Philadelphia's Italian-American mobsters. This was no doubt in part because of the historical ties between Black Mafia figures and the city's Cosa Nostra family. Importantly, it was also because in 1984 the FBI was investigating another old-time Black Muslim hustler with ties to the city's crime family and to the Black Mafia, Stanley Culbreth.

Culbreth's name was never far from the surface of any number of discussions regarding the Philadelphia underworld. By 1984, the Black Expo debacle (see Chapter 11) was a distant memory and Culbreth was serving as the executive secretary of the National Promoters Association. Culbreth, whose Muslim name was Sheik Raqeeb Atif Beyah, was running a promotions firm named Beyah Associates. According to another FBI teletype:

> Shabazz works for Don King Productions in New York and can be contacted there several times a week. In addition, [the FBI's Philadelphia office] is investigating a case entitled 'Beyah Associates, RICO' ... wherein both black and white organized crime figures in the Philadelphia area are attempting to muscle in on

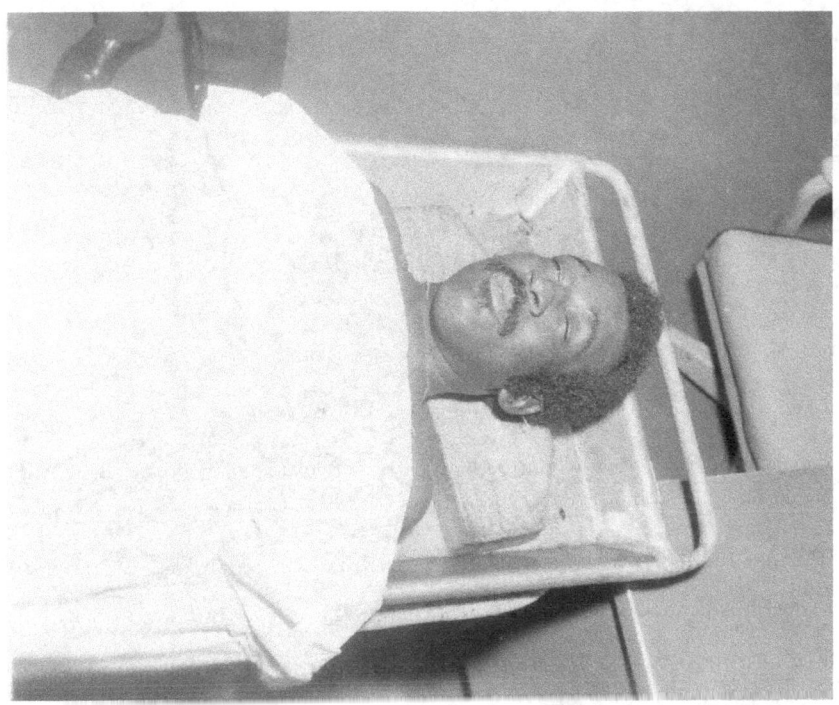

A major player in Philadelphia's narcotics trade, "Cadillac Tommy" Farrington (above) was gunned down outside Ernie's Club Paree. "Black Charlie" Russell (below left) was suspected of carrying out the hit on the orders of George "Bo" Abney, but no one was ever charged.

Soon after the murder of Tommy Farrington, it was Bo Abney's turn, when he failed to kick back enough of his drug profits to the Black Mafia. The powerfully-built hoodlum's body was found dumped on a city street (above), hog-tied with metal coat hangers. His head had been severed, probably while he was alive, and left on the steps of a neighborhood bar.

Larry Starks (above left) rose up the ranks of the Black Mafia when many of its leaders were jailed or on the lam, but he and his cousin Clarence Starks (above right) were caught on an FBI wire extorting a tavern owner.

Gene Hearn (left) was jailed in 1974 for his part in a "massive drug distribution ring" with other Black Mafia leaders. As the syndicate reeled from repeated arrests, Clarence "Squeaky" Hayman (right) tried to reassert its influence on the streets. He was shot dead.

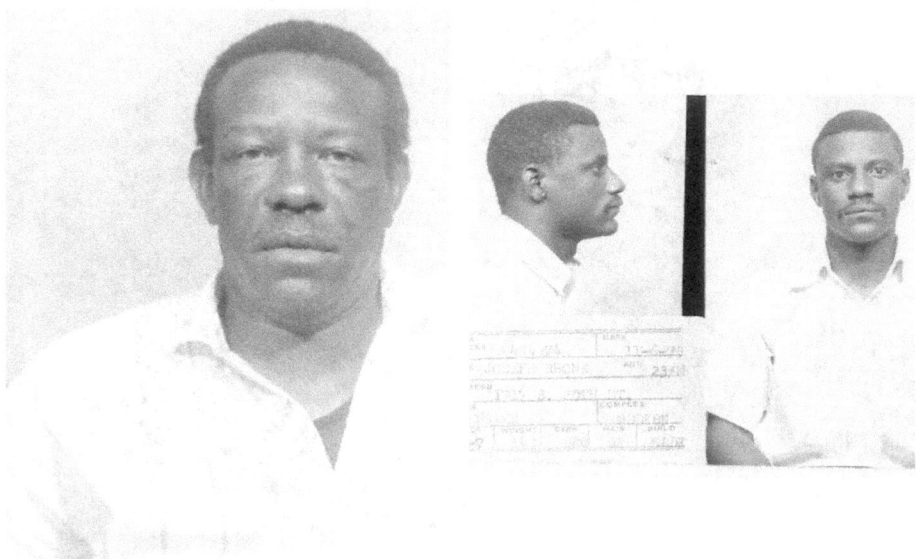

"Cadillac Willie" Rispers (top left) was a protégé of drug dealer Tyrone Palmer and intermittently worked with the Black Mafia. Jo Jo Rhone (top right) was on the run for thirteen years until his eventual capture and jailing in 1989 for two murders. One of those he killed was James Hadley (inset), who he shot in the street (below) from his own doorstep.

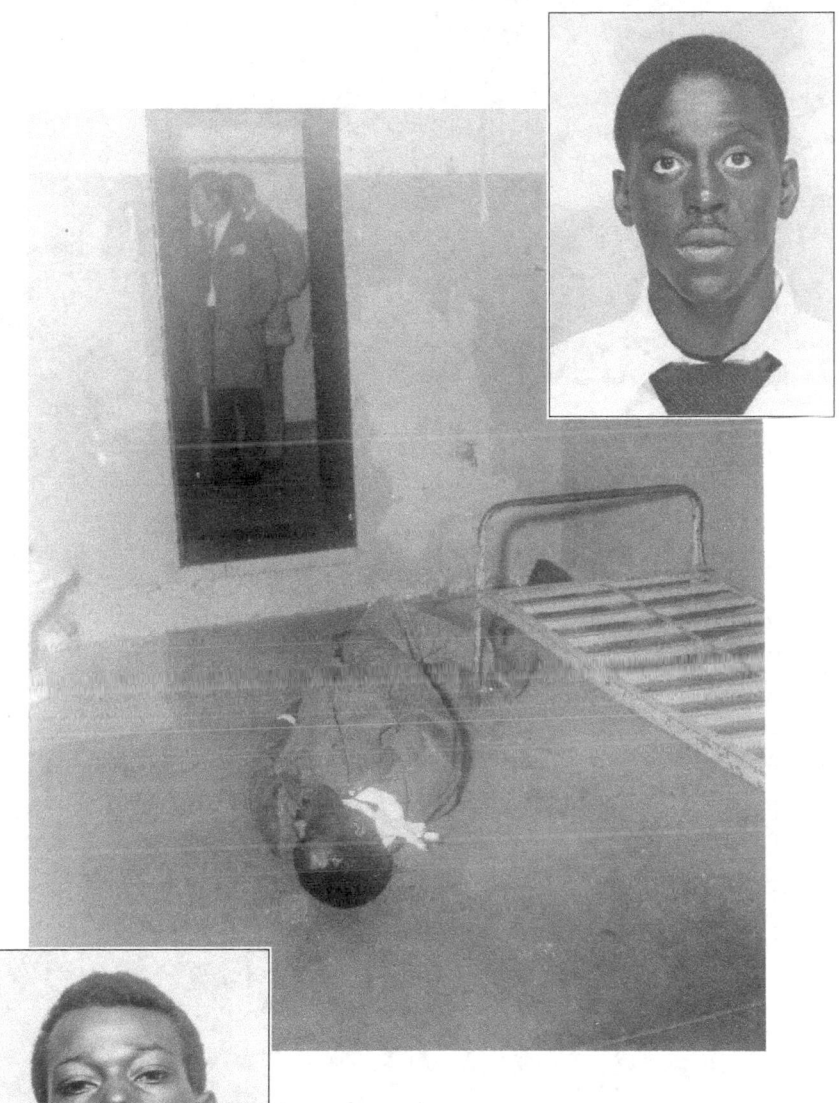

Informer James Price (inset, top right) was horrifically tortured and murdered in his jail cell by fellow inmates. John Griffin (left) was one of the three men who took part in the gruesome killing.

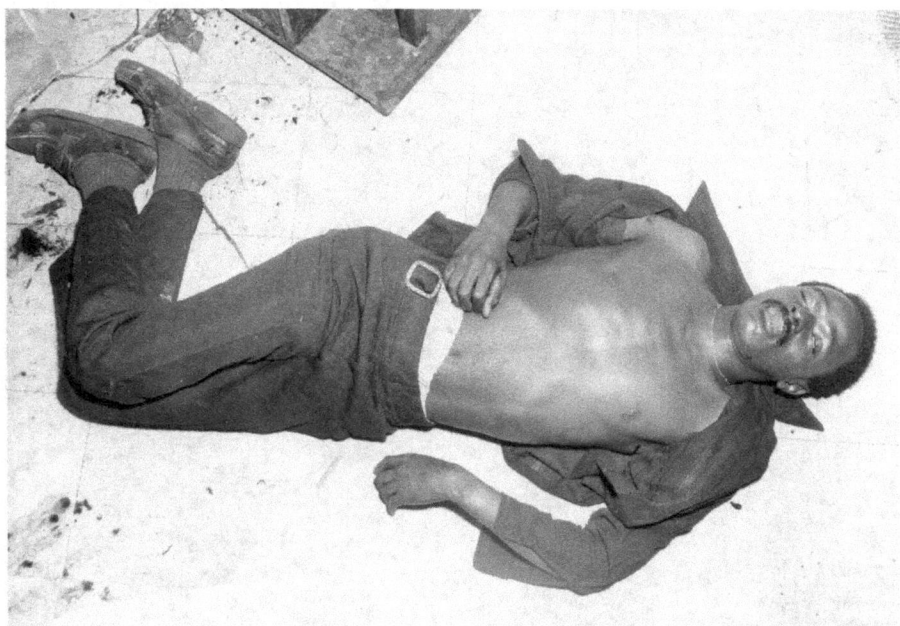

Black Brothers, Inc. secretary David "Scoogie" Mitchell survived an assassination attempt by rival mobsters, yet died in more mundane fashion, shot by his brother during an argument.

Sam Christian and Ron Harvey appeared on the FBI's "Ten Most Wanted List" in December 1973. Christian had been arrested thirty-three times and been charged in seven murders, while Harvey had amassed seventeen arrests and had skipped bail on two counts of homicide.

The outspoken Reverend Muhammad Kenyatta risked his life to take on the Black Mafia in the early 1970s, publicly labelling them "vicious, cold-blooded vermin who prey on their brothers."

Clarence Fowler, a Fruit of Islam captain, lectures gang members during a public relations shoot circa 1969. Several decades later, as Shamsud-din Ali, he became a key target in Philadelphia's federal corruption probe.

Drug dealer says he paid cash to imam's mosque

FBI TAP: IMAM MADE THREAT

Drug probe opened door for City Hall bug

ALEJANDRO A. ALVAREZ/Daily News file photo
Shamsud-din Ali is facing another indictment.

Alis facing more fraud charges

MUSLIM CLERIC IS INDICTED

SIX OTHERS ALSO NAMED IN COURT

Mob ties add twist to probe of cleric

Probe figure Imam Shamsud-din Ali appeared at 2001 pension board meeting as "friend" of bidder.

IMAM'S 'UNUSUAL' FRIENDSHIP DREW ATTENTION

TIE TO BIDDING PENSION FIRM CURIOUS

By DAVE DAVIES, BOB WARNER & ERIN EINHORN
davies@phillynews.com

WHEN THE city pension board met in early 2001 to hear a Pittsburgh company's pitch to manage $100 million in assets, an unusual figure was in the room: Imam Shamsud-din Ali, the Muslim cleric who has emerged as a prominent figure in a federal corruption probe.

The pension board decided not to entrust its assets to the firm, HT Asset Management, but participants regarded the Imam's presence as unusual.

"That's why I remember the meeting," city Finance Director

George Burrell's legal fees connected to probe will be paid by city; Story on Page 16.

and Ali emerged with the FBI raid of Ali's firm, Keystone Financial Information Services.

financial services firm.

In a separate October raid, federal agents seized numerous boxes from the city pension fund office.

Davis said she had arranged for HT Asset Management's appearance before the pension board, something she said often happens when a company wants to pitch its services or when a member of the city administration suggests it.

Davis said she believed someone recommended HT to her, but she can't remember who.

George Burrell, the administration's secretary for external affairs, who often plays a role in the selection of professional firms, said he had nothing to do with arranging the meeting.

Burrell said he was vaguely aware of the firm and knew they'd played a minor role in city bond work. Records show HT Capital Markets has earned about $41,000 on three city-related bond deals since 2000.

Davis said it was clear after the presentation the firm didn't meet the city's needs and the board never considered the company again.

A Daily News attempt over the past two days to review the meeting minutes was unsuccessful. Pension board officials said materials were stored in boxes due to a

---

Philadelphia's headline-making corruption investigation was revealed by the discovery of a secret bugging device in the Mayor's Office and involved Shamsud-din Ali, among others.

---

the contracts that are expected in the future from Don King Productions as a result of the Michael Jackson concert tour. [The FBI's office in] Philadelphia has received information that [name redacted] wants to muscle in and have a say as to which companies or businesses are awarded contracts.

Despite Culbreth's efforts, which included criticizing the Jackson tour and Don King Productions for not employing enough African-American promoters, Shabazz and King agreed to terms with a popular, longtime Philadelphia disc jockey and activist named Georgie Woods. When Woods announced that he had agreed to terms with the Jacksons Tour (the group had reunited for the tour), he did so accompanied by his "spiritual adviser," Shamsud-din Ali. Ali, of course, was one of Shabazz's early recruits in Philadelphia, and succeeded him as head of Temple 12.

Notwithstanding the Jackson-King-Culbreth fiasco, the investigation into Jeremiah Shabazz had grown considerably. Correspondence between regional FBI field offices detailed several meetings between undercover FBI agents and Shabazz and his partners at various spots in New York City and Cherry Hill, New Jersey. During one of the meetings, Shabazz asked if the supposed drug dealer was interested in the "male" or the "female," street lingo for heroin and cocaine respectively. The undercover agent told Shabazz that he was interested in the "male" only, and Shabazz said it would be no problem obtaining the product because of the contacts he had throughout the country from all of his travels. The agent paid him $500 as a deposit on the heroin sample that Shabazz was to procure in a short period of time.

The FBI's broader strategy was to get Shabazz to sell an undercover agent a quarter ounce sample of heroin for $2000 for the ostensible purpose of the agent buying a much larger quantity if the product was of high quality. The Philadelphia office of the FBI and the Strike Force agreed that he was a "significant target" because of his "involvement with all types of organized crime elements in the Philadelphia area." It was further noted that Shabazz "should not be approached until such time as a significant heroin case has been developed against [him] which would ensure an extensive period of incarceration or total cooperation on [his] part." Thus, the end game was to flip him to become a top-level informant: "Once Shabazz supplies the one quarter ounce, [the FBI's field office in] Newark will approach him for his cooperation in continued investigation of drug matters and organized crime activity." Specifically, the FBI believed that if he agreed to cooperate, Shabazz "very likely could provide information ... [concerning] Black Muslim trafficking in heroin and cocaine in the Philadelphia area [and] narcotics dealing between the Black Muslims and the ... LCN organization in the Philadelphia/Atlantic City area."

As the investigation reached a crucial junction, the FBI offices in New

York, Newark and Philadelphia coordinated the prospective deals with Shabazz, and received authorization from FBI headquarters for "buy money" for a one-quarter kilo of heroin. According to a May 1984 teletype, "The Bureau authorized sufficient funds with which to make heroin purchases from Shabazz ... which [the FBI's office in] Philadelphia estimates should be within the $50,000 to $75,000 range."

On May 9, an undercover FBI agent from the New York office met with Shabazz and an associate to discuss the prospective deal. Shabazz said he would be able to take care of the agent's drug needs and that "his people" could supply a pound or two at a time. The deal was supposed to be consummated the following week but was put off because Shabazz had to give a speech to a Muslim youth group. "Ironically, Minister Jeremiah preaches weekly on the evil of narcotics to his [congregation] and maintains a high profile in the black community as being against all narcotics," the FBI noted.

The plan was to approach Shabazz for his cooperation immediately after the deal went down, if he brought the heroin himself. The FBI also addressed the more likely situation. "If, as expected, Shabazz either sends one of his associates or is accompanied by one of his associates to make the transaction, Shabazz will have to be approached as soon as is practical." Months of negotiations between the parties took place until an undercover FBI agent received a phone call on 28 November 1984, from either Shabazz or one of his associates, who said "that he had a large sum of heroin for sale."

The agent purchased a sample of heroin from Shabazz or one of his partners on December 1. Unfortunately, the FBI has removed or heavily redacted documents that involve the resolution of the investigation into Shabazz's activities. The Bureau also refuses to discuss his role in these matters – as a suspect, defendant or informant. Shabazz was never charged, and the manner in which his voluminous FBI file has been redacted could be interpreted as suggesting that he or his unnamed primary associate provided information.

Jeremiah Shabazz wasn't the only Philadelphia Black Muslim leader discovered in the midst of the 1981-1982 investigations into Black Mafia narcotics trafficking. On 22 February 1982, Imam Shamsud-din Ali was observed talking with Lonnie Dawson and Roy Hoskins. Ali was also the topic of several conversations on court-authorized wiretaps of Dawson, Lawrence Simons and Gene Hearn. Federal agents thus had further confirmation of earlier information that stated Shamsud-din Ali was still involved in the drug trade. The debate for observers was whether Ali was simply an overseer who collected a street tax on the dealers in return for providing them protection inside the prison system, or if he was more hands-on. He has never been charged with drug offenses.

Federal authorities did not believe they had enough evidence to charge

Gene Hearn, and so he too was spared the fate of Dawson and others. In fact, FBI sources believe the prosecution of Dawson, Hoskins and others spooked him out of the drug trade. The sources also point out that Hearn had developed ties to legitimate society, and was making his name in the political arena. One of his relationships was with Mayor Wilson Goode, the city's first black mayor. Because of Hearn's background, the Mayor was forced to defend the partnership in June of 1985. Mayor Goode's press secretary said that Goode met with Hearn "regularly" because Hearn had been a "respected leader" in the community for the past seven years. This was, of course, not quite right, since Hearn had only been released from prison in 1980. Hearn was also a paid staffer on Robert Williams Jr.'s campaign for District Attorney throughout 1985. Williams's campaign director claimed that he had not known of Hearn's background because he only knew him by the name Fareed Ahmed.

★

Following the heavy round of convictions and lengthy sentences imposed in late 1984 and early 1985, the Black Mafia as an active force on the streets of Philadelphia was virtually defunct. Most of its remaining crimes came when imprisoned members got out and tried to take back their territories, and most of these attempts failed, although several members were able to regain prominence in the heroin trade. One of those who tried to take back his turf was hit man Russell Barnes. Released sometime in 1985, after serving almost ten years on heroin distribution charges, he immediately sought to re-establish himself as a powerful heroin dealer in South Philadelphia. Barnes aligned himself with remnants of the 20th and Carpenter Streets gang, and began extorting numbers house operators and drug dealers. He also hired himself out as an enforcer.

Barnes apparently overstepped his bounds when he played a role in the slaying of Edward "Boney Bill" Perry on 7 December 1985. Boney Bill worked for one of the top heroin wholesalers in the city, "Cadillac" Willie Rispers, a Tyrone Palmer protégé who intermittently worked with the Black Mafia. Rispers put out a contract on Barnes, who began wearing a bullet-proof vest and stopped traveling alone. Nevertheless, in the morning hours of 23 January 1986, he was found dead in a vacant lot in the 1200 block of South Hanson Street in Southwest Philadelphia. The trash-strewn lot sat in the middle of a downtrodden area that was dotted with burned out, boarded up and abandoned buildings. Barnes, aged thirty-seven, was lying on his back with his face covered in blood. A closer inspection showed he had been badly beaten in the face and shot three times, in the left eye, the left ear and the left shoulder.

Barnes's dress showed how the times had changed. At his death, he wore blue jeans and black Reebok sneakers – standard fare for a drug dealer at the time, and a marked departure from the stylish suits and alligator shoes of the era when he and his friends ruled the streets. The days of Superfly – and the Black Mafia – were over. An investigation into his death turned up interesting leads, but, like many other Black Mafia cases, the murder has never been solved. One informant said the hit was ordered from prison by Lonnie Dawson and/or Sam Christian, the latter of whom was rumored to be making a return to the street in the near future. Another source claimed Cadillac Willie Rispers was behind the hit and that it was over the Richard Allen Homes drug territory. In any event, Barnes's death started another war between rival drug factions involving what was left of the 20th and Carpenter Streets gang.

★

Nudie Mims remained in power at Graterford Prison. He was even credited by authorities for having a lead role in the creation of a drug gang calling itself the Junior Black Mafia [JBM]. The JBM started as a handful of cocaine dealers in the city's Germantown section in 1985, and continued to grow, filling the vacuum in the narcotics trade created by the extensive investigations into Philadelphia's crime family in the mid- to late-1980s, and the largely vanquished Black Mafia. Two of the gang's founders, James and Hayward Cole, were enforcers and runners for the Black Mafia in the 1970s. It was said that JBM leader Aaron Jones was obsessed with the popular film *The Godfather* and crafted his persona in the mold of Marlon Brando's character, Vito Corleone.

An OCU intelligence report critiqued the gang in 1988: "The JBM is a group of young black males deeply involved in drug traffic in the Philadelphia area, these members are flashy in their style and flaunt their profits, driving expensive cars mainly Mercedes and BMWs which are completely [customized] with gold trim, black windows, etc. They wear brightly colored jogging suits ... along with expensive jewelry." They were especially known for their trademark, diamond-encrusted rings bearing the initials JBM.

The gang dealt primarily in cocaine, and worked loosely with remaining factions of both the Black Mafia and the Scarfo (*nee* Bruno) crime family. Police conducting surveillance in February 1988 observed a leading JBM figure meeting with an Italian mobster inside "the LCN club-house" at 16th Street and Oregon Avenue. Informants claimed that when JBM members arrived at the clubhouse, they were "greeted as long lost friends." Sources also said that younger members of the Scarfo family, and specifically up-and-comer Joey Merlino, were working with the JBM to commandeer various drug territories throughout the city and southern New Jersey. Several JBM members attended the 1988 murder trial of mob boss Nicky Scarfo in an apparent, and rather poorly calculated, display of support. Law enforcement agencies photographed numerous JBM characters at the trial to build their intelligence on the hyper drug gang. A cocaine distributor named Earl "Mustafa" Stewart was one of the JBM's main suppliers, and his name would later come up in a larger investigation. The ultra-violent JBM was known for its motto, "Get down or lay down" – cooperate or be killed. It followed through on that pledge all too often, to its ultimate demise.

The JBM actually had little in common with its more significant forefather. Where the Black Mafia was engaged in multiple rackets, scams and illicit enterprises, the JBM dealt exclusively in narcotics. Furthermore, the successors had nowhere near the same connections with legitimate society as several Black Mafia figures. The few ties between the new group and the original crew were sporadic and fleeting, not at all the lineage and mentoring suggested by the choice of the name Junior Black Mafia.

One oft-cited JBM tie to the Black Mafia involves Michael Youngblood. "Blood," as he was known, was arrested for his involvement in the Mims-Dawson prison drug network on 29 September 1983, and agreed that day to become an FBI informant. He pleaded guilty in 1984 to conspiracy to distribute cocaine, Quaaludes and marijuana, was given a suspended sentence in January 1988, and was placed on federal probation Youngblood, a grand hustler in the mold of Major Coxson but without the entourage, played the informant system, snitching on various criminal enterprises while keeping his hand in illicit deals. In order to increase his street status, and to ingratiate himself with criminals he was seeking to incriminate, Youngblood put word out that he was one of the founders of the Junior Black Mafia, along with Nudie Mims and others. The Youngblood-JBM myth was quickly adopted by the Pennsylvania Crime Commission, which published the revelation in its reports, and by the Philadelphia press.

It wasn't true. According to his former FBI handlers, Michael Youngblood was never in the JBM, let alone one of its founders or leaders. Rather, they contend, the legend was just one of the many Youngblood-inspired cons that continue to impress. Youngblood finally caused authorities enough grief to cut him loose in March 1988, when he appeared in a TV documentary, unnamed and with his face obscured, claiming to be one of the city's top four drug dealers. During the broadcast, Youngblood also threatened to kill rival Jamaican drug dealers: "We're going to start exterminating them … I'm telling them, we're coming. Not maybe, might, or we're thinking about it. We're coming. Just think when, where, or how. Who's going to be first?" Police and federal authorities immediately suspected it was Youngblood, and arrested him days after the broadcast with eighty-six vials of crack. In September 1988, Youngblood admitted violating his probation by making the threats and holding drugs, and was sentenced to ten years in prison. Nevertheless, he would soon surface again in the broader Black Mafia story.

★

As Black Mafia links to the JBM and others emerged from time to time, another series of historical ties revealed themselves in the mid- to late-1980s. Philadelphia's volatile and mob-ridden Roofer's Union Local 30 had persisted despite the December 1980 assassination of its tough and flamboyant leader, John McCullough. Now led by Steve Traitz, the union was still under investigation for a variety of activities, including bribing judges. Traitz and other Local 30 officials were ultimately convicted on an assortment of charges, including racketeering offenses stemming from all sorts of tactics (beatings, arson, theft, terroristic threats) used to coerce and intimidate non-union contractors. Before sentencing, Traitz visited Shamsud-din Ali's Masjid to arrange protection for himself and his "colleagues" who were destined for Graterford and other Pennsylvania prisons. Ali was well known for his influence in the prison system, due in large part to his close relationship with Nudie Mims. The amorphous network didn't end there, however. Another Local 30 associate, John Berkery, had ties to several Black Mafia-related figures that went back decades. By the 1980s, Berkery was working with Raymond Martorano in the drug trade. Furthermore, Ray Martorano worked with his son, George, orchestrating narcotics deals with imprisoned leaders Lonnie Dawson and Nudie Mims.

Federal authorities documented the Traitz visit to the Masjid because they were already interested in Ali's multifarious activities. One FBI finding concerned manipulation of the state's work release programs for prisons. For a prisoner to qualify for early release from prison, he had to put together a "home plan" that showed he had a relatively stable environment to which he could return. First and foremost, the offender had to establish that he had a job lined up, or at least a realistic strategy for obtaining one. The FBI learned through informants that Black Muslims, particularly Nudie Mims, had put a system in place whereby the Masjid would sponsor Mims's followers for parole, and Shamsud-din Ali would arrange for jobs – real or, so the allegations went, fictitious – in return for favors. Ali's close relationship with Sam Staten, the head of Local 332 of the Laborer's Union, was at the heart of the arrangement. Federal investigators from the FBI and the Department of Labor concluded at the time (in the mid- to late-1980s) that, as union members alleged, Staten was using Black Muslim ex-convicts to intimidate dissident union members. A federal grand jury looked into Staten's links to "criminal elements of the Black Muslims," but no charges were lodged against him.

Staten was also the focus of another organized crime probe. Back in 1985, Ralph Costobile, a South Philadelphia builder with connections to the Scarfo crime family, paid off a Scarfo associate so that Costobile could use non-Local 332 laborers on his construction sites. "Big Ralph" Costobile turned to mobster Nicholas Caramandi, who used his contacts to get in touch with boss Nicky Scarfo, who approved the scheme and directed an associate named Saul Kane to contact Roofers Local 30 boss Steve Traitz. Traitz, the mob's "labor guy," was enlisted as the go-between with Sam Staten at Local 332, since Costobile's scheme depended on Staten's approval. According to Caramandi, Staten met with the interested parties at Costobile's bar, Big Ralph's Saloon, on East Passyunk Avenue in South Philadelphia. All parties worked out a deal that resulted in non-union laborers working Costobile's site. Costobile told Caramandi that the meeting ended with Staten agreeing to the terms, and Costobile in possession of bogus union cards for his workers. Obviously, Scarfo got a cut of the ongoing deal, and Costobile's payments typically went through Caramandi and were conveniently delivered on Friday nights at Big Ralph's Saloon, a mob hangout. According to the Special Agent in Charge of the Labor Department's Philadelphia Office at the time, "Union members who complained about Costobile using non-union laborers were beaten and also in an election in 1985, Costobile on behalf of Sam Staten, made a payoff to an individual by the name of Eddie Walton. Walton was an individual who was a candidate for business manager who was going to run against Staten. And Costobile made a payoff to him in return for Walton withdrawing his candidacy and not opposing Sam Staten."

In fact, investigators documented that Walton was told "if he did not take the money and drop out of the race [against Staten] he would be killed." "Fast Eddie" Walton no doubt knew about 332's history of violence, which included the fatal beating of a dissident union member, and accepted the payoff. Insiders who followed the Ali-Staten-Costobile-Scarfo-Traitz activities no doubt recalled the Altemose and Skyway examples that exhibited the ties binding figures from Roofers Union Local 30, Laborer's Local Union 332, the defense team consisting of Cecil Moore, Charles Peruto, Robert Simone, Stanley Branche and Gus Lacy, and racketeers like Frank Sheeran, John Berkery, Major Coxson, Junior Staino and Sonny Viner.

Though Ralph Costobile eventually pleaded guilty to his involvement in the racketeering activities, Local 332 leader Sam Staten was never charged. Staten's lawyer at the time was Ronald A. White, and the two would be under federal scrutiny again ten years later. Meanwhile, yet another old school Black Mafia figure turned up in the Staten-Costobile probe. It was discovered that in late 1984, Stanley Branche acted as a broker between Costobile and a drug dealer over a $20,000 debt the dealer owed Costobile for two pounds of methamphetamine. Branche's mention in the Costobile investigations was not remarkable, considering his involvement with this crowd over many years. The FBI took note of these events as part of a larger case they were building against Philadelphia's Italian-American crime family.

Stanley Branche and his dear friend Gus Lacy had survived a few brushes with the law over the years. In addition to the Advance Security-Redevelopment Authority scandal in the early 1970s, the two were charged in 1977 with bilking a medical school student of $5,000 in return for getting the student into Philadelphia's Hahnemann Medical College. The charges were ultimately dropped when a prosecution witness died. Branche, of course, lived an interesting life, doing edgework between the underworld and the upperworld. Among numerous other pursuits, the former activist had owned three nightspots through the years: the Rolls Royce (with Major Coxson), the Graduate (with Gus Lacy) and Bugsy Siegel's. Siegel's, named after the infamous Prohibition-era gangster, lasted less than two months.

Branche's affinity for the gangster life eventually led to his arrest for extorting drug dealers on behalf of the Scarfo family. Comically, Branche was running for Congress, with Lacy as his campaign treasurer, at the time. The key incident in the case occurred in August 1985, when Branche and Norman Lit demanded a street tax of $1,000 per week in tribute to the "downtown mob" from a Northeast Philadelphia drug dealer. The incident took place in a Dunkin' Donuts parking lot on Street Road in the Northeast, and the jury rejected the testimony of Branche's key defense witness, his pal Gus Lacy, who claimed he and Branche remained inside the store throughout the incident. One piece of evidence in the case was an FBI tape recording of a November 1986 conversation between Branche and George Botsaris, a leader of Philadelphia's "Greek mob." The tape illustrated the breadth and depth of Branche's knowledge of the underworld.

High-profile defense attorney Robert Simone, perhaps known best for his defense of mob boss Nicodemo Scarfo and other Italian-American crime figures, represented Branche. Simone had been tight with Branche and Lacy for years, and his clientele had included fringe Black Mafia players like James "Foo-Foo" Ragan, Raymond Martorano, and George Martorano. Despite the efforts of Simone, who considered Branche a "dear friend and drinking buddy," the former NAACP leader was convicted in March 1989 and sentenced to five years in federal prison. Reverend Jesse Jackson was among those who wrote letters of support for Branche's parole. Ironically, Branche's pal and defense attorney, Simone, was later convicted of racketeering, extortion and using the violent reputation of the mob to collect loan-shark debts, and was sentenced to a four-year prison term.

★

On 25 October 1989, Philadelphia police and FBI agents entered a home on Watkins Street and found Joseph "Jo Jo" Rhone asleep on a sofa. Before Rhone could reach a .38 caliber handgun lying on the floor nearby, authorities arrested him, ending his thirteen-year run as a fugitive from the Herschell Williams murder in 1975. Along the way, he had hidden in various mosques in Atlanta, Chicago and Detroit. He was charged with the April 1976 murder of James "Monk" Hadley, but the key witness against him, Lonnie Diggs, refused to testify; in 1976, when Diggs had originally named Rhone as the shooter, his mother's home was firebombed and his sister was shot. Federal authorities believed Rhone had stayed in contact with local drug dealers, especially Lonnie Dawson, William Roy Hoskins and Gene Hearn, and may have been one of their sources. He was eventually convicted of both the Williams and Hadley murders.

Meanwhile, *the* most prominent Black Mafia throwback was making an inauspicious return to the streets. Sam Christian was paroled on 4 November 1988, at the age of fifty. He tried to gain the favor of the Junior Black Mafia on numerous occasions, starting just after his release from prison. According to law enforcement sources, Christian was trying to negotiate a truce between the ever-warring factions. "Sam's back and wants to teach these kids some self-discipline," said one investigator. He was rebuffed by the young members for unknown reasons, although one law enforcement official said that he "didn't have the network, fidelity, contacts, supply or distribution" necessary to make his leadership count. One also has to wonder if the JBM crowd knew what little credibility the seminal Black Mafia had in matters of "self-discipline." Christian was arrested in July of 1990 for possession of crack cocaine, in violation of his parole, and was off the streets again.

The JBM soon followed. Law enforcement started receiving good intelligence on the gang not long after it was founded in the mid-1980s, and the Federal Strike Force was assigned to investigate the JBM in 1989. Investigators discovered the group put 100-200 kilos of cocaine, especially in the form of crack, on the streets each month. The JBM murdered several dozen people, including rivals, witnesses, innocent bystanders and their own confederates. Most of the gang's members who survived its many internecine battles were arrested in 1990 and 1991, and the remaining infrastructure was decimated in March of 1992, when twenty-six defendants went on trial for operating "a continuing criminal enterprise known as the JBM." The flash-in-the-pan quasi-successor group with a predilection for media attention and murder was vanquished for good.

*

During his twenty-one years in Graterford, Nudie Mims had corrupted the system through payoffs to guards in cash, narcotics, and sexual favors carried out in his Black Muslim "office" by prostitutes posing as religious volunteers. Women visitors would often wear religious garb to conceal the day's contraband on the odd occasion a guard was not compromised. Yet Mims also provided a service to the prison through his influence on other inmates. "Nudie keeps the lid on things and everything is under his control," said one official. "Yeah, we have drugs, prostitution ... but that's the tradeoff." Mims was the leader, or Imam, of over half of Graterford's prison population. Officials estimated the Muslim community at 1,800, while the prison's total population was less than 3,600. "Officials described him as a power unto himself, controlling other inmates through fear or respect, and the reputed overlord of part of the prison's underground economy."

In 1993, Cythnia Link was a nine-year veteran guard in Graterford Prison. At the time, Mims was a twenty-one-year veteran of the institution. Link recalled the occasion of an evacuation drill that went awry when more than 100 men refused the orders of several guards to participate. "The awesome sight of all of these people out of their cells and not budging was intimidating," she said. "They refused to move in deference to Mims. I said, 'Okay, go get Imam and tell him I need him to move these people.' He came over and moved his hand, and it was done. Then he came up to me and said, 'I move them when I need to move them.'"

Mims's reign at Graterford ended in October of 1995, when 650 state troopers and prison guards, along with thirty drug-sniffing dogs, raided the prison in an attempt to break its cycle of corruption. The search resulted in the confiscation of 200 weapons, fifty-five packets of cocaine, 122 assorted pills and six stashes of marijuana. Governor Tom Ridge estimated the cost of the effort at $2 million. Mims was among twelve inmates transferred, and was sent to the state prison at Camp Hill. He still maintained his networks, and was next "traded" to Minnesota for another inmate serving a life sentence. Pennsylvania Department of Corrections spokesman Mike Lukens said of Mims's reputation in the state system, "He was just somebody we couldn't move anywhere. He had too much influence in the prison."

Mims's influence was inextricably linked to his Black Muslim contacts on the outside, most notably Jeremiah Shabazz and Shamsud-din Ali. While the latter Imam was still on the scene, Shabazz was on the wane. The man who started Temple 12 with Malcolm X and built it into a religious and political force, before being expelled for fomenting Black Mafia activities, died of congestive heart failure on 7 January 1998. The current NOI leader for Philadelphia, Minister Rodney Muhammad, said that under Shabazz, "Philadelphia became one of the leading cities in the Nation of Islam ... A great deal of history goes with Jeremiah Shabazz as it relates to the Nation of Islam ... He was a tremendous groundbreaker and an excellent administrator."

*

As the curtain dropped on the 1990s, Lonnie Dawson was imprisoned somewhere in the Midwest or Western U.S., Nudie Mims was imprisoned in Minnesota, and the vast majority of the Black Mafia hierarchy from years past was dead, in prison, or too old to organize crime. The group's membership and power waned from the late 1970s, and without a real successor group, its members no longer commanded the attention of law enforcement and the media. Piecing together their whereabouts and contemporary activities has predictably become all the more difficult. Little was heard of the syndicate or its affiliates for a time until two of the founding Black Mafia members wound up in the news on different occasions.

Robert "Bop Daddy" Fairbanks, once "the executioner, the enforcer," made the front page of the *Philadelphia Daily News* in July 2001. The District Attorney's Office had just launched a unit targeting the city's repeat offenders. On 2 April 2001, Fairbanks was involved in a shooting that left an innocent bystander paralyzed. At the time of his arrest, he had tallied twenty-eight arrests and had served time for a 1970 homicide. "He was equally well-known to the community as a cranky bookie who allegedly ran an illegal numbers-writing business out of a nondescript, brick storefront on South 52nd Street."

On 22 January 2002, members of the Violent Traffickers Project, including members of the FBI, Philadelphia police and others, arrested Black Mafia founder Sam Christian in South Philadelphia. New York authorities had requested the Philadelphia FBI office arrest Christian, age sixty-two, on a year-old warrant for a parole violation. The notorious, once-feared, 5'10", 220 lb. gangster was described by FBI special agent in charge of drug investigations, Jim Sweeney, as gaunt and gray haired with a white beard. In a comment that served as a metaphor for the Black Mafia, Sweeney said that Christian "was a shadow of his former self."

Yet though the syndicate had been dormant for years, there were a few old heads left in the community who deftly straddled the legitimacy fence, just like in the golden days. Shamsud-din Ali watched Lonnie Dawson, Roy Hoskins and others get picked off the street in the mid-1980s, witnessed the JBM implode in the late 1980s and early 1990s, and saw Russell Barnes and Sam Christian try to take back old territories without success. Throughout, Ali allegedly kept busy with a close-knit extortion network of his own, just as he established himself as a major political power broker in the Philadelphia region. Ali, with the assistance of old-timers like Donnie Day and Darrell Jackson serving as runners on the street, was now the lone person of significance – and it seemed as though the con would go on forever. After all, he had taken over Temple 12 back in 1976, established himself in the protection and extortion rackets soon afterward, and had not faced a criminal prosecution during the more than twenty years since his return to the community.

That was about to change, as Shamsud-din Ali and the rest of the United States realized soon after the October 2003 discovery of an FBI listening device in the Philadelphia Mayor's Office.

CHAPTER 21

THE PROBE

I N THE LATE 1990s, federal agents in Philadelphia conducted a comprehensive investigation into a rap group named RAM Squad that also happened to be a narcotics trafficking organization. According to the rap group itself, and the FBI, "RAM" stood for Richard Allen Mob. RAM Squad was the successor, in name and drug territory, to the original Richard Allen Mafia, which consisted of Black Mafia members and their affiliates. RAM Squad, based in North Philadelphia's Richard Allen Homes projects, dealt in all the standard street drug fare – powder and crack cocaine, marijuana and heroin. The group caught the attention of the Feds when its founder and manager, Ronnie "Bank" Johnson, was shot and killed in September 1997 during a drug war.

Days after the hit, Joseph "Skinny Joey" Merlino, then head of Philadelphia's Italian mob, visited RAM Squad member John Wilson (*aka* Tommy Hill, his stage name) to pay his respects. Because the Feds were constantly monitoring Merlino's activities, they caught the visit and subsequent meetings between the mobster and the drug dealing rap group, including a turkey giveaway staged by Wilson and Merlino that November. Merlino put the rap group in touch with a music promoter named Stephen Epstein, who took them on as a client and orchestrated a deal with a bona fide record label, Universal Music Group. Merlino was to receive a finder's fee if the group hit it big.

RAM Squad's rise ended with the release of its 2001 CD, *Random Access Money*, which was followed by a brief tour. Despite being released and supported by a major label, disc sales were weak at about 13,000. Thus, RAM Squad lost their record deal – and then ran into a blizzard of law enforcement activity. During the early 2000s, federal authorities arrested members of their entourage, including producer Devon "Biggie" Moore, convicted of illegal arms possession, and Bank Johnson's two brothers, Van Johnson, later convicted of murder, and Chad "Ra-Tek" Johnson, later charged with murder. John Wilson, who led the group following the death of Bank Johnson, was arrested in 2003 and pleaded guilty to dealing crack cocaine.

Almost from the start of the investigation into RAM Squad, authorities were looking into who was supplying them with narcotics, and eventually placed wiretaps on the phones of major dealers Gerald "Bubby" Thomas and Kaboni Savage. Thomas and Savage were in charge of a large drug ring with connections to RAM Squad, and the two were indicted in May of 2004 along with eighteen others for their roles in a drug network that supplied hundreds of kilos of cocaine throughout the city between 1999 and 2003. Among those indicted was Dawud Bey, son of the founding Black Mafia member, and high-ranking Black Muslim, Roosevelt "Spooks" Fitzgerald.

It had been rumored for years that Bey – in the Black Mafia tradition – extorted a street tax on drug dealers in South Philadelphia. Of supreme significance to the events consuming Philadelphia's City Hall in 2004, the Thomas-Savage investigation produced an additional outcome. During the FBI and DEA probe into the drug ring, Gerald Thomas was overheard speaking with Imam Shamsud-din Ali on several occasions. The wires allegedly picked up Ali shaking down Thomas for money. On one occasion, Thomas was overheard speaking with Dawud Bey about Ali, who they referred to as "Cutty," short for Cutthroat.

"You talk to Cutty today?" Thomas asked Bey.

"Yeah," said Bey. "[Shamsud-din Ali's] walking with kings and we're out here hustling."

Thomas and Bey also met on occasion with Ali at his upscale home just outside the city, at Ali's Sister Clara Muhammad School, and at his Masjid. With the information gleaned from the narcotics wires, much of which was also provided by other sources, FBI agents applied for court approval to tap Ali's home phone, arguing the proposed wire would possibly disclose evidence regarding "the distribution of drugs ... the planning of extortion and kidnapping schemes to collect criminal proceeds ... [and] a scheme involving bribery of a public official." Federal agents could not have known where the otherwise routine narcotics investigation was about to take them when the court authorized the wiretap on Shamsud-din Ali's phone on 13 June 2001.

One month later, the FBI also got authorization to listen in on conversations on Ali's cell phone. They overheard the politically connected, business savvy Muslim cleric talking with bankers, lawyers, vendors and other significant political players. Many of these individuals would soon end up being investigated themselves. As one person said of Ali: "Being selfish, stupid, and greedy, [Ali] delivered them on a silver platter."

In no time, authorities were developing cases against Ali and his wife Faridah for a variety of offenses. Faridah was suspected of being involved in a scandal at the Community College of Philadelphia (CCP) concerning no-show teachers whose classes were supposed to be held at the Sister Clara Muhammad School. IRS agents searched the CCP office of Delores Weaver, a friend of Faridah's, and seized records related to the adult education scam. Authorities also suspected Shamsud-din Ali of using his connections to Street Administration officials to get a $60,595 kickback on a delinquent-tax collection case. Ali ran a mom-and-pop collection agency called Keystone Information Financial Services (KIFS) out of a storefront on Germantown Avenue. Meanwhile, as the Feds continued pursuing the CCP and KIFS leads, they overheard Ali on his cell phone speaking with Philadelphia power attorney and Democratic fundraiser Ron White.

One conversation between the two influential men concerned contracts at Philadelphia International Airport. Phone taps were authorized for White's office and cell phones. As a result of information gleaned from those intercepts, wiretaps were approved on the phone of Treasurer Corey Kemp, who oversaw bond work for the city, and for Ron White's law office. White so frequently discussed city business and mentioned the mayor's name that authorities sought court approval for a bug in Mayor John Street's office. U.S. District Judge Eduardo C. Robreno authorized the electronic device for the mayor's office on 18 September 2003. The public had little, if any, knowledge of these extensive law enforcement efforts when the bug was discovered in Mayor Street's office less than three weeks later.

The numerous inter-related investigations, collectively referred to as "The Probe," led initially to indictments against five people, including Faridah Ali, her daughter, Lakiha "Kiki", and son, Azeem "Osh", who were charged with stealing federal funds meant for adult education. The government alleged that Ali conspired with, amongst others, Delores Weaver, then director of the federally funded Adult Basic Education (ABE) program for the Community College of Philadelphia, to steal $224,375. Sister Clara Muhammad School was approved as a site for ABE programs, and Faridah Ali masterminded a scheme involving paying her children and others for teaching non-existent ABE classes sponsored by CCP from the Fall of 1999 through December 2001.

When the investigation into the CCP scam was disclosed to the public, Faridah Ali said, "A long time ago, they decided they wanted to bring this Muslim organization down and bring down Shamsud-din ... This is an attack on Islam." She added, "I'm being targeted because I'm Muslim. I'm African-American. I'm woman." Faridah also said, "They can send the FBI. They can send the CIA. They can do what they want, but then we fight. I only rely on Allah ... The only thing I can be afraid of is Allah. Because otherwise I'm making the federal government and my enemies who are saying these things to them, I'm making them bigger than God."

At trial, the defense list of witnesses included boxing champ Mike Tyson, Lakiha's former lover, but he was never called to testify. The Government's tapes appeared as promised, however, and ultimately sealed Faridah Ali's fate. Prosecutors were also able to demonstrate the so-called "teachers" were not physically available to teach at the supposed times and locations they listed on various documents. Notwithstanding the repeated cries of racism and bigotry, Faridah Ali and her three co-defendants were each found guilty on 27 October 2004, on all counts against them. One of the people who testified on behalf of the defense was a psychic named Valerie Morrison. Following the guilty verdicts, a juror sarcastically noted that Morrison should have warned Faridah her phones were tapped.

Much of the broader corruption probe into the so-called "pay-to-play" political system in Philadelphia has little to do with Shamsud-din Ali, though of course the investigation is ultimately traced back to intercepts of his calls with campaign fund raiser and power lawyer Ronald A. White. White and eleven others were indicted on 20 June 2004. The fifty-six-count, 150-page indictment detailed White exploiting his ties to the Street administration, especially his close relationship with City Treasurer Corey Kemp. Essentially, companies who agreed to White's demands for legal fees or retainers, or made "donations" to his charitable organization or contributions to his political affiliates, got contracts with the City. The financial contributions were shared between White and public officials. U.S. Attorney Patrick L. Meehan commented, "The nameplate on the desk of the City Treasurer may have read 'Corey Kemp' but Ron White was calling the shots."

The Government's case against White, Kemp and others was based in part on numerous wiretapped conversations. On 26 August 2003, Ron White was overheard speaking with Corey Kemp discussing the process they had employed whereby firms would either make political contributions or be excluded from obtaining City business.

"Either you down or you ain't with it," said White.

"Right," responded Kemp, "cause if they don't, if they ain't with us they ain't gonna get nothing."

Incredibly, the City Treasurer then employed the Junior Black Mafia's old motto when he continued, "You know, you just hate to say it but that's the way it is, man, I mean, this is ... election time, this is time to either *get down or lay down*, man, I mean, come on, to me, personally it's not even a hard decision" (emphasis added). Unlike when the JBM employed the saying, however, people who didn't play along with White, Kemp and gang were not assassinated, but their opportunities for work with the city were effectively terminated. [1]

U.S. Rep. Robert A. Brady was among the prominent Democrats who outwardly questioned the motivations of the Justice Department when the bug was discovered in Mayor Street's office in October 2003. Brady, the Philadelphia Democratic Party Chairman, joined with two other local Democratic congressmen, Chaka Fattah and Joseph M. Hoeffel, and wrote a letter to Attorney General John Ashcroft and FBI head Robert S. Mueller soon after the bug's discovery that stated, "The conduct of your personnel raises suspicions that this might be an attempt to intervene in and even compromise an election." *Philadelphia Magazine* caught up with Rep. Brady in the summer of 2004 to see what he thought of the probe, now that the election was long over and indictments had since been handed down – first involving the narcotics conspiracy, and more importantly those concerning municipal corruption that originated with the unrelated drug case. The politician now conceded that he simply seized on a grand political opportunity during a close campaign. "I was just spinning the shit, and it worked," he admitted.

Amongst firms being investigated in the wide-ranging federal inquiry was West Insurance, a minority-certified firm with an advisory board that has read like a Who's Who of Philadelphia's African-American power players, including Robert Bogle, Bruce Crawley, Charles Greene, Willie Johnson, Obra Kernodle, Carl Singley, Bernard West and his son Kobie West, and Fletcher Wiley. Of particular note, West Insurance's Vice President is Fareed Ahmed who, of course, was formerly known as Gene Hearn, Black Mafia drug kingpin and co-founder of Black Brothers, Inc.

Willie Johnson is one of the city's preeminent businessmen, best known for his pioneering stewardship of PRWT, a national firm that specializes in third-party payment processing and systems management services for the municipal sector. PRWT has frequently served as the minority subcontractor to larger firms seeking municipal business, including corporate giant Lockheed Martin. Johnson's firm worked in concert with a Lockheed subsidiary, Lockheed Martin Information Management Systems (Lockheed Martin IMS), that was acquired in 2001 by Affiliated Computer Services (ACS), a national firm based in Dallas that has maintained the relationship with PRWT. These ties have become fodder for discussion as inquiries into the "pay-to-play" culture persist, and also because of a threat issued to a broker in an ACS deal that was taped by the FBI investigating Imam Shamsud-din Ali.

Shamsud-din Ali approached power attorney Carl Singley in 2000 to see if Ali's firm, KIFS, could get at least a part of the city's lucrative contracts with ACS. Singley has said, "My recollection is that I was approached by the Imam and [the late U.S. Rep. Lucien 'Lu'] Blackwell about whether or not there was an opportunity for the Imam's company with ACS ... I knew of the Imam. I knew of his relationship to Lu ... He was a leader in the Muslim community and well-respected." Singley, a consultant for Lockheed Martin IMS, set up a meeting between Ali and Tom Wrigley, Senior Vice President and Managing Director of Lockheed Martin IMS's Municipal Service Division. In the early 1980s, Wrigley served as Mayor Bill Green's chief of staff, which included Singley and Willie Johnson. Wrigley met with Ali over breakfast at the posh Four Seasons hotel. For unknown reasons, Lockheed Martin never consummated a deal with Ali/KIFS. Wrigley retired in December 2001 (just after ACS acquired the firm), and was replaced by Joe Martz, who previously served as Managing Director of Philadelphia and then as the city's Chief Operating Officer under Mayor Street. Martz, ACS's managing director of municipal services, was contacted by Singley on behalf of Ali in early 2003. Martz met with Ali, who then met on another occasion with an ACS representative at the KIFS office before traveling together to the office of a firm called Universal Payment Solutions (UPS).

People familiar with the ACS/UPS/KIFS negotiations say that Ali – whom one party in the deal derisively referred to as "*Scam*sud-din" – was offering UPS access to city contracts currently governed exclusively by ACS. Throughout the Ali courting of ACS, ACS had no need for a minority subcontractor because of its longstanding relationship with PRWT. The Ali-proposed pact would apparently have been an add-on to the existing city agreement with ACS, and it would have entailed Ali receiving a finder's fee from UPS. A contract was drawn up at some point in mid-2003 just before the federal investigation into Ali's Sister Clara Muhammad School was made public that summer. The disclosure apparently troubled ACS officials, who sat on the KIFS/UPS agreement until it became clear to Ali the deal was off.

Federal authorities were by this time hot on Ali for his many activities, and were listening in on a conversation the Imam held with an undisclosed party on his cell phone when he threatened to harm a business associate that he blamed for bungling the ACS deal. The business associate has not been identified publicly, though as policy dictates, the FBI warned the person of the threat. Shamsud-din Ali was also taped making threats against Mayor Street's top aide, George R. Burrell. According to the *Philadelphia Inquirer*, Ali believed Burrell was cooperating with federal investigators and told an unidentified person that Burrell should watch himself. As in the other case, the FBI warned Burrell of the threat, and for a time a police officer was assigned to protect him around-the-clock.

The advent of Shamsud-din Ali's taped threat regarding the failed ACS bid is intriguing for reasons beyond the ongoing corruption probe. The noteworthy success of Willie Johnson's PRWT is inextricably linked to ACS. Though PRWT is said to stand for People Really Working Together, insiders know the firm's name was initially an acronym for the principals: the R, W and T stood for Raymond A. Saulino, Willie F. Johnson, and William L. Turner, three of the four founders. The P indicated an individual anyone familiar with the Black Mafia story knows well – former judge Paul Dandridge.

Dandridge, who served on the Municipal Court from 1968 to 1973 and the Court of Common Pleas from 1974 to 1984, had quite a career of public service and philanthropy behind him by the time he got involved in PRWT. In 1982, United States Senator and ex-D.A. Arlen Specter proposed his former understudy for the post of U.S. Attorney for the Eastern District of Pennsylvania, before Dandridge was removed from consideration when the requisite FBI background check raised concerns. Though numerous news articles have been written about the Specter-Dandridge U.S. Attorney bid, the reason for the FBI concerns has never been disclosed. One common speculation predictably revolves around the controversial 1972 testimonial dinner for which he was sanctioned by the state Supreme Court, though an

FBI source familiar with the situation stresses the dinner was simply one matter among others, including Dandridge's associations with Black Mafia figures, which aroused concerns. The Dandridge curiosity vis-à-vis the Ali-ACS-PRWT relationships would be just that save for yet another failed business deal involving Shamsud-din Ali.

On September 11, 2000, Paul Dandridge was hired to serve on the board of First Chesapeake Financial Corporation, then based in Philadelphia. Three days later, the firm released the following statement: "First Chesapeake Financial Corp. is buying Keystone Information and Financial Services Inc. ... Philadelphia-based Keystone provides municipal revenue recovery and revenue enhancement services, such as litigation and enforcement, lease-sharing ventures, tax discovery and census and fraud investigation. Officials for First Chesapeake, a mortgage company based in Philadelphia, said the acquisition of Keystone would allow First Chesapeake to expand its specialty portfolio, business and add a 'strongly profitable segment to First Chesapeake, CEO and Chairman Mark Mendelson said. The terms of the sale were not disclosed."

No doubt, few financial observers pieced together the fascinating history behind the First Chesapeake–KIFS deal. The newly-appointed First Chesapeake director, Dandridge, after all, knew the head of KIFS, Shamsud-din Ali, from the Black Mafia's glory days when Ali, then known as Clarence Fowler, worked under Dandridge at the North Philadelphia office of Safe Streets, Inc. This was just prior to Fowler's 1970 arrest for the murder of Rev. Smith and his five-year stint in prison before his conviction was overturned. While Fowler (Ali) was incarcerated at Holmesburg Prison, his cellmate was Darrell Anthony Jackson, who was in prison for a bank robbery he committed with the Black Mafia's murderous John Clark. It was Clark's wife who served as the Safe Streets, Inc. receptionist during the Black Mafia's exploitation of the federally-funded program run out of D.A. Specter's Office.

The First Chesapeake–KIFS agreement announced in September 2000 never materialized because the principals of First Chesapeake discovered that claims made by KIFS were misleading. According to Dandridge, "A careful review showed [KIFS] wasn't what it claimed to be." Despite the failed deal with First Chesapeake, the episode illustrates the enduring ties Shamsud-din Ali has maintained with prominent members of business and society. The legitimacy afforded Ali and his Black Mafia compatriots in the 1960s and 1970s that brought them to prominence was exhibited yet again and continued to confuse the public and intimidate those around him.

*

While running his Masjid in West Philadelphia, Shamsud-din and his wife attained a high social status, which they exhibited in a variety of ways, from attending black tie affairs with heavy-hitting political figures and celebrities to driving late model luxury cars and living in a gated suburban community in an exclusive neighborhood called Latham Park, in Melrose Park, just north of the city in Cheltenham Township, Montgomery County.

Shamsud-din has been a political force almost since he got out of prison in 1976, courted during campaigns for his endorsement and, more importantly, for his get-out-the-vote support. His ability to influence and mobilize the Muslim vote has been vital to the region's politicians, including Mayor/Governor Edward G. Rendell and City Council President/Mayor John F. Street. Ali is also (at the time of writing) the assistant *amir* (director) of, and spokesman for, the Majlis Ash'Shura, an umbrella group of some thirty-five clerics from area mosques representing different sects. As one Philadelphia political commentator remarked in 1996, "Anyone who wants to seek political office in this town should first seek Shamsud – that is the word among potential candidates."

Loosely stating that Shamsud-din Ali has become politically significant or that he and his family have built relationships with high-profile personalities does not tell the whole story. Some examples illustrate the variety, extent and duration of his connections. In 1982, Republican Governor Richard Thornburgh visited Ali's mosque during his re-election campaign. The following year, Ali traveled to Cape Canaveral in Florida to watch the liftoff of Space Shuttle Challenger, which was carrying Philadelphia-born astronaut Guion S. Bluford, Jr. Shamsud-din Ali was accompanied by music mogul Kenny Gamble, U.S. Rep. William H. Gray III, and Philadelphia School Superintendent Constance Clayton. City Councilman Lucien Blackwell and his wife/assistant Jannie were also there with Ali, whose Masjid and school sat in Blackwell's council district (Lucien Blackwell was later elected to Congress, and Jannie took over his City Council seat). Years later, in 1995, Shamsud-din and Faridah Ali were honored by several noteworthy personalities at a black tie affair for their work at Sister Clara Muhammad School. The master of ceremonies was Kenny Gamble (Luqman Abdul Haqq) and the mistress of ceremonies Valerie Morrison, psychic and former spiritual adviser to the likes of Frank Sinatra and Mexican songstress Selena. Philadelphia's Deputy Mayor praised the school's "Adopt-a-Student" program that placed Sister Clara Muhammad students in city council, the mayor's office and in business environments. Congressman Chaka Fattah donated $15,000 to the school, and then-City Council President John Street said the school was "exactly what we need in our community today. God bless you as you do His work." Jimmy Binns, the former Pennsylvania boxing commissioner and counsel for the World Boxing Association, added his praise. "We publicly support Imam Ali and his wife because they are so easy to love," he declared. "I pledge to continue to support them both physically and financially." The affair's program featured pictures of Ali's family with boxers Mike Tyson and Muhammad Ali.

Shamsud-din Ali's son, Abdul-Rafi Ali, was twenty-six years old and working in the city Register of Wills Office when he was shot and killed in the summer of 1996, apparently over a trivial neighborhood dispute. Mayor Ed Rendell eulogized Abdul-Rafi at Ali's Masjid, and said that Ali's mosque was "a force for nonviolence, a force for peace, a force for persuading a lot of young people not to get involved in drugs ... one of the most positive forces in the city."

When John Street was elected Mayor of Philadelphia in 1999, Shamsud-din Ali served on his transition team to help shape policy and advise on new personnel for "quality of life" issues. Two years later, Street appointed Ali as one of the seven members of Philadelphia Prison System's Board of Trustees, which makes decisions about how inmates are treated and how prisons are managed. According to Jimmy Binns, one of Ali's lawyers, and someone who has visited prison with him, Shamsud-din is "more revered in Graterford than he is on the streets or in the Masjid where he preaches – and not just by the inmates." According to Binns, when Ali walked into the prison, "it was as though President George Bush was going to visit the troops in Baghdad."

During the spring of 2001, Mayor Street joined U.S. Reps. Bob Brady and Chaka Fattah in celebrating the anniversary of Ali's Sister Clara Muhammad School, and District Attorney Lynne M. Abraham took out a full-page ad in the event's program book. The covert backdrop to the event was the burgeoning federal probe of Ali based on the massive narcotics investigation already well underway by the time wiretaps were approved for his phones, beginning in June 2001. According to Faridah Ali, her daughter, Lakiha, was just a few blocks from the World Trade Centers in New York City when the hijacked planes struck on September 11, 2001, and was driven from the chaotic scene by rapper-actor Ice-T. Two months after the attacks, the Philadelphia Association of Black Journalists organized a panel discussion, "Shattering the Peace: Understanding the Roots of the Sept. 11 Attacks," that featured three "scholars" including Shamsud-din Ali. Ali has also served on the Pennsylvania Attorney General's School Safety Task Force.

Shamsud-din Ali has deftly managed his political involvement while overseeing his tax-exempt Masjid. For example, though IRS rules regarding tax-exempt charities state they must not participate, or intervene, in any political campaign, Ali's Sister Clara Muhammad School received $16,200 for election work on behalf of Ed Rendell's successful campaign for Pennsylvania Governor in 2002. The school was paid for getting roughly 6,000 campaign volunteers placed on 300 vans and buses and transported to the polls on Election Day.

Faridah appears to have flexed her own political muscle in a controversial 2003 business deal. She submitted an application for MBEC certification as a disadvantaged minority-business enterprise for a firm called Elite Services, operated out of the same small office front location as KIFS, below Azeem Spicer's apartment. The application included Mayor Street and Ron White as references. On 17 July 2003, MBEC wrote to Faridah Ali explaining the office's refusal to certify Elite Services on the grounds that she had not provided financial information such as tax returns, a bank statement, and an insurance certificate. Though nothing had changed in the span of twenty-four hours, Elite Services was certified by MBEC the following day. Elite Services was up and running for the start of the Fall football season, and operated one of only twelve lucrative concession stands available to independent vendors at the new home of the Philadelphia Eagles, Lincoln Financial Field. Faridah and Azeem operated the stand, which served a Southern regional menu: fried chicken, fried fish, collard greens, potato salad, beans and water ice.

On 30 October 2003, after Shamsud-din Ali was publicly identified as one of the key subjects in the federal probe, he was honored by the Philadelphia Multicultural Affairs Congress, a division of the Philadelphia Convention and Visitors Bureau, for his "personal dedication and hard work to increase Philadelphia's share of the multicultural convention and tourism markets." Bruce Crawley, chairperson emeritus of the organization, introduced Ali at the banquet and said, "Here is a man who does great things all the time." Mayor Street was also there, and added, "If this great Congress believes Shamsud-din Ali is worthy of the award, then it should be given to him. I remind people that because there's an investigation doesn't mean anybody has done anything wrong." The looming probe also didn't deter Street from inviting Ali to join him and a few dozen supporters on stage at the Mayor's victory party following the November election. As the probe's focus turned to Ali in late 2003, councilwoman Jannie Blackwell said of the Imam, "Everyone who knows him views him as an honest person who you can count on."

An influential crowd of individuals has consistently paraded with Ali in public, in his Masjid, and in the Sister Clara Muhammad School. The collective celebrity of the Alis is perhaps best illustrated in the many photos inside their suburban mansion that show them with famous people, including former U.S. President Bill Clinton. In one photo, Shamsud-din Ali shakes hands with Clinton as John Street stands alongside, and another shows Faridah standing between Street and Clinton.

The litany of Shamsud-din Ali's high-profile affiliations likely accounted for Dawud Bey's taped remark decrying Ali "walking with kings" while drug dealer and murder suspect Bey was stuck out on the street "hustling." One could easily argue that although Ali was indeed consorting with a different crowd, he also was, in essence, hustling. The main difference, on the surface, was that Ali was legitimate and providing "consulting" and "broker" services. Insiders knew better – and so did the FBI.

CHAPTER 22 ★

THE TIES THAT BIND

O N 29 SEPTEMBER 2004, Shamsud-din Ali was indicted as the leader of a racketeering enterprise that included his wife and five others. Announcing the forty-eight-count RICO indictment, the U.S. Attorney for the Eastern District of Pennsylvania said, "This enterprise used political influence as leverage and access to people in high places as a hammer. This organization wrapped its tentacles around individuals, institutions, government entities or whomever it targeted as a source of profit, and simply applied pressure when necessary. Taxpayers wound up stuck with the bill for work that was never done. Banks were defrauded, vendors were extorted, and even contributors to a religious school were duped." He added, "This is a case where influence, access and power were used as weapons. A well-placed phone call. A meeting with a member of City Council or the Mayor's staff helped seal deals that appeared in jeopardy."

The head of Philadelphia's FBI office described the complex enterprise in six words: "Lies, kickbacks, lies, shakedowns, lies, greed."

Ali and the others were charged with a variety of related offenses that essentially derived from four scams involving the following entities: Sister Clara Muhammad School, Bowman Properties, AAT Communications, and Waste Management & Processors, Inc. The Imam and his wife allegedly pilfered an estimated $189,000 in funds that contributors and consumers thought was destined for the school, and defrauded the Community College of Philadelphia by charging $21,600 for the rent of Sister Clara Muhammad for CCP classes never taught there. These charges were in addition to the offenses for which Faridah and her children were convicted in 2004, involving bogus CCP classes. Shamsud-din and Faridah were also charged with submitting false financial information to obtain an $87,078 auto loan for a new Mercedes Benz S500 sedan. A taped comment made by Faridah Ali captured the self-inflated mindset behind the couple. "The Imam can't make a statement in a seven-year-old car," she told a relative. "A world leader can't be driving around in an old car." Lastly, both were charged with tax evasion for the period 1998-2001 for failing to disclose illegal income.

Formerly known as Rita M. Spicer, Faridah divorced from Merrill Spicer in the late 1980s, and the former couple's home just outside Philadelphia was officially turned over to her as part of the settlement. She lived there with one of the major suppliers to the Junior Black Mafia, Earl "Mustafa" Stewart (*aka* Earl Dixon). Stewart later testified that he supplied hundreds of kilos of cocaine to the JBM, and was paid in garbage bags filled with money. He often met with Shamsud-din Ali. During their time together, Rita joined Stewart ringside at boxing matches and was shuttled around in limousines. Intriguingly, she was a government informer at the time, providing information against the dealers competing with the JBM. She left Stewart in 1990, months before he was arrested, and in the summer of that year secretly married Shamsud-din Ali as his second wife under Muslim law, adopting the name Faridah, which means "Precious Gem." The secret marriage somehow wound up in the pages of the *Philadelphia Tribune*, and a public ceremony was held in October 1990. There was one problem with Shamsud-din's new marriage: his first wife, Lillian, was apparently not okay with the "second wife" concept, and she and Shamsud-din divorced in 1992. The Imam was represented in the divorce proceedings by his friend, Ron White.

Faridah Ali's son, Azeem Spicer, was convicted in 1999 for a firearms offense in a case in which he was cleared of attempted murder. In January 2001, police responded to a late-night alarm call at an apartment above Shamsud-din Ali's KIFS office. They found $30,000 worth of marijuana and cocaine, scales, 5000 baggies, and a Tech-9 semi-automatic pistol in the apartment, and arrested its resident, twenty-eight-year-old Azeem. He was held for trial on drug and weapon charges, but the D.A.'s Office dropped the weapon charge before the case went to trial. In court, Faridah Ali testified that rap groups also used the apartment, because she and Azeem ran a music production business together. A jury acquitted Azeem Spicer on the drug charges after renowned mob attorney Joseph Santaguida argued that others had access to the apartment and that the narcotics did not belong to his client.

Shamsud-din Ali's Keystone Information and Financial Services (KIFS) was founded in 1997 by the Muslim cleric and his then-partner, Marcellino Guerrero. At the time of writing, KIFS functions primarily as a collection agency and, according to Ali, initially won debt collection work from the city in 1998 during the tenure of Mayor Ed Rendell. KIFS operates out of a small, rundown storefront in the Mount Airy section of Philadelphia. The office's outside appearance is unimpressive, and the inside has been described as a "hole-in-the-wall" that houses a "meeting room" in the rear. The sparsely furnished meeting room is cordoned off from the office front by a velvet curtain drawn by hand, and is marked by a few computers atop dated metal desks, and a coffee table and sofa that each saw their best days long ago. Mirrors line the walls as reminders of the barbershop it once was.

The tiny and tattered KIFS office, in short, belies the significance of deals being vetted involving the firm. Though Ali did not have success with his proposed KIFS arrangement involving Affiliated Computer Services, he parlayed his ties to the Street administration in other negotiations, and several came under the scrutiny of prosecutors. The preeminent example of the Imam's ties to Philadelphia government officials is the Bowman Properties scandal.

By January 2001, Bowman Properties, a local real estate firm, owed the city more than $600,000 in back property taxes. Bowman head Richard W. Snowden turned to councilwoman Donna Reed Miller's top aide, Steven Vaughn, for assistance. Throughout mid-2001, Bowman Properties wrote the city twenty-two checks with a total value of $661,338 to settle the tax debt. For reasons that are unclear, the checks were delivered to Vaughn, who never forwarded them to the city. Rather, he held onto them until Shamsud-din Ali could get a contract with the city to collect delinquent taxes and thus would take credit for the Bowman payments and earn the finder's fee. Ali met with the city's Law Department and advised them that his KIFS firm had discovered a taxpayer who owed the city more than $1 million and was prepared to pay. A "discovery services" contract was drawn up between the Law Department and KIFS in June 2001 for KIFS to identify taxpayers who were currently not on the city's rolls. Ironically, the two-story building housing the KIFS office was owned by Faridah Ali, who owed the city more than $8,000 in property taxes on the building at the time.

When Ali told officials that the "taxpayer" in question was Bowman Properties, the Law Department concluded that KIFS could not earn the collection fee because the department was already aware of the debt and it was already in the process of being paid. To rescue the floundering deal, Ali employed the political connections he had been honing for years, and many of the resulting exchanges were caught on FBI wiretaps. The indictment states that Ali and his cohorts in city government pressured the department to approve the payment of fees to KIFS through the intervention of the Mayor's Office. On November 14, City officials agreed to pay five per cent of the amount collected. That was subsequently, and inexplicably, increased to ten per cent, bringing the final fee paid in March 2002 to $60,595. Two weeks later, FBI agents witnessed Vaughn meet with Ali for half an hour at Ali's suburban home, and watched as he walked out of the house carrying $2,000 in cash.

The Bowman tax collection scam was arguably not all that significant if weighed in dollar terms alone – Ali pocketed "only" $60,595. However, the Ali-induced hustling in the Bowman affair demonstrated his "juice" with the city administration. In fact, the rather modest figure in this context was arguably *more* significant, since it caused many to ponder why people in positions of authority would be willing to risk so much for a relatively trivial deal. The Bowman affair also seemed to confirm what many argued, namely that Ali had increasingly altered his extortion racket from preying on drug dealers to businessmen and politicians. Whereas the Black Mafia threatened violence if a street tax was not paid, Ali threatened to cut off access to city business and to withhold his support for political endeavors.

Another scam involved the AAT Communications Corporation, based in New Jersey, which hired KIFS in March 2000 to help them get deals at the city-owned Philadelphia International Airport. AAT successfully bid for the contract to install, lease and manage cell phone towers at the airport. Such activities compelled one publication to refer to Ali's KIFS as a "we'll-be-your-minority-partner-so-you-can-get-city-contracts firm." Further allegations of kickbacks and illegal dealing followed.

Other federal and local investigations into Shamsud-din Ali's activities, and the remaining components of the September 2004 indictment, involved some intriguing historical ties to the Black Mafia. Waste Management & Processors, Inc. (WMPI) is a sludge-hauling firm based in Schuylkill County, Pennsylvania. WMPI's Vice President is Brian Rich, grandson of coal baron John B. Rich, the victim of the most infamous burglary in Pennsylvania history. Two racketeers with Black Mafia ties were among those charged in the legendary 1959 heist. In 2002, WMPI held a sludge-hauling contract with the city and was seeking to have it renewed. Rich apparently didn't factor in the cost of using Shamsud-din Ali and John M. Johnson, a waste management consultant and Ali friend, to obtain the renewal.

According to the Government, the pair threatened "to have Shamsud-din Ali exercise his power and influence over elected and appointed officials to cause the City to terminate a renewable contract" and to prevent the company "from obtaining other contracts unless the company paid a $25,000 'bonus' to Ali and Johnson." In September 2002, Rich, Ali and Johnson met in the office of city councilwoman Jannie L. Blackwell, a long-time Ali friend and supporter. Blackwell phoned Mayor John Street about the contract and later that month Johnson told Rich his contract would be renewed. In three installments, Rich paid the $25,000.

Jannie Blackwell is someone with another remarkable connection to the story.

Michael Youngblood, after demonstrating that he was a "model prisoner," was released from prison in January 1992, serving three years and two months of what was initially a ten-year sentence. Within months of his release, Blackwell hired the multiple narcotics offender as a $30,000 per year "personal assistant." Youngblood had forsaken his name for a new one, Michael David Williams, and for a few months the curious hire went unnoticed. In early 1993, however, Youngblood was in Blackwell's company when he got in a scuffle with police. Following the incident, police discovered "Michael Williams" was, in fact, Michael Youngblood, and a media firestorm ensued. Blackwell responded to the criticism of her hire by saying, "I had heard things about his past, but I don't believe people should be penalized forever." Blackwell added that she knew Youngblood as a volunteer in her campaign and that of her husband, Congressman Lucien Blackwell.

Then-City Council President Street, a longtime friend of the Blackwells, fired Youngblood within days of the ex-con's run-in with police, against Jannie's wishes. Despite Street's action, Blackwell kept Youngblood on as an ostensibly unpaid staffer, and he kept a desk in the councilwoman's office. He was such a close adviser that he accompanied the Blackwells to a private City Hall reception – attended by only a dozen or so people – with President Clinton in May 1993. "Blood" became a fixture in City Hall, and could often be seen lurking in the hallways and chatting with Mayor Ed Rendell and other pols.

The savvy game Michael Youngblood was playing paid off in 1995 when he parlayed his influence as Blackwell's aide to become the *de facto* project manager of a large construction project. The city had partnered with a church to build a 450-bed homeless shelter in North Philadelphia, with the city footing the bill. The Deliverance Center of Hope II project was initially estimated to cost $850,000, but by mid-1997 costs had exceeded $1.75 million and the project was nowhere near completion. When the scandal was disclosed, Mayor Rendell deflected criticism from his office to other officials who were supposed to be overseeing the project. He said that he approved letting Youngblood work on the shelter project, but assumed his role would be negligible. "I wouldn't suppose Michael could be a construction manager of an $80,000 rehab," said Rendell. "He doesn't have the background for that. Certainly not for the $1.5 million rehab of an abandoned building into a shelter."

The city's homeless czar at the time said he put Youngblood on salary at $30,000 a year on the Deliverance project, and though he knew Youngblood wasn't qualified to oversee a major construction project, never protested because he "was an important staff person to councilwoman Blackwell." Other politicians and bureaucrats permitted the ex-con to take over the construction site despite the fact that he had no title, no mandate, and zero experience. The acting director of the city's Office of Emergency Shelter and Services said that it was his perception that Youngblood had direct access to Mayor Rendell. Youngblood ultimately earned $58,185 in salary before he was removed from the project. Following an FBI investigation, he was indicted and convicted in 1999 of thirty-four counts of extortion, bank fraud, tax evasion, and failure to file tax returns. A jury found that Youngblood shook down contractors for $36,468 in kickbacks, cashed forged checks, and dodged taxes on the money he extorted – and on $30,585 that Jannie Blackwell paid him out of her own pocket in 1996 and 1997 for "personal and city business tasks." Blackwell had given

Youngblood unrestricted access to her personal bank account, and he used it to cash the forged checks. After the presiding judge considered letters of support from Lucien and Jannie Blackwell, he sentenced Michael Youngblood to three years in prison.

The Youngblood story – his ties to Black Mafia leaders like Nudie Mims, his exploitation of political ties to the likes of the Blackwells and Ed Rendell, the extortion of individuals seeking city business, the requisite tax evasion, the victimization of Philadelphia taxpayers in general and the black underclass in particular, all under the guise of aiding those most in need – reads like a primer on the much larger and more significant 2004 investigation into Shamsud-din Ali.

★

In mid- to late-2001, federal authorities were hearing from a mob turncoat about meetings between Shamsud-din Ali and former Philadelphia mob boss "Skinny" Joey Merlino. According to the informant, Merlino was looking to expand into the area's narcotics scene and thought Ali would provide protection in prison. Perhaps not coincidentally, Merlino placed a half-page ad for his restaurant, the Avenue Café, in a fundraising program for Ali's Sister Clara Muhammad School back in 1996. By 2001, Merlino was sitting in prison, serving his sentence on a 1999 conviction for drug and racketeering offenses. In the summer of 2001, FBI agents overheard Ali on wiretaps discussing an upcoming meeting. Agents tracked Ali weeks later to a popular South Philadelphia restaurant called the Saloon, where the Imam met with his close friend, Laborer's Local 332 business manager Sam Staten, Sr., Wilkes Barre/Scranton crime boss William "Big Billy" D'Elia, and a business consultant named Joseph Moderski. D'Elia was the successor to the late Russell Bufalino who had numerous ties to Philadelphia labor racketeers and gangsters, including several with Black Mafia links. D'Elia had his own ties to the area's underworld, as evidenced by a 1997 meeting he arranged in Philadelphia with Merlino and other local mobsters. Such connections caused the New Jersey Casino Control Commission to ban D'Elia from Atlantic City casinos, and would cause grief for an associate of his who was interested in applying for one of the much-sought-after Pennsylvania slot machine licenses.

According to Joseph Moderski, D'Elia pitched the idea of forming a demolition company at the autumn 2001 meeting with Ali and Staten. In addition to his mob connections, D'Elia had a history of serving as a "waste broker," obtaining contracts for air space at landfills, selling that space and transportation services to waste generators and haulers, and was thus savvy to these types of deals. The plan was to obtain work from the Street administration. Months later, in March of 2002, Shamsud-din Ali and Sam Staten formed a demolition company called Clear Alley, Inc., which listed its address as 7108 Germantown Ave., the same address as Ali's collection firm, KIFS. On their MBEC application for Clear Alley, which included power lawyer Ron White as a reference, Ali and Staten identified themselves as president and secretary of Clear Alley, respectively; there was no mention of D'Elia's or Moderski's involvement or interest in the firm. Incorporation records on file at the Pennsylvania Department of State listed Staten's then sixteen-year-old son, Qa'id Ameer Staten, as a co-founder. Qa'id was a standout student at Sister Clara Muhammad School at the time, and already accepted into Howard University. The Qa'id Staten–Clear Alley situation made news because of the probe and because Qa'id was shot four times and killed in a bungled robbery attempt in April 2003 outside a pizza shop in North Philadelphia. When Qa'id was rushed to the hospital, the Statens were joined by family friends Mayor John Street and Police Commissioner Sylvester Johnson. The funeral service for Qa'id was held at Ali's Masjid.

Sam Staten and his other son, Sam Staten, Jr., respectively serve as the business manager and president of Laborer's Local 332, and each was subpoenaed to appear before the probe's grand jury. When federal agents obtained a search warrant for KIFS in October 2003, Local 332 was one of eighteen individuals/entities named on the warrant, along with Clear Alley, Philadelphia Gas Works, AAT Communications, Commerce Bank, and Philadelphia's Minority Business Enterprise Council. Until the advent of the probe, Laborer's Local 332 donated $12-15,000 annually to Sister Clara Muhammad School. Local 332 has been a major campaign contributor to John Street, supported Ron White's Youth Leadership Foundation, and, in fact, was represented by White in legal matters. When Sam Staten, Sr. was investigated regarding the labor racketeering scandal involving the Philly mob and builder Ralph Costobile in the 1980s, White defended him. Like others around him, Staten has weighty political connections, and has served on several influential boards, such as Governor Rendell's transition team in 2002.

Staten and White also appeared with Ali on the Board of Directors for Faridah Ali's proposed Liberty Academy Charter School in 2003. Faridah was listed as president, while her daughter, Lakiha "Kiki" Spicer Ali, was vice president and Faridah's son, Azeem Spicer Ali, was secretary. Among those who wrote letters of support of the school were U.S. Rep. Bob Brady (of "I spun the shit" fame) and Police Commissioner Sylvester Johnson. The FBI subpoenaed the School District of Philadelphia for documents related to Liberty Academy in July 2003, just as the proposed school's application for $5.7 million was being considered. The application was signed by *Dr.* Faridah Ali. She apparently purchased the bogus doctorate from an internet diploma mill, though this did not stop her from insisting others refer to her as "Doctor Ali." The investigation and other probes into the Alis could not have helped the proposal, which was rejected in April 2004.

Commissioner Johnson has since publicly distanced himself from Shamsud-din Ali, and said that he was on a trip to Israel when his now-retired secretary drafted the letter that stated Johnson agreed to serve on the Liberty Academy board. In an extensive April 2004 magazine article, Commissioner Johnson discussed many probe-related matters, including Shamsud-din Ali, regarding whom Johnson said, "He's a bad person. Just because he's a minister and a Muslim doesn't make him a good person." Both men, interestingly enough, joined the Nation of Islam at roughly the same time in 1965, just after Minister Jeremiah Shabazz returned from his time in the South, and both followed the path to more mainstream Islam after Elijah Muhammad's death in 1975.

One of the remaining questions concerning Shamsud-din Ali, and the tattered remnants of the once-powerful Black Mafia, involves the street-level extortion of drug dealers. The sprawling investigation into corruption in Philadelphia, after all, began with consecutive narcotics investigations of RAM Squad, its suppliers, and Shamsud-din Ali. The September 2004 indictment of Ali only fleetingly mentions proceeds derived from the illicit narcotics trade. Rather than detailing the explicit shakedown of drug dealers, the Government alleges that Shamsud-din and Faridah Ali received "cash payments obtained from individuals who were engaged in the illegal distribution of controlled substances."

Back in 1975 an FBI memo bluntly stated the position regarding Imam Shamsud-din Ali's mentor, Minister Jeremiah X. Shabazz, at that time a controversial figure whose closest allies were some of the most infamous cons Philadelphia had ever seen. People so feared Shabazz and his followers that none would go public with their accusations, resulting in the following assessment by the Bureau: "Informants in Philadelphia have reported [Shabazz] as being in charge of narcotics traffic handled by NOI members and involved in killings by NOI members. *None of this can be proved in a court of law.*" (Emphasis added.) Federal investigators are in a similar dilemma when it comes to Shamsud-din Ali. Despite countless tales of Ali extorting drug dealers by informants and street sources, the informants are considered wildcards in a court of law and more law-abiding sources are not willing to testify against the feared Imam and his crowd. What is past is apparently prologue, since no such cases were ever brought against Black Mafia members in their heyday, despite the fact that it was abundantly clear that dozens of illicit entrepreneurs, especially drug dealers, paid a protection tax to the syndicate. Interestingly, onetime RAM Squad leader John Wilson once dated Faridah Ali's daughter, Lakiha. Consequently, federal investigators have pressed him for information regarding Shamsud-din Ali, though it is unknown if Wilson has assisted in any of the Ali-related probes.

Before he was indicted, Ali was quoted as saying, "How do people wrong their souls to say all these terrible things about someone they don't know? I'm not unhappy and I'm not tormented. Believe me, God doesn't allow me to be scared." He also said, "I live with no secrets. I ain't doing nothing wrong." As for the accusations that he extorts drug dealers, he denied them emphatically and added, "I have met people who are criminally inclined. I've been to prison with people who are criminally inclined. I would believe, pleasing to God, I have turned more people's minds around than anyone we know." The Alis are not alone in their legal fight; supporters established the Ali Family Legal Defense Fund to provide economic and moral assistance. A November 2004, letter from the Defense Fund claims the cases against the Alis are an all-out offense against Islam.

In addition to battling pending federal racketeering charges, Ali is fighting to retain control over the mosque he made into his own. His leadership has been frequently criticized in recent years by some of his followers, who have voiced their complaints to W. D. Muhammad in Chicago. Muhammad said Muslims from several cities, including Philadelphia, complained that some Imams "have rejected and refused to be interested in the Islamic way of progress. They have more interest in having their people obey them and not Islam." Of Philadelphia, specifically, the respected Muslim visionary also said, "We don't have strong leadership representing Islam like we should there in Philadelphia. It's coming from my supporters. They say, 'We need you here.'" Muhammad sent an emissary to Philly to address the problem in September of 2003. Shamsud-din Ali argued that W.D. Muhammad was "grossly misinformed" about the situation, and the two remained at odds following the visit. Several former Ali followers have continued efforts to unseat him from his position at the Masjid ever since.

In 2004, a group calling itself Muslims For Truth mailed unsigned letters and copies of Ali's racketeering indictment to members of the Muslim community. The letter asks recipients to read the indictment so that they will "understand that the Muslim community has been lied to and deceived by this leadership for years," and says Faridah and Shamsud-din Ali were "stealing from hard-working and sincere Muslims." The letter adds, "We now know they were spending it on themselves, and [their] family ... Even now they continue to deceive the community and ask for financial support to defend their criminal activity." The generally hands-off board of the Philadelphia Masjid has also sought to oust Ali ever since the probes became public knowledge. Interestingly, in light of the decades-long Black Mafia history, the lawyer representing Ali in the Masjid-related court proceedings is J. Garland Giles, the son of U.S. District Court Judge James T. Giles, who, like Paul Dandridge, formerly advised the Black Mafia-infiltrated community development programs Safe Streets, Inc. and Council for Youth and Community Development, the forerunner to the syndicate's infamous Black Brothers, Inc.

The parallels between the ongoing investigations into Shamsud-din Ali and those of his mentor, Jeremiah Shabazz, thirty years ago are striking.

Both are prominent African-American Muslim clerics, politically connected within the black community and to the broader "establishment", including politicians, judges and financiers. Both have ties to celebrities and prominent sports figures, as well as to labor leaders, racketeers, and organized criminals. And both stood accused of running an extortion racket preying on drug dealers and fending off their accusers by claiming their intentions were racist and that prejudice against Islam was at the core of the investigations. Each man exploited his era's government-led initiatives to enhance the lives of poor, inner-city African-Americans. Where Shabazz benefited directly or indirectly from community development programs, Ali has done the same with minority and disadvantaged business mandates for municipal contracts.

Unlike many of his Black Mafia contemporaries, Jeremiah Shabazz was never arrested during the fabulous rise of the syndicate, largely because he was savvy enough to remain distant from the actions of his followers. Minister Jeremiah's rhetorical skills, social affiliations and political connections didn't hurt, either. His understudy and successor, Shamsud-din Ali, possesses many of the same skills and affiliations, and, indeed, has far more and weightier connections with legitimate society. Ali, however, apparently overstepped the mark and defrauded taxpayers, as opposed to illegal narcotics users, and was indicted in 2004 for extorting contractors seeking municipal business in Philadelphia. Charged in thirty-eight of the forty-eight counts in the indictment, he faced a maximum sentence of 290 years in prison.

The discovery of the FBI bug in Mayor John Street's office took place almost thirty years to the day after Gene Hearn and his fellow Black Mafia leaders opened Black Brothers, Inc. office on South Street. In 2004, he was still a man of consequence in elite, influential circles of Philadelphia, and a person of interest in the corruption probe. Meanwhile, Shamsud-din Ali – a Black Mafia figure who was honing his deal-making skills as a power broker from inside Holmesburg Prison back in 1973 while his associates in Black Brothers, Inc. were playing the system on the outside – was looking into the abyss.

EPILOGUE

MUCH HAS TRANSPIRED regarding the two unrelated prongs of "The Probe" (i.e., the Savage-Thomas drug network investigation and the municipal corruption probe) since I concluded the writing of *Black Brothers Inc.* in December of 2004. What follows is a snapshot of updates about specific individuals. I should point out at the onset that there have been numerous convictions and guilty pleas beyond those explicitly referenced below. These are not included, however, simply because they are not directly related to the story of the Black Mafia. What follows are highlights of people or activities I have deemed most significant to the understanding of the syndicate and the culture that spawned, tolerated, and supported it.

As of June 2007, more than fifty people, collectively, have been convicted or have pleaded guilty in the two investigations. For convenience, the updates below are offered by probe, in order of relevance and convenience rather than chronology.

Kaboni Savage – Gerald Thomas narcotics organization

(More than thirty persons pleaded guilty or were convicted at trial)
In May 2004, Kaboni Savage and Gerald Thomas were indicted along with eighteen others for running a massive drug network. Fourteen of the twenty defendants in the Savage-Thomas drug ring pleaded guilty before trial, including Dawud Bey. One defendant died of natural causes before trial.

Gerald "Bubbie" Thomas
Gerald Thomas died of liver cancer on 5 March 2005, at the age of fifty-five. Thomas was the drug dealer overheard on FBI wiretaps being asked for money by Shamsud-din Ali, resulting in taps on Ali's phones. Those recorded conversations ultimately led to the massive probe of municipal corruption, which had power lawyer Ron White at its center. Gerald Thomas grew up with White in the Richard Allen Homes projects, and the two were friends. Shamdud-din Ali delivered the eulogy for Thomas, who was also known as Baha Jabbar, at Ali's Masjid.

Kaboni Savage

Following his 2004 arrest, Kaboni Savage, *aka* Yusef Billa, was incarcerated in the federal detention center in Philadelphia. An eavesdropping device was installed in October 2004 near the prison cell toilet bowl in a vent between two cells with adjoining plumbing systems where Savage was being held. When Savage and others wanted to talk, they would empty water from the toilet bowls and shout through the pipes. He and the others were taped by the FBI and the Federal Bureau of Prisons. The "wiretap" was installed for sixty days and, according to an FBI agent on the case, was the first ever obtained for a prison cell.

During his trial, Savage took the stand in his own defense. On the tapes, Savage was recorded in the federal detention center as saying, "They know if they left me out for them forty-three days, they wouldn't have no case ... I knew ... who was doing what. And if I was wrong, so be it," sparking the U.S. Attorney to ask of him on the witness stand, "You were talking about killing witnesses at the time?"

Savage bluntly replied, "Yes."

Summing up the case against Savage, a U.S. Attorney said, "He's a hustler and a vicious and brutal character."

Savage was convicted of federal gun, drug, witness intimidation and money laundering charges on 16 December 2005. He led a multi-million dollar drug distribution network that brought hundreds of kilos of cocaine into Philadelphia between 1999 and 2003. The novel Savage taught his understudies how to dilute (or "re-rock", in the parlance of the street) hundreds of kilos of cocaine with the synthetic compound procaine (to "stretch the brick") and then use metal plates and a hydraulic jack to compress the cocaine to make it appear pure. The six-week trial heard evidence from 361 FBI secretly-recorded conversations involving drug transactions and money laundering. There were at least twelve tapes played for the jury in which Savage was heard making death threats. Technically, Savage was convicted along with four others in the drug conspiracy, including a real estate agent who laundered hundreds of thousands of dollars of dealers' money for more than ten years. This is in addition to the fourteen others indicted along with Savage who pleaded guilty, some of whom testified for the prosecution against Savage.

Kaboni Savage was sentenced on 27 April 2006 to thirty years in prison, five years of supervised release, was fined $5,000 and ordered forfeiture of his assets. He was facing life imprisonment and a fine of up to $12.5 million, causing some law enforcement officials to decry the sentence as insufficient. Savage will be eligible for release after serving twenty-five-and-a-half years.

Since Shamsud-din Ali had such intimate ties to Gerald Thomas and Dawud Bey, and because these key figures were so closely aligned with Kaboni Savage, it is necessary to provide at least a glimpse into the hubris and brutality for which Savage and his enterprise are known and feared. Eugene "Twin" Coleman was imprisoned on April 3, 2003 and pleaded guilty in June 2004 to conspiring to manufacture and distribute 100 kilos of cocaine, and was incarcerated. Months after the May 2004 indictments in the Savage-Thomas drug investigation, it was suspected that Coleman, who formerly worked for Kaboni Savage, was cooperating with authorities against Savage. In August 2004, Savage warned Coleman the feds might be able to protect him, but not his mother and daughter. In mid-September, Savage, speaking through the prison toilet bowl communication system, said he wanted to "kill Twin's family."

In an apparent attempt to deter Coleman from further cooperation, a fire was set to a North Philadelphia row house that contained his relatives in October 2004. The arson killed a family of six, including a fifteen-month-old baby. Three days before this horrific massacre, Savage was quoted as saying, "Twin think we gonna rock his brother. Fuck his brother. We gonna hit the nigga where it hurt." During his drug trial in 2005, Savage taunted an FBI agent, asking him "Hey, where's Twin at? How's his family?" After hearing Coleman had attended his mother's funeral, Savage was taped saying, "They should have took him and got him some barbecue sauce and poured it on them sons of bitches. I'm glad the bitch died." [in reference to Coleman's mother, cousin and four children killed in the fire.] Regarding the kids, he said, "Fuck them, fucking little baby, he should have died. His pop's a rat."

Coleman, who served time in prison throughout the proceedings against Savage, technically faced a twenty-year mandatory sentence. Because of his leading role as a cooperating witness against Savage, Coleman was sentenced in March 2006 to forty-two months in prison, ten years of supervised release, and fined $2,500. It was expected he would be released at some point in 2006 and become part of the federal witness protection program. Coleman began cooperating ten months before his family was slain, and was not deterred from testifying against Savage despite the killings and threats.

Savage's menacing words were not reserved for supposed "rats" and other witnesses. In one taped threat against a prison official, Savage said, "I want to set [the prison captain] on fire. Alive. Watch him jump around like James fuckin' Brown. Get a metal chair and some cuffs. Douse him with gasoline. Say, 'Welcome to hell, motherfucker.'"

From inside the federal detention center, Savage bragged about his many "accomplishments" – or rationalized his dire circumstances – to fellow prisoners: "I ain't got no regrets for nothing I did ... Made sure my mom didn't work. My sister ain't have to work; she's got an education. Put my wife through school, got her education. My other sister got a house. I mean the fruits of my labor ... I'm proud of that." After boasting further about various pleasantries his underworld efforts afforded him and those close to him, Savage derided the prison employees burdened with guarding him: "These guards ain't never gonna experience that. They want to be us. They just ain't got the heart. Them niggas ain't never gonna know how it feel to go to a car dealer, say 'Give me that.' You drove the finest cars, you fucked the finest broads, and you shopped in the finest fucking clothing stores. Look at the watch. You pay fifty for a watch. These motherfuckers ain't got fifty thousand dollar houses or cars, and you got this on your wrist." He added, "I like to live, man ... They're gonna die miserable."

There is an effort at moral clarity on the taped exchanges between co-defendants and murder suspects Savage and Dawud Bey. When Savage (KS) implied society made him commit crimes, Bey (DB) would have none of it.

KS: I know I didn't sell drugs because I wanted to.
DB: Yes, you did.
KS: I never wake up, say I wanna be a drug dealer.
DB: Why you couldn't a' went and got a job?
KS: Come, on, man. What am I gonna do? Work and go to school? Yeah.

Dawud Bey
Dawud Bey pleaded guilty on 7 February 2005 to distributing more than 3½ kilos of cocaine, specifically repackaging kilogram quantities of cocaine from the Thomas Savage network and selling it under 500 brands between September 1999 and April 2003. Unlike some of his confederates, Bey did not cooperate with authorities.

Even before he pleaded guilty, Bey was incarcerated along with Kaboni Savage in the federal detention center in Philadelphia. Like Savage, Bey was recorded threatening numerous people, ranging from witnesses to prison officials to family members of co-defendants he feared may testify against him. For instance, on 1 January 2005 he was taped speaking to another inmate "on the bowl" (prison speak for through the toilet system), saying, "I got thirty months to do, you understand? And when I get out, I'm gonna kill every ... rat that I know, dog. You understand that?" According to an FBI agent, witnesses "numbering in the double digits" had to be relocated for their safety as a result of threats by Bey and others in the drug ring.

Bey was sentenced in February 2006 to ten years in federal prison, fined $2,000 and ordered to forfeit $15,000. Bey was also ordered to undergo drug treatment, to obtain a high school diploma, and to have five years of supervised release. The sentencing judge, in a commentary that is applicable to countless other offenders, including many in the Black Mafia story, said, "The tapes show a person that does not match up to the man I see in court, or the man I hear about from family members. I see a man, a leader, smart, caring about his family and caring for some members of the community. But the tapes show a person who threatens to kill women and children ... in the community that Mister Bey says he cares about." Indeed, Bey remains a suspect in a high-profile homicide.

Kaboni Savage was charged with the March 1998 murder of a forty-four-year-old barber named Kenneth Lassiter, who lightly bumped into Savage's car while trying to park his own. According to another drug dealer named Tybius "Tib" Flowers, Savage was sitting in his car at the time and became enraged. He first demanded money from Lassiter, though there was little or no damage to Savage's car, and then shot him in the stomach several times with a .40 caliber semi-automatic pistol. Tib Flowers cooperated with authorities and was scheduled to testify against Savage at his murder trial. The night before the trial was to begin, Flowers was inside a black Mercury on 8th Street near Butler Street – almost precisely the same location of the Lassiter killing – when an assailant shot him several times in the head and torso with a 9mm semi-automatic pistol, killing him. Without its key witness, the government lost its case against Savage, who was acquitted of murder after a four-day trial. Federal investigators believe that "Savage arranged to have the government's key witness, Tybius Flowers, murdered," and have named Dawud Bey and another Savage associate, John Tillman, as "prime suspects" in the Flowers slaying. As the Savage trial approached, the District Attorney's Office disclosed that Flowers would be testifying. Within days, Bey and Tillman visited Savage in Philadelphia's Curran Fromhold Prison, where Savage was housed pending trial. The jailhouse visit occurred five days before the trial was to start (and thus four days before Flowers was killed). No one had been charged in the Flowers murder as of June 2007.

Municipal corruption probe

(More than twenty persons have been convicted or have pleaded guilty)

Corey Kemp
The former Treasurer for the City of Philadelphia was convicted of twenty-seven charges including conspiracy, corruption, fraud, tax evasion and other charges. The Kemp case has little to do with the case involving Shamsud-din Ali. However, he was the highest ranking public official convicted in the scandals and his case is most illustrative of the city's pay-to-play culture. The jury found that Kemp took money, Super Bowl tickets, a free deck, fancy dinners and other kickbacks in exchange for lucrative city contracts. No doubt speaking for countless taxpayers and observers, one juror said he was "struck by the extent of the corruption." Another juror said, "If the [bug] wasn't found so early, [Mayor Street] probably would have been here with the rest of them. It wouldn't have sur-

prised me a bit, just because of the way the corruption was going, and the way him and Ron White were associates."

The judge said Kemp damaged Philadelphia and its reputation, and told him, "You not only cheated the city, you not only cheated your own church, you cheated Commerce Bank, you cheated the state, you cheated the federal government." Kemp was sentenced in July 2005 to ten years in prison, $330,000 in restitution and $10,000 in fines. It was last reported Kemp was serving his time in a minimum security facility in Massachusetts.

West Insurance

West Insurance was in the news again in May 2006, when it was discovered the firm had run afoul of the city's newly-implemented ethics law regarding campaign contributions and no-bid contracts. Among other things, the new law restricts certain political donors from obtaining municipal contracts and mandates potential vendors disclose whether they've made political donations in the previous two years to incumbents and candidates for city and state office. West officials had asserted that neither the business nor any of its principal officers had made contributions to anyone, though this was not accurate. West was ultimately permitted to amend its original filing, disclosing past contributions, and the matter was apparently dropped.

Interestingly, West Insurance's brochure opens with a statement from President and CEO Kobie West that begins "We guarantee our clients absolute honesty and integrity in all matters. Our reputation is worth more to us than financial considerations." Until at least January 2007, the West brochure described Vice President Fareed Ahmed (Gene Hearn) as follows: "a recognized community leader and social activist, Mr. Ahmed is West Insurance Group's Vice President in charge of marketing. He heads up a team of executive sales staff that focuses on generating and retaining commercial business. Mr. Ahmed was formerly the Chief Operating Officer of Odyssey Waste Services, LLC, the largest minority-certified solid waste and construction demolition hauler in the State of Pennsylvania." As of July 2007, however, there is no reference to Ahmed, suggesting he is no longer with the firm.

Faridah Ali "ghost teacher" case

Faridah Ali and her children, Azeem Spicer Ali and Lakiha Spicer Ali, were each convicted for their roles in a "ghost teacher" scam (see pages 238-239), of stealing $224,375 from a federally-funded adult education program, in October 2004. In March 2005, Azeem and Lakiha were each sentenced to six months home confinement and four years of probation. Azeem and Lakiha were also respectively ordered to pay $15,000 and $25,000 in restitution. Faridah Ali was sentenced to a year of home confinement and a total of five years probation. She must also pay $30,000 restitution and a $2,300 fine.

Some of the disclosures made about the case include transcripts of FBI wiretaps. On one taped call, Faridah mentioned part of the scam to her daughter, Lakiha: "I mean, forty thousand dollars ain't nothing to be disappointed about. You make that at Community College doing nothing." In another conversation, Faridah said she was tired of "forging documents." The IRS analysis of union funds donated to the Ali's Sister Clara Muhammad School demonstrated funds were misspent. Further, the FBI taped Faridah speaking in August 2001 with her daughter about a donation from longtime friend and Laborer's Local 332 leader, Sam Staten, Sr. "I can pay some of my bills cause, ah, Sam Staten gave me a check for five thousand dollars ... and he said he's gonna try to get me another five from the union ... So, ah, now I can pay my income tax." In 2005, as she awaited trial in her husband's racketeering case, Faridah Ali was in the process of remodeling the infamous KIFS office into a restaurant.

Co-defendants in Shamsud-din Ali racketeering case

Faridah Ali, Shamsud-din Ali's wife and co-defendant, had her case severed and pleaded no contest to most of the federal racketeering, fraud and tax charges on September 26, 2005. At her February 2006 sentencing hearing, however, Ali admitted she was guilty of defrauding Community College of Philadelphia, a Mercedes-Benz dealership, and a bank. She also admitted to wire fraud, tax evasion, and filing false tax returns. Long removed from the days of professing her innocence, saying she was being investigated because she was African-American, and calling the probe "an attack on Islam," Faridah now matter-of-factly told the court, "I'm saying it publicly. I broke the law."

As the government argued in the sentencing memo for Faridah Ali, "Under the guise of performing community service, the Ali family, instead, lined their pockets with funds earmarked to help poor people of the West Philadelphia area, who they purported to serve." Authorities also pointed out the Alis owned a $650,000 home, two other properties worth $575,000, and three Mercedes Benzes. At the same time the Alis were living the life and running their scams, children at their Sister Clara Muhammad School frequently wore coats in their classrooms because the heating bills had not been paid. Faridah Ali was sentenced to twenty-four months in prison, and is currently serving time in the federal prison at Danbury, Connecticut.

Richard Meehan pleaded guilty in March 2005 to commercial bribery and to accepting $7,000 in kickbacks from Shamsud-din Ali. Meehan's former firm (Meehan was fired as a result of the scandal), AAT Communications, used Ali's firm, KIFS, to satisfy a minority set-aside program requirement in order to obtain a contract at Philadelphia International Airport. In pleading guilty to the charges, Meehan said that despite telling the city that KIFS was a twenty percent minority participant, Ali's firm performed "no actual work." In return for a $1700 monthly payment from AAT, Ali paid Meehan a monthly $500 kickback. Meehan, who did not testify against Ali during Ali's trial, was sentenced to three years' probation and received a $10,000 fine.

John Johnson, a waste management consultant and Ali friend, was convicted in June 2005 of conspiracy, extortion and attempted extortion of waste haulers.

John Salter, Shamsud-din Ali's accountant, pleaded guilty in late 2004 to bank fraud for falsifying Ali's financial records.

Steven "Wassi" Vaughn, former chief of staff to City Councilwoman Donna Reed Miller (Vaughn resigned following his indictment), pleaded guilty in April 2005 to his involvement in an illegal scheme to obtain a city debt-collection contract for Shamsud-din Ali, but denied taking money from Ali (which the government contends it would have proven if the case had gone to trial). One of the conversations taped by the government caught Vaughn speaking in March 2002 to John Christmas, an aide to Mayor Street's chief of staff, boasting about the crooked deal he managed for Shamsud-din Ali. Said Vaughn, "You know, I've always been cool with Ali, but now I'm on platinum level. You know, now that he's got all this massive freebie." Vaughn was sentenced to five months in jail, followed by five months of home confinement and $60,000 in restitution.

John Christmas, a former assistant to the mayor's chief of staff (he resigned after the indictments), was acquitted by the jury on charges of aiding Ali in one scam, and a perjury charge was later dismissed by the trial judge. Christmas' lawyer, Brian McMonagle, successfully argued his client's job was to help the Street administration give businesses owned by blacks, Hispanics, and women a greater share of government contracts in the city. McMonagle said, "[Christmas] never got a darn thing from anybody. This was a situation where the mayor's office was trying to get work for Mr. Ali, and John Christmas did his job." Indeed, a juror said as much after the verdict was announced: "We thought [Christmas] was really trying to help Mister Ali get contracts, but we didn't think he was doing anything wrong," she said. "We thought he was doing his job."[2]

Shamsud-din Ali – racketeering case
On 2 February 2005, a grand jury charged Imam Shamsud-din Ali and Faridah Ali with an additional seven counts, resulting in a fifty-five-count indictment and an asset forfeiture charge of $389,000. Shamsud-din Ali pleaded guilty to four counts of income tax evasion on April 20 that year, the day before his racketeering trial began. Ali acknowledged that he failed to report hundreds of thousands of dollars in income during a four-year period beginning in 1998. Comically, considering the KIFS hustle of the Bowman Properties tax collection, Shamsud-din Ali owed the city $3,000 for delinquent taxes even as he was garnering a bogus contract to collect delinquent taxes.

During the eight-week racketeering trial, which included more than 100 witnesses and 180 wiretapped conversations, it was disclosed the FBI investigated Ali from 1993-5, and reopened the investigation in 2000, with informants updating the Bureau in between the probes. At trial, evidence was entered alleging payments from drug dealers to Ali, his mosque, and the Sister Clara Muhammad School, run by the Alis. It was also disclosed that Ali's name came up in the early 1990s when authorities investigated the Junior Black Mafia. According to the FBI, JBM boss Aaron Jones and Ali grew close before Jones began serving a life sentence.

Ali's attorney, Jimmy Binns, unsuccessfully argued the FBI used "stale" information from the 1980s and 1990s in the affidavit for the wiretap on Ali's phone. The document also included details about the 1970 shooting death of Dr. Clarence Smith, the overturning of Ali's conviction in the case, and the problems with a retrial. Thomas A. Bergstrom, an attorney for one of Faridah Ali's co-defendants, made a similar attack on the 116-page affidavit of probable cause, claiming it "provides an historical perspective of black crime in Philadelphia, dating back to the 1960s and the so-called Black Mafia," and thus is not related to the current investigation. Bergstrom added that the allegations of Ali's drug ties are based on information from eight cooperating witnesses and six confidential informants, and that three of those witnesses were no longer cooperating.

According to some of the tapes played during the trial, Ali very much enjoyed his quasi-celebrity and position of influence in the city. On one, Ali bragged about attending Mayor Street's private party with his closest friends, then dropped name after name of who attended. Along these lines, Ali was recorded telling "business consultant" Joseph Moderski: "When I see these guys clinging to me like that, then I know that the friendship between the mayor and I ... these guys are aware of it ... They aren't gonna alienate me at all, see." He was equally proud of his reputation on the street, telling Moderski that some people "don't think that I'm altogether civilized ... and believe me, in our community, in the African-American community, nobody takes me lightly. The guy that's in the back alley with two ... nine millimeters on his hips don't take me lightly."

Several prominent figures testified on behalf of Ali's character, including A. Bruce Crawley, public relations specialist and then-chairman of the area's African-American Chamber of Commerce, Mary Mason, a legendary radio talk show host, and Patrick Gillespie, business manager for the Philadelphia Building Trades Council.

Ali was convicted on 14 June 2005 of twenty-two of the thirty-four counts he faced, including racketeering and racketeering conspiracy, and multiple counts of mail fraud and wire fraud related to illegal schemes to defraud the city, Community College of Philadelphia, and companies doing business with the city. He was acquitted on four charges, and the jury was unable to reach unanimous decisions on the eight others. Jurors said the evidence amassed against him, especially the FBI tapes, was "overwhelming". "Without the wiretaps, we might have had some reasonable doubt," said one juror, who also cited recordings taken from an FBI wire worn by one of Ali's employees. The jury forewoman said that Ali was "a man of few words, but when he had words to say, they were very incriminating." Another juror said, "As a Philadelphia taxpayer, I was angry how our own money was being spent and misused ... I was really upset that the money that was supposed to go to the children [at the Sister Clara Muhammad School] was not given to them. All of the jurors felt that way ... So many people trusted Mr Ali, and he let a lot of people down who trusted him and believed in him."

Mayor Street issued a statement following Ali's conviction, which read in part, "This case was extremely troubling because it involved a recognized community leader and long-time friend ... We respect this decision and my condolences go out to the family of Imam Shamsud-din Ali." Ali was jailed for seven years and three months on September 19, and was ordered to pay restitution of $365,000 to four victims of fraud and extortion, and to forfeit $286,646. The judge also ordered Ali to relinquish his position as director of the Sister Clara Muhammad School.

Shamsud-din Ali – the rest
In light of later developments, it is interesting to return to a meeting held at the Saloon restaurant in South Philadelphia in the Fall of 2001 between Shamsud-din Ali, Sam Staten, Sr., William "Big Billy" D'Elia, and Joseph Moderski (see page 251). The FBI learned of the gathering during their investigation of Ali, which included wiretapped conversations between Ali and Moderski in June and July 2001. Moderski, who has described himself as a "business consultant" to jailed mobster Ralph Natale, told the FBI he attended the meeting with Ali, Staten, and D'Elia at Ali's request. The edge-playing, power-broker duo had once formed a firm to recoup cash from bad checks given to city agencies, though the business never materialized. Each of the four parties from the Saloon gathering has since encountered grief from the legal system. Ali, of course, was convicted in a racketeering probe and sentenced to federal prison. During his Ali's, Sam Staten was one of those identified in court as being under active investigation by the FBI, though the status of the investigation remains unknown and authorities contacted in June 2007 would not comment on the matter.

William D'Elia was charged in November 2006 in an eighteen-count federal indictment on charges of laundering hundreds of thousands of dollars in drug proceeds via banks in the Dominican Republic from 1999 to 2006. The case has no obvious ties to Philadelphia. D'Elia faces a maximum of 245 years in prison, forfeiture of $565,000 and a $4 million fine if convicted of multiple counts of money laundering, interstate transportation of laundered money, solicitation of murder, perjury, witness tampering, obstruction of justice, conspiracy and contempt of court. The charges stem from an investigation into a convicted drug trafficker named John Doncses, who pleaded guilty in Florida in 2000 to distributing more than 100 kilos of marijuana. Incredibly, in the unending degrees-of-separation that characterize big-time city business, William D'Elia's daughter Miriam is partnered with Simone White, the daughter of the late, indicted power lawyer Ron White, and the women are the minority co-underwriting counsel on a $150 million bond deal at Philadelphia International Airport. Mayor Street's top aide, George Burrell, said he pushed for Simone White "as she stepped out on her own as a young lawyer," adding that his goal was to help a young minority woman develop expertise in municipal finance.

Like Shamsud-din Ali, Joseph Moderski ultimately wound up under investigation for shenanigans at Philadelphia International. The airport, like the waterfront and the burgeoning gaming industry, is a fertile area of pay-to-play corruption, given the numerous contracting and consulting opportunities. FBI agents had observed Moderski meeting with Ali at the Saloon yet again, this time in September of 2001, and with the airport's deputy director of aviation, James Tyrrell. Tyrrell, who has not been charged with any crimes, told the FBI that power lawyer Ron White commonly asked him to "meet with individuals who have an interest in obtaining work" at the airport. According to the FBI agent's summary of the interview, Tyrrell said he "didn't think it would be prudent not to give White what he wanted since he was good friends with [Mayor Street]." When Moderski was interviewed by the FBI in October 2003, he told them that Ron White "runs the airport" and that PHL director Charles Isdell "does whatever White wants."

Authorities later indicted Moderski and three others with fraud and conspiracy charges relating to funneling campaign contributions, including $30,000 to a political action committee controlled by White, to increase their chances of winning a contract at the airport. Moderski, whom authorities believed orchestrated the plan, ultimately pleaded guilty to conspiracy, mail fraud and wire fraud in September 2006. He was sentenced in April 2007 to fourteen months in federal prison, and ordered to pay more than $25,000 in fines and restitution.

*

With their racketeering case against Shamsud-din Ali finally over, FBI agents went public. Two in particular had heard for more than two decades that Shamsud-din Ali either influenced or headed a criminal organization at his mosque, the Philadelphia Masjid. Though drug informants had detailed payments in the hundreds of thousands of dollars to the mosque, they were afraid to testify in court because, according to FBI agent Jesse Coleman, they thought "Ali was too strong in the prison system." Another agent, Jim Sweeney, said, "Probably the most surprising thing was we weren't looking at him, but another drug gang and Ali is intercepted talking about taking drug money to City Hall." Ali spoke with major drug dealer Gerald "Bubbie" Thomas frequently, including the fateful conversation taped in October 2000 that ultimately spawned the municipal corruption probe.

Ali was taped asking Bubbie Thomas for $5,000, saying he needed the money for "Connie Little." Constance Little was a longtime aide to Mayor Street. As Ali explained to Thomas, "Well, I'll tell you everything when we ain't on the phone, but that's a very, very ... that's the person closest to the person ... She called me and told me she needs five grand." Ali rattled off the names of people from whom he thought he could get a quick $5,000. Each was known to the FBI, because they were targets of FBI drug investigations. As the FBI agent on the wires said in reflection, "I thought I had a big drug dealer, Connie Little." Agent Coleman conducted an internet search and discovered Little was Street's executive assistant and longtime confidante. Of the revelation, Coleman said, "It shocked us. That was the defining moment. You knew then you had a special case."

According to agent Sweeney, the question then was "Why is a drug organization going to deliver money to Connie Little in City Hall?" More intriguingly, on the same day as the Ali-Thomas conversation, Ali obtained a no-bid contract to collect city real estate taxes. "That kicks off the Ali investigation," Sweeney said. Authorities never determined if Little received the funds, or if the money was related to Ali's contract with the city. FBI agent Jesse Coleman eventually wound up listening to approximately 35,000 calls in the Ali case, while two other agents listened to more than 25,000 calls in the municipal corruption case. Regarding the drug proceeds funneled to Ali and his mosque, an FBI agent said, "The drug dealers were mad," because if Ali's businesses were so lucrative, the dealers howled, "how come he calls and asks me for five hundred dollars, a hundred dollars, five thousand dollars?"

★

A rival faction of Muslims unseated Imam Shamsud-din Ali and his followers in a court-supervised election in August 2006, marking the first time since his release from prison in 1976 he did not control the Philadelphia Masjid. Ali relinquished control of the Masjid on 2 October 2006, though this didn't stop him and his supporters from causing the new leadership grief in various ways, including disrupting services and leaving facilities in serious disrepair. Ali again caused a scene in March of 2007 when he appeared at Philadelphia's City Council to attend a ceremony honoring his attorney, Jimmy Binns. After the event, which was held to acknowledge Binns's work on behalf of police officers and firefighters killed in the line of duty, Police Commissioner Sylvester Johnson walked over to Ali and, according to the *Daily News*, "warmly shook his hand." Of the interesting situation, Johnson said, "I've known Shamsud-din for a lot of years and he is who he is. I respect him and that's it." Predictably, Johnson's actions and comments troubled some members of the police department, who were none too pleased their boss was commiserating with a convicted felon. The incident also confused observers who recalled Johnson saying in 2004 that Ali was "a bad person," before adding, "Just because he's a minister and a Muslim doesn't make him a good person."

As of June 2007, Shamsud-din Ali was out on bail awaiting an appeal, which was based largely on the inclusion of drug testimony. Jimmy Binns had argued this prejudiced the jury, since Ali wasn't charged with drug offenses. Binns unsuccessfully fought the inclusion of such evidence at least three times during the court proceedings, saying, "Leave out the drugs, drug dealers and drug evidence." He was referring to two drug offenders who testified they paid Ali illegal drug proceeds, and the FBI testimony which included the identification of drug dealers on fifteen wiretapped conversations. Assistant U.S. Attorney Frank Labor said, "The evidence was to establish that Shamsud-din Ali and Faridah Ali had a practice in the enterprise to regularly collect money from drug dealers for themselves." According to Binns, "If a drug dealer wants to make a contribution to the cathedral, you can't indict the cardinal."

The judge in the case asked both sides to stipulate that $400,000 deposited in Faridah Ali's account "came from an illegal source – in lieu of drug evidence," but Binns refused. Binns later told an appeals court he would have agreed to say that "these people gave money" and that Ali and his wife had abused the money given to Sister Clara Muhammad. Asked by a judge if "these people" were drug dealers, Binns replied, "I didn't want to say drug dealers." When attempting to explain why Ali would have connections to drug dealers and the like, Ali's attorney took a page out of the late Jeremiah Shabazz's oft-employed playbook, stating, "Shamsud-din Ali ministers to people who are not to the manor born."

WEST INSURANCE: GUILT BY ASSOCIATION?

D URING THE COURSE of researching Black Mafia-related matters in the current federal corruption probe several noteworthy discoveries were made that are only tangentially related to the former syndicate. Appendix A is a brief mini-analysis of networks and ties of interest relating – in varying degrees – to the wide-ranging probe. Importantly, many of these ties are perfectly legitimate and are not under investigation by authorities. The remarkable, migraine-inducing series of inter-relationships exhibited by looking into corporate and not-for-profit boards are presented for two related reasons: they illustrate the rather exclusive club of power brokers in Philadelphia, and they demonstrate the backdrop to the FBI's probe into the "pay-to-play" culture in Philadelphia.

In order to better understand what led to the FBI's interest in the related lobbying and development matters along the waterfront and elsewhere, outsiders are left to piece together the known subjects under investigation and those with ties to these firms and individuals. Unfortunately, there are dozens of firms and their subsidiaries to track down, and it is therefore prudent to focus on the pre-eminent examples of the deals unsettling authorities. Perhaps the most vivid picture of politically-connected influence can be gleaned by looking at the case of West Insurance.

In September 2004, federal authorities subpoenaed records and information from several municipal entities relating to West Insurance and others with ties to West. No one involved with West has been charged with a crime, and federal authorities have not been forthcoming with information about the investigation. Philadelphia's print media has ferreted out some curiosities that may be at the heart of the inquiries. For instance, in 2000, an insurance executive named William A. Graham IV was chosen to provide the Delaware River Port Authority's worker's compensation insurance. He planned to give a share of the deal to a minority firm he had used in the past, AV Consultants, headed by an African-American named Andre Duggin. According to Graham, one of his vice presidents met with then-DRPA risk manager Steven Curtis and the following exchange took place over the choice of minority subcontractor. Curtis said, "It's going to be West," to which Graham's VP responded, "Well, I would prefer Duggin." The terse haggling ended with Curtis bluntly saying, "No, it's going to be West." Graham relented and added West as the minority subcontractor, and kept the firm on for the next four years. On this subject, top Mayor Street aide and city contracts czar George R. Burrell said that it was common for city officials to suggest minority partners to prospective contract recipients, but that these were merely "recommendations." Graham, no doubt speaking for many such entrepreneurs seeking city business, said that rejecting the "recommended" firm "is not even something you would consider" if you were seeking a municipal contract in Philadelphia. Later asked to describe West's duties, Graham said it was a "consultative role. Like, if we would need information on some esoteric subject, we'd ask them to research it." Asked next if West Insurance had done any such "research" in the four years of subcontracting (for which West was paid $276,000), Graham said, "Not to date." The DRPA is one of the agencies that received a subpoena for records involving West Insurance.

West Insurance is the source of considerable controversy in another deal with the city. A former city official, Linda S. Berkowitz, told the *Inquirer* that she was ordered by George Burrell to add West Insurance to a consulting contract at a cost of $100,000 to the city, though there was no reason for such a move because the primary firm was capable of handling the contracted services. The following year, after Berkowitz complained that West had done little – if any – work, she was again ordered to keep West in the deal, though only for $50,000 this time. Berkowitz complied, and later said, "In 25 years [of government service], it's the only thing I ever did that I'm embarrassed about." For the city's part, George Burrell said he was simply fulfilling the Street administration's goal of hiring more minority-owned firms. Furthermore, Burrell said, he wanted to help West Insurance because it was an African-American family-run business that had recently moved to Philadelphia from Boston. Federal authorities are investigating a $10,000 check John Street received in August 1998 (when he was City Council President and planning a run for Mayor) from West Insurance founder Bernard T. West. Carl Singley, then Street's main fundraiser, traveled to New Hampshire with Street and met with West at his home where the transaction took place. The reason for the payment is at issue, with West Insurance stating it was for a speech delivered by Street regarding business opportunities in Philadelphia (West was contemplating relocating), while Singley (who had a falling out with Street sometime in 1999-2000) insists the check was a retainer for legal/consulting services for West's firms. PRWT head Willie Johnson, a West board member who has been immersed in Philadelphia's Democratic Party scene for years, arranged the payment for Street.

Bernard T. West, a native Philadelphian, founded West Insurance in 1991 in Boston, where West maintained an office after the firm relocated its headquarters to Philadelphia. West has claimed the firm is one of the largest full-service minority-owned insurance agencies on the Eastern seaboard. The firm's officers and employees have been significant political donors, especially to Ed Rendell's campaign for governor in 2002 and to Mayor Street. The role of West Insurance in the probe is interesting for a few reasons. For one thing, Bernard West was formerly president of the Boston-based Coolidge Bank & Trust. West became the subject of local and federal investigators in the early 1990s when it was disclosed he had exploited loopholes in the laws that strictly limited the types of loans bank executives obtained from the institutions they run. As the *Boston Globe* reported, "West repeatedly exploited a loophole in state banking laws to obtain $2.5 million in loans for corporations and trusts he controls." West's (3) loans to himself were a flagrant violation of the *spirit* – but not the letter -of the law. If West had loaned the funds directly to himself, each of the loans would have been illegal. State laws restricted such transactions to prevent bank officials from using their status – and depositor's money – to their advantage. Coolidge Bank & Trust was declared insolvent on October 25, 1991 and was seized by federal and state regulators. FDIC auditors estimated the loss to the Bank Insurance Fund at $92 million. Federal authorities investigated the fall of the bank, though even that was not without an interesting footnote. The top federal law enforcement official in the state at the time was U.S. Attorney Wayne Budd. Budd had to recuse himself from the investigation because he was a former law partner with Fletcher H. "Flash" Wiley, a member of the Coolidge board of directors. Budd was also involved in a downtown Boston real estate deal with West and Wiley that relied on one of the three controversial loans. The investigation was ultimately conducted by the Justice Department's Financial Institution Fraud Task Force's Boston office, and did not result in charges being filed.

Up until he split with John Street at some point in 1999-2000, West Insurance advisory board member Carl Singley was one of Street's main people. Before the split, Singley obtained stakes in three airport shops (a PGA store and two gift shops), though he insists Street knew nothing of the deals. Another influential African-American entrepreneur with interests at the airport is fellow West board member Robert Bogle. Bogle owns 40 percent of the T.G.I. Friday's restaurant in the airport's concourse. According to Bogle, he obtained his share of the investment in 1997 when Friday's officials were "looking specifically for a minority investor." Like Carl Singley, Bogle obtained his interest when Ed Rendell was Mayor and John Street was City Council President. The firms seeking opportunities at the airport were subject to the city's rules that minorities, women and disabled individuals share a "meaningful and substantial" percentage, and thus the involvement of Singley and Bogle granted their respective firms "disadvantaged business enterprise" status. As an aside, another name with dated ties to the Black

Mafia history also appears in the list of politically-connected individuals with MBEC interests at the airport – Robert N.C. Nix III. Nix, of course, is the grandson of pathbreaking Congressman – and Elijah Muhammad supporter – Robert N.C. Nix, Sr., and son of the legendary state Supreme Court Chief Justice – and close associate to Mosque No. 12 leader Jeremiah Shabazz – Robert N.C. Nix, Jr. In addition to his airport business, Nix 3d has a private law practice, serves as a member of the city real estate board, chairs the Fairmount Park Commission, and is a member of the Disciplinary Board of the Supreme Court of Pennsylvania. Nix's role in airport business became part of the broader probe story when it was discovered that firms run by politically-connected, often wealthy, individuals were getting MBEC certifications as "disadvantaged" businesses. Interestingly, if only as a window into the small fraternity of black Philadelphia elites, in 1993 Robert Bogle hired Chief Justice Nix's special assistant to serve as executive editor of the *Tribune*.

Prior to co-founding MBEC-certified Odyssey Waste in 1997, Singley represented waste hauling giant BFI in negotiations with the city. As one reporter noted at the time, "Street's personal friend and top fund raiser Carl Singley gets his cut of bond deals and trash contracts." Street responded to criticism of "helping his cronies" by stating, "I'm never going to reward my enemies. Why should I? I'm always going to reward my friends." Odyssey Waste was subcontracted on a $25 million BFI contract with the city. Asked about the appearance of impropriety, Singley remarked that Odyssey's deal was with BFI, not the city, and thus was not a political gift. Odyssey Waste was technically founded by Singley, Fareed Ahmed (president and CEO), Willie Johnson, and Tony Romano, who also ran a waste-hauling firm named Stratus Enterprises. In 2001, Odyssey and Stratus had the dubious distinction of being caught up in the Pennsylvania Department of Environment Protection's "Operation Clean Sweep", a week-long statewide inspection of waste-haulers. Odyssey was cited for 22 environment violations and fined $43,000 (7th highest in the state), while Stratus was cited for 15 environment violations and 50 safety violations, and fined $32,500 (12th in the state).

In 2002, Willie Johnson replaced Fareed Ahmed as president of Odyssey, though the former Black Mafia chieftain remained as CEO. By 2003, Ahmed was earning an impressive $110,000 salary at Odyssey, and the firm's fourth person of importance was board member Obra Kernodle. Thus, Odyssey's board mirrored that of West Insurance in that Fareed Ahmed, Willie Johnson, Obra Kernodle, and Carl Singley were all listed together. The impressive foursome also partnered together in Philacomm Cable Group, where they were joined by A. Bruce Crawley, head of the area's African-American Chamber of Commerce (AACC).[3] Back in 1995, then-Council President John Street stalled Time Warner Cable's plan to purchase Wade Communications' Philadelphia cable television system until

Time Warner agreed to sell a portion to local minority businessmen. Philacomm Cable was the firm that received the minority subcontract.

Willie Johnson has not been identified as a subject in the corruption probe, despite his involvement with West Insurance, yet his remarkable career illustrates the tight-knit clique of influential minority businessmen dominating segments of Philadelphia's municipal work. Johnson, like Carl Singley, was an official in Mayor Bill Green's administration in the early 1980s, and has donated considerably to John Street and Ed Rendell for the past ten or so years. Johnson's firm, PRWT, was founded in 1988 as a small clerical support services firm (26 employees), and its focus was initially on the public services sector. John Brophy, then an executive with Lockheed Martin Corp., was a friend of Willie Johnson's and suggested that Johnson start what became PRWT. At the time, Lockheed Martin had a contract with the Philadelphia Parking Authority to accept payments and to answer phone calls. Brophy and Lockheed gave the contract to Johnson's PRWT and the Parking Authority became the new firm's first client. In no time the firm grew exponentially to handle third-party payment processing and systems management services in cities around the country. In 1996, the Greater Philadelphia Chamber of Commerce presented PRWT with its Minority Business Advocate of the Year Award, one of many such signs of recognized success the firm received. That same year, Fletcher "Flash" Wiley joined PRWT as its in-house attorney. Prior to the hire, PRWT had been a client of Wiley's. In addition to his position in Coolidge Bank & Trust, Wiley's public sector experience was noteworthy, having served as chairman of the Greater Boston Chamber of Commerce, director of Boston's Economic Development Industrial Corp., and founder and director of the Massachusetts Governor's Commission on Minority Business Development. Wiley, of course, now sits on the West Insurance board.

Though PRWT expanded to other U.S. cities, it remained based in Philadelphia where it continued to thrive. For instance, between 1994 and 1998, PRWT raked in more than $1 million in work from the Philadelphia Housing Authority alone. In 1998, PRWT began adding private accounts to its vast municipal workload, and the firm has routinely been mentioned as one of the most successful minority-run firms in the country ever since. PRWT's longtime partner, Lockheed Martin IMS, was acquired by Affiliated Computer Services (ACS) in August 2001 for $825 million. ACS is a Fortune 500 firm with 40,000 employees that provides business process outsourcing and information technology solutions to commercial and government entities around the world, and whose annual revenue is in the billions. Following the acquisition, Willie Johnson's old friend and business associate John Brophy assumed the position of Group President for ACS State and Local Solutions, and the PRWT-ACS relationship has continued. Given the historical ties between the two firms, it is perhaps not surprising to note that West Insurance board member Charles M. Greene was once with Lockheed Martin IMS, or that he served on the board of directors at PRWT. Furthermore, Greene is Vice Chair of Cheyney University under Chair Robert Bogle of the *Philadelphia Tribune* where, fittingly, Greene is also a board member. Bogle, of course, is also a West Insurance board member, and serves on the PRWT board as well. ACS's managing director of municipal services, Joe Martz, currently sits with Bogle, Willie Johnson, and Flash Wiley on the PRWT board. Charles Greene also currently serves on the board of the Philadelphia Health Management Corporation, which is headed by another familiar name in the city's elite African-American circles, former Judge Paul A. Dandridge.

A FEW HUSTLING CATS

I N THE SUMMER of 2007, just before this updated version of *Black Brothers Inc.* was completed, Philadelphia's Democratic mayoral primary took place in advance of the November election. The ongoing municipal corruption probe was still a major issue, marking the second consecutive election affected by it. Incredibly, the circumstances surrounding the 2003 electronic bug discovery and political spin were hotly debated again. In short, there were two related areas of discontent: Firstly, what did Mayor John Street know about the bug, and thus about the investigation, in the early days of the probe when the story was being absorbed into the public's conscience? If he knew anything about the bug, when did he know, and what did he tell his supporters and the public? Secondly, when did the Street campaign adopt a strategy designed to exploit the issue of race, framing the corruption probe as an attack on an African-American mayor?

Later on the day that the listening device was first found in Street's City Hall office, on October 7, Street spoke to the press. He said, "Although I don't know what's going on here, the question that will ultimately get raised in the minds of some people is, 'Who's investigating the mayor's office?' The reality is it could be a private party. It could be a state, federal or local investigation. There's no telling what it could be. I have no idea." On October 8, FBI agents raided the home and office of Shamsud-din Ali. At a news conference soon after, Street said: "I haven't talked to anybody from the federal government." Later that day, he told two *Inquirer* reporters: "I don't know what's going on, but there's got to be something going on. I can't tell you exactly what. My position is that if the feds are conducting some sort of investigation, they ought to say it and they ought to tell the truth." On October 9, Street appeared on CNN and was asked whether he knew why the bug was planted in his office. "I don't know and I don't know that I'll ever know," he replied. On October 16, federal agents raided three city agencies and the office of Ron White. Asked later that day what authorities were investigating, Street said, "I don't know what they're looking for," and promised his full cooperation.

Street's repeated claims of ignorance predictably fanned the flames of an electorate primed to be convinced of a conspiracy to dethrone a Democratic, African-American mayor. His claims were also deliberately misleading, if not outright lies.

During the trial of Shamsud-din Ali, FBI agents were questioned on the witness stand about the scope of the corruption investigation, including the infamous bugging of the Mayor's office. Agent John R. Roberts testified the FBI placed the listening device in City Hall because there was a pattern whereby John Street and Ron White would cut short their phone conversations and say they needed to speak in private. According to Roberts, these meetings would be followed by phone calls in which White, arguably on behalf of Street, would instruct city officials about who should win city contracts, framing these deals in terms of campaign donations. Thus, the purpose of the bug was to determine whether Street was exchanging municipal contracts for campaign contributions.

"We were very interested in the conversations that ... could have occurred in Mayor Street's office between Mayor Street and Ron White in the days leading up to the election," Roberts testified. "The campaign was looking to raise funds for their re-election. We were interested in whether there was any trade-off between raising campaign funds for contracts. We thought that that may have been happening in [Street's] private offices during his private meetings with Ron White." The FBI received court authorization for the bug on September 18, but it is not known when it was put in place. The FBI planned on operating the bug until November 17, when taps on Ron White's phones would also expire.

After the trial, Roberts, the FBI agent who obtained the court order for the bug, was asked to recall the scene when he heard the bug was found on October 7. He said, "The range of emotions was incredible. You're angry. You're upset. But you're trying to think calmly and rationally." Roberts and two other case agents decided they would confront Mayor Street, admit they planted the bug, and ask him questions only about Shamsud-din Ali and city contracts. The conversation included inquiries regarding two Ali businesses that have since become synonymous with this part of the probe, KIFS and Clear Alley. When they met with the mayor shortly after the discovery, the agents didn't disclose that they applied for the listening device because they suspected Street and Ron White were trading city contracts for campaign donations. The FBI had five other wiretaps in operation at the time. Roberts said the agents wanted to "tickle the wires", copspeak for generating conversations between relevant parties who are under surveillance. Indeed, the meeting with Street worked as hoped – the following day witnessed Street and White speaking briefly on the phone about Ali's KIFS, and White making 170 other calls, each of which was monitored by the FBI.

Regarding the second area of heated debate, namely the Street campaign's playing of the race card, the issue centered around a phone conversation that took place on 10 October 2003 between Ron White and Street. The conversation was recorded on court-authorized wiretaps by the FBI, and includes an exchange where the two powerful men agree to use the "race thing" as a campaign tactic. It is presented verbatim below, but the pre-October 10 events that had already foreshadowed the tone of the campaign are presented below first. Mayor Street's publicly-professed ignorance about the probe only helped to bolster the conspiracy therories.

The bug was discovered early in the morning on October 7 and it didn't take a full day for the racist/conspiracy allegations to begin. By nighttime, John Dougherty, electricians union chief and a close Street ally, said the timing of the bugging was suspicious. The *Inquirer* ran a brief assessment the next day of how it might affect the election. Highly-regarded political consultant Larry Ceisler noted the event might buttress the "Democratic argument that this election is about national politics and those Bush Republicans will stop at nothing to keep John Street from being reelected." The paper added, "[Ceisler] predicted that Street surrogates would begin stoking the idea of a Republican conspiracy against Street as long as the FBI leaves open the possibility that he is under investigation. 'This can drive up turnout in the Democratic base, African Americans and liberal whites,' Ceisler said."

On October 9, the *Inquirer* published an article, "The bug: Who knew what and when?" which included the following:

"Do we believe that the Republican Party, both at the federal level and state level, is pulling out every stop to get Pennsylvania in 2004?" Street campaign spokesman Frank Keel said. "Absolutely. Is the Republican Party capable of dirty tricks? I think that is well documented." Lawyer Leonard Ross, a longtime friend and adviser to Street, said that "the impact will be to energize our base. Folks will get mad and come out to vote. I don't think we're going to pack up our tents and go away."

Like many Street loyalists, U.S. Rep. Chaka Fattah was phoning in his outrage to talk-radio shows, including on WHAT-AM (1340), which calls itself the "voice of the African American community." "I have never been more committed to win an election than this one," Fattah said ...

State Rep. James Roebuck, a West Philadelphia Democrat and historian, said he believed that the events would energize Street loyalists. "People remember [former FBI Director J. Edgar] Hoover and Martin Luther King," Roebuck said. "The kinds of tactics the FBI used during the most heated period of the civil-rights period was designed not to investigate the Klan but to undermine the civil-rights movement." Because of that history, he said, many in the African American community "have no confidence in the FBI."

The *Inquirer's* coverage that day also included an editorial by longtime columnist Acel Moore, which included:

> Hmm . . . people planting listening devices in the offices of black political figures . . . it reminds some folks of the era of J. Edgar Hoover, who compiled audiotapes of the Rev. Dr. Martin Luther King Jr. and other black leaders during the civil-rights era. I'm not saying this equals that. I'm saying it's eerily reminiscent, and refusing to answer questions isn't helping. What I am saying is that if the FBI continues to stonewall, this will seem like what it most probably is: a modern-day dirty political trick.

Mayor Street appeared on NBC's *Today* show and said, "I think there will continue to be a huge amount of speculation and concern that some of this is racially motivated."

On October 10, conspiracy theory seemed to be taking hold of the city's two main papers. "Suspicious," "bizarre," "convenient" and "politically motivated" were some of the words reported to describe the bug revelation. Headlines that day included "FBI probe raises questions on race, politics" (*Inquirer*), "Some suggest fed probe not colorblind" (*Daily News*), and "Evasive feds doing Street a big favor" (*Daily News* again). Two *Daily News* articles mentioned Shamsud-din Ali's known relevance in the probe and his background in the Black Mafia. Importantly, one of the articles ("Street's blackberry jam") was the first to note there were, in fact, two federal probes:

> The probe that has enveloped the mayor focuses on city contracts ... The other investigation involves drugs and focuses on Muslim cleric Shamsud-din Ali, a longtime Street supporter whose home and office were raided Wednesday by FBI investigators ... Shamsud-din Ali, whose former name was Clarence Fowler, was once a reputed Black Mafia kingpin. FBI agents from Squad 2, the FBI's drug squad, spearheaded the search of Ali's Mount Airy home and office on Wednesday ... IRS agents also participated in the search. The search warrants and affidavits say why the properties were searched and what crimes may have been committed, but they remain under seal in U.S. District Court. [An anonymous law enforcement] source would not discuss how the two investigations were related. "The thing is just so sensitive," the source said. As for the mayor, the source said, "His current problems do not involve drugs."
>
> The source said the probes stem from a long-running joint investigation by police, FBI and the IRS into drug trafficking at the Richard Allen Homes in North Philadelphia, focusing on a group calling itself RAM Squad (RAM stands for Richard Allen Mob). No

one has been charged criminally in connection with this investigation, the source said.

The other, "Islamic Imam is focus of probe," began, "Before becoming a soft-spoken, politically connected leader of Philadelphia's African-American Muslim community, Imam Shamsud-din Ali was a reputed Black Mafia kingpin named Clarence Fowler." The article discussed Ali's background in the Muslim community and briefly examined his role in the syndicate.

The *Daily News* coverage set the stage for one of the more talked about wiretapped exchanges. The relevant portion of the conversation taped on White's phone went as follows. [Note: It is assumed "Kenny" is a reference to Kenny Gamble, "Al" is a reference to the Rev. Al Sharpton, and "Bruce" is a reference to A. Bruce Crawley.]

Ronald A. White: Who's this?

Mayor John F. Street: This is Street.

White: Hey, man! What're you doing? I'm just checking on you, brother.

Street: I'm actually headed to the graveyard with the body of a deceased firefighter.[1]

White: Oh, OK.

Street: Yeah, man, it's sad. The guy was forty-three years old.

White: Oh, yeah, that's the man that had the heart attack, wasn't it?

Street. Yeah. Yep.

White: Well, I was just checking in, man, just, you know, seeing if everything was OK, if you need me to do anything.

Street: No, I'm all right. I mean, we're obviously getting ready to readjust our strategy a little bit.

White: We got to, man, we got to. We got to go all out now, John.

Street: Yeah, yeah.

White: You know, we can win this thing with just us.

Street: Oh, yeah.

White: We can win with just us.

Street: People are pretty outraged about this.

White: Oh yeah, man. We need to go all the way. I saw everybody at the [Democratic] City Committee today, and you know, whatever you all come up with, whether we need to bring in national people, whatever, man. We got to go all the way.

Street: Yeah, the national people, we're lining them up now.

White: Well, you know, Al [Sharpton] calls me every day, so let me know. Just let me know what you want.

Street. Yeah. Well, you know, I talked to Jesse Jackson yesterday and all the national people. See, up until now the national people thought this was "Yeah, yeah, yeah." But they figured we were really going to win this. You know? A little bit of a yawner. You know how everybody running scared. Man, they see this kind of stuff and they say, "Oh boy, here we go again."

White: Yeah.

Street: Yeah, here we go. So there's a lot of national interest. Then I did them couple of national shows and this thing is all in the New York Times and just everywhere. So it's going to get a lot of attention. And that'll be helpful.

White: Yeah, well, you know. That's a mess, though, about that Richard Allen stuff, so. We've got to make sure we distance ourselves from that stuff.

Street: What Richard Allen stuff?

White: You didn't see that stuff in the paper today?

Street: Uhn-uh.

White: In the paper today, they had that it was the drug people that was investigating Shamsud-din, right? And that it stems from some long investigation with a group called RAM, the Richard Allen Mob, right? And it means then it goes through all of Shamsud-din's history, the Black Muslims, the Black Mafia. I mean, it goes on and on and on. Then they got one sentence in there saying, but the mayor didn't have nothing to do with this. Right? But they put you right in that story.

Street: Really?

White: Nobody didn't tell you that?

Street: No.

White: Man.

Street: They put me in a story about Richard Allen?

White: They put you right in the story with the thing about the drugs and Richard Allen, and then say you don't have these problems. That the drug thing ain't connected to you. But they put you right in the story.

Street: Oh really?

White: Yeah, man.

Street: See, they're going too far.

White: They're going too far.

Street: Yeah.

White: But they're overstepping the line. That's going to give us the justification to do what we got to do now.

Street: Right, right.

White: We got to be sensitive, man. We didn't want to get into no race thing. They did this.

Street: Right.

White: So now we got to go with it.

Street: We don't have much choice but to go with it.

White: We got to go with it, John. We got to go with it. We got to get serious now, man. We got to go at these guys with everything we've got.

Street: Right.

White: You know?

Street: I talked to Kenny yesterday.

White: We've got to communicate, man. We've got have some strategy sessions with not just your campaign people but people like myself and Bruce and Kenny. You know? I mean, we gotta now have to talk about how we're going to do this from a black thing, you know what I mean?

Street: Well, we can do both. I mean, we can do both.

White: No, we've got to do both but we've got to do it differently, John. That's all I'm saying. Because they're going all out, man.

Street: I know. I know. We're probably going to have a little series of meetings on the weekend. I'll let you know. There's some rally that they're planning. People are already, some of this stuff people are doing it, they ain't asking us, they're just doing it.

White: Right.

Street: Which is good.

One misconception, at least in some quarters, is that the October 10 *Daily News* coverage of Shamsud-din Ali's background compelled the Street campaign to embrace a political strategy exploiting race. For instance, when the White-Street wiretap transcripts were obtained by the *Inquirer* in 2005, the paper ran a story with the headline, "White, Street saw 'race thing' as probe tactic." Though it was obviously true the taped call demonstrated Street and White agreeing to exploit race, the coverage may have been interpreted by some to mean the campaign decided *at that moment* to move forward with such a strategy. Those who insist the Democratic plot to frame the corruption probe as a racist, politically-inspired investigation was employed after October 10 must acknowledge this effort was already well underway – though perhaps less formally – before Ron White explicitly proposed the strategy to Street.

It is noteworthy the incredulity in the taped White-Street conversation is reserved for the media coverage in the *Daily News*. After all, one would also expect such sentiments for the revelation or allegation that a "longtime friend" and "recognized community leader" has a history that includes an ultra-violent crime syndicate. When White said the *Daily News* coverage "goes through all of Shamsud-din's history, the Black Muslims, the Black Mafia ... ," there was no response one might expect from John Street, such as, "Imam Shamsud-din Ali and the Black Mafia? What!" Nor did White utter any curiosity, much less shock. There was probably no such reaction because insiders know this history, despite the media's lack of sincere interest in it.

★

Which brings us to the coverage of, and reactions to, *Black Brothers Inc.* Though at first glance these may seem trivial, they are significant and deserving of some commentary because of their effect on public opinion, public policy, and on the social construction of urban history and of organized crime.

Given this book's subject matter, it was predictably first embraced primarily by an urban, localized, African-American audience. This fact was also influenced by the seminal coverage in the Philadelphia area, which appeared in the *Daily News*. The *Daily News* readership is more working class, and the paper has a far more diverse audience, than its big sister and more widely-read competitor, the *Inquirer*. According to the *Daily News*, the paper's readership is half non-white, the largest percentage of non-white readers of any U.S. daily. The responses from these readers were always intriguing, because they were commonly grounded on some "real-world" experiences and I often found myself learning a great deal from these exchanges. I don't recall a single instance where a black reader questioned why some of the book's key revelations were not covered in the news. Apparently, for them the first-, second-, and third-hand experiences, stories and legends on the street were sufficient, if not superior to anything news organizations could offer. As the book's popularity grew, its readership increasingly included white, suburban audiences, and I routinely found myself entertaining wholly different conversations and questions. Importantly, these readers almost exclusively get their local news, directly and indirectly, from one of two sources: the area's "paper of record", the *Philadelphia Inquirer*; and WHYY radio.

It is difficult to convey how many times, often in exasperated tones, in forums ranging from academic settings to soccer field sidelines to community gatherings and family picnics, I heard some version of the following question from members of this subset of readers: "I follow news/I am a news junkie/I read the *Inquirer* every day/I listen to WHYY. How have I never heard about [insert any number of revelations from *Black Brothers Inc* here]?" Similarly, one borderline apoplectic radio host went so far as to ask, in a heightened pitch, "How does someone like Shamsud-din Ali wind up in [Mayor John] Street's circle? If someone took this book, with all its documentation, to John Street, what would he say?" If these folks weren't incredulous enough when they contacted me, they almost uniformly became agitated, if not irate, when they heard these media outlets knew about the story yet made no effort to press numerous consequential political and other figures about their dubious ties to the underworld, and for whatever reason opted not to inform their respective audiences about much, if not all, of the book's timely subject matter. That organized crime is so intimately tied to, if not immersed within, Philadelphia's political culture is shocking to many people, some of whom could not credibly be called naïve. Even cynics have their limits, it turns out, and when they read about government-funded murderers, and about the backgrounds of current political operatives and the other few degrees-of-separation that exist between other "legitimate" parties and the underworld, they can't believe that despite their efforts to remain informed, they never read or heard about such note-worthy matters.

In some ways, such "under-reporting" helps authors like me, since it allows for us to fill an inviting void. Nevertheless, such poor coverage of significant historical and contemporary issues also undermines serious efforts to write history, devise theory, inform public opinion, and to affect public policy. Hopefully what follows is understood not as griping on my part but rather as an effort to address what I believe is a systemic problem in academia and in the media, namely a bizarre and troublesome mix of racism, political correctness, stereotyping, and slipshod workmanship.

Inquirer to Inquiring Minds – Nevermind

The Black Mafia and Shamsud-din Ali

On 10 October 2003, the *Philadelphia Daily News* published a story titled, "Islamic Imam is Focus of Probe," by reporters Kitty Caparella and Erin Einhorn. Though the major point of the article was simply that Shamsud-din Ali was one of the first known subjects in a burgeoning and largely myste-rious federal investigation, Ali's background in the Black Mafia was mentioned, citing a just-released academic textbook of mine to support the claim. Importantly, October 10 was a mere three days after the discovery of the electronic bug in the Mayor's Office, and just weeks before a hotly contested election. The coverage of the federal probe, therefore, had primacy and would likely be far more consequential than usual. The *Daily News* article about Ali caused a flurry of media activity, with various outlets asking me for interviews and assistance regarding the Imam and his ties to the underworld. Among this crowd were reporters of the *Philadelphia Inquirer*, with whom I would ultimately correspond for some time. Importantly, in these critical, early weeks of the probe reporting, the paper's treatment of the Ali revelations left much to be desired and raises several issues.

Among the questions posed to me by one of the *Inquirer's* lead probe reporters in this crucial period, incredibly, was: "How do we *know* there ever was a group called the 'Black Mafia'?" Notwithstanding the only reason I was sought out by the paper was because my peer-reviewed research on the topic had just been cited in the *Daily News*, I pointed to the *thousands* of articles on the syndicate housed in *Inquirer's* own archives, which brought this reply: "Well, of course there are articles. If law enforcement does something, reporters usually cover it. It could have just been that reporters were repeating what was told to them." It was apparently of no concern that the two lead *Inquirer* reporters who covered the Black Mafia story in the 1970s were each highly regarded in the profession – Jim Nicholson was an award-winning investigative reporter who garnered two Pulitzer nominations just prior to his Black Mafia reporting, and Mike Leary rose through the press ranks after his reporting on the syndicate to currently sit as the national editor at the *Baltimore Sun*.

I was also told by an *Inquirer* reporter the Black Mafia may, indeed, have been a creation of the racist Philadelphia Police in the tumultuous 1960s and 1970s. Further, I was implored to understand that following the NOI's purchase of St. Thomas More High School in 1976, which upset many Catholics in the city including numerous law enforcement officials, police may still harbor a grudge against Shamsud-din Ali since he has occupied the building ever since. Mind you, these exchanges took place in 2003, more than thirty-five years after a group of hard-core criminals organized and called themselves the Black Mafia on their way to slaying dozens of people and terrorizing entire sections of the city, and here I was attempting to convince an *Inquirer* reporter there ever was such a group. Law enforcement files and court transcripts were of little value as supporting documents, of course, if one was predisposed to believe the Black Mafia cases were concocted by law enforcement for some illegitimate and perhaps extra-legal purpose.

Other surreal exchanges followed. When I asked why the *Inquirer* had made no mention of Shamsud-din's background vis-à-vis the Black Mafia in any of the thirteen articles which discussed him in the federal probe, responses from the newspaper's personnel were almost unbelievable. These included, "It's salacious" (as opposed to substantive); "It's history, and history isn't news"; and "These are just accusations [re: his involvement in the syndicate's hierarchy]. He has never been convicted of anything." That Ali was being investigated for Minority Business Enterprise Council-related activities (his other illicit activities were not public knowledge at that very early stage of the probe) was of little concern to the *Inquirer*, despite the fact his Black Mafia confederates had quite a history of making a mockery of similar government initiatives. Importantly, within two weeks of the Ali-specific coverage's start, and as the paper was debating the merits of the organized crime context in the story, the *Inquirer* ran six other articles on organized crime: three local articles involving the city's predominant Italian-American group; and three Associated Press articles out of Boston involving Stephen "The Rifleman" Flemmi, who had pleaded guilty to racketeering charges involving ten murders while running the largely Irish Winter Hill Gang with underworld legend – and fugitive – James "Whitey" Bulger.

According to one of the *Inquirer* reporters, who like others asked not to be named for obvious reasons, there was an additional reason for the lack of Black Mafia context in the paper's early probe reporting of Shamsud-din Ali, namely the combustible mix of race and politics, a mainstay in the Black Mafia story. In a June 2007 interview, this person recalled meetings among reporters and editors on how to address the Black Mafia revelations given, in the reporter's words, the "racially-charged" federal investigation, and how such reporting might unfairly impact incumbent John Street in the looming mayoral election.

The painstaking hand wringing that apparently took place at the *Inquirer* over the reporting of a so-called "racially-charged investigation" involving a prominent African-American Muslim cleric may have been extraordinary, but in Philadelphia's social and political climate, this politically-correct reporting is not without reason. Consider the fiasco, briefly recounted below, which took place merely a year prior involving its sister paper, the *Daily News*, and the tabloid's coverage of homicide fugitives in the city.

On 22 August 2002, the *Daily News* ran a cover image featuring mug shots of fifteen fugitives wanted for murder by Philadelphia police. All of the faces were minorities, mostly African-American, sparking an outcry among some of the city's black leaders.

Importantly, at the time there were forty-one people wanted for murder, none of whom were white. This fact was no solace to some who were still ostensibly uncomfortable if not outraged with the presentation, despite the accuracy of the reporting. On August 29, a group calling itself the Coalition for Fair News Coverage deemed the newspaper "racially divisive" and announced a protest set for September 9. The group, led at least in part by A. Bruce Crawley, a longtime Street adviser and then-chairman of the African-American Chamber of Commerce, asked for the resignation of the paper's editor and managing editor.

Incredibly, the *Daily News* ran an apology the following day, written by managing editor Ellen Foley, which included this:

The coverage of our paper [on 8/22/02] carried mugshots of 15 of 41 suspects. They were African-American, Hispanic, or Asian. These 41 were identified by the Police Department's Homicide Unit as suspects for whom murder warrants were issued. There were no white people who were being sought for murder. Would we do a story again about 41 fugitives wanted for murder by the Philadelphia Police Department? Absolutely. Would we do it differently? Absolutely. The front page photos from last Thursday sent the message to some readers that only black men commit murder. That was a mistake. In addition, the stories didn't address a key question: Why are there no white suspects on the loose? That also was a mistake.

The paper's editor, Zachary Stalberg, added, "I think the cover was literally correct, but a mistake on our part because what we have to worry about is perceptions, and not just the literal truth." Stalberg added, "My perception was that it was suggesting that all people who commit murders are black males. Everyone saw it a little differently, but I can understand why people were offended by it."

The editors' comments and apologies did little to satisfy the supposedly aggrieved parties, who proceeded with their protest against the paper. Roughly 100 people demonstrated in front of the *Daily News* building, urging fellow African-Americans to boycott the newspaper for what they characterized as its "racially insensitive" coverage. Predictably – and ironically – the group included Shamsud-din Ali, who would grace the paper's cover in the near future for his own crimes. He was quoted as saying, "Don't buy [the *Daily News*] until you see a white flag on the building" in surrender. "Every time you think about it, say, 'I haven't seen a white flag; can't buy it yet.'"

Meanwhile, the newspaper's apology peeved several of its own reporters and columnists, including one who noted the paper should have said, "The victims of these killers were black, too. And if publishing the faces of these fugitives means someone will recognize them and turn them in, then political correctness be damned." Indeed, within days of the coverage, four of the fugitives profiled were arrested after readers called police. Furthermore, the story also prompted tips leading to the arrest of two other killers who weren't pictured.

Interestingly, the best summation of the ridiculous situation came from a *Boston Globe* reporter named Hiawatha Bray, who wrote the following letter to the *Daily News*. His brief and pointed comments could just as easily have been written to apply to the *Inquirer's* anxiety in reporting Black Mafia aspects of the corruption probe story one year hence:

> I'm a black journalist who could scarcely believe my eyes as I read it. A newspaper is apologizing for printing the truth? It's embarrassing and humiliating that so many murders are committed by black people, but it's the job of newspapers to publish embarrassing and humiliating truths. No newspaper editor has any business apologizing for writing truthfully about an issue of obvious public concern just because it upsets some members of the public. Get a grip, you guys.

So one can at least understand why Philadelphia's media entities may be circumspect with their reporting of stories involving race. Getting back to the 2003 coverage of Shamsud-din Ali, however, the reporting decisions remain peculiar at best.

Notwithstanding the offered explanations of "sensitivity" and the issue of a "racially-charged investigation" in the probe's early coverage, the *Inquirer* somehow came to accept history and its import to their readers, because in no less than eight articles beginning in February 2004, Shamsud-din Ali's background with the Black Mafia *was* mentioned. We'll never know what miraculously convinced the paper's reporters and editors there was once a group called the Black Mafia, and that Shamsud-din Ali played a key role in its history. One thing is certain, however, and deserves mention: the articles post-February 2004 did not need his background any more or less than those published in the seminal coverage of the investigation in the run-up to the November 2003 mayoral election. What was deemed as "history" months prior became "news", what was deemed "salacious" turned "substantive", and whatever hang-ups there were about the "racially-charged" investigation somehow subsided after the election.

Though the Shamsud-din Ali coverage eventually included some of the historical context, the same cannot be said for two other relevant parts of the story.

Dawud Bey
Dawud Bey was first identified in the *Inquirer* as a part of the probe on 21 May 2004, when he was indicted as part of the Savage-Thomas drug network. To this day, however, there has been no mention of his family background, namely that his father is Roosevelt "Spooks" Fitzgerald (*aka* Roosevelt Bey). To many observers, the fact that Bey's father was one of the more significant founding members of Philadelphia's Black Mafia is at the least intriguing. When one considers his father was a Captain in Temple 12's Fruit of Islam, which included such terrifying gangsters as Black Mafia founder Sam Christian, convicted Hanafi murderer John Clark, convicted Hanafi and Coxson slayer Ron Harvey, convicted Dubrow's Furniture murderer Nudie Mims, Black Brothers, Inc. founders Gene Hearn and Lonnie Dawson (the latter another convicted murderer), one would think this was at least noteworthy. Since another of the FOI Captains at the time, and the ultimate successor to Temple 12 head Jeremiah Shabazz, was Clarence Fowler *aka* Shamsud-din Ali, one would (wrongly) assume this is newsworthy, if not consequential. When the feds discovered drug dealers Dawud Bey and Gerald Thomas each had meetings and phone conversations with Shamsud-din Ali, the Imam became part of the drug probe. The nexus between Thomas/Bey/Ali is a key point in the story of what ultimately resulted in fifty-plus people pleading guilty or being convicted. Bey's father has not been mentioned by any authorities in the multifarious probes, though this should have had little to do with the lack of reporting historical context. The *Inquirer* itself, just seven months after the Bey coverage began, demonstrated how such background can make for compelling, if not always significant, news.

On 20 December 2004, a twenty-nine-year-old man named Rocco Marinucci was shot multiple times in an apparent narcotics transaction that may have turned into a robbery. Marinucci survived the incident, making for a fairly lukewarm story in a town that endured 1000-plus shootings and 330 homicides that year. The following day, however, the *Inquirer* blared the headline, "Mobster's son shot in South Phila. Hotel," with a story that began, "Rocco Marinucci, the son of a mobster shot and killed 22 years ago during the city's widespread mob wars, was wounded early yesterday in a South Philadelphia hotel during a suspected drug deal that went awry, police said." The paper published almost as many words about the long deceased Rocco Marinucci (his criminal background and his slaying) as they did his son's shooting, ostensibly the reason for the article. Despite the sensational coverage, the body of the story belied the hype since, according to the police official quoted in the article, the incident was "not mob-related."

There was no follow-up in the *Inquirer* regarding the 2004 Marinucci shooting and we are left to conclude the first impression was correct: this was a nondescript incident involving a person of little, if any, consequence in the city's underworld. Compare this situation with the offspring of another gangster whose heyday was roughly the same as Marinucci's. Unlike the younger Marinucci, Dawud Bey *was* a consequential person on the streets of Philadelphia, in the upper rungs of one of the city's more prominent and brutal drug rings. Bey is still a lead suspect in a high-profile murder of a government witness in a homicide case against co-defendant and drug kingpin Kaboni Savage. After his arrest, Bey continued threatening witnesses and their families from his cell, resulting in the relocation of numerous people for their safety. Furthermore, he was a target of a narcotics investigation which turned into a municipal corruption probe –he consorted with a key target of the latter, Shamsud-din Ali –that affected a mayoral election. Yet despite the weighty and far-reaching nature of the Bey-Ali story, Bey's father's role in the Black Mafia, and his role as right-hand man to Ali's mentor, Jeremiah Shabazz, have never been discussed in the *Inquirer*.

Fareed Ahmed (formerly Gene Hearn)

West Insurance was first publicly identified as a subject in the corruption probe on 14 December 2003. Since then, the *Inquirer* has published seven articles regarding the investigation of the firm, including two which explicitly discuss Fareed Ahmed (Gene Hearn) as the firm's vice president. Nevertheless, despite knowing Ahmed's background, the paper has deprived its readers of such noteworthy information. Specifically, the *Inquirer* has stated, "Fareed Ahmed, a vice president for West Insurance, is well-known in political circles for his get-out-the-vote work that helped elect Street and other politicians"; and, "Company vice president Fareed Ahmed was a key election organizer for Street." The context of the latter story vis-à-vis the pay-to-play probe can be gleaned in its first paragraphs:

Insurance executive William A. Graham IV says doing government business in Philadelphia has its own set of rules. Here's an important one: Don't argue when politicians want you to cut their friends into deals. On the Street administration's recommendation, he has dumped Republicans and put in Democrats. At the direction of a Republican-controlled agency, he ditched an African American subcontractor tied to Mayor Street and put in a Republican. Over the years, he says, he has paid hundreds of thousands of dollars to minority subcontractors who did little or no work.

Graham, who is also a heavyweight campaign donor, says paying politically wired partners is just another price of doing government jobs around Philadelphia. "This is the way it's done – on concrete work, on insurance work, on any kind of work," said Graham, whose company does $250 million in business a year. "It's just so accepted," he said. "If the only way to get to Flourtown is on the bus, you don't say, 'I'm going to take the train.'" And just about every year, someone at a government agency wants him to cut in a favored minority firm ...

To fairly critique the *Inquirer's* lack of organized crime context regarding Ahmed, one must start with two crucial assumptions. Firstly, for some time now Ahmed has been removed from the Black Mafia career which once placed him in the company of the hit squad at the Club Harlem that assassinated Fat Ty Palmer, and ultimately put him in federal prison for his role in the syndicate's "massive drug conspiracy". Secondly, West Insurance has done nothing illegal and no West official has been charged with any wrongdoing.

Having said the above, it is difficult to imagine the Ahmed situation being under-reported if he was instead, say, mobster Joey Merlino, even though Merlino was arguably less consequential than Ahmed and his Black Mafia companions in their respective heydays. It is highly unlikely Joey Merlino could: come out of federal prison after serving part of a fifteen-year sentence in a major racketeering conspiracy; immediately wind up on drug wiretaps with his mafia buddies; become a political power broker; garner government contracts, a key part of his syndicate's enterprise years prior; wind up being investigated in a massive federal probe yet again, one which includes two individuals with ties to the original conspiracy for which he served time in prison; and not have this criminal background mentioned – if not highlighted – in the *Inquirer.*

More significantly with respect to contemporary matters, Hearn/Ahmed was not only a leader in one of the city's most violent criminal organizations, he was also a leader, alongside convicted Black Mafia murderers Lonnie Dawson and Larris Frazier, of Black Brothers, Inc., a bogus "community development" organization *that exploited financial initiatives for underserved, inner city minorities.* Given the focus of the current probe, this is newsworthy to say the least. And yet, as with the Dawud Bey situation and a few others not examined here for the sake of brevity, the *Inquirer* saw fit to exclude such contextual information in their otherwise comprehensive reporting.

There is one last, and perhaps trivial, point regarding Hearn/Ahmed and Fowler/Ali that has not been mentioned in the *Inquirer*'s almost four years of reporting on the federal probes. These two individuals have the dubious distinction of being investigated by federal authorities in at least three different decades. Each was investigated in the 1970s for their suspected roles in various crimes within the Black Mafia enterprise; in the 1980s when they popped up in the investigation of Black Mafia's impressive drug network led by Lonnie Dawson; and in the 2000s when they each turned up in distinct parts of the corruption probe.

★

One might humor the idea that because the Black Mafia aspects of the various probe-related stories didn't follow the *Inquirer*'s overly simplistic "Cosa Nostra" template, the paper simply didn't "get" the underworld context. There are a few reasons this is unlikely, however. For starters, the *Inquirer* has afforded other non-Italian-American groups substantial coverage, much of which was investigated and penned by the paper's award-winning organized crime reporter, George Anastasia. More significantly, the *Inquirer*'s own archives are replete with articles on the Black Mafia and its numerous affiliates, and several of the newspaper's reporters corresponded extensively with me on numerous occasions.

It may be true that "group think" partly accounted for the lack of imagination and interest at the *Inquirer* in delving beyond the superficial aspects of the story that clearly *had* to be covered. Speaking with many media types the past few years, however, it is clear there is also commonly a trend to "pull punches" when it comes to hard-hitting, incisive reporting on the known and alleged Black Mafia ties to the corruption probe story.

Philadelphia's Black Mafia on Philadelphia Public Radio: *WHYY* Not?

The curiosities involving the *Philadelphia Inquirer*'s non-reporting of various Black Mafia-related historical and contemporary actors and activities are unfortunately part of a larger pattern, one which suggests at best stereotyping or slipshod reporting and at worst suggests biased and arguably unethical reporting. Consider the following situation that occurred in July 2005.

Larry Robin is the owner and operator of Robin's, the area's oldest independent bookstore, located in the heart of the city. Larry, a legend in the Philadelphia literary scene, is a true book lover and a devout believer in the freedom of expression. In short, he is a professional in a profession that often lacks his ethics, ethos, and drive. Larry somehow sensed the book's potential and beat his competition to the punch in getting large quantities in stock. Robin's sold so many copies the first few days of the book's release, Larry contacted me about visiting his store for a book signing event. Thrilled with the state of things, and appreciative of what Larry was doing, I gladly accepted his invitation to appear at his store on the evening of 19 July 2005.

As anyone who follows the area's politics, culture, news and anything else of consequence knows, including and especially Larry Robin, one of the leading forums for such discussions is Philadelphia PBS affiliate WHYY. In particular, WHYY radio has a popular and highly-respected program, *Radio Times*, hosted by the award-winning Marty Moscoane. Over the years, she has hosted practically everyone of note in the region, and has routinely interviewed political commentators, crime beat reporters, as well as reporters and authors who examined Italian-American and Irish-American organized crime in the city. Thus, Larry Robin suggested I appear on Marty's show in one of the days leading up to the event. Within a day of agreeing to his suggestion, following which he apparently contacted the *Radio Times* staff, the show's executive producer contacted me, expressing the urgent need to have a book and press kit to prepare for an appearance on the show. I personally drove a copy of the book and press materials down to the WHYY studios. As the days leading to the event went by, Larry checked with me to see when I'd be appearing on the radio show and with each email or phone call, I explained I had heard nary a word from WHYY since dropping off the book. Time was tight, and we didn't press the matter with the station, opting instead to concentrate on the pending appearance. The book signing was great, far more interesting than any I had attended or experienced, and had as diverse a crowd as one would have expected in the Club Harlem or Gus Lacy's Third Base back in the day.

These happenings soon became an item in a national trade newsletter, which began: "Robin's Bookstore owner Larry Robin had to dig back far – beyond even Harry Potter – to find a comparison for his Philadelphia bookstore's current bestseller, which has sold almost 500 copies in its first two weeks on sale: 'I haven't seen a book sell that much since *Tropic of Cancer*,' he said this week. The book is *Black Brothers, Inc* ... the book got a further boost at Robin's Tuesday night when its author, Sean Patrick Griffin, was, shall we say, mobbed by more than 100 people during an appearance." In the 1960s, the City of Philadelphia had asked for an injunction against the sale of *Tropic of Cancer* and Robin's was the lone place to purchase the book, resulting in astronomical sales figures at the center city outlet.

As the whirlwind of media attention continued throughout fall 2005, I asked a university public relations official to follow up with WHYY to see what happened regarding being interviewed on *Radio Times*. According to the PSU official, the reply from one of the show's producers was that the book was "too academic" for their audience. For those who are remotely in tune with public broadcasting, this rationale for not covering a true crime/organized crime read – with current, "real-world" implications for any number of goings on in the city – is just silly. This oddity also flew in the face of the dozens of other outlets clamoring for our time and energy, several of whom were national or international. Comically, I was interviewed on television via satellite for another PBS affiliate, and the shoot took place in the WHYY studios. More incredibly, the technician working the equipment in the studio was none other than the tech for *Radio Times*. As I completed the interview, which was broadcast *outside* the Philadelphia region, the tech unhooked my microphone and suggested I get in touch with *Radio Times*, since this topic would be right up their alley. Containing my laughter, I politely explained the program had demurred from covering the story, and went on my way.

One could argue *Radio Times* caters to a more upscale, wealthy, largely white audience, and the decision to spurn coverage of the book was a business decision, not unlike certain book stores who viewed *BBI* as a "black book for black audiences." Different variations of this have included such comments as, "Why would a white audience be interested in this?" Of course, I don't ever recall hearing any similar queries of Italian- and Irish-American manuscripts. Imagine something like that for a moment: "Why would an audience predominantly of non-Italian descent be interested in a book on Italian-American organized crime?" Alas, this has been explicitly asked on numerous occasions with indignation regarding the topic of Philadelphia's Black Mafia, despite the fact I would argue the syndicate was and continues to be more significant in its region than most other crime groups in U.S. history. I have no evidence WHYY/*Radio Times* adopted the stereotyping business angle, but it is no less plausible than other alternatives.

In addition to the above case studies involving cases of so-called political correctness, if not poor or biased reporting and commentary regarding African-American organized crime in general and Philadelphia's Black Mafia in particular, there have been other curiosities that demonstrate this trend. To gain an understanding of how consistently this research has faced PC concerns, consider the following.

Academia and Philadelphia's Black Mafia: Crime and *Justice*

Though academics often pen books, many disciplines, including my own, frown upon book writing in favor of presenting research findings and analyses in peer-reviewed academic journals. This is for good reason, of course, since a publisher is likely to be preoccupied with profits rather than the substance or import of the research a book contains. Furthermore, there is commonly little substantive consideration given to the merits of the validity of the book's data, the reliability of the author's methodology, and the credibility of the book's findings. Academic journals employ a process by which experts in a particular field are called upon to vet submitted research papers, each far shorter than a book, using these very criteria. Thus, academic journal articles are commonly the standard by which scholars are judged. The process of having a piece of your research, analysis, findings and writing critiqued is usually fascinating and rewarding, though it can also be frustrating, particularly since the reviewers throwing darts are anonymous and there is no opportunity for retort. With all its warts, however, the process is generally sound and fair. That is, unless you are researching a topic deemed politically-incorrect by your anonymous peers.

In 1999, I submitted a paper to one of the leading journals in my field of criminology, *Justice Quarterly*. I wrote the article to debunk the commonly-held notion among academics that African-American organized crime is a new and emerging phenomenon. The paper consisted of a brief synopsis of the Black Mafia's history and concluded with a plea for academics and policy makers to research the current MBEC phenomenon (just as we do labor unions and racketeering) because of the remarkable – and sordid – history of these types of programs. The paper's conclusion disturbed at least one *JQ* reviewer, and I thus present it verbatim immediately below.

CONCLUSION: PAST AS PROLOGUE?

The case of Philadelphia's Black Mafia, then, demonstrates that African-American organized crime is not an "emerging" trend. Further historical research on African-American groups in other locations and at other times, as well as on other ethnic groups would likely find similar results as some authors have recently noted. Such research would not only alter and improve the historical record, but perhaps more importantly for criminologists would also influence theoretical models that are based on this record.

The history of the Black Mafia suggests the need for more research into the activities of inner-city power-brokers, such as those involved in MBE programs and the current federal "empowerment/enterprise zone" initiatives being implemented throughout the nation's cities. Concerning the latter, Philadelphia has experienced serious problems with the $79 million it received from the Clinton Administration for its Empowerment Zone, which consisted of three of the city's poor neighborhoods. The city was "one of only six cities to receive Empowerment Zone funds, designed to

spur economic and community development in needy areas".
Unfortunately for taxpayers and for those targeted members of the
underclass who were to receive the benefits of these funds, there are
serious problems within the 'Zone. The FBI began investigating the
Zone in 1998 following a federal audit which found "that the city's
empowerment zone had spent thousands of dollars in ways that did
not serve anyone living in the zone, and had exaggerated the
program's accomplishments". Since then, investigations have also
started looking into a series of other "irregularities" including
numerous conflicts of interest, political cronyism, no-show jobs and
other forms of corruption and fraud.

Such massive infusions of capital have a history of fueling corruption, perhaps best illustrated in the case of post-WWII Sicily,
and if Philadelphia's ordeal is any indication of how the other
"empowerment" projects are being conducted, history is being
repeated on some level. Furthermore, the African-American victims
of these scams continue to be deprived of funds designed to assist
their collective socioeconomic plight. Research into this area of
inquiry would undoubtedly have policy-development implications
for efforts designed to avoid the further misuse of government
power and funds exploited by the Black Mafia and similar groups
in the 1960's and 1970's, and by politicians and other (frequently
organized) criminals in the 1980's and 1990's.

I made no reference whatsoever to any contemporary (then 1999) Black
Mafia activities, much less any ties to the city administration at the time,
and this was for good reason – I didn't know of any. Who knew that just
as I was penning the paper, far removed from the Philadelphia area, that
federal authorities were about to stumble upon a massive municipal corruption probe involving precisely the types of actors and activities I merely
suggested as a fertile research area?

The paper submitted to *Justice Quarterly* was simply demonstrating the
historical template for certain phenomena that have been under-researched
and that we thus would be wise to investigate as scholars. Nevertheless, this
is what an anonymous reviewer wrote in rejecting the paper: "I am ... bothered by the paper's ending, an attempt to illustrate the potential for
corruption existing in city government ... This could be misunderstood by
anyone sensitive to the fact that there is an African American administration in Philadelphia, which has never been linked to the Black Mafia."
There have also been many other examples of similar political correctness
nonsense during my ten-plus years of researching African-American organized crime, particularly during exchanges at academic conferences. One last
glaring example is illustrative.

At some point in 2000, I began proposing an academic textbook on

African-American organized crime. As the text was being considered by publishing houses, there were numerous concerns expressed regarding what was deemed sensitive subject matter, so much so that more than one publisher thought a remedy to concerns over being labeled "racist" would be to interview as many African-American victims as possible and use the comments liberally in the text. Problematically, these issues didn't subside even after a publisher had signed me to write the textbook. One fast and easy example of political correctness can be observed on the final product's cover. It features a picture of NOI Temple 12 at Park and Susquehanna in North Philadelphia, considered by many to be Black Mafia headquarters back in the day when Jeremiah Shabazz headed the region's Black Muslim community. For the textbook's cover, the publisher decided to blur the language on a sign above the mosque's front door which read, "Muhammad's Temple of Islam." Of course, any reader will grasp the oddity when they read the textbook, since I detail the ties between Temple 12, Shabazz, and the Black Mafia. Nevertheless, for the publisher, the image of an NOI temple, clearly identified as such, on the cover of a book on a crime group which used the temple as a refuge and more, was just too much.

Some of my friends and colleagues have also had difficulty with the subject matter. Two quick examples will suffice: concerns were expressed by faculty about me speaking with the media regarding the Black Mafia story because they didn't want Penn State's relationship with the African-American community adversely affected; a university official didn't want to be seen carrying "a book with a bunch of black gangsters on it," referring to *Black Brothers Inc.* Indeed, he went so far as to cover the book when it was on the back seat of his car, as to not "appear racist."

The Big Picture

Just as *BBI* hit shelves in 2005, I was approached by several film production companies interested in making the book into a film. As the book was vetted in various Hollywood settings, I got my first inklings Tinseltown had the same hang-ups as many others. Since then, there have been producers, directors, actors, and corporate suits each with their own hang-ups, and two are repeated the most. Some in Hollywood have a serious problem with a black crime syndicate being uncovered by a white reporter. These folks have emphatically stated investigative reporter Jim Nicholson would have to be African-American in the film depiction of the story, or the narrative would have to be changed to diminish Nicholson's role in favor of Rev. Muhammad Kenyatta, who could easily be given more credit in the screenplay for smashing the syndicate than was actually the case. More commonly, and more ridiculously in my view, numerous film and television people at all levels of the process have asked to remove any references to the Nation of Islam. Even those who have less hyperbolic comments express concerns about touching the subject. For instance, though overall supportive of a film adaptation of *BBI*, a Vice President of a major film studio said, "The material is potentially explosive. In careless hands, it could come across as racist or xenophobic – it often looks as though it totally debunks the Black Muslim movement in the U.S., which, while it was very corrupt, was also driven by some extremely legitimate principles and did a lot to rebuild self-respect in the black community."

Since these are only the examples I know of, it's tough to imagine what else has been said and done about *Black Brothers Inc.* in the name of political correctness. In any event, as the above narratives show, people who demur from covering this remarkable story may have legitimate fears of being called – explicitly or by inference – racist, perhaps the worst slight one can be called in American society circa 2007.

At a time when there are more than enough legitimate issues pertaining to race – especially in matters of crime and justice – it is an outrage that prominent, influential members of society can so easily exploit this situation for their own benefit. It harkens back to the 1973 exchange between intrepid reporter Jim Nicholson and one of his primary street sources concerning whether Nicholson would be labeled a racist if he continued his pathbreaking reporting on the Black Mafia. Nicholson was implored to stay on the assignment, and admonished by his African-American source: "Listen. If you never believe anything I say, believe this: *You will not get any flak whatsoever from the black community*, and if you do, it will be a few hustling cats." The point he was making holds to this day: ordinary African-American residents are hip to the con artists, whether they're on the corner or in a City Hall office, and want to see hustlers exposed for what they are. After all, these folks in the community are the very ones being hurt by the scams. As the source confidently and correctly noted, those most likely to cry "racism" are precisely those with something – status, power, financial endeavors – to lose if the con is exposed.

If only relevant parties including academics and members of the media weren't so intimidated by the browbeating so shrewdly employed by these characters, which cows such investigators from covering these individuals and entities as they – properly, and without introspection about the propriety of the research – would if we were talking, for instance, about Italian-American mobsters aligning themselves with a labor union to, say, launder ill-gotten gains and pilfer pension funds.

Notes

[1] Ron White – once described as the sun in a solar system of municipal corruption – has been denied the opportunity to defend his character in the courtroom. On 4 November 2004, he lost a battle with pancreatic cancer.

2 Within weeks of his acquittal, John Christmas was hired to serve as president of the African-American Chamber of Commerce. AACC Chairman Bruce Crawley, an outspoken critic of the corruption probe, said the hiring of Christmas was exclusively because of his talents and had nothing to with the probe. Christmas resigned 11 days after assuming the position, and wound up as the top aide to Councilwoman Jannie Blackwell. Crawley, who founded the Chamber in 1993, left the group in 2006 to concentrate on other business ventures including expanding his advertising and public relations firm.

3 In addition to Bruce Crawley, the executive committee of the AACC has included West Insurance advisory board members Robert Bogle and Willie Johnson. Laborer's Local 332 leader Sam Staten, Sr. and his longtime friend and business associate, Imam Shamsud-din Ali, also serve/d on the committee.

4 Firefighter James Allen died in an apparent heart attack while fighting a fire three days earlier.

AUTHOR'S NOTES AND ACKNOWLEDGMENTS

THIS BOOK IS the result of an inordinate number of Freedom of Information Act (FOIA) requests, hundreds of interviews, an even greater number of court transcripts, and thousands of news articles. The agencies that created the law enforcement documents include the Philadelphia, Camden (NJ), New York and Metropolitan (Washington, D.C.) Police Departments, and regional offices of the Federal Bureau of Investigation, the Bureau of Alcohol, Tobacco and Firearms, the Internal Revenue Service, the Drug Enforcement Administration, and its predecessor, the Bureau of Narcotics and Dangerous Drugs. The United States Attorney's Office for the Eastern District of Pennsylvania's Organized Crime and Racketeering Section (Criminal Division) also compiled several helpful documents, including minutes of its Strike Force meetings, as did the Office of Drug Abuse Law Enforcement.

In addition to the thousands of documents that are the foundation of this work, I have interviewed hundreds of people over the past decade or so, including numerous law enforcement officials at the local, state and federal levels. Several of these officials were a part of the initial investigations into the Black Mafia during the late 1960s and early 1970s. The officials interviewed ranged from uniformed street officers, undercover narcotics unit officers, police detectives and supervisors to investigators from district attorneys' offices and federal agencies. Local and federal prosecutors were also interviewed, in addition to numerous investigative journalists who chronicled the activities of the group in real time. Finally, interviews have been conducted with several victims of, and witnesses to, Black Mafia activities, including African-American community residents and activists.

This project has its origins in the early 1990s, back when I was juggling my time as a Philadelphia Police officer and graduate student. A small portion of the work found its way into my Ph.D. dissertation, and a bit more of it was used in an academic text, *Philadelphia's Black Mafia: A Social and Political History* (Kluwer, 2003), a copy of which found its way to Milo's Peter Walsh, who envisioned what ultimately became *Black Brothers Inc.* even before the corruption probe burst in late 2003. Thus, first and foremost, I need to thank Peter for this opportunity, and for his steady counsel and support. I am also grateful to Milo's Andy Nott for his skillful editing and encouragement.

Though the majority of the research was conducted back in the 1990s, the latter stages of the research and all of the writing took place during my tenure at Penn State Abington, where the administration provided the time and resources necessary for such an undertaking. I thus need to thank Dean Karen Sandler, Associate Dean Hannah Kliger, and Division Head Jim Smith for their support. I also need to thank my Administration of Justice colleagues John Sullivan, Lisa Morris, Patti Workman, and Patricia Collins for putting up with my wacky schedule throughout the past year-and-a-half. Other faculty have also aided the project, especially Tom Brown, Judy Newman and Tram Turner. The dedicated and pleasant staff at Penn State Abington have put up with my often-quirky requests, and I want to assure them the promised pastries are on the way. This sort of project requires the assistance of literally hundreds of people, and I acknowledged many of them in the Kluwer text. What follows is my best attempt at a laundry list of people who helped make *BBI*, as I have efficiently and affectionately come to call the book, possible. The crowd below knew what a tight schedule I was following, and all were generous and considerate in their dealings with me. I will no doubt forget someone here, particularly given the tumult of the past two years, and I apologize in advance for any such omissions.

Former investigative reporter Jim Nicholson lent his criticisms, documents, sources and, most importantly, his wisdom to much of this study. Perhaps the only person who devoted more time or energy to helping this project along is Kitty Caparella of the *Philadelphia Daily News*. Like Jim, Kitty has incredible street and law enforcement sources to go along with her steadfast work ethic, sharp mind and crafty pen. She also provided entrée to the invaluable PNI archives (the library of *Philadelphia Inquirer* and *Daily News* articles and photos), and lent perspective to much of the current goings-on in the corruption probe. I am indebted to each for the innumerable acts of collegiality and professionalism they have routinely extended to me.

Through the course of the research, I've benefited from an (often frantic) exchange of information and ideas with several other members of the media, including: George Anastasia, *Philadelphia Inquirer*; Jim Barry, CBS-3 television; Erin Einhorn, *Philadelphia Daily News*; Tyree Johnson, *Westside Weekly*; Mike Leary, *Baltimore Sun*; Maria Panaritis, *Philadelphia Inquirer*; Nicole Weisensee-Egan, *Philadelphia Daily News*; Tim Whitaker, *Philadelphia Weekly*; and Mitchell Zuckoff, *Boston Globe*. Thanks go out to all for often placing things in context and for helping resolve many historical questions.

For several years now, victims and witnesses to assorted activities of Black Mafia characters have contacted me. For a variety of reasons (e.g., their requests not to have their personal matters disclosed in print, my inability to vet their stories), I have not used their stories in the book, though on occasion their revelations led me to other sources of inquiry. I would like to express my gratitude to each of them for offering their insights. As one can imagine, understanding the complexities of the 1960s/1970s community development push is a challenge. I was aided immeasurably by some prolific minds who took part in that fascinating and controversial process, and I thus need to thank them for taking their valuable time to speak with me: Walter W. Cohen, Paul A. Dandridge, and U.S. District Court Judge James T. Giles.

In addition to the above-mentioned individuals, I want to thank numerous others who have assisted this unwieldy project (in no particular order): The dozens of current and former staffers and officials in the Philadelphia Police Department who gave of their time and who helped me answer the historical questions pertaining to the Black Mafia; current and former members of law enforcement at all levels, several of whom have maintained their own files on cases involving the Black Mafia and who shared them with me; press officers, numerous officials and staffers in the Philadelphia District Attorney's Office; agents and supervisors in the regional offices of the FBI in Boston, Chicago, Philadelphia, and Washington (D.C.); The Executive Office for United States Attorneys, and the United States Attorneys Offices for the Eastern District of Pennsylvania (Philadelphia), the District of Massachusetts (Boston), and the District of Columbia (Washington); John W. King (Griffin), son of the Black Mafia's John W. Griffin, who shared his unbelievable life experience (recounted in his *The Breeding of Contempt* [Xlibris, 2002]) and assisted in a variety of ways; several prominent attorneys who have represented or prosecuted Black Mafia actors over the years who were gracious with their time and often provided much-needed perspective to my inquiries, including Frank DeSimone, Joel M. Friedman, Clifford E. Haines, Joel S. Moldovsky, Nino V. Tinari, and Paul H. Zoubek.

Also: Evan Towles of Temple University's Urban Archives (housed in Paley Library), who patiently dealt with me for hours and hours and deserves special thanks; the staff at Penn State's Pattee Library; researchers and staffers at the Ford Foundation, who lent their files and much-needed expertise on several occasions; the delightful staff of the National Archives and Records Administration for the Mid-Atlantic region (thankfully housed in Philadelphia); the ever-resourceful and affable librarians and staffers of the Philadelphia News Inc. archives, including Michael Mercanti and Michael Panzer; Linda Uhrmann, the *Atlantic City Press*; Janet Niedosik, Atlantic County (NJ) Prosecutor's Office; Kathleen M. Higgins, Camden County (NJ) Prosecutor's Office; the Camden County Sheriff's Department; and the Pennsylvania Department of Corrections public relations office.

Lastly, though no less significantly: Philadelphia Fire Commissioner Harold Hairston and his helpful staff, especially Captain Armand Gersbach and Assistant Fire Marshal Bordes Ramseur; several current and former

Securities and Exchange Commission (SEC) and National Association of Securities Dealers-Regulation (NASD-R) officials; and several of my academic colleagues at other institutions who played a variety of instrumental roles, with Penn State historian/criminologist Alan Block leading the way. Others included: Jay Albanese, National Institute of Justice/Virginia Commonwealth University; Joe Albini, University of Nevada; Frank Hagan, Mercyhurst College; Mark Haller, Temple University; Benn Prybutok, Montgomery County Community College; Jeff McIllwain, San Diego State University; Gary Potter, Eastern Kentucky University; and Mike Woodiwiss, University of the West of England.

Despite the aid of all the aforementioned folks, the responsibility for the analyses and conclusions in the book rests with me.

*

The first edition of *Black Brothers Inc.* included *104 pages* of endnotes. This, as I suspected it might, became the source of considerable conversation – good and bad! Plenty of readers were enamored with the legwork behind, and with the handiness of, the notes. However, there were apparently more folks annoyed by their impact on the read, not to mention the added bulk. As a result, I have included only those notes needed to appropriately credit sources *explicitly quoted in the narrative*. This has only been done if the citation is an author or media outlet (i.e., not an interview, a court document, or a law enforcement document). Other notes have been edited out entirely. Thus, if readers are interested in the documents or other information left out of this edition's notes, the 2005 version should be consulted. In addition to the people listed in the earlier "Acknowledgments" section above, there are others who must be recognized. These individuals have played a part in the success of *BBI* and/or in the writing of this updated version.

It is difficult to overstate the role Larry Robin, longtime owner of Philadelphia's oldest independent bookstore, played in the early days of this book's release. At a time when bookstores were apprehensive in stocking it, and media organizations were hesitant to discuss it, Larry not only offered the book in his store, he embraced and promoted it. Area sales and related attention put the book into the mainstream, forcing many media outlets and national book chains to take it seriously. It is tough to predict how history would have treated this book without Larry's steadfast support. Other area bookstore managers were also gracious with their efforts. Thus, thanks to Rochelle Culbreath-Griffin and Lee Bendetti for getting the word – and the book – out, particularly at a time when doing so was a novel and touchy concept.

As 2005 came to an end, more outlets and forums thankfully opened themselves up to the topic and to me, and the following individuals and entities need to be thanked above all others: Marcy Cox, of Wall To Wall Productions in the UK; Wendy Daughenbaugh, of her Philadelphia-based NOBIS Productions; Brian Lockman, of the Pennsylvania Cable Network; Keith Murphy, of XM Satellite Radio's *The Power*; and the councilors and staff of the Historical Society of Philadelphia.

Chris Burrows at Milo handled all media inquiries as well as my numerous, often odd, frequently annoying, requests. He has also served as the buffer for some of the more bizarre correspondence this book has inspired. Your variegated efforts have been very much appreciated, Chris.

Numerous individuals at Penn State Abington have continually assisted in various ways. This is all the more noteworthy when you consider this has often meant making their jobs more challenging. Thanks, then, to the following (most of whom know only bits and pieces of the madness this unruly project has become): Theresa Bloom, Ross Brinkert, Gary Calore, Carol DeBunda, Bella Friesel, Lonnie Golden, Peter Johnstone, David Jwanier, Ellen Knodt and Jane Owens. Vicki Fong, of Penn State's University Relations Office, has gone beyond the call of duty for the past two years, and deserves special kudos. I would thank the great Abington staff again for all they do, but that would only remind them I never owned up to my "pastries" pledge of two years ago (still in print above).

I need to thank local film-maker – and muckraker – Tigre Hill, whose documentary *Shame of a City* is required material for anyone trying to understand Philadelphia's contemporary political scene. Tigre's outspoken support for the book has brought it to audiences who might otherwise not picked up a book on African-American organized crime.

The book was optioned in 2006 to be made into at least one major motion picture. Judy Karfiol has politely endured my ignorance of the Hollywood scene and spared me much grief as we vetted various film and television proposals for adaptations of *BBI*, and thus has my deep gratitude.

Lastly, and significantly, I want to especially thank the various internet posters and bloggers who have taken up the charge and are asking questions the media have continually refused to entertain.

Notes

Introduction

9   *You have an African-American Democratic mayor*: Erin Einhorn and Dave Davies, "A Bugs-Eye View of First 72 Hours," *Philadelphia Daily News*, November 7, 2003.
I let it rip: Einhorn and Davies, "A Bugs-Eye View of First 72 Hours".

10   *They resent that black men*: Chris Brennan, "Street, Backers Cry Plot," *Philadelphia Daily News*, October 20, 2003.
There are some people: William Bunch, Mansah M. Dean and Jenice M.

Armstrong, "Some Suggest Fed Probe Not Colorblind," *Philadelphia Daily News*, October 10, 2003.

It moved undecided voters: Thomas Fitzgerald, "Street Coasted to Victory on Back of a Bug," *Philadelphia Inquirer*, November 5, 2003.

11 *energized Street's base of black supporters*: Leonard N. Fleming, Angela Couloumbis and Michael Currie Schaffer, "Mayor Rolls to a Resounding Win in Contentious Race," *Philadelphia Inquirer*, November 5, 2003.

suspect...especially when you know: Mark McDonald, "Probe Spotlight On...Black Leaders: Criticize Coverage," *Philadelphia Daily News*, December 19, 2003.

There's no African-American mobsters: Nancy Phillips, George Anastasia and Maria Panaritis, "Dueling Images of Phila.'s Imam Ali," *Philadelphia Inquirer*, September 27, 2004.

Chapter 1

13 *During the 1940s and 1950s*: Roger Lane, "Black Philadelphia, then and now," *The Public Interest*, Summer 1992.

14 *dismal failure*: Victor S. Navasky, *Kennedy Justice* (Lincoln, NE: iUniverse.com Publishers, 2000 [1971]).

What the hell: Evan Thomas, *Robert Kennedy* (New York: Simon & Schuster, 2000).

These are the people: Tamar Jacoby, *Someone Else's House: America's Unfinished Struggle for Integration* (New York: Basic Books, 1998), quoting from Jack Newfield's *Robert Kennedy: A Memoir* (New York: Dutton, 1969).

16 *a pipeline to the federal government*: Peter Binzen, "Bowser is an Old Hand at Playing the Political Game in Philadelphia," *Philadelphia Inquirer*, November 13, 1991.

muzzle a growing number of public demonstrations: S.A. Paolantonio, *Frank Rizzo: The Last Big Man in Big City America* (Philadelphia: Camino Books, 1993).

history of excessive use of arrests: Pennsylvania Crime Commission, *Report on Police Corruption and the Quality of Law Enforcement in Philadelphia* (St. David's, PA: PCC, 1974), quoted in the Committee of Seventy, *Philadelphia Police Department Governance Study* (Philadelphia, PA: Committee of Seventy, 1998).

17 *first bad nigger in Congress*: Jacoby, *Someone Else's House*.

consistent with statements: *Muhammad Speaks*, December 30, 1962, p. 4, quoted in Karl Evanzz, *The Messenger: The Rise and Fall of Elijah Muhammad* (New York: Pantheon Books, 1999).

Confrontational and in-your-face: Acel Moore, "Under Mondesire, NAACP has risen from the shadows," *Philadelphia Inquirer*, October 12, 2000.

What we need: Jacoby, *Someone Else's House*. Jacoby is quoting a *Time* magazine article dated July 15, 1966.

18 *A lot of these numbers bankers*: WHYY-TV (Philadelphia), *Mobfathers*.

Late model Cadillacs: Thompson, "Black Café Society".

the place where straight-lifers: Elmer Smith, "'Mr. Silk' Was Family's Loving Boss, Right To The End," *Philadelphia Daily News*, May 19, 1995.

19 *Niggah, I'm not your congressman*: Chuck Stone, "Can 'Mr. Silk' & 'The Hustler' Do It?" *Philadelphia Daily News*, June 15, 1976.
    a sepia-toned Jack Armstrong: Chuck Stone, "Stanley Branche's Logical Move: to Congress," *Philadelphia Daily* News, May 2, 1978.
    wears two costumes: *Philadelphia Magazine*, September 1968.
    in the ghetto: Ron Goldwyn, "A Foot in the Door and a Hand in Everything," *Philadelphia Daily News*, June 15, 1988.
20 *Some people are saying*: Alfred Klimcke, "Black Militancy to Continue," *Philadelphia Inquirer*, June 16, 1968.
    and then was ostracized: Gaeton Fonzi, "The Man from M.O.X.I.E.," *Philadelphia Magazine*, July 1970, p. 65.

Chapter 2

22 *thick-necked bully*: James Nicholson, "The Underworld on the Brink of War: Part 1 - The Muslim Mob Gets It On," *Philadelphia Magazine*, November 1973.
24 *They would intimidate persons*: James Nicholson, "Philadelphia's Black Mafia," *The Philadelphia Inquirer*, TODAY, August 12, 1973.
25 *Touch one of my men*: Hank Messick, *Of Grass and Snow: The Secret Criminal Elite* (Englewood Cliffs, New Jersey: Prentice-Hall, 1979) quoted in Howard Abadinsky, *Organized Crime* second edition (Chicago: Nelson-Hall, 1985).
26 *religious fanatic in that he followed*: Laura Murray, "Killer of Hanafis Dies," *Philadelphia Daily News*, August 24, 1977.
30 *This is just another injustice*: Alfred Klimcke, "Negroes to Picket in Harrisburg Over Clay Bout Veto," *Philadelphia Inquirer*, June 11, 1968.
31 *we are taught*: "Muhammad Ali Here to Help Black Drive for $1 Million," *The Evening Bulletin*, August 30, 1968.
    I was a fighter: James V. Magee, "Branche Leaves Coalition, Says Job Needs College Man," *The Evening Bulletin*, January 8, 1969.
    I feel very strongly: Orrin Evans, "Black Coalition Disbands; Leaders Ask New Program," *The Evening Bulletin*, April 9, 1969.
    I would have made: Bill Alexander, "Citizen Coxson: Brass, Class and a Little Larceny on the Side," *Philly Talk Magazine*, March 5, 1973.
33 *provide an alternative*: James Laverty, "City, DA Battle for Crime Fund Allocation,' *The Evening Bulletin*, June 10, 1969
34 *I was a gang member*: William J. Spears, "The Safe Streets Project – Inroads on Phila. Gang Control?" *Philadelphia Inquirer*, February 22, 1970.

Chapter 3

35 *I'd never heard*: Thomas Hauser, *Muhammad Ali: His Life and Times* (New York: Touchstone [Simon & Schuster], 1991).
    true religion: C. Eric Lincoln, *The Black Muslims in America*, third edition (Grand Rapids, MI: Eerdmans Publishing, 1994 [1961]).
36 *like the NAACP*: Lincoln, *Black Muslims in America*.
37 *Malcolm lived in a room*: Hauser, *Muhammad Ali*.
    What we taught: Hauser, *Muhammad Ali*.

38   *intended to facilitate*: Kenneth O'Reilly, *Racial Matters: The FBI's Secret File on Black America, 1960-1972* (New York: The Free Press [Simon & Schuster], 1989).
     When somebody does: Hauser, *Muhammad Ali*.
39   *Whenever we talked*: Hauser, *Muhammad Ali*.
     induce Negroes to migrate: Karl Evanzz, *The Messenger: The Rise and Fall of Elijah Muhammad* (New York: Pantheon Books, 1999.
40   *He told me*: Hauser, *Muhammad Ali*.
     Cassius didn't have problems: Hauser, *Muhammad Ali*.
41   *I was afraid*: David Remnick, *King of the World* (New York: Random House, 1998).
     Ali understood strength: Remnick, *King of the World*.
42   *If any Muslim*: "Minister Who Knew Him best (Part I); Rips Malcolm's Treachery, Defection," *Muhammad Speaks*, December 4, 1964, quoted in Evanzz.
     a year in which: *Muhammad Speaks* quoted in Remnick, *King of the World*.
     Malcolm died according: Remnick, *King of the World*.
46   *On one side*: John W. Griffin, *A Letter to My Father* (Xlibris, 2001).

Chapter 4

48   *We have some documents*: Joseph H. Trachtman, "Racket Link Sought in Beating of Prober for Insurance Dept.," *Philadelphia Inquirer*, June 6, 1969.
     There is no question: Dave Racher and Les Fuller, "Warrant Issued in Attack on Prober," *Philadelphia Daily News*, June 30, 1969.
49   *the next Martin Luther King, Jr.*: Tyree Johnson, "Informer Serves 'Life Sentence' of His Own," *Philadelphia Daily News*, March 26, 1975.
52   *You look up and down*: Hoag Levins, "Rev. Smith Made Isle of Beauty in Bleak Ghetto," *Philadelphia Inquirer*, May 19, 1970.
53   *They could not have known*: Levins, "Rev. Smith Made Isle of Beauty in Bleak Ghetto".
54   *Foo-Foo Ragan is a numbers man*: Jim Smith, "Numbers Writer Awaits," *Philadelphia Daily News*, May 8, 1979.
55   *Don't say anything*: WHYY-TV (Philadelphia), "Mobfathers" program.
56   *If you don't shut up*: "2 Held Without Bail for Grand Jury in Holdup-Murder at Dubrow's," *The Evening Bulletin*, January 28, 1971.
57   *If a window*: "Rizzo to Beef Up Homicide Unit After Rampage in South St. Store," *The Evening Bulletin*, January 5, 1971.
     I have seen: Charles Gilbert and Gerald McKelvey, "Robbery Called Chief Motive," *Philadelphia Inquirer*, January 6, 1971.
     given the chance: Howard Goodman, "Convict Says Prosecutor Barred Blacks from Jury," *Philadelphia Inquirer*, September 3, 1992.
     It was like a Western movie: Doris B. Wiley, "'Like a War,' Clerk Says of Dubrow Scene," *The Evening Bulletin*, October 22, 1971.
     I don't understand it: Gerald McKelvey, "Why Did Bandits Shoot? Did They Lose Nerve," *Philadelphia Inquirer*, January 5, 1971.
58   *In our Mafia*: "Offbeat," *Philadelphia Inquirer*, April 8, 1975.
     one of the most bizarre: Jack McGuire, Jim Smith and Joe O'Dowd, (title unknown) *Philadelphia Daily News*, January 5, 1971.

It was one: Tom Fox, "A Savagery Revisited," *Philadelphia Inquirer*, November 23, 1978.

was an outburst: Elmer Smith, "How Race May Taint the Sense of Justice," *Philadelphia Daily News*, September 18, 1992.

62   *There are more angles*: Charles Montgomery, "Black Mafia Linked to Delco Hijacker Slaying," *Philadelphia Daily News*, July 21, 1970.

Chapter 5

69   *There used to be*: Robert Strauss, "What Does Hip-Hop Mean to a Doo-Wop Kind of Guy?" *New York Times*, March 24, 2002, section 14NJ, p. 3.

brassy nightspot: Donald Goddard, *Easy Money* (New York: Farrar, Straus and Giroux, 1978).

70   *bedlam broke loose*: Eric Pace, "4 Killed, 11 Injured As Narcotics Rings War in Atlantic City," *New York Times*, April 3, 1972.

former Black Panther: "Suspect is Named in Drug Shootout," *Philadelphia Inquirer*, April 5, 1972.

71   *they killed and killed*: Goddard.

Chapter 6

74   *best fighter in the world*: John Rawling, "The best contender who never became champion," *The Guardian* (London), January 5, 1999.

had never seen: Furman Bisher, "More a circus than a fight: Ali-Quarry in Atlanta was an event not to be upstaged," *Atlanta Journal Constitution*, January 7, 1999.

76   *They say I*: Adolph Katz, "Coxson: A Man of Mystery with a Love for Luxury Cars," *The Evening Bulletin*, June 8, 1973.

77   *His nose crinkles*: Gaeton Fonzi, "The Man from M.O.X.I.E.," *Philadelphia Magazine*, July 1970.

78   *The Negro has*: Fonzi, "The Man from M.O.X.I.E."

79   *You know what*: Fonzi, "The Man from M.O.X.I.E."

Some people can't believe: Tom Fox; "Making It," *Philadelphia Daily News*, July 22, 1970.

Hershey bar dipped: Bill Alexander, "Citizen Coxson: Brass, Class and a Little Larceny on the Side," *Philly Talk Magazine*, March 5, 1973.

80   *Some people like horses*: Donald Janson, "Camden Mayoral Hopeful Runs a Flamboyant Race," *New York Times*, April 9, 1973.

There were so many: Janson, "Camden Mayoral Hopeful Runs a Flamboyant Race."

81   *They didn't concern themselves*: Gunter David, "IRS Seizes Car, Houses of Suspected Dope Biggie," *Philadelphia Daily News*, December 8, 1972.

Chapter 7

85   *They visited me*: Bruce Keidan, "Police Protection Fails to Lessen Faith in Religion," *Philadelphia Inquirer*, February 13, 1973.

86   *My own decision*: Thomas Hauser, *Muhammad Ali: His Life and Times* (New York: Touchstone [Simon & Schuster], 1991).

if they care: Stephen Seplow, "Police Didn't Answer Call Preceding 7 Killings, Woman Says," *Philadelphia Inquirer*, January 20, 1973.

I teach Islam: Warren Brown, "Pistol Stolen Here Believed Used in Moslem Murders," *Philadelphia Inquirer*, January 21, 1973.

89 *Come on*: Karl Evanzz, *The Messenger: The Rise and Fall of Elijah Muhammad* (New York: Pantheon Books, 1999).

Why did he write: "Muslim Slayings of '73 Recalled," *New York Times*, February 23, 1974.

My father knows: Paul Delaney, "Survivor Tells How 7 Moslems Died in Washington," *New York Times*, January 25, 1973.

90 *the seed of the hypocrite*: John Sansing, "Hanafi Massacre, Hanafi Siege: How Greed, Revenge, Religious Fanaticism, and a Search for Justice Combined into a Washington Tragedy," *The Washingtonian*, February 1980.

91 *Elijah's people*: "Sect-Feud Rumors Probed in Capital," *Philadelphia Daily News*, January 20, 1973.

These people is fiends: WHYY, "Mobfathers".

92 *couldn't understand the violence*: Tom Schmidt, "7 Here Charged in Massacre," *Philadelphia Daily News*, August 16, 1973.

were jumping up and down: Evanzz, *The Messenger*.

Elijah Poole has taken: John Kifner, "Jabbar Talks of Islamic Strife Linked to Slayings," *New York Times*, January 25, 1973.

They hate us: Paul Delaney, "Leader of Hanafis Calls for Muhammad Ouster," *New York Times*, January 23, 1973.

We are the most peaceable: Bruce Keidan, "Ali Suspended, But Still Avowed Muslim," *Philadelphia Inquirer*, February 12, 1973.

They know us: "Muslim-Sect War is Denied by Leader," *New York Times*, January 29, 1973.

I loved Elijah Muhammad: Evanzz, *The Messenger*.

would sell out: Evanzz, *The Messenger*.

mean, cowardly man: Keidan, "The Troubled Stars of Islam."

95 *no part in this thing*: Helen Blue, "Black Muslim Leader Silent on 7 Suspects," *Philadelphia Daily News*, August 16, 1973.

no sane Muslim: Eugene L. Meyer, "Black Muslim 'Traitors' Warned of Vengeance," *The Washington Post*, April 5, 1974.

part of Elijah Poole's cutthroat gang: Sansing, "Hanafi Massacre."

Chapter 8

98 *If things don't*: Francis M. Lordan, "Muslim Killers Tried in Theft," *Philadelphia Inquirer*, November 15, 1974.

101 *a sad day*: Elizabeth Duff, "Witness Threatened, Won't Talk," *Philadelphia Inquirer*, October 9, 1974.

103 *What I'm gonna do*: Larry Fields, "IRS Grabs Camden Candidate's Cars," *Philadelphia Daily News*, May 19, 1972.

104 *a grade-A stool pigeon*: James Nicholson, "The Underworld on the Brink of War: Part 1 - The Muslim Mob Gets It On," *Philadelphia Magazine*, November 1973.

a thousand guys: Fonzi, "The Man from M.O.X.I.E.".

I make myself: Rod Nordland, "It's...Survival of the Fittest," *Philadelphia Inquirer*, June 9, 1973.

I'm no priest: Donald Janson, "Camden Mayoral Hopeful Runs a Flamboyant Race," *New York Times*, April 9, 1973.

He's no angel: Chuck Stone, "Camden and Coxson," *Philadelphia Daily News*, May 4, 1973.

105 *Though he says*: Janson, "Camden Mayoral Hopeful.".

To Ali, the Major's a God: "Camden Mayoralty Candidate is Unconcerned at Threat of Jail Term," *Philadelphia Inquirer*, n.d.

120 *Muhammad Ali will add*: Art Peters, "Getting Control of Camden a Major Undertaking," *Philadelphia Inquirer*, January 25, 1972.

Chapter 9

107 *We were just*: Laura Murray, "Coxson, 2 Pals Rapped Here Last Night," *The Evening Bulletin*, June 8, 1973.

108 *It's Lex*: Terry Bitman, "Tied and Gagged, Coxson's Son Fled Through Woods," *Philadelphia Inquirer*, June 9, 1973.

Hi, Sam: "'Sam' Named as Suspect," *Philadelphia Daily News*, June 12, 1973.

an execution: George L. Kerns and Francis J. Lenny, "Major Coxson Slain in Cherry Hill Home," *The Evening Bulletin*, June 8, 1973.

we had Coxson: James Nicholson, "The Underworld on the Brink of War: Part 1 - The Muslim Mob Gets It On," *Philadelphia Magazine*, November 1973.

109 *lovable rogue*: Claude Lewis, "The Doors Were Open: Business Makes It Easy for Crime Figures," *The Philadelphia Inquirer*, November 11, 1987.

probably started by some: "Muhammad Ali Next? He Blames Crank for Rumors," *Philadelphia Inquirer*, June 15, 1973.

Coxson was a good associate: Nicholson, "The Underworld.".

Surely, no life: Gerald Early, "Muhammad Ali: His Life and Times (book review)," *The New Republic*, v. 205, no. 18 (October 28, 1991).

small man with: Adolph Katz, "Coxson: A Man of Mystery with a Love for Luxury Cars," *The Evening Bulletin*, June 8, 1973.

It was an appearance: Rod Nordland, "Was Coxson Penniless?" *Philadelphia Inquirer*, June 11, 1973.

110 *His ingenuity was*: Acel Moore and Terry Bitman, "Friends Recall Coxson's Good Humor and Flamboyance," *Philadelphia Inquirer*, June 9, 1973.

I don't like: WHYY, "Mobfathers".

go underground: "F.B.I. Seizes Suspect in Coxson Slaying," *New York Times*, June 29, 1973.

111 *You can see*: Leslie Wayne, "2 Cannot Recall Statements on Coxson Killings," *Philadelphia Inquirer*, May 24, 1977.

114 *What has marked*: Joseph Busler and Charles West, "Harvey friends – an association of violence," *South Jersey*, August 18, 1973.

Chapter 10

123 *when we went*: *New York Times*, July 24, 1970, p. 18, cited in Dwight C. Smith, Jr., *The Mafia Mystique* (New York: Basic Books, 1975).

124 *Poverty and powerlessness*: Francis A. J. Ianni, *Black Mafia: Ethnic Succession in Organized Crime* (New York: Simon and Schuster, 1974).
125 *a figment of*: John F. Morrison, "'Black Mafia' Was Short-Lived," *Philadelphia Daily News*, January 24, 1986.

Chapter 11

127 *To a lot*: Joseph Busler and Charles West, "Harvey friends – an association of violence," *South Jersey*, August 18, 1973.
   major drug dealer: Gunter David, "Drug Suspect is Sought as Tax Evader," *Philadelphia Daily News*, August 17, 1973.
128 *Arrest is imminent*: Susan Q. Stranahan, "Tax Suspect's Out of Sight, IRS Team Finds," *Philadelphia Inquirer*, August 18, 1973.
   We're puzzled: Gunter David, "Black Mafia Aide Believed Hiding," *Philadelphia Daily News*, August 28, 1973.
129 *a very gifted brother*: John W. Griffin, *A Letter to My Father* (Klibris, 2001).
   scruffy: Mike Leary, "Police Say 'Black B' Is Front for Drug Dealers," *Philadelphia Inquirer*, April 7, 1974.
136 *Drugs are taking*: "Heroin at 10 Cents a Bag? It's Not Such a Far-Out Idea," *Philadelphia Inquirer*, August 30, 1971.
137 *sell heroin addicts*: "No Sales of Heroin – Specter," *Philadelphia Inquirer*, August 14, 1971.
   The idea that: Tom Wolfe, *Radical Chic & Mau-Mauing the Flak Catchers* (New York: Noonday Press, 1970).

Chapter 12

145 *Why don't you*: Mary Lovitz, "Woman Identifies Three as Husband's Slayers," *Camden Courier-Post*, October 2, 1974.
   Johnny's hair: Jane M. Von Bergen, "A Fugitive for 13 Years, Phila. Man Held in Killing of Camden Contractor," *Philadelphia Inquirer*, November 20, 1986.

Chapter 13

151 *some kind of*: Maralyn Lois Polak, "Muhammad Kenyatta: A Black Activist Marked for Death?" *Philadelphia Inquirer*, TODAY, September 1, 1974.
   The movement: Polak, "Muhammad Kenyatta."
152 *Muhammad is Muslim*: Peyton Gray, "Black Writer Finds Kenyatta No 'Phony'," *Philadelphia Daily News*, January 7, 1972.
   declared war: Acel Moore, "Black Conference Appeals For Crusade Against Crime," *Philadelphia Inquirer*, January 4, 1974.
153 *We're asking them*: Tyree Johnson, "Kenyatta Sounds Call to End 'Black Mafia'," *Philadelphia Daily News*, January 4, 1974.
158 *bloody struggle*: Tyree Johnson, "Bloody Struggle for Power in S. Phila.," *Philadelphia Daily News*, March 6, 1974.
159 *scared to death*: Jack McGuire, "3 'Black Brothers' Ambushed in S. Phila.," *Philadelphia Daily News*, March 8, 1974.
160 *They can always*: Mike Leary, "Police Say 'Black B' Is Front for Drug Dealers," *Philadelphia Inquirer*, April 7, 1974.

161 *information about police*: Tyree Johnson, "Kenyatta: Muslim Chief Linked to Black Mafia," *Philadelphia Daily News*, April 12, 1974.

taken down their sign: Tyree Johnson, "'Black Brothers' Disband-Lawyer," *Philadelphia Daily News*, April 17, 1974.

totally disappointed: "Black Brothers, Inc., Folds, Lawyer Says," *Philadelphia Inquirer*, April 18, 1974.

Nab Fugitive: "Nab Fugitive 'Black Brother'," *Philadelphia Daily News*, May 29, 1974.

Chapter 15

172 *We're supposed to*: John Sansing, "Hanafi Massacre, Hanafi Siege: How Greed, Revenge, Religious Fanaticism, and a Search for Justice Combined into a Washington Tragedy," *The Washingtonian*, February 1980.

173 *Let this be*: Eugene L. Meyer, "Black Muslim 'Traitors' Warned of Vengeance," *Washington Post*, April 5, 1974.

176 *For the guards*: J.B. Leiber, "The Unquiet Death of Charlie 77X 'Bubbles' Price," *Philadelphia Inquirer*, April 27, 1975

177 *reputation of the*: Jerome Mondesire, "Trail of Death Grows Longer," *Philadelphia Inquirer*, May 11, 1975.

The investigation really: Mike Leary, "Trail of Death Leads to Hollow Verdict," *Philadelphia Inquirer*, July 27, 1975.

178 *What was taught*: Tyree Johnson, "Black Muslims Exorcise 'Devils'," *Philadelphia Daily News*, June 17, 1975.

In the old days: Bruce Keidan, "Calm Reigns in Black Islam," *Philadelphia Inquirer*, July 4, 1975.

179 *Apparently, after years*: Tyree Johnson, "Muslim Changes Revealed," *Philadelphia Daily News*, February 20, 1978.

I read your: Letters to the Editors, *Philadelphia Inquirer*, May 25, 1975.

180 *It is no secret*: William Brashler, "Black on Black: The Deadly Struggle for Power," *New York Magazine*, June 5, 1975.

181 *Everybody in the neighborhood*: "Wounds Kill Founder of Black Mafia," *Philadelphia Inquirer*, June 18, 1975.

Chapter 16

183 *religious persecution*: "Black Muslims Accuse Inquirer of Persecution," *Philadelphia Inquirer*, August 29, 1975.

184 *We don't have to*: "Black Muslims Accuse Inquirer".

You came away: Chuck Stone, "Christians, Jews, Muslims & Crime," *Philadelphia Daily News*, September 3, 1975.

Here are the views: Chuck Stone, "Crime & Black Muslims: Another View," *Philadelphia Daily News*, September 10, 1975.

187 *clothes, money and cars*: Tyree Johnson, "A Violent Life, A Violent Death," *Philadelphia Daily News*, November 11, 1975.

193 *Police are working*: Joe O'Dowd and Jill Porter, "Police Seeking Black Mafia Hit Squad," *Philadelphia Daily News*, February 6, 1976.

Chapter 17

195 *Some of the*: Les Payne, "The Man Who Drew Cassius Clay to Islam," *Newsday*, February 16, 1997.

199 *It was a*: Sam W. Pressley, "New Muslim Leader Counts on Faith in God," *The Evening Bulletin*, July 23, 1976.

200 *very much contained*: Laura Murray, "Muslim Killers Under Guard," *Philadelphia Daily News*, March 10, 1977.

I can't tell: United Press International, "Security Tightened for Prisoners Sought in Exchange for Prisoners," *New York Times*, March 11, 1977.

203 *The Cassius Clay*: "Excerpts From Khaalis Interviews," *New York Times*, March 11, 1977.

I want those: Paul Delaney, "Hamaas Abdul Khaalis: A 4-Year Grudge," *New York Times*, March 11, 1977.

Chapter 18

206 *I work for*: Tyree Johnson, "Con Man May Be Cleaning Up Mosque," *Philadelphia Daily News*, February 20, 1978.

It's been in: Jim Nicholson, "Fiery Resurrection for Black Mafia?" *Philadelphia Daily News*, July 28, 1978.

207 *was the victim*: Jack McGuire and Kit Konolige, "Alleged Muslim Threat Eyed in Slaying," *Philadelphia Daily News*, February 15, 1978.

an old element: Nicholson, "Fiery Resurrection for Black Mafia?"

209 *You bear a*: Jack McGuire, "'Kingpin' Sought in Drug Bombings: Slayings Blamed on Pushers' War," *Philadelphia Daily News*, June 20, 1980.

210 *God did not*: Linn Washington, "Religions Hold Rally for Unity," *Philadelphia Daily News*, July 5, 1979.

212 *If we don't*: Linn Washington and Joe Blake, "Allen 'Mafia' Hires Killers to Silence Women Foes," *Philadelphia Daily News*, September 16, 1980.

Chapter 19

214 *Don't worry about*: Maria Gallagher, "Killer Says Defendants Helped Keep Tabs on Murder Probe," *Philadelphia Daily News*, May 25, 1984.

217 *If you have*: Kitty Caparella, "Drugs in Philadelphia: Prison Drug Traffic - The Light's Green," *Philadelphia Daily News*, December 21, 1984.

You knew who: Caparella, "Drugs in Philadelphia: Prison Drug Traffic."

218 *I'm just so*: Dave Racher, "'Black Mafia' Murder Witness to Testify Today," *Philadelphia Daily News*, July 28, 1982.

219 *It's a milestone*: Jim Smith, "Black Mob Bosses Get Stiff Jail Terms," *Philadelphia Daily News*, December 13, 1982.

a perfect example: Jim Smith, "Killer Sentences for 2 Drug Dealers," *Philadelphia Daily News*, December 14, 1982

put a stop: Ron Goldwyn, "Sentences Ring Out Black Mafia," *Philadelphia Daily News*, November 29, 1983.

Wittingly or unwittingly: Christopher Hepp, "Accusations Fly During First Debate," *Philadelphia Daily News*, September 27, 1983

Chapter 20

223 *Wallace changed*: Thomas Hauser, *Muhammad Ali: His Life and Times* (New York: Touchstone [Simon & Schuster], 1991).

227 *regularly*: Kitty Caparella, "Drug Dealer Listed on Campaign Staff," *Philadelphia Daily News*, June 4, 1985.

229 *We're going to*: Linda Lloyd, "Ex-Aide Freed in Subway Fracas," *Philadelphia Inquirer*, May 14, 1993.

231 *Union members who*: WHYY TV, *Mobfathers*.
    if he did not: George Anastasia, "The Scarfo Mob's Fateful into the Labor Rackets," *Philadelphia Inquirer*, September 5, 1989.

232 *dear friend*: Robert F. Simone, *The Last Mouthpiece: The Man Who Dared to Defend the Mob* (Philadelphia: Camino Books, 2001).

233 *Sam's back*: George Anastasia and Robert J. Terry, "JBM: Internal Struggles, External Rivalries," *Philadelphia Inquirer*, August 27, 1989.
    didn't have the: Kitty Caparella, "The Warlords of Crack - Old Guard Leader Makes Bid to Rule JBM: Convicted Killer an Organizer," *Philadelphia Daily News*, August 25, 1989.
    Nudie keeps: Kitty Caparella, "The JBM Mother of All Trials: Prosecution of 3 Bosses to Chronicle Rise and Fall of Organization," *Philadelphia Daily News*, March 30, 1992.

234 *Officials described him*: Julia Cass, "Second-Guessing Follows Prison Raid," *Philadelphia Inquirer*, October 29, 1995.
    The awesome sight: Rich Henson, "At Graterford, Officials Collected Stories Along with Contraband," *Philadelphia Inquirer*, October 27, 1995.
    He was just: Del Quentin Wilber, "States Swap Their Worst for Prisons' Sake," *Philadelphia Inquirer*, April 29, 1999.
    Philadelphia became: Andy Wallace, "Jeremiah Shabazz, 70, Former Nation of Islam Minister, Ali Aide," *Philadelphia Inquirer*, January 9, 1998.

235 *He was equally*: Dana DiFilippo and Dave Racher, "Cops, DA Target City's Worst Thugs," *Philadelphia Daily News*, July 30, 2001.

Chapter 21

237 *Yeah, he's walking*: Kitty Caparella and Nicole Weisensee Egan, "Ali's Wife: Ex-Fed Stoolie Sources: But It's His Tie to Drug Lords That Led to Pay-to-Play Probe," *Philadelphia Daily News*, April 16, 2004.
    the distribution of: George Anastasia and Nancy Phillips, "U.S. Sought to Link Cleric to Drug Ring," *Philadelphia Inquirer*, August 25, 2004.
    Being selfish: Caparella and Weisensee Egan, "Ali's Wife."

238 *A long time*: George Anastasia, Maria Panaritis and Nancy Phillips, "Imam's Wife, Kin Indicted in Probe," *Philadelphia Inquirer*, June 3, 2004.
    I'm being targeted: Brendan McGarvey, "Firing Back," *City Paper*, April 29-May 5, 2004.
    They can send: Nancy Phillips, George Anastasia and Maria Panaritis, "Cleric's Wife is Notified She is Fraud-Probe Target," *Philadelphia Inquirer*, April 20, 2004.

239 *The conduct of*: Thomas Turcol, Leonard N. Fleming and Nancy Phillips, "U.S. Reportedly Seeks Streets' Bank Records," *Philadelphia Inquirer*, October 19, 2003.

240 *I was just*: Stephen Rodrick, "Are You Bob Brady's Friend?," *Philadelphia Magazine*, August 2004.

My recollection is: Erin Einhorn, Bob Warner and Kitty Caparella, "FBI Tap: Imam Made Threat," *Philadelphia Daily News*, March 31, 2004.

242 *First Chesapeake*: Associated Press, "Business Briefs from Across Pennsylvania," *BC Cycle*, September 14, 2000.

244 *a force for*: Jack McGuire and Gloria Campisi, "Imam: Leave Son's Killers to Law," *Philadelphia Daily News*, July 16, 1996.

more revered in Graterford: Nancy Phillips, George Anastasia and Maria Panaritis, "Dueling Images of Phila.'s Imam Ali," *Philadelphia Inquirer*, September 27, 2004.

245 *Here is a man*: Clea Benson and Craig R. McCoy, "Street Ally Says He is Baffled by Probe," *Philadelphia Inquirer*, October 31, 2003.

Everyone who knows: "Street Stands by His Friends," *Philadelphia Daily News*, November 5, 2003.

Chapter 22

246 *This is a case*: Maria Panaritis and Nancy Phillips, "Imam Indicted with Six Others," *Philadelphia Inquirer*, September 30, 2004.

Lies, kickbacks: Kitty Caparella, "Muslim Cleric is Indicted," *Philadelphia Daily News*, September 30, 2004.

249 *we'll-be-your*: "The Federal Probe: An Explainer," *Philadelphia Independent*, August 2004.

250 *I had heard*: Peter Landry and Suzette Parmley, "Police: Jannie Blackwell Aide Has Drug Record," *Philadelphia Inquirer*, February 2, 1993.

I wouldn't suppose: Joseph Slobodzian and Cynthia Burton, "Grand Jury Indicts Aide to Blackwell," *Philadelphia Inquirer*, January 6, 1999.

was an important: Jim Smith, "Contractors: Payoffs Got job," *Philadelphia Daily News*, March 30, 1999.

253 *He's a bad*: Noel Weyrich, "The Incredible Shrinking Police Commissioner," *Philadelphia Magazine*, April 2004.

How do people: Nancy Phillips, George Anastasia and Maria Panaritis, "Dueling Images of Phila.'s Imam Ali," *Philadelphia Inquirer*, September 27, 2004.

254 *I live with*: George Anastasia, Maria Panaritis and Nancy Phillips, "Drug Probe Opened Door for City Hall Bug," *Philadelphia Inquirer*, April 15, 2004.

I have met: Phillips et al., "Dueling Images."

have rejected and: Jim Remsen, "Imam's Phila. Visit Keyed to Tension in Black Mosques," *Philadelphia Inquirer*, September 26, 2003.

understand that the: Kitty Caparella, "Muslims Split Over Support for Alis," *Philadelphia Daily News*, January 10, 2005.

Epilogue

257 *They know if they left me*: Kitty Caparella, "Toilet Bowl Talk II: Handling 'rats' & teeth," *Philadelphia Daily News*, December 2, 2005.

He's a hustler: Kitty Caparella, "Solitary drove Savage 'crazy,' lawyer says," *Philadelphia Daily News*, December 13, 2005.

258 *Twin think we gonna*: Kitty Caparella, "Drug kingpin's chilling words detailed in memo," *Philadelphia Daily News*, April 26, 2006.
I want to set: Kitty Caparella, "Spared life sentence," *Philadelphia Daily News*, April 28, 2006.
I ain't got no regrets: George Anastasia, "Jury listens to reputed drug lord's revelations on tape," *Philadelphia Inquirer*, December 4, 2005.

259 *I know I didn't*: Caparella, "Potty-talk tapes played at drug trial," *Philadelphia Daily News*, December 1, 2005.
I got thirty months: L. Stuart Ditzen, "U.S. says prisoners talked via toilets," *Philadelphia Inquirer*, August 19, 2005.
The tapes show: Kitty Caparella, "Drug dealer Bey gets 10 years: 3 years added for obstruction," *Philadelphia Daily News*, March 1, 2006.

260 *Savage arranged to have*: Kitty Caparella, "Ali Pals Wanted in 'Snitch' Slaying," *Philadelphia Daily News*, April 19, 2004.
struck by the extent: Emilie Lounsberry, "Jury's work: 'It wasn't easy'," *Philadelphia Inquirer*, May 11, 2005.

261 *You not only cheated*: John Shiffman, "Kemp gets 10 years for corruption," *Philadelphia Inquirer*, July 20, 2005.

262 *I mean forty thousand*: Anastasia, "U.S.: Bogus courses cost college $100,000," *Philadelphia Inquirer*, April 23, 2005.
forging documents: Kitty Caparella, "Ali's lawyer: Wife ran scam," *Philadelphia Daily News*, April 23, 2005.
I can pay some: Kitty Caparella, "Ali in court: Union leaders unfazed by his spending," *Philadelphia Daily News*, April 26, 2005.
I'm saying it publicly: Kitty Caparella, "Tearful Faridah Ali," *Philadelphia Daily News*, February 17, 2006.
Under the guise: Kitty Caparella, "Memo: Faridah 'didn't need' the $$," *Philadelphia Daily News*, March 15, 2005.

263 *You know, I've always*: Kitty Caparella, "He gets sentence just like Martha's," *Philadelphia Daily News*, July 7, 2005.
Christmas never got: David B. Caruso, "Defense: Mayor's office aide was doing job by helping Ali," *Associated Press*, April 21, 2005.
We thought Christmas: George Anastasia, "Acquited defendant says he felt an obligation to testify," *Philadelphia Inquirer*, June 15, 2005.

264 *provides an historical*: George Anastasia and Nancy Phillips, "U.S. sought to link cleric to drug ring," *Philadelphia Inquirer*, August 25, 2004.
When I see these guys: George Anastasia, "Imam's lawyer asks judge to dismiss racketeering case," *Philadelphia Inquirer*, May 24, 2005.

265 *Without the wiretaps*: John Shiffman, "Juror says Imam didn't respect city, neighbors," *Philadelphia Inquirer*, June 15, 2005.

266 *as she stepped out*: Marcia Gelbart, "White's daughter gets city bond deal," *Philadelphia Inquirer*, February 19, 2005.
meet with individuals: John Shiffman, George Anastasia, and Marcia Gelbart, "Airport contract is focus of probe," *Philadelphia Inquirer*, January 20, 2006.

267 *Ali was too strong*: Kitty Caparella, "How the feds nailed a crooked cleric," *Philadelphia Daily News*, September 26, 2005.
Well, I'll tell you: George Anastasia, "Ali fraud case holds mirror up to city," *Philadelphia Inquirer*, May 29, 2005.

I thought I had: John Shiffman and Mark Fazlollah, "For agents, bug case is one they can savor," *Philadelphia Inquirer*, June 19, 2005.

Why is a drug: Kitty Caparella, "How the feds nailed a crooked cleric," *Philadelphia Daily News*, September 26, 2005.

268 *Warmly shook his hand*: Gar Joseph, "From bug to blog," *Philadelphia Daily News*, March 30, 2007.

Leave out the drugs: Kitty Caparella, "Ali's lawyer says he's ready for a rematch," *Philadelphia Daily News*, July 21, 2005.

If a drug dealer: George Anastasia, "Imam asks to overturn conviction," *Philadelphia Inquirer*, July 21, 2005.

came from an illegal: Kitty Caparella, "Ali lawyer cites 'irrelevant' evidence," *Philadelphia Daily News*, April 24, 2007.

Shamsud-din Ali ministers: George Anastasia, "Imam's defense attorney says jury must know 'whole story'," *Philadelphia Inquirer*, June 4, 2005.

Appendix A

270 *It's going to be*: Joseph Tanfani and Mark Fazlollah, "Insider's Guide to Getting City Deals," *Philadelphia Inquirer*, May 9, 2004.

In 25 years: Joseph Tanfani, Mark Fazlollah and Craig R. McCoy, "Ex-Official: Street Aide Inflated Contract," *Philadelphia Inquirer*, December 14, 2003.

271 *West repeatedly exploited*: Mitchell Zuckoff, "Coolidge Insolvent; U.S. Sells It to Pioneer," *The Boston Globe*, October 26, 1991.

272 *Street's personal friend*: Scott Farmelant, "Street Smarts," *City Paper*, November 2 – 9, 1995.

Appendix B

275 *Although I don't know what's going on*: John Shiffman and Emilie Lounsberry, "Street met with the FBI early on," *Philadelphia Inquirer*, March 27, 2005.

276 *We were very interested*: Emilie Lounsberry and John Shiffman, FBI agent tells jury why Street's office was bugged," *Philadelphia Inquirer*, March 4, 2005.

The range of emotions: John Shiffman and Mark Fazlollah, "For agents, bug case is on they can savor," *Philadelphia Inquirer*, June 19, 2005.

277 *Democratic argument that this election*: Thomas Fitzgerald, "A startling distraction in race for mayor," *Philadelphia Inquirer*, October 8, 2003.

Do we believe that: Thomas Fitzgerald, Cynthia Burton and Leonard N. Fleming, "The Bug: Who knew what - and when?" *Philadelphia Inquirer*, October 9, 2003.

278 *Hmm...people planting*: Acel Moore, "FBI must clear the air now and say if Street was bug's target," *Philadelphia Inquirer*, Ocotber 9, 2003.

The probe that has enveloped: Dave Davies, "Street's blackberry jam," *Philadelphia Daily News*, October 10, 2003.

279 *Before becoming a soft-spoken*: Erin Einhorn and Kitty Caparella, "Islamic Imam is focus of probe," Philadelphia Daily News, October 10, 2003.

285 *The coverage of our paper*: Ellen Foley, "To our readers: An apology," *Philadelphia Daily News*, August 30, 2002.

286 *I think the cover*: Bill Bergstrom, "Paper apologizes but denies racial insensitivity," *Associated Press* state and local wire, August 30, 2002.

Don't buy the Daily News: Dan Geringer, "Demonstrators call for Daily News boycott," *Philadelphia Daily News*, September 10, 2002.

The victims of these killers: Jill Porter, "Victims matter, not political correctness," *Philadelphia Daily News*, September 17, 2002.

I'm a black journalist: Hiawatha Bray, "An apology – for what?" *Philadelphia Daily News*, September 4, 2002.

288 *Rocco Marinucci, the son of a mobster*: Thomas J. Gibbons, Jr., "Mobster's son shot in South Phila. Hotel," *Philadelphia Inquirer*, December 21, 2004.

Fareed Ahmed, a vice president: Joseph Tanfani, Mark Fazlollah, and Craig McCoy, "Ex-official: Street aide inflated contract," *Philadelphia Inquirer*, December 14, 2003.

Company vice president Fareed Ahmed: Joseph Tanfani and Mark Fazlollah, "Insider's guide to getting city deals," *Philadelphia Inquirer*, May 9, 2004.

INDEX

CPSIA information can be obtained
at www.ICGtesting.com
Printed in the USA
JSHW042005180321
12568JS00001B/1

9 781903 854365